THE PROVENANCE OF
THE PSEUDEPIGRAPHA:
JEWISH, CHRISTIAN,
OR OTHER?

⌄SUPPLEMENTS TO THE

Journal for the Study of Judaism

Editor

JOHN J.COLLINS
The Divinity School,
Yale University

Associate Editor

FLORENTINO GARCÍA MARTÍNEZ
Qumran Institute,
University of Groningen

Advisory Board

J.DUHAIME
A.HILHORST
P.W. VAN DER HORST
A.KLOSTERGAARD PETERSEN
M.A.KNIBB
J.T.A.G.M. VAN RUITEN
J.SIEVERS
G.STEMBERGER
E.J.C.TIGCHELAAR
J.TROMP

⌄VOLUME 105

The Provenance of the Pseudepigrapha: Jewish, Christian, or other?

by

JAMES R. DAVILA

BRILL   LEIDEN · BOSTON · 2005

This book is printed on acid-free paper.

LIBRARY OF CONGRESS CATALOGING-IN-PUBLICATION DATA

. . . .

Davila, James R., 1960-
    The provenance of the Pseudepigrapha: Jewish, Christian, or other? / by James R. Davila.
        p.   cm. – (Supplements to the Journal for the study of Judaism, ISSN 1384-2161 ; v. 105)
    Includes bibliographical references and index.
    Contents: Jewish Pseudepigrapha and Christian Apocrypha: (how) can we tell them
apart? – Did Christians write Old Testament Pseudepigrapha that appear to be Jewish? –
Jewish Pseudepigrapha – Some Pseudepigrapha of debatable origins – Conclusions.
    ISBN 90-04-13752-1 (hardback : alk. paper)
        1. Apocryphal books (Old Testament)–Criticism, interpretation, etc. 2. Apocryphal
books (Old Testament)–Authorship. I. Title. II. Series.

BS1700.D35 2005
229'.9066–dc22

                                                                                    2005052633

. . . .

ISSN 1384-2161 / ISBN 90 04 13752 1

For Rachel and Teddy

ACKNOWLEDGEMENTS

I am grateful to a number of people and institutions for their help and support as I wrote this book. The Arts and Humanities Research Board provided me with funding for a semester of research leave, which, along with a semester of leave provided by the University of St. Andrews, allowed me a year of uninterrupted work in the late stages of writing. An early draft of Chapter One was presented in the New Testament and Second Temple Judaism Seminar of the British New Testament Conference in Cambridge, England, in 2002, with George Brooke as respondent. A draft of Chapter Two was presented in the Apocrypha and Pseudepigrapha Group at the annual meeting of the International Society of Biblical Literature in Groningen in 2004. Material from Chapter Four was presented in the Pseudepigrapha Section at the annual meeting of the Society of Biblical Literature in Atlanta in 2003. The following people read drafts of sections of the book and gave me much useful feedback: Kenneth Atkinson, Ellen Birnbaum, Ingrid Hjelm, Jeffery Hodges, Ross Kraemer, Robert Kraft, Steve Mason, Alexander Panayotov, Sigrid Peterson, Karla Pollmann, Annette Yoshiko Reed, Torrey Seland, and Francis Watson. Jacques van Ruiten helped me navigate the Groningen University library during a major research foray. The feedback of the series editor, John J. Collins, was invaluable for working out the final shape of the book. Kate Donahoe prepared the indices. My thanks to all of them, to others who helped me with material that ultimately was not included in the book, and to my wife, Rachel, whose sharp editorial eye provided many corrections. Any errors of any kind that remain are, of course, my responsibility alone. My family bore the seemingly endless work hours this book involved with good cheer and loving support. It is dedicated to them.

CONTENTS *Short Cut*

There survive today in a great many medieval manuscripts (and fewer late antique ones) an assemblage of quasi-scriptural or parabiblical documents generally known as the Old Testament pseudepigrapha,[1] which deal with events, persons, and topics from the Jewish scriptures. Many, although by no means all of these texts can be shown to have been composed in the early centuries C E or earlier. Some of them found their way into the scriptural canons of this or that Christian church, but none were accepted as part of the Hebrew Bible that now forms the Jewish canon; the Old Testament of the Protestant Bible; or the Catholic Old Testament and Deuterocanonical corpus (which latter is known as the Old Testament Apocrypha to Protestants). There are various modern collections of these works, but these are etic assemblages of texts on essentially modern principles and none of them can be taken as comprehensive.[2] Nearly all of them survive only in manuscripts copied and transmitted entirely by Christians, although fragments of a few have been recovered either from the ancient scrolls from the Judean Desert or in early medieval manuscripts from the Cairo Geniza.

Some of the Old Testament pseudepigrapha are thus undoubtedly

---

[1] There is some overlap between the Old Testament Apocrypha and the Old Testament pseudepigrapha: some include the Prayer of Manasseh (not treated in this book), 3 *Maccabees*, and Psalm 151 in one collection and some in the other. The decision where to place them is ultimately arbitrary and I categorize them as pseudepigrapha rather than Apocrypha. Strictly speaking, the Christian transmission of the Old Testament Apocrypha is a problem outside the scope of this book, but the issues are very similar to those for the Old Testament pseudepigrapha and so I have paid some attention to the Apocrypha when its evidence seemed useful for the understanding of the pseudepigrapha and I have also included some observations on the Apocrypha in the Excursus to Chapter Four.   I recognize that the scholarly convention when referring to what used to be called the 'Old Testament' in Christian circles is to use the terms 'Hebrew Bible' or 'Jewish scriptures' and I do so when referring to the Hebrew Bible itself in a neutral context. I continue, however, to use the phrase 'Old Testament pseudepigrapha' because it is more strictly accurate than alternative appellations such as 'pseudepigrapha of the Jewish scriptures' or 'pseudepigrapha of the Hebrew Bible.' The Old Testament pseudepigrapha are quasi-scriptural

of Jewish origin and many of those that are preserved only in Christian manuscripts, with no Jewish fragments, are widely taken to be Jewish compositions as well. Indeed, much of the modern interest in these works has been driven by the wish to use Old Testament pseudepigrapha of Jewish origin as sources for ancient Judaism, either as background to the New Testament or as prolegomena to the rabbinic literature. These are perfectly reasonable aims, but their disadvantage is that work done on the pseudepigrapha for these reasons treats them as a means to an end rather than as subjects worthy of study in their own right. And this agenda has seriously distorted much of what has been published on them.

Perhaps the most fundamental distortion is the widespread assumptions, made especially frequently by biblical scholars seeking to use the pseudepigrapha as background to the New Testament and Christian origins, that pseudepigrapha that lack explicitly Christian content or elements, or whose explicitly Christian elements can be easily excised on redaction-critical grounds, were originally Jewish compositions. Frequently scholars assert that because a given work has no explicitly Christian features, we should assume it to be Jewish.[3] Just as frequently

works about events and people in the Jewish scriptures, which works have been transmitted, at least in their complete form, only by Christians who thought of them as related to the Christian Old Testament, not to the Jewish scriptures or the Hebrew Bible. Granted, there are books such as *3 Enoch* and the *Hebrew Apocalypse of Elijah* which were transmitted by Jews and thus are better thought of as pseudepigrapha of the Jewish scriptures (although *3 Enoch* is first and foremost a piece of Hekhalot literature), but this book is not concerned with them. I also use the term Old Testament when discussing how the Jewish scriptures were or may have been used and thought about by Christians in antiquity. [2] The main collections in English are R. H. Charles (ed.), *The Apocrypha and Pseudepigrapha of the Old Testament in English*, vol. 1, *Apocrypha*, vol. 2, *Pseudepigrapha* (Oxford: Clarendon, 1913) (abbreviated hereafter as *APOT*); James H. Charlesworth, *The Old Testament Pseudepigrapha*, vol. 1, *Apocalyptic Literature and Testaments*, vol. 2, *Expansions of the 'Old Testament' and Legends, Wisdom and Philosophical Literature, Prayers, Psalms, and Odes, Fragments of Lost Judeo-Hellenistic Works* (Garden City, N.Y.: 1983-85) (abbreviated hereafter as *OTP*); H. D. F. Sparks, *The Apocryphal Old Testament* (Oxford: Clarendon, 1984) (abbreviated hereafter as *AOT*). My colleague, Richard Bauckham, and I are currently editing a new collection of additional texts, which is provisionally entitled 'More Old Testament Pseudepigrapha.' [3] There are countless examples. I include just a few here as illustrations: O. S. Wintermute, 'Apocalypse of Zephaniah,' *OTP*, 1:497-515: 'Whatever his name, it is fairly it is asserted that if none of the obviously Christian features in a work are so central to it that they cannot be removed without damage to the sense, we should again assume that the work is Jewish and has merely been touched up during its transmission in Christian circles.[4] Neither of these assumptions leads necessarily to false conclusions, but both of them are fundamentally flawed in principle.

clear that the writer was a Jew. In the surviving portions of the text that deal with doctrines as basic as judgment for sin, intercessory prayer, and life after death, there is nothing distinctively Christian' (p. 501); G. MacRae, 'Apocalyse of Adam,' *OTP*, 1:707-19: 'Its real importance lies in the absence of any unmistakably Christian influences in its depiction of the Illuminator of knowledge, opening up the possibility that the work reflects a transition from some form of apocalyptic Judaism to Gnosticism' (p. 708); G. W. E. Nickelsburg, 'Stories of Biblical and Early-Post-Biblical Times,' in *Jewish Writings of the Second Temple Period: Apocrypha, Pseudepigrapha, Qumran Sectarian Writings, Philo, Josephus* (CRINT 2.2; Philadelphia: Fortress, 1984), 33-87: 'Although there is no convincing evidence that *Joseph and Aseneth* is a Christian composition, it is easy to see why it was preserved and transmitted by Christian scribes' (p. 71); H. F. D. Sparks: 'At all events, the author was not a Christian; for the book [of *2 Baruch*] shows no trace of Christian influence of any kind' (*AOT*, 837); Craig A. Evans, 'Scripture-Based Stories in the Pseudepigrapha,' in *Justification and Variegated Nomism*, vol. 1, *The Complexities of Second Temple Judaism* (ed. D. A. Carson, Peter T. O'Brien, and Mark A. Seifrid; WUNT 140; Grand Tübingen: Mohr Siebeck, 2001), 57-72: 'Although a few Christian interpolations have been proposed here and there [in *Joseph and Aseneth*], there is nothing distinctively Christian about the work; it reflects a strongly hellenized Judaism and was probably composed in Egypt' (p. 62). ____ [4] ____ Again, a very few examples: H. C. Kee, 'Testaments of the Twelve Patriarchs,' *OTP*, 1:775-828: 'The Christian interpolations, which number not more than twelve, and which occur in the latter part of those testaments that contain them, are conceptually peripheral to the main thrust of the document and are literarily incongruous, so that they may be readily differentiated from the original Greek text' (p. 777); E. P. Sanders, 'Testament of Abraham,' *OTP*, 1:871-902: 'The redactional activity that imparted to [recension] A, and to a lesser extent to B, late words and traces of New Testament passages, however, must be distinguished from the rewriting that produced the ancestors of the two recensions. If the late redactional activity had extended to rewriting, it would doubtless also have resulted in a pronounced Christianizing of the text, especially the judgment scene. Despite being repeatedly copied by Christian scribes, the Testament of Abraham in both recensions remains unmistakably Jewish' (p. 875); Emil Schürer, Geza Vermes, Fergus Millar, and Martin Goodman, *The History of the Jewish People in the Age of Jesus Christ (175 B. C. – A. D. 135)* (3 vols.; rev. ed.; Edinburgh: Clark, 1973-87): 'The work [the *Testament of Abraham*] should be accepted as Jewish even though the more particular elements of Jewish piety are not stressed. The Christian interpolations, which are more numerous in the long recension (A) than in the short (B), can be easily excised without affecting the coherence of the narrative, and nothing in the narrative would be unlikely for a Jewish writer' (3.2: 763-64); Craig A. Evans, *Noncanonical Writings and New Testament Interpretation* (Peabody, Mass.: Hendrickson, 1992), 27 (on the *Apocalypse of Abraham*): 'Although a Jewish work, there are some Christian and Gnostic interpolations' (cf. also p. 29 on the *Testaments of the Three Patriarchs* and p. 30 on the *Testament of Adam*). ____ [5] ____ Kraft, 'The Pseudepigrapha in Christianity,' in *Tracing the Threads: Studies in the Vitality of Jewish Pseudepigrapha* (ed. John

In two articles published in recent years, Robert A. Kraft has challenged these assumptions.[5] He has argued compellingly that, since the texts in question have been transmitted by Christians in church languages and survive in Christian manuscripts, most of them rather late, our starting point should be these manuscripts. We should try to understand these documents initially as Christian works,[6] since this was their function in the forms in which they are actually preserved; they must have meant something to their Christian tradents, whatever their origins. This is not a conclusion but a starting point: we need to understand the work in the historical, linguistic, and cultural context of the earliest surviving manuscripts and to work backwards from there only as required by needs of the particular case.[7] When working backwards we shall conclude in some – perhaps many – cases, that a given work is a 'Jewish pseudepigraphon' (i.e., that it was composed originally in Jewish circles, primarily for a Jewish audience). In other words Kraft wishes to reverse the burden of proof: rather than assuming that a given work is a Jewish composition until demonstrated otherwise, it behooves us to consider it a Christian composition unless demonstrated to be Jewish. Kraft's methodology has been used profitably in a number of recent works, for example Daniel C. Harlow's book on *3 Baruch*, Ross Shepard Kraemer's book on *Joseph and Aseneth*, and David Satran's book on the *Lives of the Prophets*.[8] Similar points have been made for the last half-century by Marinus de Jonge, especially with regard to the *Testaments of the Twelve Patriarchs*.[9]

C. Reeves; SBLEJL 6; Atlanta: Scholars Press, 1994), 55-86; idem, 'The Pseudepigrapha and Christianity Revisited: Setting the Stage and Framing Some Central Questions,' *JSJ* 32 (2001): 371-95. —— [6] That is, 'Christian apocrypha.' The proposal to group Old Testament pseudepigrapha authored by Christians with New Testament apocrypha under the rubric 'Christian apocrypha' is a useful heuristic device that I will follow in this book. See Éric Junod, 'Apocryphes du NT ou apocryphes Chrétiens anciens?' *ETR* 58 (1983): 409-21; idem, '"Apocryphes du Nouveau Testament": une appellation erronée et une collection artificielle,' *Apocrypha* 3 (1992): 17-46. ——
—— [7] I would add that in cases where the earliest attestation of a pseudepigraphon is an undoubted quotation in another work, we should usually try in the first instance to understand that pseudepigraphon in the same context as that of the writer who quoted it. ——
—— [8] —— Harlow, *The Greek Apocalypse of Baruch (3 Baruch) in Hellenistic Judaism and Early Christianity* (SVTP 12; Leiden: Brill, 1996); Kraemer, *When Aseneth Met Joseph: A Late Antique Tale of the Biblical Patriarch and His Egyptian Wife, Reconsidered* (Oxford: Oxford University Press, 1998); Satran, *Biblical Prophets in Byzantine Palestine: Reassessing the 'Lives of the Prophets'* (Leiden: Brill, 1995). —— [9] —— Some of the relevant works include De Jonge, *The Testaments of the Twelve Patriarchs: A Study of their Text, Composition and Origin* (2nd ed.; Assen/Amsterdam: Van Gorcum, 1975); idem (ed.), *Studies on the Testaments of the Twelve Patriarchs: Text and Interpretation* (SVTP 3; Leiden: Brill, 1975); and idem, *Pseudepigrapha of the Old Testament as Part of Christian Literature: The Case of the Testaments of the Twelve Patriarchs and the Greek Life of Adam and Eve* (SVTP 18; Leiden: Brill, 2003).

It should be emphasized that the question of the origin of Old Testament pseudepigrapha transmitted solely by Christians is an important one, not only for our understanding of the texts in question, but also for related fields such as New Testament studies, rabbinics, and the history of the religions of late antiquity in general. It is certainly important to keep in mind that Christianity evolved out of Judaism and therefore it is by no means always easy or even desirable to draw a firm line between early Christianity and ancient Judaism. Nevertheless, if we fail to establish the origins of an ancient pseudepigraphon as precisely as is in our power or we accept a more precise conclusion about its origin than the evidence warrants, we are doing a disservice to scholarship. To take a cogent example, it matters very much to a number of fields of study whether *Joseph and Aseneth* is a first-century C E -or-earlier Egyptian Jewish composition or a third-century C E Syrian Christian one. It matters also whether we can tell with any confidence!

In conversations with other scholars, one of the points I have had the most difficulty getting across is where the burden of proof lies in this sort of inquiry and why. I am often asked why we should assume a Christian origin for a given pseudepigraphon and require proof to regard it as anything else. Why should we not refrain from assuming anything about its origin? In one sense this question makes a valid point: we should always hold all reasonable possibilities in our minds and refrain from letting one of them ossify into an unwarranted orthodoxy. But in another sense the question misses the point. To take the same example, we have positive

---

[10] Kraemer comments on the political implications of research on the origins of ancient Jewish and Christian texts: 'The tendency to assume that texts known to be transmitted by Christians are of Christian (as opposed to Jewish) composition, in the absence of clear evidence for Jewish composition, could easily be construed as a form of Christian hegemony and as Christian expropriation of Jewish traditions. As more and more scholars have become sensitive to the potential for anti-Judaism that lurks in the methodological morass of distinguishing Jewish from Christian in the Greco-Roman world, it may also be the case that the classification of ambiguous texts as Christian carries with it potentially disturbing implications, with the ironic result that we may be far too quick to catalogue as Jewish texts those whose origins are far less apparent.' (*When Aseneth Met Joseph*, 238.) This is an important point that bears underlining. I hope I have made it quite clear that my agenda in developing the methodology in this book is to improve our knowledge of ancient Judaism by showing how we may use our sources more critically and therefore more accurately. This field would be ill served if we were either to refrain from going where the evidence leads us or to go farther than the evidence merits merely to avoid offending well-meaning but ultimately counter-productive politically correct sentiments.

proof that *Joseph and Aseneth* in the long Greek recension was used by Syrian Christians in the sixth century C E: two Syriac manuscripts of it survive from that century, one of which refers to it being translated from Greek (see Chapter Four). It meant something to these Christians; indeed, they found it important enough to translate it into Syriac. Therefore, in that context it functioned as a Christian work and this should be our starting point for understanding it. In the case of all Old Testament pseudepigrapha transmitted solely by Christians the same point can be made: these documents were read, copied, and presumably valued by Christians. This is not a possibility, it is a material fact. We should extrapolate backwards from this fact to earlier origins only on the basis of positive evidence.

The purpose of this book is to ask what sort of positive evidence leads us to extrapolate a Jewish origin for a pseudepigraphon transmitted by Christians; to ask under what circumstances it is possible in principle to demonstrate a Jewish origin for such works; and, no less important, to ask under what circumstances are unable to tell whether the work was originally a Jewish, a Christian, or another kind of composition. In other words, I seek to establish what we can know and how we know it, and what we cannot know and why we know we cannot know it. A central thesis behind my approach is that that for the purpose of reconstructing ancient Judaism a false negative is less harmful than a false positive. By this I mean that, on the principle of moving cautiously from the known to the unknown, if a given work *may* be a Jewish composition but may also be from Christian or other hands, we are better off *not* using the work for our reconstruction of ancient Judaism, or at least separating out its evidence and giving it less weight. It is best that we limit the evidence used in our reconstruction to works we can accept as Jewish with confidence. The reason for this position ought to be clear: if we focus on securely Jewish works we will gradually build up an understanding of ancient Judaism which, while it has many lacunae, will be largely uncontaminated by irrelevant and misleading data. As our reconstruction improves, we may be able to go back to works we set aside and come to a better-informed decision about whether or not they are Jewish. And in the meantime these sidelined works remain useful for reconstructing forms of ancient Christianity. The alternative would be to try to reconstruct ancient Judaism using any work that *could be* Jewish, in which case we very likely would inadvertently include texts of Christian or other non-Jewish origin, contaminating our data with false information and making it considerably more difficult to improve our understanding.[10]

Mathematical proof is, of course, impossible in the humanistic disciplines, but the standard I am aiming for in this book is *to accept particular works as Jewish only when this is established beyond reasonable doubt on the basis of positive evidence.*

The book takes the following form. Chapter One reviews the question of the relationship between Judaism and gentile society and religion, Christian or otherwise. It formulates a methodology and criteria ('signature features') for distinguishing Jewish literary works, especially pseudepigrapha, from works by others such as gentile Christians, other gentiles (e.g., polytheists and 'God-fearers'), Jewish-Christians, Samaritans, etc., in cases where this is possible.

Chapter Two applies an 'empirical models' approach to the question of whether Christians wrote Old Testament pseudepigrapha whose Christian origin is undetectable; that is, either works in which such undeniably Christian features in them are so few and peripheral as to tempt modern scholars to excise them as secondary redactions, or works that contain no explicitly Christian features at all. The chapter draws on ancient Christian sermons, scriptural commentaries, and poetic epics to ascertain how Christians actually handled such matters in their writings.

---

[11] Note that the titles and abbreviations used for the works of Philo are those found in *The SBL Handbook of Style* (ed. Patrick H. Alexander et al.; Peabody, Mass., 1999), 78.

Chapter Three applies the methodological advances from the first two chapters to isolate a corpus of Old Testament pseudepigrapha that are of Jewish origin beyond reasonable doubt. Chapter Four looks at six pseudepigrapha that are widely accepted to be Jewish compositions but for which, to a greater or lesser degree, the case for Jewish origins falls short of being convincing. The works of Philo of Alexandria and Flavius Josephus as well as the Old Testament Apocrypha are also considered briefly in Excurses to Chapters Three and Four.[11] Chapter Five summarizes the book's conclusions.

Although I have tried to consider as wide a range of primary evidence as possible, there is some material that I have ignored or to which I paid relatively little attention. I have not addressed the Old Testament pseudepigrapha preserved primarily in Old Church Slavonic, because I do not control this language or its cultural context. I have had little to say about Coptic Gnostic Old Testament pseudepigrapha because this corpus has its own unique set of challenges that are best addressed elsewhere on their own terms. And I have not devoted much space to the Greek quotation-fragments of historians and poets preserved in the writings of authors such as Josephus, Clement of Alexandria, and Eusebius of Caesarea, because, again, this material presents its own problems that are best addressed in a study devoted entirely to them. Likewise, the Islamic transmission of Old Testament pseudepigrapha is an important but vast topic that is outside the scope of this book.

CHAPTER ONE

INTRODUCTION

In this chapter, I wish to take Kraft's position as a starting point and to explore its implications and develop it. Given that Jewish pseudepigrapha transmitted by Christian tradents must have meant something to those tradents; that it can be argued that no literary work is perfectly consistent in itself; and that readers often can tolerate a great deal of cognitive dissonance when reading a text, especially one with spiritual or canonical authority (witness the Christian exegesis of the Pentateuch), what sorts of things tell us that we need to work backward from the manuscripts we have started from? More specifically, what *positive evidence* might indicate to us that the Christian apocryphon in our hands originated as a Jewish pseudepigraphon? What factors might lead us to consider a work Jewish, Christian, some mixture of the two, or something else? What is the range of possible categories of authorship from the second temple period through late antiquity? Who had the means, motive, and opportunity to compose Old Testament pseudepigrapha and what were the processes of transmission of these works once they had been written? The purpose of this chapter is to work out the range of possibilities, to propose some methodological principles for sorting them out, and to explore the limits of what we can know.

My approach will be somewhat roundabout and will review some heavily trodden ground, but it aims to make explicit how we know what we know, so that we can also make clear what we do not know. First, I formulate criteria for identifying Jewish compositions on the basis of external evidence and use them to delineate a preliminary corpus of Jewish works. Then I survey the evidence for the complex relationships of Judaism with the gentile world and early Christianity. Next, I set

---

¹ Cohen, 'Ioudaios, Iudaeus, Judean, Jew,' in *The Beginnings of Jewishness: Boundaries, Varieties, Uncertainties* (Berkeley, Calif.: University of California Press, 1999), 69-106; and 'From Ethnos to Ethno-religion,' in ibid., 109-39.

Jewish Pseudepigrapha
and Christian Apocrypha:
(How) Can We Tell Them Apart?

out what I see as the range of possible origins and authorships of ancient Old Testament pseudepigrapha. Finally, I formulate a methodology for assessing the origins and authorship of individual Old Testament pseudepigrapha.

2   EXTERNAL CRITERIA
AND A PRELIMINARY CORPUS

I proceed from the assumption that Judaism developed out of the religion and culture of Iron Age Israel and Persian period Judea, and that the bulk of the collection now known as the Hebrew Bible was composed and redacted into various forms, some surviving today, during this same period (c. 1000 – 300 B C E). The Hebrew term *Yehudi* (as well as Aramaic *Yehuday*) originally had the sense of 'someone from the tribe of Judah.' In the second temple period, with the effective demise of the tribal system, these words took on the geographical sense of a 'Judean,' someone who lived in or came from the region of Judea but who also shared the national or ethnic identity that went with that geographical origin. This is also the earliest sense of the Greek *Ioudaios*. Shaye J. D. Cohen argues that only from the first century B C E onward does the word take on a political sense: the *Ioudaioi* could enfranchise outsiders as citizens; and a cultural or religious sense: the *Ioudaioi* as a community that an outsider could join by subscribing to a set of beliefs, practices, and social connections and disconnections.[1] Whether or not we accept the specifics of his argument, over time the word clearly developed political and religious nuances beyond the basic geographical sense.

I use 'Jews' here to refer to the people who reckoned themselves to be the Judean ethnic and cultural heirs of ancient Israel, whether or not their literary works use the term 'Jew' (many works in the Qumran library, for example, do not), and 'Judaism' to refer to the ethnic and religious identity of these people. My primary chronological focus begins with the time of Alexander the Great (late fourth century B C E) and continues through the Tannaitic period to the end of the third century CE, since allegedly Jewish pseudepigrapha are generally assigned to sometime in this period. However, sometimes I carry the analysis somewhat earlier, into the Persian period, and later, up to the rise of Islam in the early seventh century, and occasionally even slightly beyond.

If we want to know how to identify ancient Jewish literature, the logical first step is to identify verifiably ancient Jewish manuscripts, manuscripts that survive from the second temple and Hellenistic pe-

[2] Obviously, composition in the pre-Christian era rules out composition by a Christian. But to anticipate some of the discussion later in this chapter, the possibility remains that a pre-Christian work with Jewish content could have been written by a gentile proselyte, a God-fearer, or a sympathizer. However, the pre-Christian Jewish literary manuscripts isolated in this section are nearly all in Hebrew or Jewish Palestinian Aramaic, were found in the contexts of Jewish collections of literature, and show no sign of gentile polytheistic origin. They can safely be regarded as Jewish literary works. [3] Official publications of the Dead Sea Scrolls may be found in the Discoveries in the Judean Desert Series (Oxford: Clarendon, 1955–). A convenient hand edition of the nonbiblical scrolls, with the original text and an English translation, had been published by Donald W. Parry and Emanuel Tov (eds.), *The Dead Sea Scrolls Reader* (6 vols.; Leiden: Brill, 2004-2005). [4] For a survey of the contents of the Qumran library, see James C. VanderKam, *The Dead Sea Scrolls Today* (Grand Rapids, Mich.: Eerdmans, 1994), 29-70. [5] Yigael Yadin, *The Ben Sira Scroll from Masada* (Jerusalem: Israel Exploration Society and the Shrine of the Book, 1965); Yigael Yadin, Joseph Naveh, and Yaacov Meshorer, *Masada: The Yigael Yadin Excavations 1963-1965: Final Reports*, vol. 1, *The Aramaic and Hebrew Ostraca and Jar Inscriptions; The Coins of Masada* (Jerusalem: Israel Exploration Society/Hebrew University of Jerusalem, 1989). The official publications of the literary texts from Masada are also in the Discoveries in the Judean Desert Series. [6] The principal publications include: P. Benoit, J. T. Milik, R. de Vaux, et al., *Les grottes de Murabba'at/Excavations by the Jordan Department of Antiquities, École Biblique et Archéologique Française and Palestine Archaeological Museum* (DJD 2; Oxford: Clarendon, 1961); Naphtali Lewis, Yigael Yadin, and Jonas C. Greenfield, *The Documents from the Bar Kokhba Period in the Cave of Letters*, vol. 1, *Greek Papyri; Aramaic and Nabatean Signatures and Subscriptions* (Jerusalem: Israel Exploration Society/Hebrew University of Jerusalem: Shrine of the Book, 1989); Emanuel Tov, *The Seiyâl Collection. 1, The Greek Minor Prophets Scroll from Naḥal Ḥever (8 Ḥev XIIgr)* (DJD 8; Oxford: Clarendon, 1990); Hannah M. Cotton and Ada Yardeni, *Aramaic, Hebrew and Greek Documentary Texts from Naḥal Ḥever and Other Sites, with an Appendix Containing Alleged Qumran Texts (The Seiyâl Collection II)* (DJD 27; Oxford: Clarendon, 1997); Ada Yardeni, *Textbook of Aramaic, Hebrew and Nabataean: Documentary Texts from the Judaean Desert and Related Material* (Jerusalem: Hebrew University, Ben-Zion Dinur Center for Research in Jewish History, 2000); Yadin et al., *The Documents from the Bar Kokhba Period in the Cave of Letters: Hebrew, Aramaic, and Nabatean-Aramaic Papyri* (Jerusalem: Israel Exploration Society/Hebrew University of Jerusalem and Shrine of the Book, 2002). [7] For basic information on the texts (including both Tannaitic and Amoraic literature) and bibliography see Günter Stemberger, *Introduction to the Talmud and Midrash* (Edinburgh: Clark, 1996). Though I pay relatively little attention to the Amoraic literature, I do not believe the picture of Judaism formulated below would be greatly changed if I had included more on it. [8] Josephus was regarded as Jewish by Suetonius and

riods. There are some very obvious external criteria (i.e., not based on content) which can establish with virtual certainty that a given ancient work is Jewish: if a work with clear Jewish themes and content (i.e., pervasive knowledge of and interest in material and themes in the Hebrew scriptures) survives in manuscripts copied in the pre-Christian era;[2] if a work survives from the pre-Christian era or even the Hellenistic/Roman periods in Hebrew, the language of the Jewish scriptures; or if a copy of the work is preserved in a physical context that is undoubtedly Jewish (the Qumran library is of course the best example). If we use these straightforward criteria to establish a preliminary corpus of ancient Jewish literature, we come up with something like the following:

a   The Dead Sea Scrolls recovered from caves near the Wadi Qumran[3] These include manuscripts of all books of the Hebrew Bible apart from Esther and perhaps Nehemiah; sectarian Jewish writings, presumably of the group or groups who collected the library and hid it in the caves; and other ancient Jewish texts that seem not to be of sectarian origin.[4]

b   The documentary and literary texts recovered from Masada[5]

c   The documentary and literary texts of the Bar Kokhba era recovered from caves in the Judean Desert[6]

d   Texts preserved in highly fragmentary manuscripts among the Judean Desert manuscripts but fully in later primary or secondary translations These include the Book of the Watchers; the Astronomical Book; the Animal Apocalypse; and the Epistle of Enoch (all of which survive in 1 [Ethiopic] Enoch) as well as Jubilees, Tobit, Ben Sira/Ecclesiasticus, and the Epistle of Jeremiah. None of these survives intact in ancient copies and only the last survives complete in its original language, but the spot-checking allowed us by the ancient (and, in the case of Ben Sira, medieval) fragments of the original confirms that they have been transmitted reasonably accurately in translation.

e   Tannaitic rabbinic literature[7] Such works are preserved in late manuscripts but are written in Hebrew and Aramaic and were transmitted exclusively in Jewish circles.

Another external criterion is less conclusive, but worth taking into account. It is reasonable to take it at least as a working hypothesis that works by a named and dated Jewish author which are extensively quoted with attribution by numerous later Christian authors are in fact Jewish. I have in mind, of course, the two large corpora of texts attributed to the first-century CE historian Josephus and the slightly earlier philosopher Philo of Alexandria.[8] Ultimately, these corpora are accepted as Jewish on internal grounds (on which more below) as much as external. But the overwhelming evidence for the existence of these works in antiquity in much the same form we have them today, mostly in late manuscripts, should give us reasonable confidence that they are mostly genuine works of the attributed authors. For any specific passage we must, of course, pay close attention to issues of textual criticism before accepting a given text as original. For a more detailed discussion of the origins of the works attributed to Philo and Josephus and the grounds for accepting them as Jewish, see the Excursus in Chapter Three. I draw on Philo and Josephus as Jewish texts in the rest of this chapter, although I do not take them into account when formulating 'signature features' at the end of the chapter.

In addition, quotation as Jewish in a certainly Jewish text, or transmission of a work in second temple or postbiblical Jewish circles *supports* the genuineness of a work as an originally Jewish text. This criterion is potentially useful as collateral evidence but is not in itself decisive. Jewish writers sometimes quote with approval or make use of non-Jewish works. For example, the fifth-century BCE Jewish Aramaic archive recovered from Elephantine in Egypt included a copy of the obviously (by its content) non-Jewish *Story of Aḥiqar*,[9] and Aḥiqar is mentioned with approval in Tob 1:21-22 and even claimed as Tobit's nephew. If we take into account quotations in Josephus, we could add a number of works to the list, such as the *Letter of Aristeas* and 1 Maccabees. (I shall, however, not include the last two works in my preliminary corpus, although I do argue for their Jewish origin later in this book.)

In this section I have established a preliminary corpus of ancient Jewish literature, isolated on the basis of solid external criteria. It does not take into account ancient Jewish inscriptions or material culture, both

and the early Christian authors who cite him by name. The case of Philo is more complex: Josephus does not cite Philo's works but says he led the embassy to Gaius and clearly takes him to be a Jew. Clement and Origen cite Philo by name without calling him a Jew, although Clement may imply it in one passage. Later Christian authors believed that Philo was a convert to Christianity and even a bishop. Nevertheless, in both cases the external and internal evidence converge to show with overwhelming probability that both authors were Jewish and wrote in the first century CE. [9] The setting of *Aḥiqar* in both the fifth-century BCE version from Elephantine and the later recensions is the gentile polytheistic Assyrian royal court. [10] Sanders, *Paul and Palestinian Judaism: A Comparison of Patterns of Religion* (London: SCM, 1977), 422. [11] Sanders, *Judaism: Practice and Belief, 63 BCE – 66 CE* (London: SCM, 1992), 47-303. For of which deserve full-scale treatments but which are outside the scope of this book. Perhaps the most important limitation of the corpus is that most or all of the texts come from Palestinian Judaism. It is possible that Tobit and the Epistle of Jeremiah are Diaspora works, but even so the Diaspora is not well represented. Nevertheless it is a beginning, from which known quantity we can work to the unknown, and it will serve as the basis for exploring the questions of 'common Judaism' and 'the parting of the ways' between Judaism and Christianity in the next two sections.

THE PROBLEM OF 'COMMON JUDAISM'

Taking the preliminary literary corpus as a starting point, can we then say that it provides evidence for a cohesive thought world that we are justified in thinking of as 'common Judaism,' a Judaism shared by the writers of all the texts, whatever their differences? It has been argued at length by a number of scholars that such a common Judaism existed in the centuries on either side of the Common Era. I take the writings of two, E. P. Sanders and James D. G. Dunn, as representative.

Sanders takes the view that the core of ancient Judaism can be summed up in the concept of 'covenantal nomism':

‹The 'pattern' or 'structure' of covenantal nomism is this: (1) God has chosen Israel and (2) given the law. This law implies both (3) God's promise to maintain the election and (4) the requirements to obey. (5) God rewards obedience and punishes transgression. (6) The law provides for means of atonement, and atonement results in (7) maintenance or re-establishment of the covenantal relationship. (8) All those who are maintained in the covenant by obedience, atonement, and God's mercy belong to the group which will be saved. An important interpretation of the first and last points is that election and ultimately salvation are considered to be by God's mercy rather than human achievement.›[10]

Elsewhere he spells out his concept of the major characteristics of common Judaism in detail. Based on the chapter headings of the section with that title, these include the temple, priests and Levites, sacrifices, the festivals, tithes and taxes, worship, the sabbath, circumcision, purity, dietary rules, and charity and love. He sees covenantal nomism as the theological core of Judaism and finds a widespread hope for a future age in which God rules over the earth and restores Jewish prosperity.[11]

Dunn offers 'four pillars of second temple Judaism' as representative of common Judaism:[12]

a   Monotheism .... There is only one God, who rules the world, and the many gods of the more tolerant polytheists of the ancient world are idols that may not be worshiped and who are unworthy of worship, either because they do not exist at all or they are angels subordinate to God or are really aspects of God's character.

b   Election .... God has chosen the people of Israel alone as his own covenant people to whom he has given the Promised Land.

c   Covenant and Torah (Sanders's 'covenantal nomism') .... The covenant between God and Israel is centrally focused in the Torah: the revelation and instruction of God to Israel. By the period that concerns us, Torah was embodied in the written Pentateuch of Moses, on whose text extensive oral and written commentary was already being composed. The Torah gave Israel distinctiveness, a sense of privilege, and focused laws and rituals that marked them off from others (chiefly circumcision, observation of the Sabbath, and food laws).

d   Land focused in temple .... The temple in Jerusalem stood at the center of the national worship of God. It had political, economic, and religious functions, especially notably the priestly and sacrificial system.

These two accounts of common Judaism cover the major elements that can reasonably be advanced: the One God's election of the people of Israel and his covenantal relationship with them; the revelation of Torah and the requirement to obey its commandments and follow its rituals (including especially, circumcision, the sabbath, tithes, festivals, ritual purity, and dietary rules); the giving of the Promised Land and the establishment of the temple and its atoning sacrificial cult and priesthood.

---

more discussion of many of these issues, see idem, *Jewish Law from Jesus to the Mishnah: Five Studies* (Philadelphia: Trinity, 1990). Recent attempts to interact with, challenge, and refine Sanders's work include Mark Adam Elliott, *The Survivors of Israel: A Reconsideration of the Theology of Pre-Christian Judaism* (Grand Rapids, Mich.: Eerdmans, 2000); and D. A. Carson, Peter T. O'Brien, and Mark A. Seifrid (eds.), *Justification and Variegated Nomism*, vol. 1, *The Complexities of Second Temple Judaism* (WUNT 140; Tübingen: Mohr Siebeck, 2001). .... [12] Dunn, *The Partings of the Ways: Between Christianity and Judaism and Their Significance for the Character of Christianity* (London: SCM, 1991), 18-36. .... [13] .... Boccaccini, *Beyond the Essene Hypothesis: The Parting of the Ways Between Qumran and Enochic Judaism* (Grand Rapids, Mich.: Eerdmans, 1998). See also idem, *Middle Judaism: Jewish Thought, 300 B.C.E.–200 C.E.* (Minneapolis: Fortress, 1991); and *Roots of Rabbinic Judaism: An Intellectual History, from Ezekiel to Daniel* (Grand Rapids, Mich.: Eerdmans, 2002). .... [14] .... Nickelsburg, 'Enochic Wisdom: An Alternative to the Mosaic Torah?' in *Hesed*

If we compare this common Judaism to the evidence of our preliminary corpus of Jewish literary texts we find a close degree of correspondence but also a number of difficulties. Most of the texts do consistently share precisely the concerns laid out by Sanders and Dunn as common Judaism, but one corpus in particular shares them to a much lesser degree. This leads me to the work of Gabriele Boccaccini, particularly in his book *Beyond the Essene Hypothesis*.[13] Boccaccini has attempted to demonstrate that the Judaism of the second temple period included two major trends or streams, which he calls 'Zadokite' and 'Enochic' Judaism. According to *Zadokite Judaism* the world is a good place (as per Genesis 1); evil only arose from the sin of Adam and Eve in the Garden of Eden (as per Genesis 2-3). The hero of Zadokite Judaism is Moses, and the Mosaic Torah or divine instruction in the Pentateuch is centrally important. The Jerusalem temple is a microcosm of the universe, and its ritual cult and the Zadokite priesthood that maintains it are also centrally important. *Enochian Judaism* presents evil as arising when fallen angels corrupted the world and seduced human women, as in the myth of the giants found in the Book of Giants, the Book of the Watchers, and elsewhere (cf. Gen 6:1-4). The hero of the Enochians is the pre-Flood patriarch Enoch (cf. Gen 5:18-24). The Enochians may have had priestly connections and they certainly show interest in priestly matters, but they are hostile to the second temple and to the Zadokite priesthood who administer it. They show little interest in the Mosaic Torah, focusing instead on the divine wisdom revealed to Enoch in his visions. Boccaccini argues that the Dead Sea Scrolls were collected and preserved by an extremist sect of Enochic Judaism (which had meanwhile accepted the importance of Mosaic Torah alongside Enoch's revelations). If true, this means that the Dead Sea Scrolls, our largest corpus of certainly Jewish literature, was collected by a rather untypical group with somewhat fringe views. Presumably it would contain both extremist sectarian literature (e.g., the Community Rule) and older foundational literature (e.g., scriptural and Enochic books) but would leave out the rival Zadokite literature. Thus the sample of works in the Qumran library is skewed both in what it contains and what it omits. Many of the elements of Sanders's and Dunn's common Judaism apply more readily to Zadokite than to Enochic Judaism. Indeed, George W. E. Nickelsburg has argued persuasively and at length that Enochic Judaism (as represented in the Enochic works in our preliminary corpus) rejected the Mosaic Torah and was actively hostile toward the Jerusalem temple in the period in question.[14]

Not all scholars accept the concept of ancient common Judaism. Jacob Neusner, in particular, has rejected this approach and has preferred to speak of a greater or lesser number of 'Judaisms' instead. In an essay explaining the concept of 'a Judaism' rather than 'Judaism' he writes: ‹ As I said, a Judaism therefore constitutes the world view and the ›
way of life that characterize the distinctive system by which a social ›

Ve-Emet. Studies in Honor of Ernest S. Frerichs (ed. Jodi Magness and Seymour Gitin; Atlanta: Scholars Press, 1998) 123-32. See also his *1 Enoch 1: A Commentary on the Book of 1 Enoch, Chapters 1-36; 81-108* (Hermeneia; Minneapolis: Fortress, 2001), 50-54, 57-60. This position has not gone without challenge. Richard Bauckham has disputed that the Enochic literature presents Enoch and his revelations as an alternative to Moses and the Torah on the grounds that *1 Enoch 1-5* in particular alludes to Deuteronomy 33 and other scriptural covenantal materials and places the theophany on Mount Sinai. These points lead Bauckham to assert, with Lars Hartman, 'that chs. 1-5 evoke God's covenant with Israel as their "referential background"' ('Apocalypses,' in Carson et al. (eds.), *Justification and Variegated Nomism*, 1:135-87, quotation from p. 142). This much is true, but I believe Bauckham is missing the point of the passage. It is Enoch who is receiving these covenantal revelations, not Moses. And the theophany of Yahweh on Mount Sinai is an ancient Israelite tradition that is not necessarily associated with the revelation of the Mosaic Torah (cf. Judges 5 and Psalm 68). The fact that Enoch sees a Sinaitic theophany undermines the connection of Sinai with Moses. According to the Book of the Watchers, Enoch was associated with covenantal revelations and Mount Sinai long before Moses.   Other evidence could be cited in the literary texts against the idea of a monolithic Judaism. For example, Jack T. Sanders has argued that the Israelite wisdom tradition, which he takes to have been originally independent from the Mosaic Torah, is still imperfectly amalgamated with the Torah in the second temple period: 'When Sacred Canopies Collide: The Reception of the Torah of Moses in the Wisdom Literature of the Second-Temple Period,' *JSJ* 32 (2001): 121-36. But the evidence of the Enoch literature makes my point, and I am content to rest my case on it for the moment. More evidence of variety within Judaism is cited in later sections of this chapter.____ ¹⁵___ Neusner, *Ancient Judaism and Modern Category Formation: 'Judaism,' 'Midrash,' 'Messianism,' and Canon in the Past Quarter-Century* (Lanham, Md.: University Press of America, 1986), 19. See also ibid., pp. 1-24. Neusner lays out his approach in outline as applied to the entirety of Jewish history in *The Way of Torah: An Introduction to Judaism* (4th ed.; Belmont, Calif.: Wadsworth, 1988), xi-xvii, and recently in greater detail and with reference to the Qumran library in 'What Is a Judaism? Seeing the Dead Sea Library as the Statement of a Coherent Judaic Religious System,' in *Judaism in Late Antiquity*, part 5, *The Judaism of Qumran: A Systemic Reading of the Dead Sea Scrolls* (ed. Alan J. Avery-Peck, Jacob Neusner, and Bruce D. Chilton; 2 vols.; HO Section One: The Near and Middle East 56-57; Leiden: Brill, 2001), 1:3-21. He responds in detail to Sanders's criticisms of his work in *Judaic Law from Jesus to the Mishnah: A Systematic Reply to Professor E. P. Sanders* (South Florida Studies in the History of Judaism 84; Atlanta: Scholars Press, 1993), esp. chaps. 7-10.___ ___ ¹⁶___ Smith, 'Fences and Neighbors: Some Contours of Early Judaism,' in *Imagining Religion: From Babylon to Jonestown* (Chicago: University of Chicago Press, 1982), 1-18, 135-41.___ ___ ¹⁷___ Martin Goodman presents graphic views of various models of ancient Judaism in 'Modeling the "Parting of the Ways,"' in *The Ways that Never Parted: Jews and Christians in Late Antiquity and the Early Middle Ages* (ed. Adam H. Becker and Annette Yoshiko Reed; TSAJ 95; Tübingen: Mohr Siebeck, 2003), 119-29. The chart on

group of Jews sorts out its affairs. True, these several systems produced ›
by different groups of Jews assuredly do exhibit traits in common. For ›
example, they universally appeal to the same Hebrew Scriptures. But ›
in fact points in common underline the systems' essential diversity. For ›
if we ask a group to specify those verses of Scripture that it finds critical ›
and to explain their meaning, we rarely hear from one a repertoire of ›
verses found equally central in the system of some other distinct group. ›
Still less do the interpretations of verses of Scripture among the several ›
groups coincide. It follows that, in the history of Judaism, we identify ›
different Judaisms. Whether we deal with a long period of time, such as ›
a millennium or a brief period of just a few centuries, the picture is the ›
same.›[15]

I have considerable sympathy with Neusner's approach, which seeks
to understand the Judaism of a given text on its own terms rather than
attempting to fit it somehow into a larger category of 'Jewish texts' in
general. Nevertheless, I believe he overcompensates for the variety within Judaism: the fact that he uses the plural of the word 'Judaism' assumes
that there is cohesion between his various Judaisms which requires
explanation. They are in some sense exemplars of the same thing. As he
frankly acknowledges, his Judaisms share a great deal with one another.
In one sense I see the point of Neusner calling such groups 'Judaisms,'
but in another sense they are clearly forms of 'Judaism.'

In short, we come to an impasse: a 'monothetic' definition of common
Judaism in antiquity does not seem to work; that is, no satisfactory
definition of Judaism based on a *sine qua non* or core essence can be formulated. But at the same time, the various Judaisms or forms of Judaism
share enough between them to justify their membership in some elusive
broader category of Judaism. I believe that Jonathan Z. Smith, in his
article, 'Fences and Neighbors: Some Contours of Early Judaism,' has
pointed to a way forward.[16] He proposes that classification of religions
should follow a 'polythetic' rather than a 'monothetic' approach. Polythetic classification is an idea borrowed from biology. Rather than
attempting to find an essence common to every member, it is based on
a broad grouping of characteristics or properties. A member of the class
being defined must have many of these characteristics, but no single
characteristic is necessarily possessed by every member. Most members
share characteristics with many other members, but some members have
nothing in common with some others. There will also be some borderline cases, which have a few of the characteristics but not enough to
justify accepting these cases as members of the class.[17] With a polythetic

classification, we can look for both general trends shared in antiquity by many or most Jews and clusters of traits that identify different Jewish groups. Some important widely shared traits include

a worship of the God of Israel alone;

b the acceptance of certain books as Jewish scriptures given as revelation by this God;

c the acceptance of a historical narrative drawn from those scriptures;

d the following of the customs, laws, and rituals mandated in those scriptures;

e participation in or support of the temple cult in Jerusalem;

f self-identification as a Jew;

g membership in and acceptance by a particular Jewish community; and

h acceptance of Palestine as the Holy Land.

Such elements compose a 'common Judaism' in that virtually every form of Judaism will have some of them, but some forms will have more than others, different forms of Judaism will emphasize different elements in different ways, and some forms of Judaism may emphasize features that are not characteristic of 'common Judaism.' But there is no single element, no sine qua non, which must be present in every form of Judaism. To take Boccaccini's typology as an example, Zadokite Judaism accepted all the elements listed above in ways that seem relatively uncomplicated in light of rabbinic and post-rabbinic Jewish tradition, whereas Enochic Judaism, while accepting the same historical narrative and probably many of the same scriptures, focused on the elements associated with Enoch rather than Moses and some of the Enochic literature is openly hostile to the temple cult. It seems to have accepted the concept of a covenant (perhaps associated with Enoch or Abraham rather than Moses) and a Levitical priesthood, but the relationship of the latter to the Zadokite priesthood remains unclear. But despite these differences, let us not forget that, according

p. 127, 'Self-perceptions,' gives a good visual representation of a polythetic understanding. ___ ___ [18] ___ Boccaccini, *Beyond the Essene Hypothesis*, 81–117. ___ ___ [19] ___ Some recent important works on Paul include Alan F. Segal, *Paul the Convert: The Apostolate and Apostasy of Saul the Pharisee* (New Haven: Yale University Press, 1990); Daniel Boyarin, *A Radical Jew: Paul and the Politics of Identity* (Berkeley: University of California Press, 1994); James D.G. Dunn (ed.), *Paul and the Mosaic Law* (WUNT 89; Tübingen: Mohr Siebeck, 1996); John G. Gager, *Reinventing Paul* (Oxford: Oxford University Press, 2000); James D.G. Dunn (ed.), *The Cambridge Companion to St Paul* (Cambridge: Cambridge University Press, 2003). ___ ___ [20] ___ Obviously, I am making vast generalizations about an extraordinarily complex set of historical questions. It is difficult to know where to begin citing to Boccaccini's reconstruction, the Enochians and Zadokites had enough in common to effect a considerable rapprochement in the late second temple period.[18] I work with a polythetic understanding of Judaism in the remainder of this book and speak of 'common Judaism' in the nuanced sense outlined above.

4

EARLY CHRISTIANITY
AND THE PARTING OF THE WAYS

We move, then, to the questions of the early relationship between Judaism and Christianity and how and when the latter developed out of and eventually branched off from the former. Can we define Christianity? I fear that the problem is in many ways similar to that of finding a common Judaism. We can perhaps postulate a core, in that identification with Christianity or the Jesus movement involved belief in Jesus as a (broadly understood) divine mediator with a redemptive function. The specifics of both elements were worked out in different ways. Jesus was the human Messiah or the incarnate God or an angel or a descending/ascending redeemer, etc., who functioned as eschatological redeemer, atoning sacrifice, or revealer of gnosis, etc. (Any comprehensive definition of modern Christianity would be still more diffuse: perhaps simply self-identification as a Christian along with the belief that Jesus was somehow important.) The Jesus movement originated in Palestinian Jewish circles but within a generation it began to be appropriated by gentiles. Here the Apostle Paul played a central role: he established a gentile version of the Jesus movement which featured Jesus as the source of salvation through his death and resurrection, which lifted the requirement of following Jewish ritual law at least for gentiles, and which looked forward to a glorious eschatological return of Jesus.[19] Broadly speaking, the early Jesus movement thus developed two streams: a strictly Jewish one, the Jesus movement as a Jewish party or sect, and a gentile movement spread by Paul and his followers which adopted the Jewish scriptures but taught the veneration of Jesus and the abandonment of Jewish ritual law, and for obvious reasons quickly lost interest in Jewish national identity. The long-term fate of the Jewish Jesus movement is unclear. It seems to have died out eventually, although, as we shall see, it lasted longer and had more influence on gentile Christians than is often recognized. The gentile movement is ancestral to all subsequent forms of Christianity (although of course with great and rapidly increasing differentiation built around the basics summarized above).[20]

In support of this general picture I can cite the article by L. V. Rutgers, 'Jewish Literary Production in the Diaspora in Late Antiquity: the Western Evidence,' in which he argues for the Jewish origin of an anonymous Latin treatise composed roughly in the late fourth century, the *Collatio Legum Mosaicarum et Romanarum*.[21] To make his case he surveys Christian patristic literature through the fourth century for the views of the fathers on the Mosaic law. He finds a general agreement that the Decalogue, the 'first law' that was given to Moses on his first ascent of Sinai, was still valid for Christians. However, the remaining Pentateuchal laws, including the ritual laws so central to Judaism, were given during Moses' second ascent of Sinai after the golden calf episode (Exodus 32). This 'second law' was given to the Jews as a punishment to keep them in line after their idolatrous sin, and it was not to be followed by Christians. This widespread patristic view detailed by Rutgers is in accord with the general picture I have outlined above. Christians accepted

bibliography on the first several centuries of the development of the Christian Church. I will limit myself to a single recent collection of essays: Philip F. Esler (ed.), *The Early Christian World* (2 vols.; London: Routledge, 2000). In what follows I nuance my treatment of early Christianity considerably, although always with a focus on its relationship with ancient Judaism. ___ ___[21]___ Rutgers, 'Jewish Literary Production in the Diaspora in Late Antiquity: The Western Evidence,' in *The Hidden Heritage of Diaspora Judaism* (2nd ed.; Contributions to Biblical Exegesis and Theology, 20; Louvain: Peeters, 1998), 235-84. For some criticisms of this piece, which however, do not affect its main thesis, see Jan M. Bremmer, 'Review Article: The Manifest and Hidden Heritage of Judaism,' *JSJ* 31 (2000): 45-64, esp. pp. 63-64. ___ ___[22]___ The classic work on the subject is Marcel Simon's *Verus Israel: A Study of the Relations between Christians and Jews in the Roman Empire (135-425)* (Oxford: Oxford University Press, 1986). Translation of French original by H. McKeating (Paris: Boccard, 1964). See esp. pp. 85-91, 163-73. More recently see Dunn, *The Partings of the Ways*; idem (ed.), *Jews and Christians: The Parting of the Ways A. D. 70 to 135* (WUNT 66; Tübingen: Mohr Siebeck, 1992); Giovanni Filoramo and Claudio Giantto (eds.), *Verus Israel. Nuove prospettive sul giudeocristianesimo* (BCR 65; Brescia: Paideia Editrice, 2001). ___ ___[23]___ I use the phrase 'non-Christian gentiles,' cumbersome though it is, to underline a point: the term 'pagan' implies a false unity for the largely polytheistic gentile world in this period. Gentile polytheists did not begin to regard themselves as 'pagans' until the second and third centuries CE, when they began to identify themselves as a group over against Christians. 'Non-Christian gentiles' is an etic term, since they did not think of themselves primarily in relation to Christians or Jews, but as Greeks, Egyptians, Babylonians, or even Alexandrians or Antiocheans, whether atheists or worshipers of one or more gods. But 'non-Christian gentiles' distinguishes them for my purposes from Jews and Christians without implying that they held to a third 'pagan' religion. See John North, 'The Development of Religious Pluralism,' in *The Jews among Pagans and Christians in the Roman Empire* (ed. Judith Lieu et al.; London: Routledge, 1992), 174-93, esp. pp. 187-88. ___ ___[24]___ North, 'The Development of Religious Pluralism,' 187.

Jesus as a divine redeemer and adopted the Jewish scriptures, but rejected the Jewish ritual law.

In general, and this has been shown in numerous publications by many scholars in the last century, early Christianity *in its (retrospectively) orthodox forms as represented by the patristic authors* accepted the idea of monotheism (at least by its own lights), rejected the temple and ritual cult, rejected the Torah apart from the Ten Commandments, and allegorized the national identity of Israel and the priesthood to apply to itself.[22] Let this stand for the moment as an initial approximation of the evidence. There can be no doubt that the situation was more complex than this, and part of the task of this chapter is to nuance the picture of early Christianity's relationship to Judaism.

5

JEWS AND NON-CHRISTIAN GENTILES:
PROSELYTES, GOD-FEARERS, SYMPATHIZERS,
AND SYNCRETISTIC JEWS

In this section I examine the ways in which Jews interacted with non-Christian gentiles[23] in antiquity and the implications that their modes of interaction have for how they might have composed Old Testament pseudepigrapha. An important factor that explains much of the evidence I shall be reviewing in the next two sections of this chapter is a change in the social structure of the Greco-Roman world. It is discussed by John North, who writes:

‹The broad contention of this chapter is that we can illuminate the › religious history of this period best by recognizing a new religious › situation, in which the individual had to make his or her own choices › and in which, as a result, the location of religious power became far › more contentious, far more open to negotiation than it had been in › the traditional Graeco-Roman world. This created a situation of com- › petition and potential conflict between religious groups based on a › voluntary commitment, which had not existed before.›[24]

In other words, generally speaking, the ethos of the Greco-Roman world developed away from religious self-identification by nation-state, city-state, or ethnicity, to a more complicated situation of pluralism: rather than being embedded *a priori* by accidents of birth and location in a predetermined religious monopoly, people found themselves in something much more like a free market of religions in a (comparatively) open society. Faced with competition, the ancient national religions had to adapt, evolve, and sometimes borrow from competitors in order to thrive or even survive. There was no doubt some fuzziness of religious boundaries between the ancient national religions, but language differences, national boundaries, and the embeddedness of religious traditions in the social fabric served to keep national religions national. But by the late second temple period these barriers were beginning to break down: Greek, and later Latin, were widely used, and empire brought transnational government structures and elements of social identity which made it easier to separate out ethnic and religious traditions as entities in themselves. (This is not, of course, to dismiss the limits imposed on many people's choices by patronage and kinship.) Judaism, along with other national religions, had to come to terms with the changes. This is a major complicating factor for understanding the relationship between Judaism, gentile polytheism, and early Christianity.

I have broken this section down into four categories:

a proselytes (gentiles who have converted formally to Judaism);

b God-fearers (a controversial category, usually taken to mean gentiles with a close, and perhaps to some degree formal, connection with Judaism which falls short of full conversion);

c sympathizers (gentiles with an interest in Judaism but no formal commitment); and

d syncretistic Jews (Jews who adopt gentile religious traditions to a greater or lesser degree).

As we shall see, these groupings, which are traditional ways of talking about the problem, are to some degree arbitrary. However, I find them useful as heuristic devices. I am not claiming that all these terms were

---

.......²⁵...... North, 'The Development of Religious Pluralism,' 183-84....... ....²⁶..... Cohen, 'Crossing the Boundary and Becoming a Jew,' in *The Beginning of Jewishness*, 140-74 (rpt. of *HTR* 82 [1989]: 13-33)....... ....²⁷..... Ibid., 168-74....... ......²⁸...... Much evidence is discussed by Paul F. Stuehrenberg in 'Proselyte,' *ABD*, 5:503-5. Joyce Reynolds and Robert Tannenbaum also have a detailed discussion of proselytism in *Jews and Godfearers at Aphrodisias* (Cambridge Philological Society Supplement 12; Cambridge, England: Cambridge Philological Society, 1987), 43-45, although it is weighted somewhat uncritically toward the later, clearer rabbinic standard. See also Shaye J. D. Cohen, 'Respect for Judaism by Gentiles according to Josephus,' *HTR* 80 (1987): 409-30, esp. pp. 416-27; Paul Figueras, 'Epigraphic Evidence for Proselytism in Ancient Judaism,' *Imm* 24/25 (1990): 194-206; William Horbury, 'A Proselyte's *Heis Theos* Inscription Near Caesarea,' *PEQ* 129 (1997): 133-37; Terence L. Donaldson, 'Jerusalem Ossuary Inscriptions and the Status of Jewish Proselytes,' in *Text and Artifact in the Religions of Mediterranean Antiquity: Essays in Honor of Peter Richardson* (ed. Stephen G. Wilson and Michel Desjardins; Waterloo, Ontario: Wilfrid Laurier University Press,

---

used with these senses in antiquity. Nor do I imply a moral judgment, positive or negative, by using terms such as 'sympathizer' or 'syncretistic.' Other classifications could be applied. North proposes a general classification for social/religious groups which asks

a   how clearly the group's structure makes it autonomous;

b   what level of commitment the group demands of its members;

c   to what degree the group espouses values and principles inimical to those of the larger society; and

d   to what degree the life of the group is based on rituals, calendars, and dietary customs different from those of the larger society.[25]

Cohen has laid out a seven-point classification of gentile interest in Judaism.[26] These are

a   'admiring some aspects of Judaism';

b   'acknowledging the power of the god of the Jews';

c   'benefiting the Jews or being conspicuously friendly to Jews';

d   'practicing some or many of the rituals of the Jews';

e   'venerating the god of the Jews and denying or ignoring all other gods';

f   'joining the Jewish community'; and

g   'converting to Judaism and "becoming a Jew."'

He also attempts to map this typology onto something like the categories I use in this section.[27] The classifications of both North and Cohen are useful as well and I draw on them from time to time, but the four categories I outlined at the beginning of this paragraph provide the overall structure of my treatment.

PROSELYTES OR CONVERTS .... In the modern discussion an ancient convert to Judaism is usually referred to as a 'proselyte,' and I will use this term here, although with some reservations. By it I mean someone joined the Jewish community to the point of assimilating to it entirely and effectively becoming a Jew. By the Tannaitic period, a clear standard of conversion had been promulgated in rabbinic circles, which included acceptance of the Torah, circumcision for men, and immersion. There was also the tradition that converts had been required to offer a sacrifice as long as the temple stood. Amoraic literature describes a detailed conversion ceremony. One can debate what the exact prerabbinic requirements for conversion were, whether they always included immersion and circumcision (the latter, of course, did not apply to women anyway), and whether the proselyte was indeed viewed by Jews as a full Jew. Josephus, Philo, some ancient gentile writers, and a few inscriptions mention proselytes or gentile converts to Judaism.[28] The details are not terribly important for my purposes, except to establish that such converts existed in our period of interest.

In terms of North's classification, proselytes or converts to Judaism would be entering a well-defined group with strong boundaries. Judaism was universally recognized as a discrete ethno-religious body with its own privileges and disabilities; it demanded of converts a very high level of commitment, including rejection of past religious and national affiliations; it promoted monotheism, an unusual doctrine elsewhere in the Greco-Roman world, where adherence to the cult of the emperor was compulsory and polytheism was the norm; and it required adherence to a distinctive calendar, a distinctive ritual cult (including, at least under normal circumstances, circumcision), and distinctive dietary rules. Proselytes stand at the most committed end of Cohen's classification, although there seemed to be some disagreement as to whether either Jews by birth or the proselytes themselves considered them to be fully and unambiguously transformed into Jews. But the category of proselyte or convert is the least problematic one in this section: a convert is sufficiently absorbed into the Jewish community that we generally would be hard pressed to distinguish pseudepigrapha written by one from pseudepigrapha written from someone born into Judaism. For my purposes, authorship by a convert would almost certainly be undetectable and can be regarded as Jewish authorship.

2000), 372-88; Judith M. Lieu, 'Circumcision, Women, and Salvation,' *NTS* 40 (1994): 358-70. ....
.... [29] .... For a detailed review of the issue and the literature through the mid-1980s, see Reynolds and Tannenbaum, *Jews and Godfearers*, 48-66. .... [30] .... A. T. Kraabel, 'The Disappearance of the "God-Fearers,"' *Numen* 28 (1981): 113-26; idem, 'Greeks, Jews, and Lutherans in the Middle Half of Acts,' *HTR* 79 (1986): 147-57; Max Wilcox, 'The "God-Fearers" in Acts – A Reconsideration,' *JSNT* 13 (1981): 102-22; Philip F. Esler, *Community and Gospel in Luke-Acts: The Social and Political Motivations of Lucan Theology* (Cambridge: Cambridge University Press, 1987); Joseph B. Tyson, 'Jews and Judaism in Luke-Acts: Reading as a Godfearer,' *NTS* 41 (1995): 19-38. ....
.... [31] .... The inscription was published by Reynolds and Tannenbaum in *Jews and Godfearers at Aphrodisias*. For subsequent discussion see Walter Ameling, *Inscriptiones Judaicae Orientis*, vol. 2, *Asia Minor* (TSAJ 99; Tübingen: Mohr Siebeck, 2004), 70-112. .... [32] .... Figueras, 'Epigraphic Evidence for Proselytism,' 202-203. .... [33] .... For discussion see Cohen, 'Respect for Judaism by Gentiles,' 417, 425-26. .... [34] .... *Sat.* 14.96-106. See Menachem Stern, *Greek and Latin Authors on Jews and Judaism* (3 vols.; Jerusalem: Israel Academy of Science and Humanities, 1974-84), #254. ....
.... [35] .... Cited by Augustine in *Civ.* 6.11 = Stern, *Greek and Latin Authors*, #186.

GOD-FEARERS ....In the secondary literature the term God-fearers (θεοσεβεῖς), inspired in no small part by usages in the book of Acts, has traditionally been used to refer to gentiles who associated themselves with the Jewish community, including the synagogue, were sympathetic to monotheism, followed Jewish Law as far as it suited them, yet did not become proselytes or convert so as to identify themselves fully with Judaism and leave behind their gentile background.[29] The nature and even existence of the God-fearers, however has been stridently debated in recent years. That the evidence of Acts is open to more than one interpretation can scarcely be denied.[30] The import of the epigraphic evidence is also contested. The lapidary inscription from the city Aphrodisias in ancient Caria (Asia Minor) which was recovered in the 1970s was argued by its editors to date to the third century C E and to provide evidence for gentile 'God-fearers' (θεοσεβῖς = θεοσεβεῖς) associated with the local Jewish community. But the inscription may well have been produced some centuries later than this and at most it indicates that in late antiquity some gentiles (perhaps including Christians) may have participated in group projects with Jews in Aphrodisias and these gentiles were known as 'God-fearers.' Whether such a title existed in the Hellenistic period is another matter.[31]

Other inscriptions do offer some collateral evidence for God-fearers as an ancient category, but even these do not give us quite enough information to be certain of the usage.[32] Nevertheless, apart from the epigraphic evidence, there is sufficient evidence for such gentiles in antiquity if we do not insist that they be called by the title 'God-fearers.' Josephus asserts that in Antioch the Jews 'were always attracting to their religious ceremonies a great multitude of Greeks and they made these in some manner a part of themselves' (B.J. 7.3.3 §45) and that no gentile city or nation lacked some who kept the sabbath, the Jewish fasts and 'lighting of lamps,' and many of the Jewish dietary rules (C. Ap. 2.39 §282).[33] Philo may refer to 'proselytes' who do not go as far as circumcision and these may be better regarded as God-fearers (QE 2.2). Juvenal refers to a convert who becomes circumcised; the convert's father does not go so far but does observe the sabbath and abstain from pork.[34] Seneca also asserts that gentiles 'throughout the world' followed Jewish laws and customs, even though most of these gentiles did not themselves understand the reasons for the customs.[35]

This and other evidence has led a number of scholars to take a less skeptical viewl, acknowledging that there were indeed gentiles who had a close association with Judaism and the synagogue, and expressing considerably more openness to the possibility for a core historicity of the gentile God-fearers portrayed in Acts.[36] But I am content to rest my analysis on the other evidence and set Acts aside: there were gentiles in antiquity who liked Judaism well enough to associate themselves more or less closely with the Jewish community by observing Jewish laws and rituals and, at least sometimes, by involvement with the local synagogue. Some, perhaps many, of the men were not circumcised. What they were called does not matter for my purposes, but for the sake of simplicity I will call them 'God-fearers.' In terms of North's classification, these adherents to Judaism seem to have been tolerated by the Jewish community and allowed to interact with it on quite a close level even though they did not convert and give up their former social identity to adopt a fully Jewish one. In other words, although Judaism seems to have demanded a very high level of loyalty and conformity of converts, it was quite tolerant of lesser levels of commitment as well. As for Cohen's classification, we may assume that God-fearers accepted the first two elements (admiring Judaism and acknowledging the power of its god). They also were openly friendly and beneficent to Jews (c); practiced some, but not necessarily all, Jewish rituals (d); and they venerated the god of the Jews (e), although it is not clear that they always denied or ignored other gods. We do not know if any of them joined the Jewish community (e.g., by nominal conversion for the sake of marriage to a

---

[36] Thomas M. Finn, 'The God-fearers Reconsidered,' CBQ 47 (1985): 75-84; John G. Gager, 'Jews, Gentiles, and Synagogues in the Book of Acts,' HTR 79 (1986): 91-99; J. Andrew Overman, 'The God-Fearers: Some Neglected Features,' JSNT 32 (1988): 17-26. In addition, J.M. Lieu discusses the usage of the word θεοσεβής in antiquity in 'The Race of the God-Fearers,' JTS 46 (1995): 483-501. [37] For this usage of 'sympathizers,' see Folker Siegert, 'Gottesfürchtige und Sympathisanten,' JSJ 4 (1973): 109-64, esp. pp. 147-51. The rabbinic 'fearers of heaven' (יראי שמים) may belong either in this category or in the category of God-fearers; the information we are given about them is not sufficient for us to be able to place them more specifically. See Siegert, 'Gottesfürchtige,' 110-26; Lieu, 'The Race of the God-Fearers,' 484-85. [38] See also John G. Gager, 'The Dialogue of Paganism with Judaism: Bar Cochba to Julian,' HUCA 44 (1973): 89-118; Wolf Liebeschuetz, 'The Influence of Judaism among Non-Jews in the Imperial Period,' JJS 52 (2001): 235-52. [39] Stephen Mitchell, 'The Cult of Theos Hypsistos between Pagans, Jews and Christians,' in Pagan Monotheism in Late Antiquity (ed. Polymnia Athanassiadi and Michael Frede; Oxford: Clarendon, 1999), 81-148. Paul R. Trebilco, in Jewish Communities in Asia Minor (Cambridge: Cambridge University Press, 1991), 127-44, accepts that there is some evidence for Jewish influence on the cult of Theos Hypsistos, but such influence is rejected by Margarita Tacheva-Hitova, Eastern Cults in Moesia Inferior and Thracia (5th Century BC–4th Century AD) (EPRO 425; Leiden: Brill, 1983), 190-215. [40] The philosophical Hermetica are

Jew) (*f*) but in general they did not convert formally to Judaism (*g*). We cannot by any means rule out the possibility that well-educated God-fearers wrote Old Testament pseudepigrapha.

SYMPATHIZERS .... I use the term 'sympathizers' here to mean gentiles who were in some way well disposed toward Judaism, at least enough to be influenced by it. Unlike converts or God-fearers, some gentiles clearly were attracted to elements of Judaism without feeling the need to abandon polytheism or develop a relationship with a Jewish community.[37] Some of the evidence reviewed in the previous section could also apply to such gentiles, although we have no way to distinguish them very clearly from the God-fearers.[38] But it is more relevant for my purposes to review some epigraphic and literary evidence for non-Christian gentiles who observed Jewish customs or made use of Jewish themes.

The *Theos Hypsistos* cult may give us evidence of a transition from God-fearers to sympathizers.[39] This is a cult of worship that is widely attested over a broad range of social classes in the eastern Mediterranean region and the ancient Near East from at least the first to the fifth century C E. The evidence for the cult consists of nearly three hundred inscriptions, several excavated sanctuaries, and patristic testimonies. The worship of *Theos Hypsistos* or merely *Hypsistos* had strong monotheistic tendencies, although often this god was identified with Zeus as well, and veneration of subsidiary gods or angels is attested. The terminology of the cult, including the titles of the deity himself, seems to show Jewish influence, and according to Gregory of Nazianzus (*Or. Bas.* 18.5; PG 35.990) some adherents observed the sabbath and Jewish dietary rules. Mitchell is inclined to identify the Hypsistarians with the God-fearers, and there is circumstantial evidence to support the identification, but this may be simplistic. As he recognizes, it is frequently impossible to tell whether a given Hypsistarian inscription is Jewish, judaizing, or gentile polytheistic, and the cult may have had room for all three. Given the physical evidence for Hypsistarian sanctuaries, it may be that that at least some of these people were gentiles who had no formal connection with a Jewish community but who drew on Jewish traditions and who adapted the concept of monotheism for their own purposes, often explicitly identifying this one god as Zeus. I would consider these sympathizers rather than God-fearers.

As to literary texts that provide evidence for sympathizers, I will limit myself to two examples. The *Poimandres* is a late antique Greco-Egyptian work of popular philosophy in the Hermetic tradition.[40] In it the god after whom the treatise is named (apparently to be identified with Hermes Trismegistus) reveals to an unnamed human being a gnostic path of enlightenment and apotheosis and, in the process, presents a cosmogony that clearly relies in part on the L X X version of the creation story in Genesis 1. The thematic echoes are obvious and the verbal echoes are clear in the Greek text. Other parallels to Jewish literature outside the scriptures have also been advanced.[41] The *Poimandres* is a work of philosophical polytheism which was significantly influenced by the L X X of Genesis and perhaps also by Jewish tradition, but we have no reason to conclude that the author was Jewish, a fallen-away convert, or even knew a Jewish community personally, nor do we have any good reason to date the work more precisely than somewhere in the Hellenistic to late antique period.[42] The simplest explanation of such evidence that we have is that the author was a member of a Hermetic conventicle who had direct or indirect access to the Greek text of Genesis and who perhaps picked up some knowledge of other Jewish traditions through means we cannot now reconstruct, and who incorporated some of these traditions into a philosophy and a written work.

The Greek magical papyri provide us with additional evidence for gentile polytheists interested in Jewish (and Christian) traditions.[43]

translated with commentary by Brian P. Copenhaver in *Hermetica: The Greek* Corpus Hermeticum *and the Latin* Asclepius (Cambridge: Cambridge University Press, 1992). The Hermetic literature, philosophical and technical, is discussed by Garth Fowden in *The Egyptian Hermes: A Historical Approach to the Late Pagan Mind* (cor. ed.; Princeton: Princeton University Press, 1993). [41] For scriptural parallels and parallels to Philo of Alexandria, see C. H. Dodd, *The Bible and the Greeks* (London: Hodder & Stoughton, 1934), 99-169; R. P. Festugière, *La révélation d'Hermès Trismégiste* (4 vols.; Paris: Lecoffre, 1944-54), 2:521-54. For other parallels to allegedly Jewish literature see Birger A. Pearson, 'Jewish Elements in *Corpus Hermeticum* I (*Poimandres*),' in *Studies in Gnosticism and Hellenistic Religions Presented to Gilles Quispel* (ed. R. van den Broek and M. J. Vermaseren; EPRO 91; Leiden: Brill, 1981), 336-48. [42] Contra Pearson, 'Jewish Elements,' 347-48. [43] Karl Preisendanz, *Papyri Graecae Magicae: Die Griechischen Zauberpapyri* (2nd ed.; 2 vols.; Stuttgart: Teubner, 1973-74); Hans Dieter Betz (ed.), *The Greek Magical Papyri in Translation, Including the Demotic Spells* (2nd ed.; Chicago: University of Chicago Press, 1992). [44] Preisendanz, *Papyri Graecae Magicae*, 1:64-180; Betz (ed.), *The Greek Magical Papyri*, 36-101. [45] Following the translation of M. W. Meyer in Betz (ed.), *The Greek Magical Papyri*, 62. [46] For discussion of the spell of Pibechis, see M. Gaster, 'The Logos Ebraikos in the Magical Papyrus of Paris and the Book of Enoch,' *JRAS* 33 (1901): 109-17 (which draws parallels to the oath of creation in *1 En.* 69:16-25 and suggests—wrongly, I think—that the spell was translated from Hebrew); and Daniel Sperber, 'Some Rabbinic Themes in Magical Papyri,' *JSJ* 16 (1985): 93-103, esp. pp. 95-99.

PGM IV is a large fourth-century papyrus from the Anastasi collection, evidently recovered from Thebes along with some other magical papyri in the nineteenth century.[44] Its basic religious orientation is Greco-Egyptian, with invocations and references to gods such as Helios, Thoth, the Fates, Horus, Hermes, Aphrodite, Kore, Osiris, Selene, and Kronos, and references to numerous Egyptian and Greek figures and stories. But it draws eclectically on other traditions as well: it includes the Mithras Liturgy (475-829) and mentions the Mesopotamian underworld deity Ereshkigal (1417). And, now and again, it refers to Jewish and Christian traditions: the divine names IAO, PIPI (the Tetragrammaton read backward as Greek letters), Sabaoth, and Adonai appear; angels and archangels are mentioned; one spell is entitled 'Trance of Solomon' (850-929), but although the spell claims to be a 'procedure of Solomon,' its religious content is otherwise Greco-Egyptian; there is a reference to 'the great god who shone in all the world, flashing toward Jerusalem, Lord IAO' (1220-23); and there is a Coptic invocation, 'Hail, God of Abraham; hail God of Isaac; God of Jacob; Jesus Chrestos,' and a call to drive out Satan (1231-41).[45] The most striking such passage in this manuscript is 'A proved (spell) of Pibechis for those demonized' (3007-86), which includes an adjuration of 'the god of the Hebrews, Jesus,' and refers to paradise; 'Osrael' (= Israel); a garbled account of the ten plagues and the pillar of fire and cloud which led the Israelites in the wilderness; 'the seal of Solomon which he put on the tongue of Jeremiah'; various demonic forces including a 'Pharisaios'; the crossings of the Jordan River and the Red Sea through Sabaoth; the cherubim; and holy Jerusalem. The user is adjured not to eat pork and is assured that the spell is 'Hebraic.'[46]

These references do not prove that the writers were directly in touch with either Jews or Christians, but the taboo against eating pork is clearly poached from Judaism and the legend of the Seal of Solomon comes from postbiblical Jewish tradition. The editor of this manuscript was a Greco-Egyptian polytheistic practitioner of ritual power, but one very open to outside traditions, including Judaism.

The evidence for sympathizers surveyed in this section is open to a range of possible interpretations, but even taking these into account it demonstrates that there were gentiles with an interest in Judaism which fell short of that of the God-fearers, at least as narrowly construed above. By North's typology the Hypsistarians show signs of being an autonomous group who espoused something approaching monotheistic worship and who may have followed some Jewish rituals. We do not know what level of commitment was asked of members, but available evidence does not point to it being high. Moreover, it is not even clear that they sought a formal relationship with Judaism or felt obligated to make any exclusive commitment to its principles. By Cohen's typology, the most we can claim is that they may have admired some aspects of Judaism (a) and acknowledged the power of the Jewish god (b), and some of them may have practiced some Jewish rituals (d).

The philosophers and magicians (or better, 'practitioners of ritual power')[47] display a yet more attenuated relationship with Judaism. We could, if we wish, with Pearson take the Hermetic philosopher who wrote the *Poimandres* as an apostate God-fearer, but I prefer a more conservative understanding of the data in which we can assume no commitment of any type to Judaism or its principles, although the philosopher may have been part of a Greco-Egyptian Hermetic conventicle whose nature and commitment level remain obscure. This philosopher admired some Jewish theology, particularly the creation myth in Genesis (Cohen's a) but any resulting veneration seems to have been applied to Hermes Trismegistus rather than the Jewish God. The Greco-Egyptian practitioners of ritual power who composed, transmitted, and used the

---

[47] For a critique of the term 'magic' and a defense of the use of the phrase 'ritual power' as a more useful category in which to place 'magical' literature and practice, see James R. Davila, *Descenders to the Chariot: The People Behind the Hekhalot Literature* (JSJSup 70; Leiden: Brill, 2001), 32-42. [48] It is difficult to find a satisfactory terminology for these matters: traditionally Jews who sympathize with gentile religious traditions or even abandon Judaism to adopt a gentile cult and identity have been termed syncretists and apostates. A more neutral nomenclature might refer to them as sympathizers and converts to gentile cults. I have used the traditional terminology because I find it counterproductive to redefine too many terms for the sake of addressing issues of tangential import to the authorship of Old Testament pseudepigrapha, the real focus of this chapter. No moral judgment is intended by these usages. [49] Rajak, 'Jews and Christians as Groups in a Pagan World,' in *The Jewish Dialogue with Greece and Rome: Studies in Cultural and Social Interaction* (AGJU 48; Leiden: Brill, 2001), 355-72, esp. pp. 358-62. The strategies of the *Avodah Zarah* for dealing with the gentile world are discussed by Moshe Halbertal in 'Coexisting with the Enemy: Jews and Pagans in the Mishnah,' in *Tolerance and Intolerance in Early Judaism and Christianity* (ed. Graham N. Stanton and Guy G. Stroumsa; Cambridge: Cambridge University Press, 1998), 159-72. See also Guy G. Stroumsa, 'Tertullian on Idolatry and the Limits of Tolerance,' in ibid., 173-84, which compares and contrasts the levels of tolerance toward gentile polytheism in the works of Tertullian and in the *Avodah Zarah*. Peter Schäfer analyses the Yerushalmi's *Avodah Zarah*, concluding that it is largely based on rabbinic interpretations of the Hebrew Bible and tells us very little about the actual life-situation of Jews in Palestine in that period: 'Jews and Gentiles in Yerushalmi Avodah Zarah,' in *The Talmud Yerushalmi and Graeco-Roman Culture* III (ed. Peter Schäfer; TSAJ 93; Tübingen: Mohr Siebeck, 2002), 335-52. [50] Boccaccini, *Beyond the Essene Hypothesis*, 129-62; Leonard J. Greenspoon, 'The Dead Sea

Greek magical papyri drew on Jewish scriptures and Jewish traditions for their own purposes, but their knowledge of them is superficial and it seems quite unlikely that they cultivated a formal or informal relationship with any actual Jews. They acknowledged the power of the God of the Jews (Cohen's *b*) as a source of textual and ritual power to be drawn on along with many other traditions and therefore admired some aspects of Judaism insofar as they thought these aspects provided them with power (*a*).

SYNCRETISTIC JEWS ⸳⸳⸳⸳⸳⸳ ⸳⸳⸳⸳⸳⸳ Thus far in this section we have looked at ways in which non-Christian gentiles interacted with Judaism in antiquity. The flip side of the coin is the question of how Jews interacted with the gentile world and the temptations within it. The theoretical range of possibilities extends from complete rejection of gentile ideas to mild interest in elements potentially compatible with Judaism to compromise with inimical gentile institutions when expedient (such as participation in polytheistic cults) to outright severance (or ejection) from the Jewish community ('apostasy').[48] But to what degree was the possible range of responses actually acted out by Jews?

Diaspora Jews may well not have followed the strict rabbinic rules concerning interaction with gentile polytheists, as has been pointed out, for example, by Tessa Rajak. The Mishnaic tractate *Avodah Zarah* required Jews to set off a theoretical neutral space between themselves and gentiles, in which Jews neither benefited nor derived benefit from polytheists or their religions. Although this neutral space allowed some flexibility for mutual interaction, the rabbinic rules still forbade participation in polytheistic festivals and sacrifices or even chatting with a polytheist around the time of one of their festivals.[49] Following these rules would have been extremely difficult and impractical, and Rajak finds it likely in principle that Diaspora Jews would have been more flexible in an environment where they were a minority trying to conduct their business and lives without giving offense to a majority with very different values.

Some ancient Jews were careful to avoid contamination, as far as they were able, with any kind of gentile influence. The people who wrote the Qumran library seem to fall into this category. No non-Jewish works were found among the surviving scroll fragments, nor are there any advocating or sympathetic to a Hellenizing ideology. The Qumran sectarians appear to have eschewed gentile traditions entirely and even to have avoided the Greek language to an extraordinary degree, although not completely.[50]

Philo of Alexandria was a Greek-speaking Jew who was vastly more Hellenized than the Qumran sectarians, yet he remained devoted to Judaic praxis. Although he adopted and applied the Greek concept of allegorization to scripture, he drew heavily on Greek philosophy, especially Plato's *Timaeus*. Philo also drew distinctions within different polytheistic systems; finding Greek religion more tolerable than Egyptian, he nevertheless advocated full observance of the ritual laws and, at least in theory, subordinated his Platonism to the Hebrew scriptures.[51]

There is ample evidence for Jews at times taking the route of expediency when confronted with gentile institutions that took minor participation in polytheistic cults for granted. For example, in 127 C E a Jewish woman named Babatha, whose personal papers were recovered from the Cave of the Letters associated with the Bar Kokhba revolt, evidently

Scrolls and the Greek Bible,' in *The Dead Sea Scrolls after Fifty Years: A Comprehensive Assessment* (ed. Peter W.Flint and James C.VanderKam; 2 vols.; Leiden: Brill, 1998-99), 1:101-27; James C.VanderKam, 'Greek at Qumran,' in *Hellenism in the Land of Israel* (ed. John J.Collins and Gregory E.Sterling; Christianity and Judaism in Antiquity 13; Notre Dame, Ind.: University of Notre Dame Press, 2001), 175-81. For the issue of Hellenization in Jewish Palestine in general, see the classic work by Martin Hengel, *Judaism and Hellenism: Studies in Their Encounter in Palestine During the Early Hellenistic Period* (2 vols.; London: SCM, 1974). [51] Maren R.Niehoff, 'Philo's Views on Paganism,' in Stanton and Stroumsa (eds.), *Tolerance and Intolerance*, 135-58. [52] Papyrus Yadin 16.34 in Lewis et al., *The Documents from the Bar Kokhba Period in the Cave of Letters*, 1:65-70. For other examples see Ross S.Kraemer, 'On the Meaning of the Term "Jew" in Greco-Roman Inscriptions,' *HTR* 82 (1989): 35-53, esp. pp. 41-42; Steven G.Wilson, 'ΟΙ ΠΟΤΕ ΙΟΥΔΑΙΟΙ: Epigraphic Evidence for Jewish Defectors,' in Wilson and Desjardins (eds.), *Text and Artifact*, 354-71, esp. p.365; Rajak, 'Jews and Christians in a Pagan World,' 366-67, 368, 369, 364, and 369. [53] Laurence H.Kant, 'Jewish Inscriptions in Greek and Latin,' *ANRW* 2.20.2 (1987), 671-713, esp. pp. 683; Kraemer, 'On the Meaning of the Term "Jew,"' 41-42; idem, 'Jewish Tuna and Christian Fish: Identifying Religious Affiliations in Epigraphic Sources,' *HTR* 84 (1991): 141-62, esp. pp. 155-58; Margaret H.Williams, 'The Meaning and Function of *Ioudaios* in Graeco-Roman Inscriptions,' *ZPE* 116 (1997): 249-62, esp. p.253. [54] Mordechai Margalioth, *Sepher Ha-Razim: A Newly Recovered Book of Magic from the Talmudic Period* (Jerusalem: Yediot Achronot, 1966; Hebrew), 76, 99; Michael A.Morgan, *Sepher Ha-Razim: The Book of the Mysteries* (SBLTT 25; SBLPS 11; Chico, Calif.: Scholars Press, 1983), 38, 71. [55] J.J.Collins, 'Artapanus,' in *OTP*, 2:889-903; Carl R.Holladay, *Fragments from Hellenistic Jewish Authors*, vol. 1, *Historians* (SBLTT 20; SBLPS 10; Chico, Calif.: Scholars Press, 1983), 189-243. The problem of evaluating fragments of ancient Jewish authors quoted by later Christian and non-Christian gentile writers is somewhat different from the problem of evaluating the origins of relatively well-preserved ancient pseudepigrapha, and the latter problem is the subject of this book. I hope to return to the methodology of studying quotation-fragments in the future. I consider a number of allegedly Samaritan quotation-fragments later in this chapter.

saw no difficulty in swearing an oath 'by the *genius* of the Lord Caesar,' as recorded in a declaration of ownership of property.[52]

Evidence of such participation by Jews is also found in circumstances that seem not to have been compulsory. The polytheistic phrase *dis manibus* ('to the shades of the departed') may be attested on Jewish epitaphs.[53] Polytheistic elements are attested in Jewish incantations of ritual power. *Sepher Ha-Razim*, the 'Book of Mysteries,' a Hebrew compendium of such incantations and recipes from roughly the Talmudic era, provides examples. A ritual for questioning a ghost requires the practitioner to invoke the aid of the 'spirit of the "Ram-Bearer" (Κριοφόρος, transliterated into Hebrew letters),' a name for Hermes (1.178). Later in the work a Greek invocation to Helios is transliterated into Hebrew (IV. 61-63).[54]

The fourth-century church historian Eusebius quotes three Greek fragments from the work *On the Jews* by the gentile historian Alexander Polyhistor (mid-first century BCE) which purport to summarize material from a work by an otherwise unknown Jewish writer named Artapanus, who may have been from Egypt (*Praep. ev.* 9.18, 23, 27). These fragments retell material from the scriptural stories of Abraham, Joseph, and Moses in a rather garbled form. They report that Moses was the teacher of Orpheus, that he divided Egypt into thirty-six nomes and set up the cults and priesthoods of the various gods in each, and that he was identified with Hermes. We are at two removes from Artapanus and would perhaps be wise not to rely too heavily on his evidence, but he may be an example of a well-educated Jew who produced a highly syncretistic literary retelling of scriptural stories.[55]

REFLECTIONS ....For my purposes proselytes – gentiles who converted to Judaism to the point of renouncing gentile social and religious ties and who (if male) were circumcised – were effectively Jewish. God-fearers – gentiles who associated themselves with Judaism and perhaps with the synagogue, but without necessarily renouncing polytheism or adopting Jewish practices fully – are a more complicated problem: we may assume them to have been well informed about Judaism but not necessarily to have had views or followed practices that would have been approved of by the Jewish communities with which they were in contact. Hypsistarians may have been as well informed as God-fearers (some of them may have *been* God-fearers), but their connections with Judaism and actual Jewish communities may also have been far more tenuous. The Greco-Egyptian Hermetic philosophers and practitioners of ritual power may have derived their information about Judaism from reading the Greek translation of the Jewish scriptures and from folklore about Jews. They may have known real Jews – even Jewish practitioners – but there is no need to postulate that they did. Let us connect the dots. The boundary between proselyte, God-fearer, sympathizer, and vaguely interested polytheist was a permeable continuum, and we have good reason to believe that many or most of the points on this continuum not represented in our evidence were nonetheless occupied by real people somewhere and sometime in antiquity.

Likewise, I have illustrated that from the Jewish side there was a continuum of attitudes toward gentiles and gentile polytheism, ranging from thoroughgoing rejection to thoroughgoing adoption. As with gentile sympathy for Judaism, the examples selected above occupy a sufficient number of points on the continuum to confirm that we should connect the dots and conclude that a similar Jewish continuum existed in the period in question. It does not, however, tell us where the majority of Jews belonged on it. It might be tempting to assume that most of them fell into the range of the more strictly observant, such as the Qumran sectarians, Philo, and the rabbinic sages. But this would be an assumption: we simply do not know where the average Jew in Palestine or in the Diaspora stood on such matters or whether Jews in the middling or the less observant sectors of the continuum were common or uncommon.

Who among all these people would have been in a position to write Old Testament pseudepigrapha? I am afraid any of them who were sufficiently well educated could have done so. Indeed, it has been suggested that the sapiential work *Pseudo-Phocylides* was composed by a God-fearer. Written in the name of a sixth-century B C E Ionic poet, this Greek work is clearly a pseudepigraphon, one that shows familiarity with the Greek scriptures. But the morality is generic and most of the scriptural rules it alludes to are moral principles congenial to a Hellenistic environment. The Decalogue is summarized in lines 3-8, but there is no mention of sole worship of the Jewish God or observance of the sabbath.

---

[56] P. W. van der Horst, *The Sentences of Pseudo-Phocylides* (SVTP 4; Leiden: Brill, 1978); idem, 'Pseudo-Phocylides,' OTP, 2:565-82. [57] T. Baarda, 'The Sentences of the Syriac Menander,' OTP, 2:583-606.

Admonitions to help one's enemy with a fallen beast of burden (140; cf. Exod 23:5) or to refrain from sex with one's stepmother, the concubines of one's father, one's sister, or the wives of one's brothers (179-83) are derived from the Holiness Code (Lev 18:8-9, 16) and the story of Reuben (Gen 35:22; 49:4) but would be acceptable to many gentiles as well. Only the commands not to take the mother bird from the nest (84-85; cf. Deut 22:6-7) and not to eat meat torn by wild animals (147-48; cf. Exod 22:31) can be counted as strictly Jewish *halakhah*. But the first might have been included to give a scriptural-sounding verisimilitude to the piece, and both are the sort of praxis that a God-fearer or sympathizer might voluntarily adopt. I see nothing in this work that rules out authorship by a Christian (cf. Acts 15:29; 1 Cor 5:1), a sympathetic non-Christian gentile, or a Jew.[56]

Likewise, the Hermetic philosopher who wrote the *Poimandres* and the Greco-Egyptian practitioners of ritual power who composed, edited, and collected the incantations in PGM IV had both a literary bent and an interest in Judaism. Granted, these particular polytheists had such a sketchy knowledge of the subject that it is unlikely they could have produced Old Testament pseudepigrapha that looked convincingly Jewish. But the question is made more complex by Jews sympathetic to polytheism. Reference to the gods does not automatically exclude Jewish authorship. *Sepher Ha-Razim* was composed in Hebrew and transmitted in Jewish circles; but although it is almost certainly by a Jew, it contains incantations that invoke Greek gods. One of them is transliterated from Greek, so this was a language familiar to the author or the author's source. A somewhat better-informed, sympathetic gentile polytheist and a somewhat more syncretistic Jew who wrote in Greek could conceivably have written similar Old Testament pseudepigrapha with polytheistic tendencies and we would not be able to distinguish their origins. The *Sentences of the Syriac Menander* illustrates my point.[57] It is a pseudepigraphon attributed to the fourth-century BCE Athenian playwright and is filled with generic moralizing, much of it apparently derived from the Jewish scriptures. Nevertheless, it also refers sympathetically to Homer (78-93) and condemns priests who despise their gods (262-64). Was it written by a syncretistic Jew or a sympathetic polytheist? We do not know. And, finally, it is worth noting that Jews sometimes adopted gentile polytheistic literary works and made them their own. A premier example, as noted earlier in this chapter, is the *Story of Aḥiqar*.

6

JEWISH-CHRISTIANITY AND
JUDAIZING GENTILE CHRISTIANITY

JEWISH-CHRISTIANITY .... The problem of 'Jewish-Christianity' has long occupied scholars, and a vast bibliography has been generated on it.[58] To keep this chapter from expanding beyond all reasonable bounds I must focus the treatment of the subject very carefully. There has been much debate on how to define Jewish-Christianity; I use the term to mean Jewish followers of Jesus who accepted him as Messiah but maintained their Jewish ethnic identity and continued to observe the Jewish ritual cult as they understood it to apply. The question I wish to ask is, to what degree, if at all, can texts – specifically Old Testament pseudepigrapha – written by such people be isolated as a separate category? How can they – or can they – be distinguished not only from Jewish or Christian compositions, but also from Jewish texts that have been interpolated by Christian tradents or absorbed into Christian compositions and from works by judaizing gentile Christians?

An initial point, which may be made by noting an article by Raymond E. Brown, is that we must think in terms of 'Not Jewish Christianity and Gentile Christianity but Types of Jewish/Gentile Christianity.'[59] He shows that we should be thinking, not in terms of a bipolar distinction between Torah-observant Jewish and non-observant gentile Christianities, but of a continuum between observant and non-observant Christians, whether Jewish or gentile. He isolates four or five points on this continuum:

......[58]...... I will not attempt to review the history of scholarship on this subject. Recent surveys include J. Carelton Paget, 'Jewish Christianity,' *CAH*, 3:731-75; and David G. Horrell, 'Early Jewish Christianity,' in Esler (ed.), *The Early Christian World*, 1:136-67. ...... [59]...... Brown, 'Not Jewish Christianity and Gentile Christianity but Types of Jewish/Gentile Christianity,' *CBQ* 45 (1983): 74-79. Some additional attempts to define and describe early Jewish-Christianity include A. F. J. Klijn, 'The Study of Jewish Christianity,' *NTS* 20 (1974): 419-31; Bruce J. Malina, 'Jewish Christianity or Christian Judaism: Toward a Hypothetical Definition,' *JSJ* 7 (1976): 46-57; Stanley K. Riegel, 'Jewish Christianity: Definitions and Terminology,' *NTS* 24 (1978): 410-15; Simon C. Mimouni, 'Pour une définition nouvelle du judéo-christianisme ancien,' *NTS* 38 (1992): 161-86. ...... [60]...... Much of the New Testament, including the Gospels of Matthew and John; the letters of Paul, James, Jude, and John; and perhaps the book of Revelation, presumably would fit somewhere on this continuum, although it is not clear just where to place each text and in any case this is not important for my purposes. The main point is the existence of the continuum and its implications for the study of the Old Testament pseudepigrapha.

---

a Christians, whether Jewish or their gentile converts, who were fully observant of the Mosaic Torah (including circumcision), a form that maintained a strong connection with Jerusalem and spread at least to Galatia and Philippi.

b Partially observant Christians who did not require circumcision but required followers to keep some aspects of Jewish ritual purity. This form too had a close relationship with Jerusalem and was connected especially with James and Peter, although it spread widely elsewhere and seems to have been followed by Barnabas and John Mark.

c Christians who required neither circumcision nor the following of Jewish dietary rules, but who (probably, like types *a* and *b*) observed rules against marriage among close relatives, observed Jewish festivals and the temple cult, and did not require Jewish members to eschew circumcision and Torah observance. Paul in his milder statements (such as in Romans) fits this type.

d Hellenist Christians who did not observe any of the Jewish ritual law or cult. This type, which moved from Jerusalem into Samaria and beyond, is exemplified in an early stage by Paul in Galatians and later by the Gospel of John and the Letter to the Hebrews and is the branch from which gentile Christianity developed as a separate religion.

e Brown mentions also the Alexandrian Christianity of Apollos, as reported in Acts 18:24-25, which seemed not to know of baptism in the name of Jesus or receiving of the Holy Spirit, as another possible point on the continuum.

One could either debate elements in Brown's schema or attempt to nuance or add to it. Rather than doing either, I will simply underline the main point: first-century Jewish and gentile Christianity comprised a continuum when it came to the divisive issue of to what degree Jewish-Christians should follow the legal and ritual prescriptions of Judaism and gentile Christians should adopt Judaism as an ethnic and religious identity as part of conversion to Christianity. Brown's five points are to a degree arbitrary, identified through the accident of our surviving sources, but they plot a line, the points of which we must assume were occupied by individuals and communities now lost to us: there was a continuum in first-century Christianity between full Torah observance and retention or adoption of Jewish ethnic identity on the one pole and complete rejection of both on the other pole, a continuum very similar to the one we have already seen for Judaism in the same period.[60]

The existence of the former pole already raises a potential problem for the question of distinguishing between Jewish and Christian pseudepigrapha. A concrete example would be useful here: let us take the writer of the Gospel of Matthew, who in his surviving work makes it explicit that Torah observance is still required of the followers of Jesus (5:17-20; 23:1-3) and who refers to participation in the temple sacrificial cult (5:23-24); deletes the nullification of ritual purity regulations which Mark puts in the mouth of Jesus (Matt 15:17 // Mark 7:19); speaks approvingly of rigorous tithing (23:23); and alludes to the importance of the sabbath, which we may assume his readers kept (24:20). He does not accept details of the halakhic praxis of some other Jews (e.g., 15:20), but Jews commonly disagreed on such minor points. The writer does not mention circumcision, either because it was taken for granted or because he did not consider it important. We also do not know whether he expected gentile converts to follow the Torah. The writer of Matthew is thus a Torah-observant Christian who wrote a major religious work in the late first century.[61] It would not be taking a great liberty to imagine the author of Matthew writing another work, a pseudepigraphon about, say, visions of Moses. Quite likely such a work would include Jewish signature features. The author might have included *vaticinia ex eventu* or editorial foreshadowings regarding Jesus and early Christian theology, or he might consciously have written the work as though he were a figure

---

[61] Studies of the Gospel of Matthew in its Jewish context include William David Davies, *The Setting of the Sermon on the Mount* (Cambridge: Cambridge University Press, 1964); Reinhart Hummel, *Die Auseinandersetzung zwischen Kirche und Judentum im Matthäusevangelium* (BEvT 33; Munich: Chr. Kaiser, 1966); Amy Jill-Levine, *The Social and Ethnic Dimensions of Matthean Salvation History* (Lewiston, N.Y.: Mellen, 1988); J. A. Overman, *Matthew's Gospel and Formative Judaism: The Social World of the Matthean Community* (Minneapolis: Fortress 1990); David L. Balch (ed.), *Social History of the Matthean Community: Cross-Disciplinary Approaches* (Minneapolis: Augsburg Fortress, 1991); Graham Stanton, 'Matthew's Christology and the Parting of the Ways,' in Dunn (ed.), *Jews and Christians: The Parting of the Ways*, 99-116; idem, *A Gospel for a New People: Studies in Matthew* (Edinburgh: Clark, 1992); J. Leslie Houlden, 'The Puzzle of Matthew and the Law,' in *Crossing the Boundaries: Essays in Biblical Interpretation in Honour of Michael D. Goulder* (ed. Stanley E. Porter, Paul Joyce, and David E. Orton; Biblical Interpretation Series 8; Leiden: Brill, 1994), 115-31; David E. Orton, 'Matthew and Other Creative Jewish Writers,' in ibid., 133-40; Anthony J. Saldarini, *Matthew's Christian-Jewish Community* (Chicago: University of Chicago Press, 1994); David C. Sim, 'The Gospel of Matthew and the Gentiles,' *JSNT* 57 (1995): 19-48; Hans Kvalbein, 'Has Matthew Abandoned the Jews? A Contribution to a Disputed Issue in Recent Scholarship,' in *The Mission of the Early Church to Jews and Gentiles* (ed. Jostein Ådna and Hans Kvalbein; Tübingen: Mohr Siebeck, 2000), 45-68. I am grateful to Louise Lawrence for her advice on my bibliography on Matthew and Judaism. [62] The following information is derived from A. F. J. Klijn and G. J. Reinink, *Patristic Evidence for Jewish Christian Sects* (NTSup 36; Leiden: Brill, 1973);

from or in the period of the Jewish scriptures and avoided all mention of Christian matters. In the first instance we in the twenty-first century might recognize the work's true nature and label it 'Jewish-Christian,' but we might also, especially if the Christian elements were few and peripheral, be tempted to excise them as secondary in order to reconstruct a pristine Jewish work. And in the second instance we would not even need to resort to surgery: the *Visions of Moses* might give us positive evidence of being a pristine Jewish work, with no indicators to the contrary.

This scenario highlights some of the difficulties in reconstructing the origins of Jewish-Christian literature. But two qualifications are necessary. First, there is a sense in which the imaginary *Visions of Moses* ought to be taken as a Jewish work: if a fully Torah-observant Christian who either belonged to or (in the case of a gentile convert) was assimilated into an observant Jewish community, the work can legitimately be labeled 'Jewish,' insofar as the writer was fully informed about and assimilated to that Jewish community. Or, to turn the point around, it might be clearer to say that pseudepigrapha that give positive signs of being Jewish and no positive signs of being Christian could still in principle come from a very broad range of forms of Judaism, including fringe or borderline cases like that of the author of Matthew (or, perhaps more problematically, the 'type *b*' semi-observant Christianity of James or Peter or their Jewish or gentile followers).

The second point is that, although the author of Matthew might conceivably have produced an Old Testament pseudepigraphon that misled us into thinking it was strictly Jewish rather than Jewish-Christian in origin, it would also be possible for an ancient (non-Christian) Jewish writer to produce a pseudepigraphon that was undoubtedly Jewish but was extremely unlikely to be Jewish-Christian. If, for example, an explicitly Torah-observant author presented an eschatological scenario or a theodicy that is highly difficult to reconcile with (unmentioned) belief in Jesus as Messiah, we would be justified in considering the work Jewish but not Jewish-Christian. Similarly, if the internal evidence of the work placed it soundly in the pre-Christian era, the same conclusion would apply. Absolute certainty is impossible in our field, but such cases would shift the balance of probability to a point beyond reasonable doubt.

When we move to the second century and beyond, the problems we find are similar. The traditional picture of Jewish-Christianity, based mainly on patristic and rabbinic testimony, is of two groups, the 'Ebionites' and the 'Nazoraeans' or 'Nazarenes.'[62] We are told by Irenaeus that

the Ebionites used only the Gospel of Matthew, but they denied both
the virgin birth and that Jesus was God incarnate, and they rejected Paul
as an apostate from the Law. They engaged in careful exegesis of the
prophets. They followed the Jewish Law and customs, including circumcision, and 'adored Jerusalem as though it were the house of God.'[63]
Origen notes of the name Ebionites that its Hebrew meaning is 'poor
ones,' and reports that this group kept the Jewish dietary laws, that they
celebrated Easter on the same day as the Jewish festival of unleavened
bread (in imitation of Jesus), that some of them believed in the virgin
birth whereas others did not, and he repeats some information already
given by Irenaeus.[64] Epiphanius, along with many other patristic writers, refers to 'Ebion,' the, probably imaginary, eponymous founder of the
group. He reports that the Ebionites engaged in immersions for ritual

Ray A. Pritz, *Nazarene Jewish Christianity: From the End of the New Testament Period until Its Disappearance in the Fourth Century* (StPB 37; Leiden: Brill/Jerusalem: Magnes, 1988). Some other im-
portant recent studies include Wolfram Kinzig, '"Non-Separation": Closeness and Co-operation
Between Jews and Christians in the Fourth Century,' *VC* 45 (1991): 27-53, esp. pp. 29-35; Martinus
C. de Boer, 'The Nazoreans: Living at the Boundary of Judaism and Christianity,' in Stanton and
Stroumsa (eds.), *Tolerance and Intolerance*, 239-62; Simon C. Mimouni, 'I nazorei a partire dalla notizia 29 del *Panarion* di Epifanio di Salamina,' in Filoramo and Gianotto (eds.), *Verus Israel*, 120-46;
Richard Bauckham, 'The Origin of the Ebionites,' in *The Image of the Judaeo-Christians in Ancient
Jewish and Christian Literature* (ed. Peter J. Tomson and Doris Lambers-Petry; WUNT 158; Tübin-
gen: Mohr Siebeck, 2003), 162-81; Joseph Verheyden, 'Epiphanius on the Ebionites,' in ibid., 182-
208. [63] Klijn and Reinink, *Patristic Evidence*, 19-20, 102-107; quotation from p. 105.
[64] Ibid., 23-25, 124-35. [65] Ibid., 28-39, 154-55, 160-61, 174-97. [66] George
Howard, 'The Gospel of the Ebionites,' *ANRW* 2.25.5 (1987), 4034-53; A. F. J. Klijn, *Jewish-
Christian Gospel Tradition* (VCSup 17; Leiden: Brill, 1992), 65-77. [67] Klijn and Reinink,
Patristic Evidence, 21-23, 25-28, 39-43. [68] Taylor, 'The Phenomenon of Early Jewish-Chris-
tianity: Reality or Scholarly Invention?' *VC* 44 (1990): 313-34, esp. pp. 321-25. [69] Klijn and
Reinink, *Patristic Evidence*, 44-52, 154-55, 160-61, 169-75, 206-11, 217-29; Pritz, *Nazarene Jewish
Christianity*, 9-94. For the Gospel of the Nazoreans see A. F. J. Klijn, 'Das Hebräer- und das
Nazoräerevangelium,' *ANRW* 2.25.5 (1987), 3997-4033; idem, *Jewish Christian Gospel Tradition*,
86-115. [70] Pritz, *Nazarene Jewish Christianity*, 95-107; Reuven Kimelman, 'Birkat Ha-
Minim and the Lack of Evidence for an Anti-Christian Jewish Prayer in Late Antiquity,' in *Jewish
and Christian Self-Definition*, vol. 2, *Aspects of Judaism in the Graeco-Roman Period* (ed. E. P. Sanders
with A. I. Baumgarten and Alan Mendelson; London: SCM, 1981), 226-44, 391-403; Lawrence
H. Schiffman, *Who Was a Jew?* (Hoboken, N. J.: Ktav, 1985), 69-73; Philip S. Alexander, '"The Parting of the Ways" from the Perspective of Rabbinic Judaism,' in Dunn (ed.), *Jews and Christians:
The Parting of the Ways*, 1-25; William Horbury, 'The Benediction of the *Minim* and Early Jewish-
Christian Controversy,' in *Jews and Christians in Contact and Controversy* (Edinburgh: Clark, 1998),
67-101 (rpt. of *JTS* 33 [1982]: 19-61); Liliane Vana, 'La *birkat ha-minim* è una preghiera contro i
giudeocristiani?' in Filoramo and Gianotto (eds.), *Verus Israel*, 147-89.

purity; they forbade asceticism; they did not eat meat; they used the 'Hebrew Gospel,' from which he quotes passages. Epiphanius also makes use of a corrupted form of a book, the *Periodoi Petrou*, which he attributes to Clement, and another book, *Anabathmoi Iakobou*, in which James is said to have rejected the temple cult in Jerusalem. Epiphanius does not distinguish clearly among the groups he claims to describe and his comments should perhaps be used with caution.[65] He also quotes seven times from a gospel used by the Ebionites. Its ancient title is unclear but the modern convention is to refer to it as the 'Gospel of the Ebionites.' It appears to be a Greek harmony of the Synoptic Gospels, edited to reflect the Ebionite vegetarianism and antipathy toward the Jerusalem sacrificial cult.[66] A number of patristic writers emphasize that the Ebionites kept the Law on the ground of following the example of Jesus. Other comments on the Ebionites by other writers are either of dubious value or repeat the information given by these three witnesses.[67] We do not know to what degree the name Ebionites is a blanket term for different Jewish-Christian groups. Joan E. Taylor even raises the possibility that they were judaizing gentile Christians (on whom more below).[68]

We learn what we know about the Nazoraeans mainly from Epiphanius and Jerome, the former of whom drew on literary sources rather than firsthand knowledge for his account. Jerome claims to have had some contact with them, although he too used literary sources. The Nazoraeans lived in Syria and perhaps Jordan (Pella) and survived at least into the third century and perhaps into the fourth. They continued to observe Jewish Law, including circumcision and sabbath, but accepted Paul as an apostle and the resurrection and deity of Jesus, and they, or some of them, may also have accepted the virgin birth. They seem to have continued the use of Hebrew (or possibly Aramaic) and had a Gospel in this language to which Jerome refers frequently, although it is not clear how well he himself knew it. He also quotes from Nazorean exegesis of passages in Isaiah and refers tantalizingly to an apocryphon of Jeremiah in the group's possession. According to Jerome they knew of and disapproved of the rabbinic houses of Shammai and Hillel.[69] Passages in the Babylonian Talmud refer to a town of Nazarenes, Kefar Sechaniah, in the Galilee and tell of a second-century resident named Jacob who quoted an agraphon of Jesus. At least one early version of the twelfth benediction of the Amidah (the *birkat ha-minim*) curses not just 'sectarians' (*minim*) but also *Notzrim* (cognate and perhaps to be identified with the *Nazaraei*); a version containing 'Nazarenes' was known to Epiphanius and Jerome.[70] Other patristic evidence for Jewish-Christian groups could be cited, but these two are the best founded and give us some idea of what such groups may have been like.

It seems likely that some Jewish-Christian literature has survived apart from the patristic testimonies. Richard Bauckham has argued that the *Apocalypse of Peter* is a Jewish-Christian work from the time of the Bar Kokhba revolt, based on its interest in discerning which is the true and which the false Messiah, its concern with martyrdom, its hope for the future conversion of Israel, and its apparent rejection of the earthly temple cult.[71] The concern with Israel does offer some support for a Jewish background, although the long section on postmortem punishments in Chapters 7-12 says nothing about halakhic sins such as sabbath-breaking and eating forbidden foods, and this weakens the case.

Likewise, there have been attempts to reconstruct sources behind the Pseudo-Clementine *Recognitions* and *Homilies*. Some have argued that both the *Periodoi Petrou* and the *Anabathmoi Iakobou* (mentioned above) were sources of the Pseudo-Clementine literature and that they can be reconstructed at least to some degree, but this is debated.[72] More to the point, the Pseudo-Clementine literature in its surviving forms provides important testimony to fourth-century authors who found earlier Jewish-Christian literary sources worth editing and transmitting.[73] The *Homilies* seem to require the observance of Jewish ritual purity regulations, such as washing after sexual intercourse and to 'keep (the regulations concerning) menstrual impurity' (7.8.1-3; 11.28-30); not to

[71] Bauckham, 'The *Apocalypse of Peter*: A Jewish Christian Apocalypse from the Time of Bar Kokhba,' *Apocrypha* 5 (1994): 7-111; idem, 'Jews and Jewish Christians in the Land of Israel at the Time of the Bar Kokhba War, with Special Reference to the *Apocalypse of Peter*,' in Stanton and Stroumsa (eds.), *Tolerance and Intolerance*, 228-38. [72] For discussion, see Robert E. Van Voorst, *The Ascents of James: History and Theology of a Jewish-Christian Community* (SBLDS 112; Atlanta: Scholars Press, 1989); F. Stanley Jones, *An Ancient Jewish Christian Source on the History of Christianity: Pseudo-Clementine Recognitions 1.27-71* (SBLTT 37; SBL Christian Apocrypha Series 2; Atlanta: Scholars Press, 1995); Bauckham, 'The Origin of the Ebionites,' 164-71. [73] Annette Yoshiko Reed gives a preliminary analysis of the Pseudo-Clementines from this perspective in '"Jewish Christianity" after the "Parting of the Ways": Approaches to Historiography and Self-Definition in the Pseudo-Clementines,' in Becker and Reed (eds.), *The Ways That Never Parted*, 189-231. In the comments that follow I draw on this article and also on her paper, 'Fire, Blood, and Water: Demonology and Halakha in the Pseudo-Clementine *Homilies*,' presented at the annual meeting of the American Academy of Religion in Atlanta on 23 November 2003, of which she has kindly given me a copy.

partake of food offered to idols, that which dies of itself or is torn by wild animals, and strangled meat (7.8; 8.19); and refraining from eating with gentiles because of their impure life (13.4). The *Epistle of Peter to James*, associated with the *Homilies*, extols the eternal validity of the Law, excoriates Paul (without naming him), and requires that the *Homilies* be communicated only to the circumcised (2-4.1). A review of history put in the mouth of Peter in the *Recognitions* (1.27-71) rejects the validity of animal sacrifice (1.34-39) and blames Paul for instigating the martyrdom of James (1.69-70).

Thus there was a range of Torah-observant Jewish-Christians in the ancient world in the first several centuries C E. Some of these groups survived after the first century and held on to their Jewish ethnicity and observance of *halakhah*, even though they seem to have disagreed on issues of Christology and the legitimacy of the Apostle Paul. Some, but apparently not all, refrained from eating meat and were hostile toward the Jerusalem temple cult (or at least its memory). The important point for my purposes is that the existence of Torah-observant Jews who also followed Jesus creates complexities for our analysis of possible Jewish pseudepigrapha. These complexities have been outlined above in the discussion of the Gospel of Matthew. But I think it is fair to say that judaizing *gentile* Christians complicate the matter even more.

JUDAIZING GENTILE CHRISTIANITY ⸺ ⸺ From the earliest stages of Christianity there have been some gentile followers of Jesus who, to a greater or lesser degree, willingly followed Jewish ritual and halakhic customs as well. According to Chapter 15 of the book of Acts, a Jerusalem council required gentile converts to abstain from blood and meat that had been strangled (along with idolatry and sexual immorality). Whatever we make of the historicity of the Jerusalem council, it is clear enough that Paul opposed other followers of Jesus who required gentile converts to be circumcised and to follow Jewish dietary laws (Rom 2:25-29; 3:29-30; 4:9-12; Gal 2:1-21; 5:2-12; Phil 3:2-3). Such debates continued beyond the first century. Ignatius, bishop of Antioch, who was martyred in Rome during the reign of Trajan and who wrote seven letters to various churches on the journey to his martyrdom, warned his Magnesian readers not to live according to Judaism, following old practices such as the sabbath (*Magn.* 8-10), and cryptically admonished the Philadelphians not to heed anyone who 'interprets Judaism' to them, 'For it is better to hear Christianity from a man who has circumcision than Judaism from one uncircumcised' (*Phld.* 6:1). The exact meaning of this sentence has been debated, but its most natural sense is that the second part refers to gentile Christians who advocated a partial adherence to the ritual Law. The circumcised in the first part of the sentence appear to be Jewish converts to Christianity, but nothing in the sentence implies that they expected gentile Christians to follow Jewish Law. It is unclear whether

----

[74] William R. Schoedel, *Ignatius of Antioch: A Commentary on the Letters of Ignatius of Antioch* (Hermeneia; Philadelphia: Fortress, 1985), 16, 20-21, 118-27, 200-203; Paul J. Donahue, 'Jewish Christianity in the Letters of Ignatius of Antioch,' *VC* 32 (1978): 81-93; Mark Edwards, 'Ignatius, Judaism and Judaizing,' *Eranos* 93 (1995): 69-77; Enrico Norelli, 'Ignazio di Antiochia combatte veramente dei cristiani giudaizzanti?' in Filoramo and Gianotto (eds.), *Verus Israel*, 220-64.

[75] Thomas B. Falls, *Writings of Saint Justin Martyr* (FC 6; Washington, D.C.: Catholic University of America Press, 1948), 218-19; Graham N. Stanton, 'Justin Martyr's Dialogue with Trypho: Group Boundaries "Proselytes" and "God-fearers,"' in Stanton and Stroumsa (eds.), *Tolerance and Intolerance*, 263-78, esp. pp. 271-73.

[76] It is worth noting that there is secure evidence for ancient gentile Christians who looked forward to the eschatological restoration of Jerusalem and the rebuilding of the Jewish temple. Jerome (confirmed by Theodoret of Cyrus) informs us that both Jews and judaizing Christians or 'half-Jews' (*semiiudaei*) held such views, naming his contemporary, Apollinaris, bishop of Laodicea, as an example of the latter. Some Christian chiliasts (Cerinthus and Nepos) even anticipated the restoration of the sacrificial cult. See Robert L. Wilken, 'The Restoration of Israel in Biblical Prophecy: Christian and Jewish Responses in the Early Byzantine Period,' in Neusner and Frerichs et al. (eds.), *'To See Ourselves as Others See Us,'* 443-71.

[77] Paul W. Harkins, *Discourses against Judaizing Christians: Saint John Chrysostom* (FC 68; Washington, D.C.: Catholic University of America Press, 1979); Wayne A. Meeks and Robert L. Wilken, *Jews and Christians in Antioch in the First Four Centuries of the Common Era* (SBLSBS 13; Missoula, Mont.: Scholars Press, 1978), 25-36, 83-127; Robert L. Wilken, *John Chrysostom and the Jews: Rhetoric and Reality in the Late 4th Century* (Berkeley, Calif.: University of California Press, 1983); Adele Monaci Castagno, 'I giudaizzanti di Antiochia: bilancio e nuove prospettive di ricerca,' in Filoramo and Gianotto (eds.), *Verus Israel*, 304-38.

[78] A. P. Hayman, 'The Image of the Jew in the Syriac Anti-Jewish Polemical Literature,' in Neusner and Frerichs et al. (eds.), *'To See Ourselves as Others See Us,'* 423-41, esp. pp. 434-38; idem, *The Disputation of Sergius the Stylite Against a Jew* (2 vols.; CSCO 338-39; Scriptores Syri 152-53; Louvain: Corpus Scriptorum Christianorum Orientalium, 1973), 2:76.

[79] Other discussions of the evidence for judaizing gentile Christians include: Figueras, 'Epigraphic Evidence for Proselytism,' 205-206; Pieter W. van der Horst, 'Jews and Christians in Aphrodisias in the Light of Their Relationship in Other Cities of Asia Minor,' in *Essays on the Jewish World of Early Christianity* (Freiburg, Switzerland: Universitätsverlag/Göttingen: Vandenhoeck & Ruprecht, 1990), 166-81; Kinzig, '"Non-Separation,"' 35-43; Judith Lieu, 'History and Theology in Christian Views of Judaism,' in Lieu et al. (eds.), *The Jews among Pagans and Christians*, 79-96; Stephen G. Wilson, 'Gentile Judaizers,' *NTS* 38 (1992): 605-16; Louis H. Feldman, 'Proselytism by Jews in the Third, Fourth, and Fifth Centuries,' *JSJ* 24 (1993): 1-58, esp. pp. 9, 22-41; Reuven Kimelman, 'Identifying Jews and Christians in Roman Syria-Palestine,' in *Galilee Through the Centuries: Confluence of Cultures* (ed. Eric M. Meyers; Duke Judaic Studies 1; Winona Lake, Ind.: Eisenbrauns, 1999), 301-33; Wilson, 'Epigraphic Evidence for Jewish Defectors,' 365-67; Maren R. Niehoff, 'Circumcision as a Marker of Identity: Philo, Origen, and the Rabbis on Gen 17:1-14,' *JSQ* 10 (2003): 89-123, esp. p. 108.

Ignatius' judaizing opponents were the same as his docetic opponents or a different group, but this does not matter for my purposes.[74] Later in the second century (the conversation is set during the Bar Kokhba revolt) Justin Martyr acknowledged in the *Dialogue with Trypho* 47-48 that there were both Jewish converts to Christianity who continued to follow the Law and gentile Christians who, at the behest of Jewish-Christians, chose to live according to the Law. Justin believes that both groups would be saved (the former only if they did not attempt to persuade gentiles to follow the Law) but he says that not all Christians held this view.[75]

Some of the most striking evidence for judaizing gentile Christians comes from a series of eight sermons preached by John Chrysostom of Antioch in the late fourth century. Traditionally known as sermons *Against the Jews*, their wrath is directed mainly at Christian judaizers, although considerable invective is directed at Jews themselves as well. The first two sermons were given in the fall of 386 and the fourth through eighth in the fall of 387. The third sermon was preached just before Lent in 387. Chrysostom admonished his congregation against celebrating Jewish festivals and fasts (1 i 5; 1 vii 5; 2 i 1; 3 iii 1; 7 i 3; 8 v 4); worshiping in the synagogues (1 v 5-8; 6 vii 3-4; 8 viii 7-9) or swearing oaths in them (1 iii 4-5); going to Jews for healing of illness (1 vii 6-11; 8 v 6 - viii 6); submitting to circumcision (2 ii 4; 3 iii 1); celebrating Easter at the same time as the Jewish Passover (3 iii 3, 6, vi 12); and hoping for the rebuilding of the temple (5 passim; 7 ii 2).[76] Friendly contact between Jews and Christians and adoption of Jewish customs by Christians were clearly common enough in Antioch to be a source of great vexation to Chrysostom.[77]

His fulminations seem not to have had any great long-term effect on Syrian Christians, since as late as the eighth century we find judaizers being roundly condemned by Sergius the Stylite near Emesa in much the same terms as those used by Chrysostom. Christians were associating with Jews in the synagogue and participating in Jewish festivals.[78]

This survey of evidence for Judaizing gentile Christianity is far from complete, and much more could be cited: there is evidence in other church fathers such as Barnabas, Origen, Ephrem, and Jerome; there is epigraphic evidence; and there is evidence in the church canons.[79] But, again, the material covered suffices to demonstrate that some gentile Christians throughout antiquity were very interested in Judaism and adopted Jewish customs as they pleased while holding on to their Christian identities.

Reflections......... .... Our evidence for Jewish-Christianity and judaizing gentile Christians occupies a range of points between the putative parting of the ways between Judaism and gentile Christianity. We know that some Jews and some gentile Christians, rather than parting decisively, maintained communication. Some Jews adopted and preserved a belief in Jesus as Messiah or divine mediator while maintaining their ethnic identity and praxis. Some gentile Christians found Judaism attractive and adopted Jewish customs to go with their Christianity. Indeed, given both the paucity of our evidence and the filtering of it through both Christian and Jewish circles which really had parted from one another, it appears that there was a continuum between Judaism and Christianity throughout antiquity. Indeed, a recent collection of essays is entitled *The Ways That Never Parted.*[80]

Whether or not we go so far as to say that the ways never parted at all, the existence of this continuum rather than universally accepted sharp boundaries has implications for our study of the Old Testament pseudepigrapha: the question of whether a pseudepigraphon is Jewish or Christian becomes much more difficult, if not entirely irrelevant. It might be tempting to take the view that the question is not worth asking, that it is hopeless to try to establish the origins of a given work in anything like these terms. But I think this position goes too far. It is clear, for example, that the Mishnah, the Tosefta, the Midrashim, and the Hekhalot literature are 'Jewish.' It is clear also that the anti-judaizing homilies of Chrysostom as well as most ancient sermons and biblical commentaries by named patristic authors are 'Christian.' The reason we can assign such identities to these works is that they were written by people to whom such distinctions did matter. The traditionally authoritative sources in both Judaism and Christianity were written by Jews and Christians for whom the ways had indeed parted. These were the Jews and Christians towards the extremities of the continuum for whom the difference mattered and who, to borrow a concept from Reuven Kimelman, invested their energies in 'boundary maintenance.'[81] Much of the literature preserved from antiquity, almost certainly a dispropor-

---

......[80]...... Becker and Reed (eds.), *The Ways That Never Parted*. Note also Judith Lieu, '"The Parting of the Ways": Theological Construct or Historical Reality?' *JSNT* 56 (1994): 101-19.......
......[81]...... Kimelman, 'Identifying Jews and Christians,' 303-306....... ......[82]...... Kimelman, 'Identifying Jews and Christians,' 314-15.

tionate amount, was written by boundary maintainers. They wrote self-consciously as either Jews or Christians, whether implicitly (especially for the former) or explicitly (especially for the latter), in opposition to one another. Nevertheless, we have no reason to believe that boundary maintainers were the only ones who could write Old Testament pseud-epigrapha. Educated people from anywhere on the continuum would be capable of that. Indeed, as noted above, we have explicit testimony from Jerome that the Nazoraeans possessed a now lost apocryphon of Jeremiah.

So, if Judaism and Christianity had such porous borders that the space between them was really a continuum, isolating Jewish pseudepigrapha from Christian apocrypha is possible only toward either end of the con-tinuum, the regions that focus on boundary maintenance. We should expect a priori to find a large number of texts that cannot be identified in these terms because they come out of the space between. We may be able to assign some of these texts to specific intermediate points on the continuum: if a pseudepigraphon explicitly advocates the following of Jewish *halakhah* and vegetarianism, recognizes Jesus as the Messiah, and rejects the doctrine of the virgin birth, it may make sense to pigeonhole it as 'Ebionite.' But more often we may have to hold several quite disparate possibilities as equally likely.

Two other points are worth mentioning. First, Kimelman raises the possibility of Torah-observant gentile Christians whom he calls 'bib-licizers' rather than 'judaizers.' Such Christians, having converted to Christianity and accepted the authority of the scriptures, would then of their own accord have adopted some of the laws and rituals found in the Jewish scriptures merely because they were scriptural and could be argued to be ratified by parts of the New Testament, such as Matt 5:17-19. We need not assume that they had contact with any actual Jews.[82] I know of no verifiable cases of biblicizing Christians (and such cases would be extremely difficult to verify), but we cannot rule out the trou-bling possibility that even an Old Testament pseudepigraphon that makes use of Jewish scriptural law could have been written by a bibliciz-ing gentile Christian who had no direct knowledge of Judaism. To be confident that a work is Jewish or judaizing, we would have to show it contained demonstrably Jewish traditions that go beyond the scriptures.

Second, if a work has only one or two allusions to matters with which we might expect Jews to be concerned but not Christians (matters such as Torah and Jewish ritual), this is not enough to establish authorship by a boundary-maintaining Jew, even if there are no Christian elements in the work. Even the most orthodox of boundary-maintaining Christians occasionally referred to such matters in surprisingly positive terms. For example, as we shall see in Chapter Two, the fourth-century Syrian church father Ephrem the Syrian, no lover of Judaism, takes Moses and his wife to task in his commentary on Exodus for not circumcising their son when the Lord had commanded it (Exod 4:24-26). He also opens the first of his Hymns on Paradise with praise of Moses and the Law.[83] We cannot rely on isolated comments but must look for a pattern of features and converging lines of evidence to ascertain whether a work was written by a boundary-maintaining Jew.

7   NON- OR QUASI-
      JEWISH ISRAELITES

In addition to these traditions that either emanate out of or are parasitic on Jewish tradition, there are two groups that have been argued to descend from an Israelite origin but to be, to a greater or lesser extent, independent of the Judean or Jewish tradition: the Samaritans and the Galileans.

---

[83] Edward G. Mathews, Jr., and Joseph P. Amar, with Kathleen McVey, *St. Ephrem the Syrian: Selected Prose Works* (FC 91; Washington, D.C.: Catholic University Press of America, 1994), 234-36; Sebastian Brock, *Hymns on Paradise: St. Ephrem* (Crestwood, N.Y.: St. Vladimir's Seminary Press, 1998), 77. [84] John MacDonald, *The Theology of the Samaritans* (London: SCM, 1964), 15-24. Ingrid Hjelm, *The Samaritans and Early Judaism: A Literary Analysis* (JSOTSup 303; Copenhagen International Seminar 7; Sheffield: Sheffield Academic Press, 2000), 239-72. [85] Recent archaeological work has now established the existence of a citadel and a temple on Gerizim in the second temple period. See Yitzhaq Magen, 'A Fortified City from the Hellenistic Period on Mount Gerizim,' *Qadmoniot* 19 (1986): 91-101 (Hebrew); idem, 'Mount Gerizim – A Sanctuary City,' *Qadmoniot* 23 (1990): 70-96 (Hebrew); idem, 'Mount Gerizim and the Samaritans,' in *Early Christianity in Context: Monuments and Documents* (ed. F. Manns and E. Alliata; Studium Biblicum Franciscanum Collectio Maior 38; Jerusalem: Franciscan Printing Press, 1993), 91-148. The Mount Gerizim excavations are still being published. See also Ingrid Hjelm, 'What Do Samaritans and Jews Have in Common? Recent Trends in Samaritan Studies,' *Currents in Biblical Research* 3 (2004): 9-62, esp. pp. 16-17, 19-21, 30; idem, *Jerusalem's Rise to Sovereignty in Ancient Tradition and History: Zion and Gerizim in Competition* (JSOTSup 404; CIS 14; London: Clark, 2004). [86] Ferdinand Dexinger, 'Samaritan Eschatology,' in *The Samaritans* (ed. Alan D. Crown; Tübingen: Mohr-Siebeck, 1989), 266-92. [87] MacDonald, *The Theology of the Samaritans*, 276-310; I. R. M. Bóid, 'The Samaritan Halachah,' in Crown (ed.), *The Samaritans*, 624-49; Reinhard Pummer, 'Samaritan Rituals and Customs,' in ibid., 650-90.

The Samaritans...... ......The home of the Samaritans is the biblical region in the central hill country known as the hill country of Ephraim, north of the hill country of Judah and south of the lower Galilee. According to their own traditions, the Samaritans are the descendants of the northern tribes of Israel who either avoided deportation by the Assyrians in 722 B C E or who were shortly afterward allowed by an Assyrian king to return from exile and re-establish worship on Mount Gerizim. They themselves trace the split with the southerners to the time of Eli, who set up a sanctuary in Shiloh rival to the authorized one on Mount Gerizim. The biblical account implies that they were the miscegenated descendants of the foreign polytheists who were imported into the region by the Assyrians.[84] It is irrelevant for our purposes which version of their origins is closer to the truth. By the second temple period the Samaritan and Judean communities found themselves frequently in conflict with one another, but they remained in close contact, even at times intermarrying, much to the chagrin of Judean nationalists such as the author of the book of Nehemiah (Neh 13:28). A temple along the lines of the Jerusalem temple was built by the Samaritans on Mount Gerizim during the second temple period and was destroyed by John Hyrcanus in the late second century B C E.[85] During the second temple period, relations between Samaritans and Jews gradually deteriorated. We may reasonably suppose that Samaritans were increasingly distinguishable from Jews during the closing centuries B C E and into the early Common Era, as both groups shored up the boundaries between them.

Our sources indicate that the ancient Samaritans considered themselves to be the descendants of Israelites and the 'guardians' of the Mosaic traditions. They worshiped the God of Israel, revered the Pentateuch as their scripture and Moses as the mediator of its revelation, and believed that God had appointed Mount Gerizim rather than Jerusalem as the chosen site for his exclusive worship (hence the temple built on Gerizim). Their ideology favored northern Israel and was actively hostile to Judean traditions. They also had a distinctive eschatology that involved a messianic figure known as the *Taheb* or 'one who is to come.'[86] We have good reason to believe that the Samaritans had their own halakhic traditions, but the surviving Samaritan halakhic works are all very late and we have little positive evidence for Samaritan *halakhah* in our period of interest. In antiquity they appear to have followed basic Jewish customs such as circumcision, sabbath observance, and rules for ritual purity, and to have had their own Zadokite priesthood as well.[87] We also know that the Samaritans had their own calendrical system and that they seem to have celebrated the major scriptural festivals, although not the festivals of Hanukkah or Purim.[88]

A number of points of Samaritan belief could, if they figured in a

[88] Sylvia Powels, 'The Samaritan Calendar and the Roots of Samaritan Chronology,' in ibid., 691-742; T.C.G.Thornton, 'The Samaritan Calendar: A Source of Friction in New Testament Times,' *JTS* 42 (1991): 577-80; Ferdinand Dexinger, 'Samaritan and Jewish Festivals: Comparative Considerations,' in *New Samaritan Studies of the Société d'Études Samaritaines: Essays in Honour of G.D.Sixdenier, III-IV* (ed. Alan D.Crown and L.Davey; Studies in Judaica 5; Syndey: Mandelbaum, 1995), 57-78. [89] Ze'ev Ben Hayyim, 'Samaritan Hebrew–An Evaluation,' in Crown (ed.), *The Samaritans*, 517-30; Rudolph Macuch, 'Samaritan Languages: Samaritan Hebrew, Samaritan Aramaic,' in ibid., 531-84. [90] This is not to say that the mere appearance of the Greek term Ἀργαριζίν demonstrates Samaritan authorship. It does not, since it has been shown by R.Pummer that this and similar Greek transliterations were used also by non-Samaritans ('ΑΡΓΑΡΙΖΙΝ: A Criterion for Samaritan Provenance?' *JSJ* 18 [1987]: 18-25). It is the ideological *use* of Mount Gerizim as the central place of worship which is a telling indicator of Samaritan origin. [91] For example, Ruth Jacoby has argued the probability that the modern Samaritan custom of using the plant species mentioned in the Torah for the Sukkot holiday, rather than the four species used in rabbinic Judaism, is ancient, based on iconographic evidence from ancient Samaritan oil lamps. See her 'The Four Species in Jewish and Samaritan Tradition,' in *From Dura to Sepphoris: Studies in Jewish Art and Society in Late Antiquity* (ed. Lee I.Levine and Zeev Weiss; Journal of Roman Archaeology Supplementary Series 40; Portsmouth, R.I.: Journal of Roman Archaeology, 2001), 225-30. Crown has also noted some differences between Samaritan and rabbinic *halakhah* in the matters of circumcision and sabbath and Passover observance, although it is not certain how ancient some of these differences are ('Redating the Schism between the Judaeans and the Samaritans,' *JQR* 82 [1991]: 17-50, esp. p. 21 n. 11). See also idem, 'Qumran, Samaritan *Halakha* and Theology and Pre-Tannaitic Judaism,' in *Boundaries of the Ancient Near Eastern World: A Tribute to Cyrus Gordon* (ed. Meir Lubetski, Claire Gottlieb, and Sharon Keller; JSOTSup 273; Sheffield: Sheffield Academic Press, 1998), 420-41, in which he uses cautious and sometimes lateral readings of a wide range of ancient and more recent sources to attempt to reconstruct some pre-Tannaitic Samaritan *halakhah*. Reinhard Pummer looks at differences between ancient Jewish and Samaritan religious material culture in 'How to Tell a Samaritan Synagogue from a Jewish Synagogue,' *BAR* 24.3 (1998): 24-35. Some Dosithean sectarian halakhic and calendrical peculiarities are also noted by Jarl Fossum in 'Sects and Movements' in Crown (ed.), *The Samaritans*, 293-389, esp. pp. 305-307, 310-12, 332; and idem, 'Dustan and Dosithean Halakha,' in Crown, Pummer, and Tal (eds.), *A Companion*, 78-80. [92] Ross S.Kraemer has raised the possibility that *Joseph and Aseneth* could be of Samaritan provenance in her article 'Could Aseneth Be Samaritan?' in *A Multiform Heritage: Studies on Early Judaism and Christianity in Honor of Robert A.Kraft* (ed. Benjamin G.Wright; Scholars Press Homage Series 24; Atlanta: Scholars Press, 1999), 149-65. I consider her arguments in Chapter Four, below. It has also been argued that *Aramaic Levi*, a fragmentary work known from the Qumran library and the Cairo Geniza, had a Samaritan provenance, although the most recent proponent admits forthrightly that the evidence consists only of a 'concentration of northern place names' and some other 'tantalizing hints.' See Robert A.Kugler, 'Some Further Evidence for the Samaritan Provenance of *Aramaic Levi* (1QTestLevi; 4QTestLevi),' *RevQ* 17/65-68 (1996): 351-58; quotations from pp. 351 and 358, respectively.

literary work, distinguish it from a Jewish document. A work written in the Samaritan dialect of Aramaic might well be classified immediately as Samaritan if it contained specific Samaritan linguistic features, but Samaritan Aramaic is often indistinguishable from contemporary Jewish Palestinian Aramaic. A Samaritan work composed in Greek or translated into Greek would be still more difficult to classify. A work composed in Samaritan Hebrew but then transmitted for a lengthy period by Jews who thought in Talmudic Hebrew might also be difficult to isolate on linguistic grounds.[89] Perhaps the most obviously Samaritan feature would be acceptance of Mount Gerizim as the place of the central sanctuary.[90] Use of exclusively Samaritan theological jargon (such as *Taheb*) would be another, assuming it appeared in transliteration in a work written in a language other than Aramaic or Hebrew. It is more difficult to isolate other uniquely Samaritan elements that would survive translation. Strong preference for Israelite traditions and hostility to Judean ones could be a indicator of Samaritan authorship. Uniquely Samaritan *halakhah* and ritual or calendrical observances, in the rare cases they can be isolated, would be as well.[91] More general factors, such as an interest in the geographical area of ancient Samaria, would also be of ancillary value, although not of great force in themselves.

But after all this has been said, the fact remains that much of Samaritan belief and praxis would under many circumstances be indistinguishable from Judaism, especially to those at some distance from the tradition: ancient gentile Christians would have had little interest in making fine distinctions in matters of *halakhah* or Jewish belief, and we modern scholars, although prepared to do so, possess too few early sources to be able to with any great confidence.

FRAGMENTS OF SAMARITAN DOCUMENTS? ⸺ A number of quotation-fragments preserved by the church historian Eusebius have been assigned to Samaritan authorship by some modern scholars. Even though these are not precisely Old Testament pseudepigrapha as understood in this book, they can to some degree serve our purpose as test cases for establishing Samaritan authorship of works transmitted by Christians.[92] The most persuasive case is made for the fragments of 'Pseudo-Eupolemus.' Eusebius transmits (via Alexander Polyhistor) a number of fragments of a work on the Judean monarchy by a Jewish author named Eupolemus, perhaps to be identified with Judah the Maccabee's ambassador to Rome (1 Mac 8:17; 2 Mac 4:11). But one of these fragments has a rather different character from the rest, and it has been argued that

53

it, along with another fragment whose author is not named, comes from the pen of another writer, perhaps a Samaritan. The passage attributed to Eupolemus (*Praep. ev.* 9.17.2-9) relates stories about the giants and the Tower of Babel as well as Abraham, Melchizedek, and some antediluvian patriarchs. Euhemerized Greek myths and other nonbiblical traditions are correlated with these stories, although the world view of the fragment is firmly monotheistic and well within the range of the possible even for boundary-maintaining Hellenistic Judaism. The key point is that after Abraham rescued the hostages taken captive by the 'Armenians,' 'he was welcomed as a guest by the city in the temple of Argarizin, which is to be translated "mountain of the Most High."' The syntax of the Greek sentence is not entirely clear, but the intent to identify the 'Salem' of Gen 14:18 with Mount Gerizim rather than Jerusalem is obvious.[93] R. Doran, however, argues against a Samaritan provenance for the fragment and believes it to be from the work of the actual Eupolemus.

---

[93] For discussion and bibliography, see Ben Zion Wacholder, *Eupolemos: A Study of Judaeo-Greek Literature* (Cincinnati, Ohio: Hebrew Union College–Jewish Institute of Religion, 1974), 2-3, 6-7, 22-24, 46, 71, 87, 104-105, 135, 162, 205-206, 287-93; Holladay, *Historians*, 157-87. [94] R. Doran, 'Pseudo-Eupolemus,' in *OTP*, 2:873-82, esp. p. 875. [95] Pummer, 'ΑΡΓΑΡΙΖΙΝ: A Criterion for Samaritan Provenance?' [96] Y. Magen, L. Tsfania, and H. Misgav, 'The Hebrew and Aramaic Inscriptions from Mt. Gerizim,' *Qad* 33 (120): 125-32 (Hebrew); Hjelm, 'What Do Samaritans and Jews Have in Common?' 20. [97] If the second fragment attributed to Pseudo-Eupolemus (*Praep. ev.* 9.18.2) is by the same author, it too, of course, was written by a Samaritan. But despite the similarity of content, the second fragment itself has no indication of Samaritan authorship, and I take no position on its origins. [98] For a recent discussion with bibliography, see Michael Daise, 'Samaritans, Seleucids, and the Epic of Theodotus,' *JSP* 17 (1998): 25-51. See also Hjelm, *The Samaritans and Early Judaism*, 138-46. For English translations and commentary, see F. Fallon, 'Theodotus,' *OTP*, 2:785-93; Carl R. Holladay, *Fragments from Hellenistic Jewish Authors*, vol. 2, *Poets* (SBLTT 30; SBLPS 12; Atlanta: Scholars Press, 1989), 51-204. [99] Van der Horst, 'Moses' Throne Vision in Ezekiel the Dramatist,' *JJS* 34 (1983): 21-29, esp. p. 28 n. 47; idem, 'Some Notes on the *Exagoge* of Ezekiel,' *Mnemosyne* 37 (1984): 354-75. In more recent work he sees 'no reason at all to regard' authors besides Pseudo-Eupolemus and Theodotus as Samaritan; see his 'The Samaritan Languages in the Pre-Islamic Period,' 178 and n. 3. Nina L. Collins also finds Samaritan authorship doubtful on the basis of Ezekiel's calendar; see her 'Ezekiel, the Author of the *Exagoge*: His Calendar and Home,' *JSJ* 22 (1991): 201-11, esp. p. 210. For English translations and commentary, see R. G. Robertson, 'Ezekiel the Tragedian,' *OTP*, 2:803-19; Holladay, *Poets*, 301-529. [100] Wayne A. Meeks, 'Moses as God and King,' in *Religions in Antiquity: Essays in Memory of Erwin Ramsdell Goodenough* (ed. Jacob Neusner; SHR 14; Leiden: Brill, 1968), 354-71; Joseph P. Schultz, 'Angelic Opposition to the Ascension of Moses and the Revelation of the Law,' *JQR* 61 (1970-71): 282-307; Crispin Fletcher-Louis, '4Q374: A Discourse on the Sinai Traditions of Moses and Early Christology,' *DSD* 3 (1996): 236-52.

He points out that the LXX identifies Salem with Shechem in Gen 33:18 and therefore he concludes that the fragment merely sides with the opinion that Salem was in the valley of Shechem rather than Jerusalem, but this does not prove that its author was a Samaritan.[94] It is true that the LXX makes this identification, and it is also true that the Greek phrase Ἀργαριζίν, written as a single word, was not used only by Samaritans.[95] Nevertheless, Doran does not address some important points. The writer not only locates Melchizedek's sanctuary in the region of Shechem, he identifies it specifically with Mount Gerizim, which he calls 'mountain of the Most High.' This is not a neutral geographical note, it is an ideological assertion about the holiness of the place and its suitability as the site of God's temple which would be unimaginable in the mouth of a Jew in the second century BCE. Indeed, the epigraphic evidence indicates that the Samaritan temple was dedicated to YHWH El Elyon, 'YHWH, God Most High.'[96] Despite the brevity of the fragment, it contains a very strong indicator of Samaritanism. The working hypothesis that it was written by a Samaritan is robust and is our best starting point.[97]

Three other fragmentary works quoted by Eusebius have been argued to be Samaritan. The epic poem by Theodotus, which deals with the city of Shechem and presents its defeat by Levi and Simeon in a positive light, has been taken by some to be an anti-Samaritan piece and by others to be a composition by Samaritans hostile to Shechem.[98] Rather than trying to adjudicate between the various proposals, I will simply point out that there is nothing in the surviving fragments of the work of Theodotus which either could not have been written by a Jew or must have been written by a Samaritan. One can make a plausible case for either provenance; the arguments turn on subtle reconstructions of the history and social background of a period and region that are still very imperfectly understood, and recent literature recognizes and attempts to come to terms with the real-life complexities of the situation. My aim in this chapter is to work out the limits of what we can know beyond reasonable doubt, and the most I can say is that the work of Theodotus falls outside that range.

The *Exagoge* of Ezekiel the Tragedian is usually assigned an Alexandrian provenance, but a Samaritan origin has been proposed as well. Pieter W. van der Horst has suggested that the possibility should remain open, given the similarities between the exalted Moses of the *Exagoge* and the exalted Moses documented in later Samaritan tradition.[99] Indeed, the possibility should remain open, but given the exaltation of Moses in Jewish literature as well,[100] any case for Samaritan origins would have to be argued on the basis of specific parallels to Samaritan theology. Moreover, Freudenthal's suggestion that Cleodemus Malchus was a Samaritan is based on specious or erroneous grounds (chiefly 'syncretism,' along with a highly implausible association of Heracles with the Tyrian god Melkart worshiped on Mount Gerizim) and to my knowledge this view is no longer argued by any scholar.[101]

THE GALILEANS...... ...... North of Samaria and separated from it by the Jezreel valley is the region known as the Galilee (perhaps because it was 'ringed' about to the north by gentile settlements), the northernmost area of the central hill country. Although very little literature from the pre-Tannaitic period has been assigned by scholars to Galilee, George Nickelsburg has argued for such a provenance for Chapters 12-16 of the Enochic Book of the Watchers.[102] If one Old Testament pseudepigraphon may have emerged from ancient Galilee, it is worthwhile to consider whether Galileans should be understood as Jews or whether they preserved a coherent non-Jewish Israelite identity.

The issue arises primarily because Richard Horsley promotes the view that there is a direct line of continuity between Israelite culture after the destruction of the northern kingdom of Israel in 722 B C E and Galilean

...... [101] ...... R. Doran, 'Cleodemus Malchus,' OTP, 2:883-87; Holladay, Historians, 245-59. ....
...... [102] ...... Nickelsburg, 'Enoch, Levi, and Peter: Recipients of Revelation in Upper Galilee,' JBL 100 (1981): 575-600, esp. pp. 585-87; idem, 1 Enoch 1, 238-47. .... [103] ...... Richard A. Horsley, Galilee: History, Politics, People (Valley Forge, Penn.: Trinity, 1995), 19-52; idem, Archaeology, History, and Society in Galilee (Valley Forge, Penn.: Trinity, 1996), 15-42; idem, 'The Expansion of Hasmonean Rule in Idumea and Galilee: Toward a Historical Sociology,' in Second Temple Studies III: Studies in Politics, Class and Material Culture (ed. Philip R. Davies and John M. Halligan; JSOTSup 340; Sheffield: Sheffield Academic Press, 2002), 134-65. In his earlier work Seán Freyne seemed to accept much the same scenario, although it mattered less for his purposes, and he has moved to a less robust view of the ethnic and cultural continuity of Galilee in his later work. See his Galilee from Alexander the Great to Hadrian 323 BCE to 135 CE (2nd ed.; Edinburgh: Clark, 1998 – originally published in 1980), 16-56, Galilee, Jesus and the Gospels: Literary Approaches and Historical Investigations (Philadelphia: Fortress, 1988), 169-70; idem, 'Galileans, Phoenicians, and Itureans: A Study of Regional Contrast in the Hellenistic Age,' in Collins and Sterling (eds.), Hellenism in the Land of Israel, 182-215, esp. pp. 195-99. ...... [104] ...... Horsley, Galilee, 137-57, 244. Freyne is more positive about the possibility of Galileans tithing and making pilgrimage, although he acknowledges that the evidence is far from unequivocal; see Galilee from Alexander the Great, 293-97; idem, Galilee, Jesus and the Gospels, 178-90. ...... [105] ...... Horsley, Galilee, 50, 107, 148-49, 236-37, 245-46, 251-52; idem, Archaeology and History, 173-74.

culture in the Hasmonean period onward. Although the population may have been somewhat mixed, a significant proportion of it must have been of north Israelite descent. Rejecting as inconclusive the archaeological evidence of surface surveys for a massive depopulation of the region until the Persian period, he argues for the continuity of the later inhabitants with the northern Israelites. When incorporated into the Judean temple-state by the Hasmoneans, the Galileans probably shared some Israelite traditions with the Judeans, but after many centuries of separate transmission, the two cultures must have been quite different, and it is difficult to believe that the resocialization could have been very thoroughgoing.[103] Although granting some degree of cultural overlap, Horsley disputes that the Galileans tithed to the Jerusalem priesthood or made pilgrimage to the Jerusalem temple in any significant numbers, or that they followed the 'laws of Moses,' as understood by the Judeans, before the Hasmonean annexation. Differences in halakhic customs can be documented in the Mishnah.[104] Although lacking a native royal or priestly aristocracy, Galileans would have passed on their own popular and unofficial variants of northern biblical traditions. As evidence for their Galilean transmission, Horsley points to their transmission in the Jesus tradition and in Josephus' accounts of the movement led by Judas the Galilean and of other stories in which Galileans were involved. Horsley even speculates that the continuing propensity of Galileans to revolt against their overlords well into late antiquity was due to their cultivation of Israelite covenantal ideals and traditions of resistance to foreign rule.[105]

Whatever the archaeological merits (or not) of the case for continued occupation of Galilee by Israelites between 722 and the Hasmonean period, I think it is fair to say that Horsley's reconstruction of the survival of Israelite traditions in Galilee is intrinsically improbable. We are asked to believe that northern traditions also known from the Hebrew Bible were transmitted orally for six centuries by a population with no royal court or cult, yet somehow these traditions remained recognizable enough to give some religious commonality between Jews and Galileans in the second century BCE. I would expect that over such a long period the northern oral tradition would have diverged from the southern nearly to the point of unrecognizability. Moreover, even if we were to grant such a highly implausible fidelity of oral transmission, we could hardly assume that the northern tradition remained static. Surely new prophets and prophecies, new heroes, and new legends would have arisen during this time, and some would have gained a canonical status in the oral cycle equivalent to the stories paralleled in the Jewish scriptures; yet we find no trace of a postbiblical Galilean cycle of sacred legends.

Horsley's evidence for his reconstruction falls far short of proof. It is true enough that such first-century Galilean traditions as we have from the Gospels and Josephus make use of northern figures and tales – a fact that can be explained adequately by Galilean interest in local traditions – but the same material was used in Judea.[106] Moreover, in our earliest sources – Mark and Q – Jesus is portrayed as drawing also on Judean as well as Jewish traditions from long after the fall of the northern kingdom: Isaiah, including Deutero-Isaiah (Matt 11:5 // Luke 7:22; Mark 7:6-7; 9:48; 11:17); Judean psalms (Mark 1:11; 12:10-11, 35-37; 15:34); Micah (Matt 10:35-36 // Luke 12:51-53); Zechariah (Mark 14:27); Malachi (Matt 11:10 // Luke 7:27; Mark 1:2); and Daniel (e.g., Mark 13:14, 26; 14:62). The halakhic discussions he engages in assume the same Mosaic Torah as was used by his Judean contemporaries, one which did not exist in the late eighth century BCE to be transmitted independently in the north (e.g., Mark 1:43-44; 10:2-9, 17-19; 12:18-27, 29-31). He does not dispute the *texts* of their traditions but only their *meanings*. And Jesus and other Galilean figures do not refer to authoritative nonscriptural Galilean prophets and stories, if such existed.

The later in time we search, the less likely it becomes that an ancient northern oral cycle lies hidden behind our sources. It is true that the Mishnah recognizes differences between rabbinic and Galilean *halakhah*, but as Lawrence H. Schiffman has shown, Galileans and Judeans ultimately shared the same halakhic system with very minor variations, with the Galileans in many cases holding the more stringent view.[107]

In other words, the existence of Horsley's independent Galilean tradition is not supported by common sense or by such evidence as we have. We have no reason to believe that putative Old Testament pseudepigrapha composed in Galilee would have content notably different

---

[106] Freyne, *Galilee, Jesus and the Gospels*, 193-97. Jonathan L. Reed, 'Galileans, "Israelite Village Communities," and the Sayings Gospel Q,' in Meyers (ed.), *Galilee Through the Centuries*, 87-108, esp. pp. 104-108. [107] Lawrence H. Schiffman, 'Was There a Galilean Halakhah?' in *The Galilee in Late Antiquity* (ed. Lee I. Levine; Cambridge: Harvard University Press, 1992), 143-56. Martin Goodman reaches a similar conclusion in 'Galilean Judaism and Judaean Judaism,' *CHJ*, 3:596-617.

Jewish pseudepigrapha & Christian Apocrypha:
(How) Can we tell them apart?

from works composed by Judeans. Such halakhic differences between Galileans and Judeans as existed were minor and would be unlikely to stand out to us. One could perhaps argue that a given work originated in Galilean circles if it showed particular interest in Galilean geography and northern scriptural traditions (1 *Enoch* 12-16 is one possible example), but ultimately such a case would remain speculative and such works can still reasonably be classed as Jewish for our purposes.

8

THE RANGE OF
POSSIBILITIES

At this point I have surveyed sufficiently the state of the question for ancient Judaism, along with my interpretation of the implications of our current understanding. We have seen that social and intercultural relations between Jews, gentiles, and Christians in the Greco-Roman period and late antiquity were as complex as social and intercultural relations in the modern world. This is, of course, what we should assume in the first place, but often this basic point is lost when scholars work with our sources for the ancient world. I found few sharp borders but rather a series of continua in most of the relationships explored: from interested gentile to Jew; from Jew to gentile; from Jew to Christian; and from gentile Christian to Jew. There may not have been a clear 'parting of the ways' between Judaism and Christianity in antiquity. And Jewish relations with the non-Christian gentile world were complex. Our picture of all these relationships has been distorted because most of our Jewish and Christian sources have been passed down by Jews and Christians after late antiquity, when the ways had parted, and these Jews and Christians transmitted such ancient literature as was congenial to them: mostly work by Jews and Christians who occupied the extremes of the continuum – what became the mainstreams – and for whom, therefore, the ways had parted early on. These are what I refer to as 'boundary-maintaining' Jews and Christians. Our picture of them is comparatively clear; it is the continuum between them (and between Jews and gentiles) which remains poorly defined and poorly understood due to the paucity of our sources. But lack of source material should not lead us to conclude that those who occupied the inner portion of these continua were few in number. If we could somehow map the continua as graphs and knew where to assign every person in antiquity as a point on a graph, what would be the composition of the curves? Would boundary-maintainers take up a larger portion on either side? We cannot assume that this would be so. It is possible that they would occupy only the corners of a bell curve. Yet it is primarily the literary works of the boundary-maintainers which we have some hope of confidently assigning a place.

The parting of the ways between Samaritanism and Judaism developed gradually but seems to have been more or less complete by the fourth century C E. By this time Jews and Samaritans had established the boundaries between them in a way that leaves little room for a middle ground or for confusion between them. There was, however, a significant overlap in their beliefs and praxes and we cannot be confident that we can always tell a Samaritan pseudepigraphon from a Jewish one.

Two groups that could be distinguished from Jews in theory can in practice be treated as Jewish for my purposes. Proselytes, although regarded both by Jews and by themselves belonging to a slightly different and perhaps inferior category, would be likely to write pseudepigrapha indistinguishable from Jewish pseudepigrapha. As for Galileans, I find no convincing evidence that they preserved an independent northern Israelite corpus of traditions. We can expect that works by Galileans would, for the most part at least, be indistinguishable from works by Jews.

Taking these conclusions and all the data studied thus far in this chapter, let us now look at the range of possible origins for an ancient Old Testament pseudepigraphon. We should harbor no illusions that in every case, or even in many cases, we shall be able to recover the actual origin of a given pseudepigraphon. On the contrary, for the most part we can hope only to isolate pseudepigrapha written by boundary-maintaining Jews and Christians or by non-Christian gentiles who were fairly poorly informed about Judaism. For many works we shall have to be content with laying out a narrower or wider range of possible origins. In this section

---

108 Theoretical studies of the redaction criticism of apocryphal and pseudepigraphic works include Gillis Byrns Coleman, 'The Phenomenon of Christian Interpolations into Jewish Apocalyptic Texts: A Bibliographical Survey and Methodological Analysis' (Ph. D. diss., Vanderbilt University, 1976); and James H. Charlesworth, 'Christian and Jewish Self-Definition in Light of the Christian Additions to the Apocryphal Writings,' in Sanders et al. (eds.), *Jewish and Christian Self-Definition*, 2:27-55, 310-15. Note also Robert A. Kraft, 'Christian Transmission of Greek Jewish Scriptures: A Methodological Probe,' in *Paganisme, Judaïsme, Christianisme: Influences et affrontements dans le monde antique* (Paris: Boccard, 1978), 207-26.

I propose some methodological principles for working out or working toward the origins of Old Testament pseudepigrapha. As we shall see, even with all these caveats, this method will provide useful results, both in terms of sorting out the range of possibilities and isolating a corpus of pseudepigrapha that are of unambiguously Jewish origin.

Taking all this into account, what possible categories of authorship and text can we imagine for ancient Old Testament pseudepigrapha, and how might one type of author have redacted the work of another? The range of possibilities seems to me to be approximately the following. I am assuming that the works in question are Old Testament pseud-epigrapha, not New Testament apocrypha – that they are meant to be read as works written in the Old Testament period, generally by Old Testament figures, rather than in the New Testament period by apostles, Jesus, and so on. I also assume in all cases that, whatever their origins, the works were transmitted in Christian circles; thus a work such as 3 *Enoch*, written in Hebrew and transmitted by Jews, does not come under consideration.

1 A Jewish composition could have been written (a) either containing what I will call Jewish 'signature features,' elements and views expres-sed that are characteristic of boundary-maintaining Judaism but were typically rejected by boundary-maintaining Christianity, or (b) lacking such signature features.

2 A Jewish composition may have undergone minor Christian redactional changes during its transmission. These could include (a) additions with Christian signature features (elements typical of Christianity but re-jected by common Judaism); (b) additions that do not include any Christian signature features; (c) inadvertent or deliberate deletions of Jewish signature features; and (d) other deletions. In other words, a Jewish work could have been changed by Christian tradents to look either more Christian or less Jewish.[108]

3 A Christian composition could have been written containing numer-ous Christian signature features.

4 A Christian composition could have been written containing only a few Christian signature features, such that it is indistinguishable from 2a.

5 A Christian composition could have been written without any Chris-tian signature features (for example, to give an air of verisimilitude to a work written in the name of an Old Testament character).

At least superficially, works in the categories 1b and 5 could be read as either Jewish or Christian works, whatever their actual origins.

6 A Jewish composition may have been heavily reworked by Christian tradents. It may have originated (a) with Jewish signature features (i.e., as 1a) or (b) with no Jewish signature features (i.e., as 1b). In the latter case it would be indistinguishable from 3 above.

7 Works may have been composed by Torah-observant Jewish believers in Jesus ('Jewish-Christians'). Such works could contain both Jewish and Christian signature features and might be impossible to distinguish from 2 or 6 above (as well as, in some cases, 1 and 3-5 above, and 8-9 below!). They could also have been redacted along the lines described in 2 and 6 above.

8 Works may have been composed by judaizing gentile Christians – that is, gentile believers in Jesus who also had an active interest in Jewish culture and who chose to observe at least some Jewish practices such as synagogue worship, the sabbath, Jewish festivals, Jewish dietary laws, and even circumcision. Moreover, some gentile Christians may have been 'biblicizers' who adopted Jewish customs from the scriptures without any contact with a Jewish community or Jews at all. Both gentile judaizing Christians and biblicizers could have written Old Testament pseudepigrapha that were sympathetic to Jewish matters rejected by boundary-maintaining Christians. As with 7, such works could be impossible to distinguish from 1-6 above (as well as 7 and perhaps even 9) and could be redacted along the lines described in 2 and 6.

9 Works may have been composed by non-Jewish Israelites (Samaritans). It seems likely that Samaritan signature features could be formulated so that Old Testament pseudepigrapha written by Samaritans could often, but not necessarily always, be distinguished from Jewish pseudepigrapha. Samaritan pseudepigrapha could thus potentially be confused with 1 above and could be redacted along the lines of 2 and 6. At times it may be possible to show that a work originated in the Galilee, but otherwise I see no reason to regard Galilean Old Testament pseudepigrapha as something other than Jewish pseudepigrapha.

10 It is not impossible that works with scriptural overtones could have been composed by (a) sympathetic non-Christian gentiles (i.e., sympathizers and God-fearers) or (b) syncretistic Jews, Christians, or gentile polytheists who mixed and matched to formulate their own religious observances as it pleased them. The authorship of works written by such

people could only be determined, if at all, upon close examination of the text in question.

11 There are various highly unlikely scenarios that remain possible in principle: a composition by a gentile (Christian or otherwise) who for some reason learned Hebrew and wrote the work in that language; an apparently Christian work actually written by a Jew who for some reason intended to fool Christians with it and succeeded; a Christian work adopted and redacted by Jews and then transmitted either by Christians or by Jews, and so on. There may also have been sects or groups in antiquity about whom no knowledge survives today, yet their members may have produced Old Testament pseudepigrapha now in our possession. We should keep such possibilities in mind, although it is reasonable to discount them in the absence of strong evidence for one in the case of a given pseudepigraphon.

At first glance these results may seem discouraging. On the one hand, nearly every possibility listed above could, under some circumstances, be mistaken for nearly every other possibility. In some cases Jewish works may lack Jewish signature features; in some cases Christian compositions may not show any Christian signature features; redacted Jewish works may be indistinguishable from Christian compositions; Jewish-Christian and judaizing Christian or polytheistic gentile works may appear to be Jewish; Samaritan works may appear to be Jewish, and so on. But on the other hand, in some cases it is possible to limit the options of authorship and origin and even to be reasonably confident that a composition is Jewish. When Jewish signature features are present we can reasonably postulate either Jewish authorship outright or at least significant Jewish influence on the writer, however the text may have been transformed during its transmission. In some cases we may be able to postulate Jewish authorship and accurate transmission with a good deal of confidence. In other words, positive criteria may isolate texts more likely to be Jewish in origin, but negative criteria (such as lack of Christian signature features) have much less, if any weight. The next step is to work out a methodology for filtering actual Old Testament pseudepigrapha in our possession through the range of possibilities.

9

THE WAY FORWARD:
METHODOLOGICAL PROPOSALS

In this section I propose some methodological principles for approaching the origins of Old Testament pseudepigrapha transmitted solely by Christians. My guiding assumptions are those given in the introduction. It is preferable to eliminate some genuine Jewish works from consideration if we cannot be sure of their genuineness, than to mistake Christian or non-Christian gentile works for Jewish ones. A false positive does more harm to our reconstruction of ancient Judaism than a false negative. In cases where the balance of probability is arguable, we need to flag the doubtful status of the works as Jewish and avoid using them as key evidence for our theories. And it is better to lay out an accurately circumscribed range of possible origins for a given work than to try to defend a specific origin when it goes beyond the evidence to do so.

Based mainly on the contents of the externally verified corpus of Jewish texts collected in the beginning of this chapter (informed by the discussion of common Judaism and the parting of the ways), I suggest

---

[109] Corresponding Christian signature features are somewhat more straightforward and would include such things as favorable mention of Jesus, the virgin birth, the crucifixion, the resurrection, the church, and the apostles; hostile references to the falling away of the Jews; and quotation from or clear allusion to the New Testament or other early Christian literature. See also Robert A. Kraft, 'Setting the Stage and Framing Some Central Questions,' *JSJ* 32 (2001): 371-95, esp. pp. 385-86. One point of difficulty is to decide what constitutes an 'allusion' to a Christian work. Here I follow Konrad R. Schaefer's definition: 'Allusions are limited to a word, a brief phrase, or an image that constitutes an indirect reference but can sometimes be traced to a source. Allusive reference may be intentional or it may be an echo. The essence of conscious allusion is the author's intention to recall previous oracles [the context is citation in Zechariah 14 of previous prophetic oracles] with their context; once the reader recognizes the reference, the horizons for comprehension are expanded. . . . A single word or a phrase can be an echo, often unintentional, which results from the use of stock language in common circulation. The author reflects or replicates ideas that can be found in previous literature, but he may be unaware of the background source, and he does not wittingly advert to the original' ('Zechariah 14: A Study in Allusion,' *CBQ* 57 [1995]: 66-91, quotations from p. 69). I consider an allusion – a deliberate reference to a Christian text with the intention of bringing it to the reader's mind – to be a Christian signature feature, but do not consider an echo – the repetition of a word or a phrase that may be from an earlier source, but with no intention of drawing attention to that source – to be one. Scarcely a single ancient Jewish text in a language used by Christians could not be found to have an apparent echo of the New Testament in it. I discuss some specific cases of allusions and echoes in Chapter Two.

the following criteria as positive signs – signature features – of Jewish authorship (primarily, but not entirely exclusively, boundary-maintaining Jewish authorship).[109] The object is to apply these criteria to pseudepigraphic texts transmitted in Christian circles which are preserved in manuscripts dating from late antiquity or (more often) the Middle Ages, composed in or translated into languages used by Christian churches, using the criteria for positive assessment to isolate works that are likely to have a Jewish origin. All of these are internal criteria, that is, they are based on the contents of the texts rather than facts external to them:

I   A work with substantial Jewish content of any kind and strong internal evidence that the work was composed in the pre-Christian era. Such works could not have been composed by Christians but in principle could originate from sympathetic non-Christian gentiles.

II   Compelling evidence that the work was translated from Hebrew, which, as far as I can tell, was used in antiquity only by Jews. Compositions in Hebrew by Jewish-Christians remain a possibility. Jews also wrote works in Aramaic and Greek, but Hebrew was the Jewish national and religious language. (Naturally, works demonstrably composed in Hebrew, even if preserved only in another language, should also be regarded as Jewish. But compelling proof of translation from Hebrew is very difficult to come by and is an issue that cannot be dealt with at length in this book.)

III   Sympathetic concern with the Jewish ritual cult (especially priesthood, temple, ritual purity, calendar, festivals, sabbaths, and circumcision).

IV   Sympathetic concern with Jewish law/Torah and *halakhah*. (This criterion overlaps to a large degree with III above).

V   Concern with Jewish ethnic and national interests, particularly self-identification as a Jew, polemics against gentile persecution of Jews, and internal Jewish polemics.

A few caveats: first, when applying criteria III-V we should, if possible, try to distinguish the voice of the author from the viewpoint of a scriptural narrator or character such as Moses, Solomon, Ezra, and so on. A Christian or non-Christian gentile author could place concerns or viewpoints in the mouth of a scriptural narrator or character which the author did not wholeheartedly share, so it is more significant if the authorial voice addressing the intended audience shows sympathetic concern with Jewish ritual law or takes a position on Jewish nationalist issues. A consistent representation of scriptural characters with such concerns can often be taken as a sign of boundary-maintaining Jewish authorship, but we must pay close attention to whether the narrator is at the same time silent on such matters or whether the author gives us other grounds for doubting that his or her viewpoint is the same as that of the characters or even the narrator.[110]

Second, when applying criteria III-IV we must keep in mind the possibility of authorship by non-Jewish biblicizers: Christians (and perhaps conceivably even non-Christian gentiles) who adopted Jewish ritual and laws based strictly on their scriptural authority and without any direct acquaintance with Jews or Judaism. Thus, even sympathetic concern with scriptural ritual and laws is not an infallible indicator. To be confident that a work is Jewish we should also be able to show it contains Jewish elements that are not strictly scriptural, such as nonscriptural festivals or refinements of ritual observances, nonscriptural calendrical observances, polemics against other Jewish groups in matters of *halakhah*, or concern with Jewish nationalist issues.

Third, one must beware of Christian allegorical treatments of issues relevant to criteria III-V, which do not count as evidence of Jewish composition. One must also distinguish internal Jewish polemics from Christian polemics against Judaism as well as Christian polemics against gentile polytheistic religions. Both Jews and Christians condemned idolatry, and such condemnation does not count as a Jewish signature feature.

VI Certain features may also allow us to distinguish Samaritan pseudepigrapha from Jewish pseudepigrapha. Signs of Samaritan origins would include composition in the Samaritan dialect of Aramaic (if we are fortunate enough to have the text in its original language); acceptance of Mount Gerizim as the proper place for the central sanctuary; the use of Samaritan theological jargon; the use of Samaritan legend, myth or eschatology; hostility toward Judaism and preference for Israelite over Judaic traditions; the use of uniquely Samaritan ritual, legal, and calendrical traditions; and an interest in the region of Samaria. Some of these would have more force than others, and some would be much easier to establish than others.

---

[110] For a useful theoretical discussion of such reader-response concerns see Bas M. F. van Iersel, *Mark: A Reader-Response Commentary* (JSNTSup 164; Sheffield: Sheffield Academic Press, 1998), 14-29.

As noted above, we can generally treat pseudepigrapha of Galilean origin as Jewish and we may well have no way of knowing that a work comes from Galilee. In some cases, however (such as, perhaps, the Book of the Watchers), interest in specifically Galilean geography or Israelite traditions may hint at an origin in the region of Galilee.

Using these criteria, it should be possible in many cases (although by no means in all) to isolate composition categories

1a (boundary-maintaining Jewish compositions with Jewish signature features) from 5 (Christian compositions with no Christian signature features);

2a (Jewish compositions with minor Christian additions including Christian signature features) from 3-5 (Christian compositions with many to no Christian signature features); and

3 (Christian compositions with numerous Christian signature features) from 6a (Jewish works with Jewish signature features and heavily redacted by Christians).

The criteria give us no means to distinguish 1a (boundary-maintaining Jewish compositions with Jewish signature features) from 2b-c-d (Jewish compositions with minor additions not involving Christian signature features and minor deletions). In some cases textual criticism and redaction criticism may allow us to catch some of these changes. But we always run the risk that even works that appear to be clear cases of 1a (Jewish works with Jewish signature features) may have alterations along the lines of 2b-c-d (Jewish compositions with minor additions not involving Christian signature features and minor deletions). The criteria also do not give us the means to distinguish 6b (Jewish works with no Jewish signature features and heavily redacted by Christians) from 3 (Christian compositions with numerous Christian signature features).

Works by Jewish-Christians (7), depending on whether they included Jewish or Christian signature features, might easily be confused with anything in categories 1-6 (see the preceding paragraph). Presumably in some cases, such as when a work espouses specifically Ebionite doctrines such as vegetarianism, the denial of the virgin birth, and rejection of the Apostle Paul, we might be able to label it as Jewish-Christian, but more often we would be unable to place it further within the continuum and outside the range of the boundary-maintainers. And if a work could be shown to be of pre-Christian origin or to have a clearly Jewish *Sitz im Leben* (as do, for example, the Dead Sea Scrolls), we may be able to eliminate category 7 as a possibility.

Works by gentile Christian Judaizers (8) would also frequently be easily confused with works in categories 1-6. But if a pseudepigraphon could be shown to have been composed before the rise of Christianity or if it showed a high degree of Jewish nationalist polemic, especially with a clearly Jewish *Sitz im Leben*, we may be able to eliminate category 8 as a possible origin.

I suspect that in most cases we could distinguish a Samaritan pseudepigraphon (9) from a Jewish pseudepigraphon, especially if it were composed later rather than earlier. But there may well be cases where the two could not readily be told apart.

Works by non-Christian gentile Judaizers (10a) could also be difficult to distinguish from 1 (Jewish compositions with or without Jewish signature features), 2b (Jewish compositions with additions that do not include Christian signature features), and 5 (Christian compositions with no Christian signature features), especially if the writer was careful to eschew blatant references to polytheistic religion. But in such cases we would probably be dealing with a well-informed gentile writer, i.e., a God-fearer or a dedicated sympathizer. Pseudepigrapha containing overt references to polytheistic religion could be written either by interested polytheistic gentiles (such as some composers of the Greco-Egyptian magical papyri) or by Jews or Christians with syncretistic interests (for example, the syncretistic Jewish composer of *Sepher Ha-Razim*) (10b). Our starting point should be the social context of the manuscripts which preserve the works but, barring unusual evidence, such as compelling proof of translation from Hebrew, I see no way to tell 10a (gentile sympathizers and God-fearers) from 10b (syncretistic Jews, Christians, or gentile polytheists) if a work has polytheistic references.

Based on all the above, I propose the following five principles as working hypotheses when we analyze Old Testament pseudepigrapha.

A Pseudepigrapha with extensive or pervasive positive Jewish signature features and no Christian signature features provide the best case for attribution to category 1 (compositions written by boundary-maintaining Jews). In such cases we should look for converging lines of evidence that would distinguish them from categories 7-10. With luck, we may be able to isolate a number of works that we can assign to boundary-maintaining (and perhaps even other) Jews.

B Pseudepigrapha with extensive or pervasive positive Samaritan signature features may reasonably be considered to be Samaritan compositions. Our knowledge of both ancient Judaism and ancient Samaritanism is imperfect enough that it remains possible that we will mistake Samaritan works for Jewish works. Although I know of no works with both Samaritan signature features and Christian signature features, such works could in theory have been intrusively edited by Christian tradents, or composed by Samaritanizing Christians or imperfectly assimilated Samaritan converts to Christianity.

C Texts with polytheistic elements are likely to belong somewhere in category 10, and it would be very difficult to narrow their origins down further. They were not produced by boundary-maintaining Jews or Christians.

D Texts with signature features of both Judaism and Christianity could in principle be regarded as belonging to categories 2, 6, 7, or 8 (conceivably even 9), and further analysis may or may not narrow down the possibilities.

E All other pseudepigrapha, including those with neither Jewish nor Christian signature features, should be understood (as an initial working hypothesis) in the context of the earliest preserved manuscript or earliest quotation of the work in question. In almost all cases where the origin is ambiguous, this would involve reading the work first as a composition by some type of boundary-maintaining Christian.

These five starting points are imperfect for a number of reasons. Principle A may treat as Jewish pseudepigrapha Jewish works that have been altered by Christian tradents who nevertheless did not add Christian signature features. Principle B does not guarantee that we will distinguish every Samaritan work from a Jewish work. Principles B, C, and D leave us with a frustratingly large range of possibilities. And principle E may lead us to treat real Jewish works that lack Jewish signature features as Christian compositions. But nevertheless, the use of these principles would force us to apply a methodological standard that is considerably more rigorous than the intuitive one generally applied at present in the study of these works, one that would be far more likely to weed out false positives.

The following are some limitations to the analysis:

a The sources to be analyzed need to be well preserved and of substantial length. Highly fragmentary or very short works are less likely to preserve the positive features needed for even a preliminary analysis.

b Genre should be taken into account. For example, Jewish wisdom literature is less likely to contain distinctively Jewish material than halakhic
literature, and Christian works with eschatological interests, especially
those explicitly involving comprehensive eschatological scenarios and
eschatological redeemers or divine mediators, are more likely to include
direct references to Jesus than Christian rewritings of Old Testament
stories; therefore a lack of Christian signature features in eschatological
works is more interesting than their absence from rewritten scripture.

c Texts set in the pre-Mosaic period may deliberately avoid reference
to Torah-related issues, even if by Jews.

d Texts set in the pre-Abrahamic period may deliberately avoid reference
to Torah-related and nationalist issues, even if by Jews.

e Analysis of translated texts (i.e., most of the Old Testament pseudepigrapha) is highly dependent on the reliability of the translation.

f Gentile Christianity of antiquity (including boundary-maintaining
gentile Christianity) encompassed a wide geographical range and an
extended span of time and was represented by many types, movements,
and degrees of boundary maintenance. Christian apocrypha could have
originated in many different social circumstances, and works of Old
Testament pseudepigrapha need to be studied on a case-by-case basis
with this in mind.

g It should be noted that these criteria are best applied on a detailed and
case-by-case level. It would not be enough, for example, to show that
a work made positive reference to the temple cult or circumcision. Such
might be a preliminary hint of a possible Jewish origin, but one would
have to show that such views were uncharacteristic of the earliest social context indicated by the manuscripts, and exploration of such
social contexts might help suggest other possibilities.

Finally, I should draw out some implications of this methodology.
Of Old Testament pseudepigrapha transmitted solely by Christians,
those texts that we can label with confidence as 'Jewish' are mostly
the ones strongly concerned with boundary maintenance, and it will
thus be these that make the main contribution toward reconstructing
ancient Judaism. This is an unfortunate fact, but it arises inevitably from
the nature of our evidence: if we start with the Christian manuscripts
in which these works are now preserved and only work backwards to a

Jewish origin as the evidence requires, Jewish works superficially congenial to Christianity, at least in their surviving form, will be largely undetectable. We may suspect that some works of this kind are Jewish but we cannot be confident that they are, and so, at best, we should pigeonhole them in a 'possible' or 'doubtful' category whose evidence must be used with much more circumspection. In some cases it may be possible to isolate Jewish pseudepigrapha superficially congenial to Christianity, for example, if we can show that the work must have been written in the pre-Christian era. But in other cases, perhaps many, we must remain in doubt and proceed with appropriate caution. In particular, with regard to mining Jewish pseudepigrapha for the historical and cultural background of the New Testament, we should limit ourselves to using either works that can be shown to have been composed before the rise of Christianity or later works that can be placed far on the Jewish end of the continuum in the direction of boundary maintenance. (The later the work or the more uncertain its date, the less likely it is to have any relevance for the New Testament, even if it is Jewish.) The evidence of other texts should be used much more cautiously, if at all. This approach is necessary in order to prevent any Christian pseudepigrapha from being included in our corpus as false positives.

10

CONCLUSIONS

This chapter has confronted some of the most difficult problems associated with ancient Jewish and Christian pseudepigrapha and, indeed, with our understanding of ancient Judaism and Christianity in general. I believe that I have advanced the discussion. First, I proposed a set of intuitively obvious external criteria for establishing which ancient documents can safely be regarded as Jewish. Using these, I laid out a preliminary corpus of Jewish literary works, which include the Hebrew Bible; the Dead Sea Scrolls; such literary texts as have been recovered from Masada and the manuscript caches of the Bar Kokhba era; the texts in 1 Enoch; the books of Jubilees, Tobit, Ben Sira, and the Epistle of Jeremiah; and the Tannaitic rabbinic literature. Most, perhaps all, of these are of Palestinian origin.

I have used this preliminary corpus to evaluate scholarly attempts to find a 'common Judaism' in antiquity. Accepting Smith's paradigm of a 'polythetic' Judaism, I argued that common Judaism should be regarded as a group of elements of praxis, belief, and national identity which were widely accepted in ancient Judaism, even though no single element would be found in all forms of Judaism, some forms of Judaism would have more of these elements than others, and some would emphasize ideas and practices not included among the elements of common Judaism.

I then set out a preliminary typology of the range of possible authorship for ancient Old Testament pseudepigrapha, taking into account potential Jewish, Christian, non-Christian gentile, and Samaritan origins and redaction. Rather than finding sharp divisions, I found a series of continua between Judaism and non-Christian gentiles and between Judaism and Christianity. There is some evidence for compromises between Samaritanism and Christianity, and we cannot entirely rule out such relationships between Samaritanism and Judaism, although in this case the lines between the two were drawn rather more sharply than

---

[111] In late antiquity Samaritans sometimes converted nominally to Christianity to advance their careers. Note, for example, the senator Arsenius, who converted to Christianity during the reign of Justinian but continued to practice the Samaritan religion. See Alan D. Crown, 'The Byzantine and Moslem Periods,' in Crown (ed.), *The Samaritans*, 55-81, esp. pp. 64-65; idem, 'The Samaritan Diaspora,' in ibid., 195-217, esp. p. 211.

in the others.[111] Galileans and proselytes may be regarded as effectively Jewish.

Despite the lack of a sharp and definitive divide between Judaism and Christianity in antiquity, it proves possible to speak of varieties of each early on which focused on the maintaining of boundaries from one another and from gentile polytheism. After antiquity, boundary-maintaining Judaism and boundary-maintaining Christianity became the norms and it was the boundary maintainers who transmitted to us almost all of the Jewish and Christian literature from antiquity, filtering it by omission and rewriting according to their own agendas.

With this orientation to the history of the transmission of ancient Jewish and Christian literature, in particular the Old Testament pseudepigrapha, I have formulated a set of internal criteria for isolating boundary-maintaining Jewish pseudepigrapha. In Chapters Three and Four I shall apply them to selected Old Testament pseudepigrapha that have been handed down to us by Christian tradents in antiquity as well as to some related works. But first, Chapter Two will analyze the transmission of Christian pseudepigrapha in the light of 'empirical models,' looking at how certain verifiably Christian works on the Old Testament were passed down in Christian circles.

EMPIRICAL MODELS FOR
THE CHRISTIAN COMPOSITION OF
OLD TESTAMENT PSEUDEPIGRAPHA

Did Christians write Old Testament pseudepigrapha in antiquity? If so, did they always include Christian signature features, or might they sometimes have written them strictly from an Old Testament and therefore apparently Jewish perspective? To put it in terms of reader-response criticism, need the perspective in pseudepigrapha written by Christians always have reflected the world view of the author, or might it sometimes have been presented according to the world view of an Old Testament narrator (one who had not had revelations of future New Testament events and doctrines) or even that of the characters in Old Testament stories? Might a Christian author have avoided references to Christian matters for other reasons as well? On the face of it, there is no obvious reason why a Christian author would have to have included Christian signature features in a work that dealt with the Old Testament. Nevertheless, as we have already seen, scholars who study the Old Testament pseudepigrapha have often assumed not only that whatever is not obviously Christian is Jewish, but even that a work with only a few Christian signature features which can be excised without serious harm to the flow of thought was also originally Jewish.

This chapter sets out to test such assumptions empirically by looking at what verifiably Christian authors *actually did* when they wrote on Old Testament topics. It is inspired by a comment by Robert A. Kraft in a

---

[1] Kraft, 'Setting the Stage and Framing Some Central Questions,' JSJ 32 (2001): 371-95, the quotation is on p 389. I am grateful to Professor Kraft for his permission to take up the research problem he outlines here, reworking it to some degree to suit my own purposes. He, of course, is not responsible for the result. [2] Tigay (ed.), *Empirical Models for Biblical Criticism* (Philadelphia: University of Pennsylvania Press, 1985).

Did Christians Write
Old Testament Pseudepigrapha
That Appear to Be Jewish?

recent article on the problem of the transmission of the Old Testament pseudepigrapha and related works:

‹Numerous sermons have survived from various authors and/or ›
recorders. Some of them deal with 'Jewish' topics and folkloristic ›
themes – the asceticism of Joseph, the leadership of Moses, the artistry ›
of David. To what extent did the homilists rely on identifiable sources, ›
and how much did they contribute, de novo, to the resultant presenta- ›
tion? Somewhere in my filing cabinets are notes on some 4th and 5th ›
century Christian sermons, examined with an eye to distinctively ›
'Christian' traits that might betray their origins. Some were obviously ›
Christian, but not all. Why shouldn't a Christian narrator, for whom ›
Jewish scriptures and traditions were also home territory, be expected ›
to produce compositions that bear consistently 'Jewish' features?›[1]

Kraft's proposal to examine ancient Christian sermons to see what they can tell us about the use of the Old Testament by Christians is promising. Sermons are comparable in length to some of the shorter Old Testament pseudepigrapha and they sometimes retell Old Testament stories. The sermons may serve as plausible, if not entirely perfect, analogies for Old Testament pseudepigrapha. I expand on his idea by analyzing a range of verifiably Christian texts of various genres (including sermons, biblical commentaries, and verse epics on biblical subjects) which focus on Old Testament matters by retelling or making extensive use of Old Testament stories but which, either as whole works or, in the case of the commentary and one of the poems, in selected discrete episodes, show little or no interest in Christian matters (or, more concretely, display few or no Christian signature features). The point is to gain some insight into what sort of Old Testament pseudepigrapha ancient Christians might have written by examining some of their uses of the Old Testament in similar works that we are confident they did write.

My agenda and approach are similar to those of Jeffrey H. Tigay in his book *Empirical Models for Biblical Criticism*.[2] The object of the essays in this book is to look at examples of ancient literature which illuminate the process of the creation of the literature of the Hebrew Bible, especially the Pentateuch, and which provide real-life analogies to this literature and allow us to test theories concerning the composition and editing of biblical texts, especially the Documentary Hypothesis. As he explains in the preface:

‹Together these studies, based on texts whose evolution can be ›
documented by copies from several stages in the course of their devel- ›
opment – in other words, on *empirical models* – show that many literary ›
works from ancient Israel and cognate cultures were demonstrably ›
produced in the way critics believe that biblical literature was pro- ›
duced. This point alone, however, could have been made with less ›
effort. The aim of this book is not simply to demonstrate the validity ›
of a particular approach to biblical literature, but to illustrate, by ›
means of case studies, the kind of research that this approach involves. ›
The book is not merely an argument but a casebook which aims to ›
convey a feeling for what was likely to happen in the development of ›
biblical texts, and to suggest how further studies of this type might ›
be undertaken.›³

The texts studied in Tigay's book include the Epic of Gilgamesh, the Samaritan Pentateuch, the Septuagint, Neo-Assyrian royal inscriptions, and Tatian's Diatessaron.

My primary aim in this chapter is to demonstrate on similar empirical grounds that the danger of Christian works being mistaken for Jewish ones is real: Christians could write works that had few Christian signature features that can be excised easily on redaction-critical grounds; they could write works that contained no Christian signature

---

³ Ibid., xi-xii, emphasis in original. This book builds on concerns articulated earlier in Tigay's book *The Evolution of the Gilgamesh Epic* (Philadelphia: University of Pennsylvania Press, 1982). ⁴ For the second-century, perhaps Jewish-Christian, *Apocalypse of Peter* see J. K. Elliott, *The Apocryphal New Testament: A Collection of Apocryphal Christian Literature in an English Translation* (Oxford: Clarendon, 1993), 593-615; Richard Bauckham, 'The *Apocalypse of Peter*: A Jewish Christian Apocalypse from the Time of Bar Kokhba,' *Apocrypha* 5 (1994): 7-111. For the Coptic work of the same name from Nag Hammadi, see James Brashler and Roger A. Bullard, 'Apocalypse of Peter (VII, 3),' in *The Nag Hammadi Library in English* (ed. James M. Robinson; 3rd ed.; San Francisco: Harper & Row, 1988), 372-78. ⁵ For the third-century Greek *Apocalypse of Paul* see Elliott, *The Apocryphal New Testament*, 616-44. For the Coptic work of the same name from Nag Hammadi, see George W. MacRae, William R. Murdock, and Douglas M. Parrott, 'The Apocalypse of Paul (V, 2),' in Robinson (ed.), *The Nag Hammadi Library*, 256-59. ⁶ Elliott, *The Apocryphal New Testament*, 645-51.

features whatever; Christians could be concerned primarily with exegetical issues rather than homiletic ones; some Christian works on the Old Testament drew frequently on Jewish exegesis; and Christians could adopt a superficially Jewish perspective simply in order to maintain the literary integrity of the story they were telling. My analysis not only makes the case for this main point but also explores more generally some empirical evidence for how Christians approached the retelling and adaptation of Old Testament materials, how far they would go in being sympathetic toward them, and what strategies they used when dealing with Old Testament matters that were uncongenial to boundary-maintaining Christianity.

First I ask some general questions about Christian production and transmission of parabiblical works and consider how empirical evidence drawn from specific Christian works and authors can help answer them. Second, I look at three Christian sermons, two by John Chrysostom and one by Augustine of Hippo, which deal with Old Testament matters with only scant reference to Christian matters, using them as an analogy for Old Testament pseudepigrapha whose Christian elements have traditionally been excised on redaction-critical grounds. Third, I examine three Christian works that display Christian signature features but which also contain substantial retellings of Old Testament episodes that are in themselves devoid of Christian signature features. These are Ephrem's Syriac commentaries on Genesis and Exodus and the Latin biblical epic *Heptateuchos* (especially its retelling of the book of Leviticus), attributed, probably pseudonymously, to Cyprianus Gallus. Fourth, I consider a single late-antique Latin epic poem that contains no Christian signature features in its entirety: *De Martyrio Maccabaeorum*, a retelling of the story of the Maccabean martyrs attributed, again probably pseudonymously, to Hilarius or Victorinus. The last two categories provide analogies for putative Old Testament pseudepigrapha written by Christians but lacking any Christian signature features.

2

SOME PRELIMINARY QUESTIONS

My first preliminary question is: *Did Christians write parabiblical works on Old Testament matters?* The answer to this question is undoubtedly yes. We have a number of Old Testament pseudepigrapha that were clearly composed by Christians. First, Christians took up an ancient biblical and Mediterranean genre, the apocalypse, and made it their own. We have apocalypses attributed to Peter,[4] Paul,[5] Thomas,[6] and

Bartholomew,[7] as well as various Christian apocalypses attributed to the Old Testament figures Daniel[8] and Ezra,[9] and involving the prophet Elijah.[10] The *Odes of Solomon* is an early (perhaps second-century) Christian liturgical work preserved fully only in Syriac, although it is debated whether it was composed originally in Syriac or Greek.[11] We see that Christians wrote *Sibylline Oracles* from the interpolated material (if that is what it is) in *Sib. Or.* 1.324-400 and elsewhere, and in the short hymn to Christ cited by Lactantius and preserved as book 6 of the *Sibylline Oracles*.[12] It is now generally agreed that the *Ascension of Isaiah*, a work of rewritten scripture containing a visionary ascent, was composed by a Christian in Greek in the second century, although it may incorporate an earlier Jewish source.[13] The *Testament of Solomon* is a late-antique Christian work in Greek. Its date is uncertain, although a version of Chapter 18 survives in fragmentary papyri of the fifth or sixth century.[14]

---

[7] Ibid., 652-72. [8] Matthias Henze, *The Syriac Apocalypse of Daniel: Introduction, Text, and Commentary* (Studien und Texte zu Antike und Christentum 11; Tübingen: Mohr Siebeck, 2001); G.T. Zervos, 'Apocalypse of Daniel,' *OTP*, 1:755-70. Lorenzo DiTommaso has isolated twelve to sixteen apocalypses of Daniel in various languages which he argues should probably be dated no later than the seventh to the ninth centuries, at least one of which (now preserved in Armenian) was composed before 600. See his *The Book of Daniel and the Apocryphal Daniel Literature* (SVTP 20; Leiden: Brill, 2005), 96-97. [9] M.E. Stone, 'Greek Apocalypse of Ezra,' in *OTP*, 1:561-79; J.R. Mueller and G.A. Robbins, 'Vision of Ezra,' in *OTP*, 1:581-90. [10] For the Coptic apocalypse see O.S. Wintermute, 'Apocalypse of Elijah,' in *OTP*, 1:721-53. It may incorporate earlier Jewish elements but, if so, they are rewritten so extensively as to constitute a new work. [11] J.H. Charlesworth, 'Odes of Solomon,' in *OTP*, 2:725-71. The work's pseudepigraphic attribution to Solomon may or may not go back to the author, but it is early and widespread. [12] John J. Collins, 'Sibylline Oracles,' in *OTP*, 1:317-472, esp. pp. 330-44; 406-7. [13] Jonathan Knight, *The Ascension of Isaiah* (Guides to Apocrypha and Pseudepigrapha; Sheffield: Sheffield Academic Press, 1995); Richard Bauckham, 'The Ascension of Isaiah: Genre, Unity and Date,' in *The Fate of the Dead: Studies on the Jewish and Christian Apocalypses* (NTSup 93; Leiden: Brill, 1998), 363-90. [14] D.C. Duling, 'Testament of Solomon,' in *OTP*, 1:935-87. The *Testament of Solomon* is a compendium of exorcistic lore which borrows elements from the genre 'testament' but does not conform to it completely. See Dennis C. Duling, 'Solomon, Testament of,' *ABD*, 6:117-19. [15] This evidence is collected by Bruce M. Metzger in 'Literary Forgeries and Canonical Pseudepigrapha,' *JBL* 91 (1972): 3-24, esp. pp. 14-15. [16] For a critical edition, see Miroslav Marcovich, *Pseudo-Justinus: Cohortatio ad Graecos; De Monarchia; Oratio ad Graecos* (Berlin: de Gruyter, 1990), 79-100. For an older edition, see Ioan. Carol. Theod. Otto, *S. Iustini Philosophi et Martyris Opera quae Ferentur Omnia* (2 vols; Jena, 1847-49), 2:122-55. There is an English translation by G. Reith in *ANF*, 1:290-93. The spurious passages attributed to Greek authors are translated by M. Lafargue, 'Orphica,' in *OTP*, 2:795-801, esp. pp. 800-801; and by H. Attridge, 'Fragments of Pseudo-Greek Poets,' in *OTP*, 2:821-30.

This evidence suffices to show that Christians did indeed sometimes compose Old Testament pseudepigrapha.

My second preliminary questions is, *Did ancient Christians ever directly attribute Old Testament pseudepigrapha that lacked any Christian signature features to named Christian authors?* If the question is understood narrowly, a yes answer would imply that a Christian writer had deduced not only that a quasi-Old Testament work was a forgery, but also that it was a forgery by a Christian even though it contained no Christian content. This chain of inference would be extremely unlikely unless the actual author were still living and had been exposed and confessed. I know of no such case involving a quasi-Old Testament work. There is one example involving a New Testament apocryphon. According to Tertullian, the author of the *Acts of Paul and Thecla* was convicted and confessed to the forgery, losing his office as a result, but he defended himself by saying that he did it out of love for Paul. Bishop Serapion of Antioch rejected the *Gospel of Peter* as a Docetic forgery around the year 200. Likewise, the *Apostolic Constitutions* refers to books forged by heretics in the name of Christ and the disciples, and Cyril of Jerusalem refers to 'falsely inscribed' gospels apart from the canonical ones.[15]

There is, however, an early apologetic work whose evidence seems to me to be relevant but which has not, as far as I know, previously been brought to bear on this subject. The short Greek treatise *De Monarchia* (Περὶ Μοναρχίας) is attributed in the manuscripts (which are late) to the second-century Christian apologist Justin Martyr, although it is generally agreed that he was not the author.[16] The author sets out to prove the truth of monotheism to a polytheistic implied-reader, using only quotations from polytheistic Greek literature. The bulk of the quotations, however, are forgeries assigned to known authors or characters such as Pythagoras, Aeschylus, Sophocles, Philemon, and Orpheus. The work never quotes from either the Old or the New Testament and never refers to any specifically Christian doctrines, but it opposes idolatry and views God as the creator and eschatological judge. The spurious passages may have come from a single *gnomologion* that was also used by Clement of Alexandria. This source may well have been of Jewish origin, although for our purposes it does not matter whether it was Jewish or Christian. The Old Testament background of some of the quotations is clear: the one attributed to Aeschylus in Chapter 2 pictures God as a raging fire (cf. Deut 33:2; Exod 13:21, 19:18), as shrouded in darkness (cf. Exod 20:21), and as coming in a storm theophany (cf. Psalm 29); one attributed to Philemon in Chapter 3 declares the name of God to be unutterable, as in the Jewish tradition; another assigned to Philemon in Chapter 4 alludes to the Decalogue in warning against adultery, theft, murder, and the coveting of one's neighbor's wife, house, female or male slave, or cattle (cf. Exod 20:13-17). Miroslav Marcovich also finds 'several allusions to the expressions of the New Testament,' but I would class these as echoes rather than allusions.[17] It would be stretching the definition to regard *De Monarchia* as an Old Testament pseudepigraphon, but Charlesworth does include many of its sources in his *Old Testament Pseudepigrapha*, and it is a work that alludes to the Old Testament but at most only echoes the New Testament.

All this is of interest because in the early fourth century the church historian Eusebius of Caesarea knew the *De Monarchia*, which he calls 'The Sovereignty of God' (Περὶ θεοῦ Μοναρχίας). Recognizing it as dependent on both the scriptures and the Greek writings, he lists it among Justin Martyr's works with no indication that he doubted its

[17] Marcovich finds the following allusions: to 2 Tim 3:4 in *De Monarchia* 1.6; to Rom 1:20 in *De Monarchia* 1.7-9; to Eph 1:19 in *De Monarchia* 2.52; and to 2 Tim 3:2 and some other passages in *De Monarchia* 6.24 (*Pseudo-Justinus*, 82). But these are actually very general echoes, at most adding up to a word or two, and they show no effort to bring specific passages to the mind of the reader. Marcovich also has the 'impression' that one passage imitates an expression by Clement of Alexandria (ibid.), but again this would constitute at best only an echo. (For the distinctions between quotation, allusion, and echo, see Chapter One n. 109). [18] It is perhaps worth noting that the Latin biblical epic poems of approximately the fifth century are attributed to Christian authors even when, in the case of *De Martyrio Maccabaeorum*, they contain no Christian signature features. But not too much should be made of this, inasmuch as the attributions may have been added by Carolingian editors. It is, of course, interesting that these editors saw no difficulty in assigning such texts to Christian authors, but this point tells us nothing directly about attitudes in antiquity when the Apocrypha and pseudepigrapha relevant to this book were being composed. I shall have more to say about the Latin biblical epics later in this chapter. [19] Harlow, *The Greek Apocalypse of Baruch (3 Baruch) in Hellenistic Judaism and Early Christianity* (SVTP 12; Leiden: Brill, 1996), 80-86. [20] I follow the Greek text of Emmanuel Amand de Mendieta and Stig Y. Rudberg, *Basilius von Caesarea: Homilien zum Hexaemeron* (GCS 2; Berlin: Academie Verlag, 1997). There is an English translation by Blomfield Jackson, in *The Treatise de Spiritu Sancto, the Nine Homilies of the Hexaemeron and the Letters of Saint Basil the Great, Archbishop of Caesarea* (NPNF 28; Edinburgh: Clark/Grand Rapids, Mich.: Eerdmans, 1996 [rpt. of 1894 edition]), 51-107, and a facing-page Greek and French edition by Stanislas Giet in *Basile de Césarée: Homélies sur l'Hexaéméron* (SC 26; Paris: Cerf, 1949). Robert W. Thomson has edited the Syriac version and translated it into English in *The Syriac Version of the Hexaemeron by Basil of Caesarea* (2 vols.; CSCO 550-51; Scriptores Syri 222-23; Louvain: Peeters, 1995). Thomson evaluates this translation as follows: 'The Syriac version of Basil's *Hexaemeron* does not follow the Greek closely. It rather expands the original in a discursive manner, without greatly changing the sense of any passage. Such a style is not uncommon in early Syriac literature' (*The Syriac Version*, 1:vi).

authorship (*Hist. eccl.* 4.18). So an important Christian historian of late antiquity did not find it implausible that a fellow Christian might compose a literary work without either reference to any Christian doctrine or any quotation or allusion to the New Testament if it suited that author's purposes to do so. This offers at least some indirect support to the notion that Christians could have composed Old Testament pseudepigrapha without including any Christian signature features in them.[18]

My third preliminary question has to do with the transmission and interpolation of Old Testament pseudepigrapha. It is well established that Christians sometimes interpolated material into Jewish works to make them sound more Christian, that is, by adding material that contains Christian signature features. Such additions are found, for example, in 4 *Ezra* 7:28-29, Ps 96:10 (LXX 95:10), and, with a much heavier hand, in the Greek *Testament of Levi*. That being the case, *Did Christians also sometimes interpolate Christian material into* Christian *works in order to give them a stronger or more appropriate Christian flavor?* On the face of it, there is no reason to suppose that they did not or could not have, and in recent years this possibility has been widely acknowledged in relevant cases. For example, the book of *3 Baruch*, which is preserved in Greek and Old Church Slavonic versions, shows some Christian signature features in both versions but, by and large, these features do not overlap in the two versions. It is reasonable to reconstruct a Greek *Vorlage* that lacked Christian signature features entirely, but which was independently Christianized by interpolation in the Greek and Slavonic manuscript tradition. Whether or not the original Greek version was a Jewish or a Christian composition must be determined on other grounds. This is the position taken by Daniel C. Harlow in his monograph on *3 Baruch*.[19]

It is worthwhile to pause briefly over a single example of a work by a known Christian author which was subjected to this sort of editing during its transmission. Basil of Caesarea's *Hexaemeron*, a fourth-century collection of nine Greek homilies on the six days of creation in the first chapter of Genesis, survives in its original Greek, but also in a Syriac translation that was in existence by the early eighth century.[20] The *Hexaemeron* covers basic exegesis of the opening chapter of Genesis, along with numerous digressions on scientific and philosophical matters and an occasional homiletic comment. References to explicitly Christian matters are not terribly common, but are scattered throughout the work. Comparison of the two versions shows that the Syriac writer introduced a number of Christian interpolations. In 2.8, the Syriac adds the phrase 'as the apostle said, that he will show to the ages to come' as well as quotations of Heb 4:8 and 4:9. In 6.3 it adds two sentences on darkness as the dwelling of the tormented, with quotations from Heb 10:27, attributed to 'the apostle,' and from Matt 25:41, 22:13/25:30, attributed to 'our Lord.' In 6.4 the Syriac adds material from Luke 12:54-55 to a quotation in the Greek of Matt 16:3. In 8.8 the Syriac transforms 'the assembly' (τὸν σύλλογον) of the Greek into 'the congregation of the church' (ܪܕ݂ܢܬ݁ܝ ܩܢܬܠ݂). Specific references to 'the Son' are added by the Syriac to passages in the Greek which allude, or can be construed to allude, to Christ (2.8; 3.2; 3:4). The concluding doxologies, which vary in content from homily to homily in the Greek, are filled out in the Syriac to contain fully Trinitarian formulas (3.10; 7:6; 8:8).

Here we have a case of a Christian document whose translation Christianizes it further, mainly by adding quotations from the New Testament, and also subtly shifts its theology in a more explicitly Trinitarian direction. The changes fit well in the context and might not be noticed if we had only the Syriac. This case shows that our initial instinct is correct: Christian writers could and did further Christianize earlier Christian texts. The temptation to do so to a Christian text that lacked any Christian signature features would, of course, be all the greater.

This point leads to my next question, a twofold one which brings us to the central concerns of this chapter. First, *Did Christians write Old Testament pseudepigrapha with few enough and tangential enough Christian signature features that these features could be mistaken for secondary redactions?* and second, *Did Christians produce Old Testament pseudepigrapha without including any Christian signature features at all?* Again, there is no a priori reason why they should not have done either. Depending on the agenda of an individual writer and the nature and length of an individual work, there may have been little or no reason to include explicitly Christian content. There may also have been incentives *not* to include it. An author writing in the name of an Old Testament character and wishing to convince contemporaries of its verisimilitude might well have avoided anachronistic references to Christian matters. It is true that Christians sometimes put *vaticinia ex eventu* in the mouths of Old

---

21. Translated in OTP, 1:589 and OTP, 2:160-61, respectively. 22. This problem has also been noted by Ross Shepard Kraemer, *When Aseneth Met Joseph: A Late Antique Tale of the Biblical Patriarch and His Egyptian Wife, Reconsidered* (Oxford: Oxford University Press, 1998), 251-52.

Testament figures in the name of prophecy (e.g., *Vis. Ezra* 38; *Ascen. Isa.* 3:13-31[21]), but this is a risky strategy, and we need not assume it was always followed. But the purpose of this chapter is not to speculate on what ancient Christians might have done and why, but to examine what they actually did. Do we have any positive evidence, then, that they wrote quasi-Old Testament works along these lines?

Taken broadly, the first part of the question – whether Christians ever wrote on the Old Testament while introducing only a few, easily excisable, Christian signature features – can be studied fairly straight-forwardly and, as we shall see, the answer is yes. I analyze three works of this sort below in Section 3. But the second part – whether Christians wrote on the Old Testament without including any Christian signature features – is a considerably more difficult problem, and we should pause to consider the methodological issues.

The fundamental difficulty is, if we – as we must – exclude content as a criterion, how can we prove that an ancient work is a Christian com-position? Even if the work was transmitted with a title that attributes it to a known Christian author – indeed, even as part of a larger corpus by that author – one can always dispute the genuineness of the attribution, if for no other reason than the work shows no interest in Christian mat-ters.[22] If the content is not explicitly Christian, we can only be certain that the work is by a Christian author if it is attributed to a named and well-known writer and the attribution is secure on other grounds, such as its being an integral part of a corpus (e.g., one of a series of sermons on a biblical book), its conforming closely to the style of other works by that writer, or its being mentioned or even quoted by contemporaries or near contemporaries or even by the author him- or herself as being by that author. I have found no works whose authorship is this secure which lack Christian signature features entirely, although, as we shall see, one sermon by Augustine of Hippo comes extremely close.

Another approach would be to find long works by Christian authors (whether anonymous or attributed to specific writers) which contain Christian signature features, but which also include episodic stretches of narrative which lack such features. Evidence of this sort would establish that Christian authors sometimes told whole Old Testament stories without making reference to Christian matters, although it would not prove that they wrote complete works without doing so. A study of these episodes would also shed light on how Christian authors interpreted and reformulated Old Testament stories and might give us a better under-standing of the range of exegetical possibilities we can expect to find in

Old Testament pseudepigrapha by Christians. I analyze extended passages from three works of this kind in Section 4.

A third approach would be to find anonymous (or pseudonymous) works on Old Testament subjects which lack Christian signature features but which can be argued to be of Christian origin on other grounds. I shall consider one case of this type in Section 5. The text is a Latin epic poem that deals with an Old Testament story – the Maccabean martyrdoms – in a genre that is otherwise known in Latin only in Christian circles of late antiquity. In such cases one can always argue as a matter of principle that the work is a Jewish composition accidentally incorporated into a Christian context, but I will make the case that this is extremely unlikely.

Through the use of empirical models I wish to establish that Christian writers could and did write narratives on Old Testament subjects which included few or even no Christian signature features. The heuristic importance of this point for the study of the composition and transmission of Old Testament pseudepigrapha is obvious.[23]

3

CHRISTIAN WORKS WITH ONLY A FEW, EASILY EXCISABLE CHRISTIAN SIGNATURE FEATURES

TWO HOMILIES BY JOHN CHRYSOSTOM John Chrysostom, the fourth-century Greek-speaking priest of Antioch and Bishop of Constantinople whom we have already met in Chapter One, was one of the most prolific writers of the early church. Among his many works are about 150 homilies or sermons on Old Testament topics, including a

---

[23] I have consulted a great many ancient Christian works written in various languages and of various geographical origins and in a number of genres (including sermons, biblical commentaries, liturgies, poetic compositions, chronicles, and apologetic treatises). Only the most interesting results are presented in this chapter. [24] See Robert C. Hill, *Saint John Chrysostom: Homilies on Genesis* (3 vols.; FC 74, 82, 87; Washington, D.C.: Catholic University of America Press, 1985-92), 1:2-7. The standard biography of John Chrysostom is by Chrysostomus Baur: *John Chrysostom and His Time* (2d ed.; London: Sands, 1959-60). [25] J.-P. Migne, *Patrologia Graeca*, vols. 53-54, *S. P. N. Joannis Chrysostomus IV* (Paris, 1862); Hill, *Homilies on Genesis*. I cite the texts according to the paragraph enumeration of Hill, and quotations are from his translation unless otherwise noted. [26] PG 53-54:451-56; Hill, *Homilies on Genesis*, 3:56-65.

series of nine and another of sixty-seven on Genesis. The two homilies discussed here are from the second series, which may be the first set of sermons he delivered, while still a deacon.[24] There is no critical edition of this corpus, so my sources for them are Minge's *Patrologia* and Robert C. Hill's English translation.[25]

The rubric of the first sermon considered here, number 51 in the series, is the Greek text of Gen 26:1. The sermon covers the story of Isaac in Gen 26:1-11, although it frequently rambles off the subject. It consists of approximately twenty-six hundred Greek words.[26]

It opens with a brief reference to an earlier sermon that dealt with the godliness of Rebecca and the story of Esau's foolish sale of his birthright to Jacob, which incident is held up as an example of God's foreknowledge. In addition John tells his audience that after the firstborn of Egypt were destroyed during the tenth plague, all subsequent firstborn children of the Jews had to be offered to God in the persons of the priestly tribe of Levi, which, John asserts, perhaps not with impeccable chronology or logic, shows the importance of the firstborn and the privilege lost by Esau since he could not control himself properly. He then notes as an aside that the ancients, by God's wisdom, used to foreshadow important events in the lives of their children by the names they gave them.

Moving then to the story in Genesis 26, John summarizes the basic situation: there was a famine in the time of Isaac, so he went to Gerar, as his father Abraham did. God warned him not to go to Egypt and promised to be with him and bless him and give him the land. This promise came as confirmation of God's oath to Abraham: God promised to give land and blessing to Abraham's descendants, because he kept God's commandments and left his own country, and moreover, even when it seemed contrary to nature, he believed God's promise that he would have descendants and this was reckoned to him as righteousness. At God's behest, Abraham drove out Hagar and Ishmael and then unquestioningly set out to sacrifice Isaac himself. Isaac was thus inheriting the promises made to Abraham because of Abraham's obedience.

Once in Gerar, Isaac played the same trick on the gullible king Abimelech as did his father Abraham: he passed his wife off as his sister. It may even be that he was forewarned by his father to do so. But the king caught him fondling Rebecca and, remembering the earlier episode, rebuked him, but also issued an order that the people not interfere with Isaac and that his wife not be molested. John takes this as an illustration of the providence of God. He then compares Abimelech to King

Nebuchadnezzar, who praised the three Hebrew children after they were delivered from the fiery furnace. God's power is illustrated by his making their enemies praise his servants.

The last two paragraphs of the sermon each contain one reference to Christian matters. Summarizing the sermon, §17 asserts that these examples demonstrate God's benevolence: rather than abandoning his servants, he protects them miraculously and, when he wishes to, he exalts them over those acting against them. John adds: 'This happened also with the apostles: those who arrested and arraigned them, as if gnashing their teeth at them, said to one another, 'What shall we do to these people?' (Acts 4:16) They had them in their hands, but were at a loss to proceed further.' So the power of virtue and the weakness of evil are illustrated.

Paragraph 18 exhorts the readers or hearers to make much of virtue and flee evil so as to gain future good from on high. The homily concludes: 'May it be the good fortune of us all to attain this, thanks to the grace and loving kindness of our Lord Jesus Christ, to whom with the Father and the Holy Spirit be glory, power, and honor, now and forever for ages of ages. Amen.'

Two points are worth highlighting. First, Chrysostom, who, as we saw in Chapter One, was quite hostile to contemporary Jews and Judaism, presented in a positive light the promise to Abraham of the land and a multitude of descendants to possess it, and he also took for granted the legitimacy of the Levitical priesthood. The reason is obvious: the land of Israel and the priesthood are important Old Testament themes, and Chrysostom regarded them as legitimate *in their biblical context*, even though he rejected their validity for Judaism in the Christian era. But since this was a sermon on a biblical text, he proceeded in good Antiochene fashion to interpret the text without feeling the need to bring up the very different status of Abraham's children in the present, a status he would have assumed his congregation to be aware of already, and about which he preached at length in another series of sermons. This case shows that we must evaluate carefully all positive references to Jewish matters in Old Testament pseudepigrapha to determine whether they could be affirmations of biblical truths by Christian

---

[27] PG 53-54:547-58; Hill, *Homilies on Genesis*, 3:224-42.

writers, who otherwise might be quite anti-Semitic, rather than affirmations of Judaism by Jews.

Second, neither of the two brief passages containing Christian signature features is integral to the flow of the narrative and, under other circumstances, they could easily be excised as secondary additions. The point of §17 is made just as well without any reference to the apostles. As for §18, adding or expanding a doxology at the end of the work would be a convenient way to appropriate it to a Christian editor's agenda. We have seen that the Syriac translator of the homilies in Basil's *Hexaemeron* did just this. The lesson is that we must proceed with extreme caution when using redaction criticism: it is quite capable of flagging passages as secondary when they are actually an original element.

The second sermon, number 64 in the series, has a summary of Gen 41: 46-49 as its rubric and it covers the story of Joseph from this point up to 45:24. It consists of approximately fifty-five hundred Greek words.[27]

It begins by noting the rewards that Joseph received for his patience and his other virtues and asserts that the names he gave his children also illustrate his God-fearing attitude. His wisdom in first saving and then selling the grain led to the fulfillment of his dream, for it caused his father to send his remaining sons, apart from Benjamin, to Egypt in order to buy grain. John speculates on whether God might have caused the brothers not to recognize Joseph and explores Joseph's conversation with them as he tried to get news of his father. Joseph was afraid that Benjamin was missing because the brothers had done to him what they did to Benjamin's full brother, Joseph, so Joseph took one brother hostage and sent the others away with orders to come back with Benjamin. John commends Joseph for his shrewdness. The guilty reaction of the brothers, we are told, illustrates the nature of sin: first it blinds, but then, when it is too late, it accuses. Reuben blamed his other brothers and told them, 'See, there is an accounting for his blood' (Gen 42:22), an odd statement that implies that the brothers had killed him and which John takes pains to explain: the brothers killed Joseph in intent if not in act. Joseph bound Symeon and took him hostage as part of his strategy to learn what had become of Benjamin and whether the attitude of the other brothers had changed toward the sons of Rachel. He was kind to them not only by selling them the grain but also by returning their money in their sacks, and this had the effect of making them feel that events were conspiring to punish them for their sin against Joseph.

Presently the brothers arrived home, the grain began to run low, and poor Jacob, who had already given up Joseph as lost, began to despair of Symeon and Benjamin as well despite Ruben's pledging the life of his two sons against the life of Benjamin. Jacob rebuked his sons for telling the Egyptian about Benjamin but they protested that they felt they had to tell him every detail truthfully, since they were under suspicion of spying. John takes pains to explain Jacob's curious statement 'As for me, just as I had no children, so I have none now' (Gen 43:13-14 LXX). But eventually the danger of starvation compelled him to allow the brothers to return to Egypt and to take Benjamin along. Once there, they told the steward about the returned money in their sacks, but he reassured them that no one would pursue charges against them, 'for we have received the payment in full.'[28] Joseph greeted them and, seeing his full brother, retired to another room to cry. He washed his face, then returned and ordered the meal to be served. He ate by himself, since, as the biblical account says (Gen 43:32), it was an abomination for Egyptians to eat with Hebrews, but he seated the brothers in correct order by age, to their perplexity, and gave Benjamin five times more food than the others. Then after the meal, Joseph continued to pursue his carefully crafted strategy by planting their money in the brothers' bags and his divination cup in Benjamin's in order to test how the brothers would treat Benjamin when it would seem to be in their interest to abandon him to his fate.

The brothers, of course, passed the test: Judah, in fulfillment of Joseph's dream, stepped forward and, addressing Joseph as a slave would his master, offered himself in exchange for Benjamin. Joseph, now satisfied as to their regard for both Jacob and Benjamin, revealed himself. The brothers were dumbfounded and feared that he would take vengeance on them, but he forgave them and reassured them that in his view God had arranged it all for the good. When Pharaoh heard, he and his

---

[28] Hill misunderstands this passage in §19 and mistranslates the phrase καὶ γὰρ τὸ ἀργύριον πεπληρώμεθα as 'we are satisfied with your repayment.' The steward did not accept their repayment. [29] Space does not permit a detailed analysis of any more of Chrysostom's homilies on Genesis, but others could be treated similarly. Homily 20 is devoted to the story of Cain (Gen 4:16-26) and it consists of about 4150 Greek words (PG 53-54:166-74; Hill, Homilies on Genesis 2:35-49). There is a sentence that quotes 1 Tim 6:10 in §16; another that refers to the apostolic admonition in 2 Cor 8:14 (§19); and the last sentence is a Christian doxology. All three references could be excised as glosses without disturbing the flow of thought. Homily 46 deals with the

whole household were delighted and ordered Joseph to have his father brought back to Egypt at once. Joseph sent his brothers home, warning them not to quarrel along the way.

Once again Christian signature features occur only in the last two paragraphs of the sermon. Paragraph 32 explains Joseph's admonition to mean that they should not blame one another for the things that happened but should remember that Joseph had forgiven them and be kind to one another. John continues:

‹Who could adequately admire the virtue of this good man who › fulfilled in generous measure the moral values of the New Testament? › What Christ recommends to the apostles in these words, 'Love your › enemies; pray for those who abuse you' [Matt 5:44], this man even sur- › passed. I mean, not only did he give evidence of such wonderful love › for those who did away with him as far as they could, but he did every- › thing to convince them that they had not sinned against him.›

The paragraph goes on to praise Joseph for his extraordinary philosophy and love for God, in that he saw the course of events to be God's way of fulfilling his dream and of saving his family.

Paragraph 33 draws the moral that the audience should regard trials as a sign of God's solicitude and should be grateful to God for troubles and distress as an opportunity for him to show his care for them. The sermon concludes, 'May it be the good fortune of us all to attain this, thanks to the grace and loving kindness of our Lord Jesus Christ, to whom with the Father and the Holy Spirit be glory, power, and honor, now and forever, for ages of ages. Amen.'

It is remarkable how much of this long homily consists of straightforward paraphrase and basic exegesis. Chrysostom is also concerned to explain difficult details of the biblical text, and to speculate on the inner states of the characters, especially the motivations and strategies of Joseph. He aims throughout to show how God guided events inexorably toward the fulfillment of Joseph's dream. There is some hermeneutical material, but it consistently derives its lessons narrowly from the Old Testament stories and does not attempt to Christianize the instruction until the very end, when Joseph's attitude is held up as an example of the New Testament precept to love one's enemies. But this passage can be excised without interrupting the flow of thought and, again, under other circumstances, could easily be argued to be a secondary addition. Likewise, the sermon concludes satisfactorily if everything in the last sentence after 'May it be the good fortune of us all to attain this' is deleted as a Christian gloss.[29]

Augustine of Hippo preached an enormous number of sermons in his lifetime. More than seven hundred of these survive in written form, most of them transcribed at the time of preaching by stenographers (about whom we know much less than we would like). These were formed into various collections that were gathered together in the thirteenth and fourteenth centuries and published in the monumental Maurist edition in the second half of the seventeenth century. The fifty sermons on the Old Testament were reedited by Dom Cyrille Lambot in 1961 and have recently been translated by Edmund Hill.[30] Sermon 48 was preached at Carthage, apparently in May of a year late in Augustine's life, perhaps 420. It is brief for one of his sermons (about 1,450 words, which Hill suggests would have taken fifteen to twenty minutes to present).[31] The title reads 'A sermon held on the Lord's Day in the Basilica of Celerina: of the words of Micah the prophet, where it is said, "What worthy thing shall I offer to the Lord? Bending of the knee to God on high"... etc.' Augustine begins by extolling the divine utterances, from which he exhorts his audience to receive as much as they are able and to impart what they receive without malice (§1). He then reflects on Micah 6:6-8, referring also to Wis 7:13, 16; Ps 55:11; and Sir 20:24 (§2). Augustine takes up the prophet's answer to the question 'that you do judgment and justice' and concludes that his hearers should offer themselves to God: by doing what God commands, they find in themselves both judgment and justice. Rather than taking credit for their good deeds and blaming God for their failings, which is perverse judgment and blasphemy, not judgment at all, they should praise God for their good deeds and blame themselves for their failings, which is right judgment, the only real judgment. Next he takes up Psalm 72 (LXX;

---

story of Sarah and Hagar (Gen 21:6-20) and consists of about twenty-eight hundred Greek words (PG 53-54:422-28; Hill, *Homilies on Genesis* 3:3-13). Paragraph 16, which deals with envy, is fully Christian: it contrasts the envy of the Devil, which led to the fall, with the love of the Lord, which led to human salvation. But the whole paragraph, as well as the concluding Christian doxology at the end of §17, can be removed as secondary without creating any difficulties.　　[30]　Lambot, *Sancti Aurelii Augustine: sermones de vetere testamento* (CCL 41; Turnhout: Brepols, 1961); Hill, *Sermons I (1-19) on the Old Testament* and *Sermons II (20-50) on the Old Testament* (The Works of Saint Augustine: A Translation for the 21st Century, III 1-2; Brooklyn, N.Y.: New City Press, 1990).　　[31]　Lambot, CSL 41, 606-11; Hill, *Sermons II (20-50)*, 327-32.　　[32]　*Sed quod nunc est in occulto, post erit in manifesto.*

E v Psalm 73), which serves as the core text of this sermon (§3). The narrator of the psalm asserts that the God of Israel is good to the upright, but reports that he himself almost stumbled because he gazed on the peace of sinners and envied them. The fact that evil people have good things led him to be displeased with God. This leads the psalmist to question whether God knows about human affairs (§4). Augustine explains that the psalmist fastens on the question of whether he has chosen a just life in vain. The evil rejoice, while he is scourged, and this leads him to doubt whether human concerns even reach God. This thought, however, comes from a perverse heart, not an upright one, and from plausible but unsuitable reasoning (§5). Nevertheless, he is brought back from the brink by the authoritative proclamation of the saints, for he recognizes that this thought leads him to 'condemn the generation of' God's sons: Moses, the patriarchs, and the prophets, all God's sons, had no such thought. What, therefore, is the psalmist to do (§6)? He undertakes to ascertain whether God is both just and aware of human concerns, a matter that is both momentous and difficult. The answer only comes to him when he enters the sanctuary of God and understands the final state of the wicked (§7). The faithful and pious person realizes that even though one does not know why God does what he does, one should not be led by human reasoning to condemn divine authority. 'For it is most certainly to be believed by faith that it is not possible for God to be perverse and unjust. So, entering by faith into the sanctuary of God, entering so as to believe, you learn so as to understand. For so he says, "Until I enter into the sanctuary of God," by which faith enters.' The final outcome will be fair, with the good properly distinguished from the evil. 'But what is now in hiding, afterwards shall be in evidence.'[32] Augustine calls his audience to enter God's sanctuary with him that he may teach them what he has been taught; that although good people endure many external evils, evil people, even if surrounded by an abundance of goods, still have to endure their own evil souls, and so cannot be regarded as happy (§8). Earthly things are good but do not make one a good person, but carrying out judgment and justice will. Augustine admonishes his hearers to seek to be good people among their transitory earthly goods, rather than being evil people among them and perishing with them. He then promises, God permitting, later to take up some other matters that follow from this sermon, but closes it so as not to weary his audience with its length. (The promise is kept in sermon 49 in the same series.)

This is a fascinating, and admittedly very rare, case of an ancient sermon whose attribution to a named and well-known Christian author is not in doubt, yet which does not refer once to a single explicitly Christian doctrine or quote from the New Testament or any other early Christian literature. It is not a long sermon, but neither is it so very short. In it Augustine speaks from within the world of the prophet and the psalmist and draws from their words only the lessons that he imagines they intended.

I can think of three elements in the sermon that one might argue to betray its Christian authorship, but none strike me as compelling. First, in §5 Augustine refers to the 'saints' or 'holy ones' (*sancti*), meaning the patriarchs and prophets of the Old Testament. It is true that this usage is far more common in early Christian literature, but it is not unknown in ancient Jewish literature. The term 'holy ones,' referring to people, appears once in the Hebrew Bible in Ps 34:10 (34:9 EV), and it is applied to human beings also in Tob 8:15; 3 *Mac* 6:9 (variant reading); 1 *Enoch* 100:5; and often in the Similitudes of Enoch (e.g., 1 *En.* 48:7) and perhaps in the Qumran Songs of the Sabbath Sacrifice (although the last is controversial).[33]

Second, in §7, Augustine extols the virtue of faith and urges his audience to have faith that God is just. One might argue that this passage has a very Christian ring to it, and so it does, but such ideas were present also in Hellenistic Judaism. For example, Philo praises Abraham in very similar terms in *Abraham* §§262-76: 'the only unfailing and secure good is faith in God' (§268); this faith is 'the queen of the virtues' (§270); and he warns that 'he who has believed in these things [bodily and external matters] disbelieves in God, he who disbelieves in them has believed in God' (§269). Philo and Augustine are both Platonists in the scriptural tradition and their thoughts about faith are similar.

---

[33] James R. Davila, *Liturgical Works* (Eerdmans Commentaries on the Dead Sea Scrolls 6; Grand Rapids, Mich.: Eerdmans, 2000), 100. [34] In the Latin Vulgate, *Non enim est occultum quod non manifestetur.* Versions of this saying also appear in Matt 10:26; Mark 4:22, and *Gos. Thom.* 5-6, but the closest verbal similarity is found in the Lucan verse. [35] Note that both passages make use of the roots *seminare* ('to sow') and *radix* ('root'). For a defense of 4 *Ezra* as a boundary-maintaining Jewish work, see Chapter Three below. [36] I discuss the range of possible origins of the *Testament of Abraham* in Chapter Four below. [37] If space permitted, I could present other examples of Christian works that can easily be redacted into faux Jewish ones. For example, two Latin epic poems, dealing with the story of Sodom and that of Jonah are found in Carolingian manuscripts and may have been composed as late as the late sixth century, quite likely as a pair by the same author. They are ascribed either to Cyprian or Tertullian, although they seem at some point in their transmission to have been anonymous. The Latin texts

The closest we come to a sure Christian signature feature is the line 'But what is now in hiding, afterwards shall be in evidence.' This alludes to the Synoptic saying of Jesus which appears in Luke 8:17 as 'For there is nothing hidden that shall not be made evident.'[34] The adverbial phrase 'in hiding' (*in occulto*) is similar to the noun 'hidden' (*occultum*), and the adverbial phrase 'in evidence' (*in manifesto*) is similar to the verb 'be made evident' (*manifestetur*). On the one hand, that Augustine is alluding to the Lucan passage can scarcely be doubted, given all that we actually know about the sermon. On the other hand, a scholar wanting to defend the Jewish origin of an Old Testament pseudepigraphon that contained this allusion to a New Testament passage could point out that the verbal similarity is not close – it involves only two word roots, neither in the same grammatical form as the New Testament verse – and the general sentiment is congenial to Jewish eschatological thought. For example, the futility of hoping that one's sins will be hidden at the final judgment is a theme of the Epistle of Enoch (*1 En.* 98:7-8; 104:7-8). The apparent allusion could be a coincidence, or it could be a scribal assimilation of the passage to the Lucan verse during copying. Neither argument could be dismissed out of hand. Early Christianity and ancient Judaism shared many themes and ideas, and often these were expressed independently in similar language. The parable of the sower in Mark 4:3-9 in the Vulgate and the comparison of human beings with the seeds sown by the farmer in *4 Ezra* 8:41 make similar points and share some verbal similarities, yet they are completely independent.[35] Likewise, it appears that the original text of *T. Abr.* A 11:2 // B 8:12 has been brought closer, at least in recension A, to Matt 7:13. Whether there was an allusion to Matt 7:13 in the original text is not clear.[36] Often we simply cannot be sure whether an apparent allusion to a New Testament passage is one in fact, and this particular one is sufficiently general in theme and dissimilar in wording for one – again, in another context – to regard it with skepticism.

All this being the case, I was tempted to place this sermon at the end of the chapter as an example of a work on the Old Testament by a named Christian author which contained no Christian signature features, but I have kept to the route of prudence and accepted the phrase as an allusion rather than an echo, and therefore as a signature feature. Nevertheless, it should be stressed that if this level of Christianization and no more were present in an unattributed parabiblical narrative having to do with the Old Testament, it is virtually certain that some scholars would argue that it was a Jewish pseudepigraphon.[37]

REFLECTIONS .... I am not, of course, suggesting that these sermons, which are integral parts of larger corpora that are universally accepted as genuine, are anything but Christian compositions by Chrysostom and Augustine. Rather, I am using these documents, first, to highlight the fact that Christians were capable of dealing at length with Old Testament stories on their own terms, as stories to be understood. Even in sermons, a genre in which we should expect explicitly Christian hermeneutical concerns to be in the foreground, a Christian writer could concentrate virtually exclusively on retelling the story, explaining difficult points in the narrative, and deriving very basic and generic moral instruction from it. Second, Christians respected the Old Testament and its characters as precursors to Christ and treated elements of the old dispensation as valid on their own terms for their own times, such as when Chrysostom speaks with apparent approval of the blessing of

were published by Rudolph Peiper in *Cypriani Galli Poetae Heptateuchos* (CSEL 23; Vienna, 1881), 212-20 (*De Sodoma*) and 221-26 (*De Iona*). A critical commentary on the former has also been published by Luca Morisi, *Versus de Sodoma: introduzione, testo critico, traduzione e comento* (Edizioni e saggi universitari di filologia classica 52; Bologne: Pàtron Editore, 1993). English translations of both, based on an inferior Latin text, have been published by S. Thelwall in *ANF*, 4:127-32.   *De Sodoma* is a poem of 166 lines (a little less than eleven hundred Latin words) and is entirely devoid of Christian signature features apart from a possible allusion or echo of Heb 1:14 in lines 28-29, which refer to angels as 'youths in form, who both were spirits in ministry' (*forma iuuentes qui spiritus ambo ... ministerio*). But angels are considered ministering spirits in Jewish tradition as well. Compare, for example, *3 En.* 47:1, which refers to 'the souls of the angels and the spirits of the ministering ones' (נשמתן של מלאכים ורוחן של משרתים); see Peter Schäfer, *Synopse zur Hekhalot-Literatur* [TSAJ 2; Tübingen: Mohr Siebeck, 1981], §67, MS V228). *De Iona* contains 105 lines (a little less than seven hundred Latin words) and may be incomplete, since it carries the story only up to Jonah's arrival at Nineveh (although the surviving version does seem to bring the piece to a narrative conclusion). Line 55 seems to refer to Matt 8:24 and the end of the work describes Jonah as a sign of the Lord's heavenly glory or (a variant reading) his driving away of death, echoing Matt 12:38-41. If one wished, one could delete the Christian references as secondary additions with no harm to the sense. Other noteworthy discussions of *De Sodoma* and *De Iona* include Dieter Kartschoke, *Bibeldichtung: Studien zur Geschichte der epischen Bibelparaphrase von Juvencus bis Otfrid von Weißenburg* (Munich: Fink, 1975), 37-38; Ralph Hexter, 'The Metamorphosis of Sodom: The Ps-Cyprian "De Sodoma" as an Ovidian Episode,' *Traditio* 44 (1988): 1-35; and D. M. Kriel, '*Sodoma* in Fifth Century Biblical Epic,' *Acta Classica* 34 (1991): 7-20.   In addition, S. P. Brock and S. Hopkins have published 'A Verse Homily on Abraham and Sarah in Egypt: Syriac Original with Early Arabic Translation,' *Mus* 105 (1992): 87-146. This homily retells the story of Abraham and Sarah's encounter with Pharaoh in Genesis 12 in a form strikingly independent of both rabbinic and patristic tradition, one that gives an unusually central role to Sarah. Apart from a single reference in line 36 to the Samaritan woman of John 4, neither the Syriac nor the Arabic translation contain any Christian signature features.

Abraham's descendents, their possession of the land, and the Levitical priesthood. As we have seen in Chapter One, these comments in no way imply that he approved of the Jews and Judaism of his own time. Third, when Christian authors wrote works in which they concentrated on Old Testament content, they were capable of limiting references to Christian matters (Christian signature features) to asides, brief conclusions or doxologies, and subtle echoes that, because of their marginal nature, could easily be mistaken by a modern scholar as secondary glosses or adaptations to be removed by redaction criticism in order to recover the pristine Jewish text they interpolated. Therefore redaction criticism must be used with rigorous methodological controls, and we should be wary of its results. Fourth, sometimes things that one might think of as obvious Christian signature features – such as faith as a central virtue, references to human beings as 'saints,' and even some apparent echoes of New Testament passages – turn out to have close parallels in ancient Jewish thought. Given how few sources for ancient Judaism survive – especially for Greek- and Latin-speaking Hellenistic and Greco-Roman Judaism – we should accept ideas as Christian but certainly not Jewish only with great caution and after the most careful scrutiny.

4 CHRISTIAN WORKS WITH EPISODES THAT LACK ANY CHRISTIAN SIGNATURE FEATURES

EPHREM THE SYRIAN'S COMMENTARIES ON GENESIS AND EXODUS .... Ephrem the Syrian was born in Nisibis in the first decade of the fourth century. Late in life he moved to Edessa, and he is remembered for his time there as a zealous opponent of heresies. He died in 373 while coordinating a relief effort for the poor of the city during a famine. He was a prolific author, and even though most of his writings have perished, the surviving corpus is very large indeed. His poetic works are renowned for their beauty. He appears to have written commentaries on most of the books of the Bible, although only those on Genesis and Exodus survive today, and only the one on Genesis comments on the entire text. Their translators into English comment:

‹As both of the commentaries translated here bear witness, › Ephrem's method of exegesis is not intended to provide a continuous, › verse by verse, exposition of the biblical text. Rather, Ephrem dwells › on texts that have a particular theological significance for him, or › whose orthodox interpretation needs to be reasserted in the face of ›

contemporary heterodox ideas. For example, the two accounts of cre- ›
ation together with the narrative concerning Adam and Eve in the gar- ›
den occupy fully a third of the *Commentary on Genesis*. On the other ›
hand, much of the Patriarchal narratives are treated summarily or not ›
at all. In the *Commentary on Exodus* chapters 22 and 26–30 of Exodus ›
are not treated at all and chapter 15, the Canticle of Moses, is merely ›
paraphrased without comment.›³⁸

Ephrem's commentaries generally focus on straightforward exegesis
of the text; references to explicitly Christian matters tend to be few and

---

³⁸ Edward G. Mathews, Jr., and Joseph P. Amar with Kathleen McVey, *St. Ephrem the Syrian: Selected Prose Works* (FC 91; Washington, D.C.: Catholic University of America Press, 1994), 43-44. This work discusses the life of Ephrem on pp. 12-37 and these commentaries on pp. 42-44. The *Commentary on Genesis* is introduced and translated on pp. 59-213 and the *Commentary on Exodus* on pp. 217-65. All quotations are from this translation unless otherwise indicated. The Syriac text of the commentaries has been edited and translated into Latin by R.-M. Tonneau in *Sancti Ephraem Syri: In Genesim et In Exodum commentarii* (CSCO 152-53; Scriptores Syri 71-72; Louvain: Durbecq, 1955). Other translations of Ephrem's works into English include Kathleen E. McVey and John Meyendorff, *Ephrem the Syrian: Hymns* (CWS; Mahwah, N.J.: Paulist, 1989); and Sebastian Brock, *Hymns on Paradise: St. Ephrem* (Crestwood, N.Y.: St. Vladimir's Seminary Press, 1998). Important general treatments of Ephrem include Robert Murray, *Symbols of Church and Kingdom* (London: Cambridge University Press, 1975); and Sebastian P. Brock, *The Luminous Eye: The Spiritual World Vision of Saint Ephrem* (rev. ed.; Kalamazoo, Mich.: Cistercian Publications, 1992).

³⁹ Mathews and Amar, *Selected Prose Works*, 134-46; Tonneau, *Sancti Ephraem Syri*, 1:55-65. Ephrem also discusses the Flood from a more Christian perspective in Hymn on Paradise 2.12-13; Hymn on the Nativity 1:23, 47-48, 56-58; 7.7; and Hymn on Virginity and on the Symbols of the Lord 8:14. ⁴⁰ According to *Gen. Rab.* 26.2, God prevented Noah from engaging in sex until he was five hundred years old, so that if his descendants proved to be righteous they would not require too many arks to be saved. In what follows I have cited a number of parallels to Jewish traditions in Ephrem's work. These are some of the more plausible and striking ones suggested by the English translators, as well as a few I have noticed myself, and are intended to be illustrative rather than comprehensive. ⁴¹ At this point Ephrem refers back to a remark in IV.2 of the commentary. In *Gen. Rab.* 26.5 and *Tg. Neof.* 6:2, 4, the 'sons of God' in Genesis 6 are taken to be human judges. Cf. Ephrem's Hymn on Paradise 1:11 and Hymn on the Nativity 1:48.

⁴² According to *Gen. Rab.* 26.6, God reduced the lifespan of human beings to encourage them to take thought for their mortality and to repent. ⁴³ Cf. Ephrem's Hymn on Virginity and on the Symbols of the Lord 29:6. ⁴⁴ Noah was a herald to the generation of the Flood according to *Gen. Rab.* 30.7. ⁴⁵ Cf. the similar explanation in *Aris.* 162-66: unclean animals are by nature 'injurious' (κακοποιητικὸς). ⁴⁶ According to *Tg. Onq.* 6:3, the one hundred twenty years were an extension granted to humanity to see if they would repent. According to *Gen. Rab.* 32.7 and *Tg. Neof.* 7:10, the extra seven days were given to allow for mourning over Methuselah. ⁴⁷ Rabbinic traditions indicate that copulation in the ark was forbidden and that the dog, the raven, and Ham disobeyed this rule and were punished (*Gen. Rab.* 36.7; *b. Sanh.* 108b). ⁴⁸ The chronology in *Gen. Rab.* 33.7 follows the same calculation as Ephrem's regarding the length of time in the ark and the lunar and solar years.

---

far between. There are whole episodes that lack any Christian signature features. I summarize and comment on three such episodes: Noah's Flood, the story of Joseph, and the early life of Moses.

Noah's Flood .... The story of the Flood is covered in Ephrem's *Commentary on Genesis* VI-VII in approximately twenty-three hundred Syriac words.[39] Ephrem tells us that Noah preserved his virginity for the first five hundred years of his life,[40] but the sons of Seth commingled with the daughters of Cain[41] and their wives did likewise, with the result that God lowered their life spans from nine hundred years to one hundred twenty.[42] The vigorous Sethian line infused energy into the feeble Cainite line and produced mighty men. Because of the corruption of human beings, God determined to blot out all life. Ephrem is careful to present God's repentance in a theologically acceptable form: God was not sorry because he had failed to foresee this outcome, but because he had now to kill the human sinners, whom he still loved, as well as the innocent animals.[43]

It took Noah one hundred years to build the ark, during which he warned his generation of the coming flood and lived an exemplary life before them.[44] After that God told him to enter it with his family and seven pairs of all clean animals and one pair of all unclean animals. Ephrem explains that God declared the gentle animals to be clean and the vicious animals to be unclean.[45] The animals came to the ark, miraculously prevented from conflict with one another, while the sinners gathered to watch – but to amuse themselves, not to repent. Indeed, God gave that evil generation ample time to repent, even though he shortened the original grace period by twenty years to just a century. He then extended this by a week, because the wonders the people saw in that week were worth another twenty years of delay.[46] God himself closed the door after the Flood began, so as to prevent those left behind from coming in a panic and breaking the door down. The people and the animals maintained their chastity while on the ark,[47] but came out after the Flood to be fruitful and multiply. After the ark landed on Mount Qardu and the ark's passengers had been inside her for exactly a year,[48] God told Noah to empty the ark. Noah offered a sacrifice of clean animals, which were obedient to him. We are not to suppose that God literally enjoyed the smell of the burnt offerings, but rather that he approved of Noah's simplicity of heart and thus promised never to bring such a flood again.

God restored the natural cycle of the year, blessed Noah and his sons, and gave them the rule that they should not eat flesh still containing its life, that is, that meat to be eaten should be slaughtered and drained of blood.[49] Indeed, God established three covenants with Noah: the prohibition of the eating of blood; 'one of the resurrection, that their blood will be required of the animals';[50] the law that murder was to be punished by execution; then, in addition, the covenant of the rainbow, which was the sign of God's promise not to destroy the world again with a flood.

Noah's drunkenness is explained by the fact that he had had no wine for a long time – by Ephrem's calculation, at least six years.[51] He explains the mystery of Canaan being cursed by Noah, even though Ham committed the offense, by concluding that the reference to 'his youngest son' was to Canaan, since Ham was the middle son, and that Canaan had seen his grandfather's nakedness and told others about it. Therefore Ham was merely deprived of a blessing, but Canaan was cursed. Noah blessed Shem and Japheth, but the Canaanites were ultimately reduced to slavery in the time of Joshua.

The Joseph Story The story of Joseph up to Jacob's arrival in Egypt (Genesis 35:5-46:34) is covered in Ephrem's *Commentary on Genesis* XXXIII-XL in approximately thirty-one hundred Syriac words.[52] As a boy, Joseph brought a bad report about his brothers to his father, and his brothers hated him for it. Then Joseph dreamed his dreams (Ephrem is careful to explain the apparent inconsistency of Rachel bowing down to him when she was already dead), with the result that the brothers faked his death and sold him to the Arabs,[53] who, in turn, sold him in Egypt a few days later.

The commentary then digresses to the story of Tamar, as in Genesis 37. After the story of Er, Onan, and Shelah is summarized, we are told that

---

[49] Note that this is one of the few Jewish ceremonial precepts presented in a New Testament book as applying to Christians (Acts 15:29). [50] Mathews misunderstands the phrase, translating it 'one of retaliation, that God will require the blood of animals' (VI.14). The point of the passage is that at the resurrection, all animals who ate human flesh will have to give it back, as is made clear in VI.15. [51] The understanding that Gen 9:22 refers to a 'street' is found here, in the Syriac Peshitta, and in *Tg. Onq.* 9:22 and *Pirqe R. El.* 23. [52] Mathews and Amar, *Selected Prose Works*, 182-98; Tonneau, *Sancti Ephraem Syri*, 1:95-109. Ephrem interprets the Joseph story in a Christian light in two brief references in the Hymns on Virginity and on the Symbols of the Lord 18.6; 21.9-11. [53] *Tg. Onq.* and *Tg. Ps.-J.* 37:27-2; *Gen. Rab.* 91.6; and Philo, *Joseph* 15 also report that Joseph was sold to Arabs.

Tamar wanted not marriage but the blessing of the Hebrews in order to make her faith victorious. Fearing that she was suspected in the deaths of Jacob's two sons, she prayed for God to help her to seduce Jacob. Her prayer impelled him, against his normal custom, to have congress with a prostitute. As a result of their union, Tamar became pregnant and was taken out by the Hebronites to be burned. But when informed privately that he was the father, Jacob marveled at her faith. Realizing that his sons had been evil but she was innocent, he took her in but did not have sex with her again, nor did he marry another woman.

Meanwhile back in Egypt, Joseph was sold to Potiphar and prospered in his household. When Potiphar's wife tried to seduce him and failed, accusing him falsely, she had her husband throw him into prison. Joseph, we are told, could have fled back to his father's house but stayed so as not to be shamed and in order to find out how his dreams would turn out. There he brought prosperity to the other prisoners. When he correctly interpreted the dreams of Pharaoh's chief baker (who was executed) and chief butler, the latter, having been restored to his place, forgot about Joseph. Two years later, however Pharaoh had disturbing dreams, which brought to mind the butler's fellow-prisoner. Joseph was brought out to interpret them and Pharaoh, reading between the lines of Joseph's recommendation that he select a wise man to administer the plan to stockpile the grain during the years of plenty, gave Joseph his own signet ring along with control over the whole land. It chanced that Potiphar was present at this scene, and he went home to report events to his wife and share his fear of reprisals. She confessed her sin to her husband but expressed confidence that Joseph would punish only herself, if anyone, and she was hopeful that he would not take revenge even on her.

According to plan, Joseph gathered grain for the worldwide famine. In due course the famine led Jacob to send his sons to Egypt, where Joseph recognized them. Accusing them of being spies, he demanded that they bring their younger brother back with them (on the theory that eleven stars bowed down to him in his dream, so Benjamin must come to him too) and arrested Simeon, both as a hostage and as a source of information about what they had told their father after they had sold Joseph into slavery.

The brothers returned to their father and found their money in their sacks of grain. Jacob was sorely grieved by the turn of events and, after the food was used up, assented only with the greatest reluctance to send Benjamin with his brothers to Joseph. Upon their arrival, the brothers alerted the steward to the apparent mix-up concerning their payment, but he reassured them and spoke kindly to them. Joseph joined them, asked about their and their father's welfare, and after excusing himself briefly to weep in private, sat to eat by himself and seated the brothers in proper order according to age, giving the impression that he had accomplished this by means of his divining cup.[54] Then the next morning, as in the biblical story, the brothers departed but were caught with Joseph's cup in Benjamin's sack. They were brought back to Joseph, who denounced them for claiming to be righteous but stealing his cup, which crime he had discovered by divination, and he decreed that as punishment Benjamin would be kept in Egypt as a slave.

Judah lamented to Joseph until Joseph was moved to send everyone else out of the room and to reveal himself to his brothers, speaking in Hebrew, and he ordered them to return to their father to tell him that the dream and more had been fulfilled, and that Joseph was now ruler of the whole of Egypt.

Pharaoh and all his princes were pleased, and Joseph sent his brothers to bring back their father, admonishing them not to bicker – that is, not to blame one another – along the way. Upon their arrival home, the brothers had to explain Joseph's situation and their part in it to their father, but he forgave them. God told Jacob not to fear the sorcery of the Egyptians and promised that his descendants would return to the Promised Land. Jacob and his household then packed up and went to

[54] This is the sense of the Syriac in section XXXVII.7. The divining cup is also used for this purpose in *Tg. Ps.-J.* 43:33 and *Gen. Rab.* 92.5; 93.7. [55] Mathews and Amar, *Selected Prose Works*, 223-36; Tonneau, *Sancti Ephraem Syri*, 1:124-33. Ephrem gives a brief homiletic reading of this biblical passage in Hymn on Paradise 14.6. A considerably longer stretch of Ephrem's treatment of the life of Moses is devoid of Christian signature features: the first one appears in section XII, in which the institution of Passover is applied typologically to the life of Christ. But the section considered here ends at a more natural point in the narrative. [56] *Exod. Rab.* 1.18 also reports that the astrologers of Pharaoh predicted the coming of a savior of the Hebrews and that he would be put in peril by water, and Josephus refers to a similar prophecy by an Egyptian priest (*Ant.* 2.205). [57] Christians valued martyrdom, but ancient Jewish literature did as well, as is shown by 4 Mac 6-7 and 4 Maccabees. For a crown to be given to the Maccabean martyrs, see 4 Mac 17:11-16. For 'confession' of Judaism as in this passage, see 2 Mac 6:6. [58] *Tg. Onq.* and *Tg. Ps.J.* 1:19 mention the shrewdness of the Israelite women, but not the midwives specifically. [59] According to *Tg. Ps.-J.* 2:5, God sent a plague of skin inflammation against the Egyptians, and as a result Pharaoh's daughter went down to the Nile to cool herself. [60] *Exod. Rab.* 1:28-29 also says that the Egyptian Moses killed was a cruel taskmaster.

Egypt. Joseph met him and informed Pharaoh that they were owners of cattle, so as to have them settle in Goshen, away from idolaters.

The Early Life of Moses⸺ ⸺ The early life of Moses, from his birth to his return to Egypt following exile and his initial meeting with the Hebrew elders, is covered in sections I-I v of Ephrem's *Commentary on Exodus* in approximately two thousand Syriac words.[55] Ephrem tells us that both Satan and Pharaoh's diviners realized that the time was approaching for the fulfillment of the prediction to Abraham (i.e., in Gen 15:13-14) that after four hundred years of slavery and oppression in another land, his descendants would come out and that other nation would be punished.[56] Pharaoh was greatly disturbed by this prophecy and by the vast increase in the Hebrew population, and as a result he put them under hard labor. Issuing the decree that all male Israelite babies were to be killed, Pharaoh ordered the Hebrew midwives to kill them as they were born. Expecting to receive the 'crown of confession,'[57] however, they disobeyed, and they survived due to their shrewd handling of the situation and were blessed with fecundity.[58] The rivers were filled with dead babies and their corpses lay heaped on its banks, but still the Hebrews multiplied.

Moses' mother hid him for as long as possible after his birth, then put him in a basket and prayed to God not to let Pharaoh destroy the seed that God had blessed. Miriam stayed nearby to see what would happen to the baby in the river, sharing her family's confidence that God would see to it that someone would find and save the beautiful baby. It was an unusually warm day[59] and Pharaoh's daughter, who was incapable of having children of her own, was led by God to go down to the river to bathe at a different time from usual so that she would find baby Moses, whom she adopted as her son. Miriam arranged for his own mother to act as his nurse and in due course Moses completed his education. Although he was a beautiful boy, he stammered. He knew the truth about his own origins not only from his circumcision, but also from what his mother and sister had told him. As an adult he killed and buried the cruelest Egyptian taskmaster,[60] but when he tried to break up a fight the next day the one who was in the wrong accused him of the murder before many witnesses, since the rescued man had revealed it to others out of love for Moses. Pharaoh heard and in a rage set out to have Moses killed. Moses fled to Midian, where he helped the daughters of a local priest when herdsmen tried to take water from them at the well. The father invited Moses into their home and in due course Moses married the daughter Sephora, who, however, persisted in her father's religion and only permitted one of her two sons to be circumcised. Moses named one son (Gershom) in honor of his escape and sojourning in a foreign land and the other (Eliezer) in honor of his deliverance from Pharaoh. At this point, back in Egypt, the Hebrews realized that thirty years beyond the four-hundred-year deadline had passed. They prayed to God and were answered.

Ephrem goes to some effort to explain, not entirely clearly, why both an angel and God are said to have spoken to Moses out of the burning bush. God spoke from the bush because it could not be made into an idol. God ordered Moses to meet with Pharaoh, who would not listen, but nevertheless the Hebrews would plunder the Egyptians and the promise to Abraham would be fulfilled.

Moses asked for signs with which to convince his hard-hearted people. God responded with the sign of his staff turning into a snake, the sign of his hand turning leprous, and the ability to turn water into blood, and then at Moses' request also gave him eloquence. Moses went back to Midian, where he waited to return to Egypt until God informed him that everyone there who had sought to kill him was dead. Then Moses started on the way to Egypt with his wife and two sons. God told him to warn Pharaoh that unless Pharaoh sent Israel, God's firstborn son, to God, God would kill Pharaoh's firstborn. Then at night the Lord sought to kill Moses because he had not circumcised his second son. Since the vision on Horeb Moses had not had intercourse with his wife, and both Moses and God were displeased with her for preventing the circumcision of her son. Moses should have ignored her wishes, but because he did not, an angel came to kill him. Seeing this, his wife circumcised the boy and appeased the angel. Moses scolded her and then sent her and the two boys back to Midian. Then the Lord sent Aaron to meet Moses, just as had

[61] *Commentary on Genesis* XXXIV.2-3. [62] *Commentary on Exodus* IV.4. [63] Ibid., II.2. [64] Herzog, *Die Bibelepik der lateinischen Spätantike: Formgeschichte einer erbaulichen Gattung* (Theorie und Geschichte der Literatur und der schönen Künste, Texte und Abhandlungen 37; Munich: Fink, 1975), xix-xxxiii. This book is published as 'volume 1,' but a second volume has not been published and the author is no longer living. [65] A critical text was published by Peiper in CSEL 23, 1-211. Peiper discusses the manuscript tradition on pp. i-xxix, and Hexter has a useful analysis of the manuscripts in their social context in 'The Metamorphosis of Sodom,' 26-35. See also Herzog, *Bibelepik*, xxv-xxxii; Kartschoke, *Bibeldichtung*, 34-35, 99; Michael Roberts, *Biblical Epic and Rhetorical Paraphrase in Late Antiquity* (ARCA 16; Liverpool: Cairns, 1985), 92-96. This epic has never been translated into a modern

been predicted, and they assembled the elders of their people and showed them miracles, and they put their faith in Moses as God had promised.

As with Chrysostom's sermons, Ephrem's commentary shows a strong interest in basic biblical exegesis and the explanation of difficult passages with no particular hermeneutical interest. The high density of parallels to Jewish, especially rabbinic, exegesis is striking. It seems likely that Ephrem had access to Jewish targums or midrashic works and that he drew on them frequently. In addition, a number of times he alludes to Jewish customs or ideas of which he would have disapproved in the present, but which he presents in a positive light in their biblical context. In the Joseph story Tamar longs to participate in the blessings of the circumcised Hebrews and is self-conscious of her own origin among the uncircumcised.[61] Likewise, Sephora is condemned for preventing the circumcision of Moses' second son.[62] And in her prayer, Moses' mother refers to the line of the Hebrews as the seed that God blessed.[63] Christians had access to Jewish exegesis and were capable of drawing on it freely. Allusions to Jewish exegetical traditions are by no means proof of Jewish authorship. And Christians could make positive references to Jewish institutions and Jewish ethnicity if these were viewed in the context of the Old Testament period.

THE HEPTATEUCHOS *OF PSEUDO-CYPRIANUS* .... A considerable corpus of epic poetry on biblical themes was produced in Latin in late antiquity. Following Reinhart Herzog, we can divide it into three groups. The first can be labeled 'canonical' and consists of works by Juvencus, Sedulius, Arator, and Avitus. The second consists of 'non-canonical' works, those produced by named authors which survive only in a narrow manuscript base. These include works by Claudius Marius Victorius, Blossius Aemilius Dracontius, and Proba. Third are the non-canonical and pseudepigraphic works on various New Testament and Old Testament subjects.[64] It is the third category that is of interest in this chapter. The pseudepigraphic Latin epics on Old Testament themes seem mostly to have been written in or around the fifth century. Herzog believes that, whether or not their authors were known originally, once these works had been rejected from the canon they circulated anonymously until they were collected together in the Carolingian era, when they were assigned to well-known pre-Ambrosian prose authors.

The *Heptateuchos* is a five-thousand-line epic (about 32,500 Latin words) which paraphrases the Pentateuch, Joshua, and Judges.[65] It is untitled in the manuscripts; the title it goes by today is modern. Apparently the original work also included other Old Testament prose books: Kings, Chronicles, Judith, Esther, and book(s) of the Maccabees are mentioned in some library catalogues, and a few lines of poetry on Kings and Chronicles survive.[66] Some manuscripts assign the work to a Cyprianus, but nothing more is known about the author. Herzog is probably correct in concluding that this is a pseudepigraphic attribution to Cyprian of Carthage. It is generally agreed on various grounds that the *Heptateuchos* was composed during the fifth century, probably in Gaul.[67]

The *Heptateuchos* is an extended paraphrase of the Bible in ornate Latin poetry, and references in it to explicitly Christian matters are few and far between. Indeed, Jacques Fontaine has in passing raised the possibility that the author was a Western Jew or a 'Judaizing Christian,' but he did not argue the case and his suggestion has not been received with any enthusiasm.[68] The epic does have a few explicit references to Christian matters. The three 'men' who visited Abraham are interpreted as the Trinity in *Genesis* 611-12, 634. Christ is mentioned in *Exodus* 413 and *Numbers* 106.[69] The epic was transmitted under a Christian, if probably pseudepigraphic, name (at least in the manuscripts we have) in a genre whose use in Latin is attested only by Christians, and it made use of the Old Latin version of the Bible. It is difficult to be sure what Fontaine means by 'Judaizing Christian,' but such close analysis of the work as has been done up to now points to its being a Christian composition by a writer who kept close to the biblical narrative voice but whose interests as a Christian show through by what the writer chose to emphasize and

language apart from a fragment of Genesis, corresponding to lines 1-165 of Peiper's edition, which was translated into English by S. Thelwall in *ANF*, 4:132-35, and short quotations of a few lines here and there in other scholarly works. __ __ [66] __ Peiper, CSEL 23, i-ii, 209-211. The lines from Job should be deleted: see Roberts, *Biblical Epic*, 95 n. 134. __ __ [67] __ Herzog, *Bibelepik*, 52-60. __ __ [68] __ Fontaine, *Naissance de la poésie dans l'Occident chrétien: Esquisse d'une histoire de la poésie latine chrétienne du IIIᵉ au VIᵉ siècle* (Paris: Études Augustiniennes, 1981), 247: 'Faudrait-il imaginer cet anonyme impénétrable comme un Juif d'Occident, soucieux de ne pas laisser aux chrétiens le monopole de l'expression épique? ou comme un chrétien judaïsant?' Daniel J. Nodes notes Fontaine's comment without sympathy in *Doctrine and Exegesis in Biblical Latin Poetry* (ARCA 31; Leeds: Cairns, 1993), 83 n. 14. __ __ [69] __ Roberts, *Biblical Epic*, 95 n. 136; Herzog, *Bibelepik*, 118. Nodes has shown that in the section on Genesis, the epic poet interacts with and builds on the ideas of patristic writers (*Doctrine and Exegesis*, 25-36, 83-87). J. M. Evans offers some observations along the same lines in *Paradise Lost and the Genesis Tradition* (Oxford: Clarendon, 1968), 137-42. __ __ [70] __ Roberts, *Biblical Epic*, 119-21, 185-86. __ __ [71] __ Peiper, CSEL 23, 104-15.

neglect. Examples pointed out by Michael Roberts are the abbreviation of cultic material in the legal traditions and the emphasis on the virginity of Jephthah's daughter.[70] As already pointed out, a difficulty with this chapter is that any Christian texts that lack, or have only a few, Christian signature features can always be argued on those points alone to be Jewish. But the consensus at present is that the *Heptateuchos* was written by a Christian. One could perhaps think of the writer as 'judaizing' in the sense that he or she strove to keep close to the narrative viewpoint of the Old Testament, but for reasons given below I see no need to assume that the writer was a judaizer in practice, which is how I would use the term. My analysis below of the section on *Leviticus* offers considerable support to the current consensus.

Space does not allow for a complete analysis of the *Heptateuchos*, although one is a desideratum for the problem posed in this chapter, so I will narrow my focus in what follows to a close reading of the section on *Leviticus*, which consists of 309 lines (about two thousand Latin words).[71]

The first nine lines introduce the book, paraphrasing only Lev 1:9; 5:7,11 and 8:24. Then there is a summary of the story of Nadab and Abihu from Leviticus 10 (lines 10-27). A summary of the food laws in Leviticus 11 follows, but a detailed account is given only of birds, and the poet, in a rare personal aside, complains of the difficulty of rendering such matters in metrical verse (lines 28-36). Next comes an account of the laws of female impurity after birth in Lev 12:1-7 (lines 37-50; the rules for male circumcision are mentioned in 39-41), the rules regarding leprosy in Leviticus 13-14 (lines 51-68), and the impurity rules concerning male and female fluxes in Leviticus 15 (lines 69-94).

The scapegoat ritual for the Day of Atonement in Leviticus 16 is summarized briefly (lines 95-107). Of Leviticus 17, only the rule forbidding the eating of blood in vv. 3-14 is mentioned (lines 108-13). The writer then turns to the Holiness Code and discusses the incest laws and the laws against homosexuality and bestiality of Leviticus 18 (lines 114-139) and the laws regarding gleaning of fields, theft, perjury, paying of wages, the abuse of the disabled, the rebuking of a brother, mixed kinds, seduction, tree fruit, divination, tattoos and branding, making one's daughter a prostitute, respect for elders, and just measures, all of which are found in Lev 19:9-29, 31-36 (lines 140-95). Of Leviticus 20, only the prohibition against ventriloquists in v. 6 is noted in line 196. As for Leviticus 21, the priestly rules forbidding certain practices in mourning for the dead and forbidding marriage to a prostitute or an adulteress in vv. 5-9 are generalized to everyone, although the rules regarding the marriage of the high priest are applied to him alone (lines 197-210). Then the writer refers to purity before the altar and the curtain, although it is not clear if the original limitation of the rules to priests in Lev 22:3-4 and 21:23 is intended here (lines 211-15a). A reference to the rules for eating holy things in Lev 22:9, 12-14 follows (lines 215b-22), while the account of the Jewish festivals in Leviticus 23 is ignored entirely. Then the lighting of the sanctuary discussed in Lev 24:2 is filled out with new details (lines 223-26), followed by a garbled version of the story in Lev 24:10, 11, 14 of the half-breed Israelite (here, simply a 'Hebrew') who cursed God's name (lines 227-35). From Lev 25:25-54 we find an account of the rules for the release of indentured servants during the Jubilee and the redemption of those who sell themselves into servitude (lines 236-65). The blessings for obedience and curses for disobedience found in Lev 26:3-44 are then outlined (lines 266-96). The poem concludes with a summary of the laws of the valuation of devoted persons and things in Leviticus 27 (lines 297-309).

This section of the *Heptateuchos* is a remarkable passage that consistently maintains the narrative voice of the book of Leviticus and addresses the ancient Israelites as the implied readers.[72] Once, with regard to food taboos, the narrator even uses a first-person plural pronoun: 'To the people He (God) specified rules of common sustenance: and what

---

[72] In the Excursus at the end of Chapter Three, I compare Josephus' paraphrase of Leviticus in *Ant.* 3.188-286 to the paraphrase in the *Heptateuchos*. My conclusions there support my contention here that the *Heptateuchos* was written by a Christian. References below to Josephus assume the discussion in this excursus. [73] *Communis populo distinguit regula victus: /et quid vel liceat vel fas adsumere non sit, /eloquitur, quem nostra etiam conuiuia morem /caelesti sub lege tenent* (lines 28-31a). Herzog seems to think that in this passage the Christian author breaks character and speaks for him- or herself. Granted, the 'also' could be taken to distinguish the speaker's group from the 'people' in line 28, but the point of lines 30a-31a is that the speaker's group *keeps* these prescriptions, in which case the speaker seems to be the narrator of Leviticus, and the 'also' merely indicates that God specified the rules and the Israelites also kept them. See Herzog, *Bibelepik*, 116. Karla Pollmann has suggested to me in a private communication that the sense of the passage is that Christians keep the Jewish food laws, but under heavenly law, in other words, interpreted spiritually. She cites a work by Novatian of Rome, *De cibis Judaicis* (*ANF*, 5:645-50), as a Christian source that teaches that Christians should understand the Jewish food laws spiritually as a means of moderation and exhortation to moral conduct. The passage is not very clear, and her interpretation may well be correct. If so, *Leviticus* is not a unit that lacks Christian signature features entirely, but my exegesis of it as a Christian interpretation of the biblical book of Leviticus is confirmed.

is either permitted or is unlawful to receive, He pronounced, which custom our common meals also keep under the celestial law.'[73] At times the narrator addresses this reader in the second person indicative or imperative: regarding incest (122, 131); bestiality (135); rebuking one's brother (156-65); the mixing of kinds (166-70); use of the fruit of a grafted tree (179-81); tattoos, brandings, making a daughter a prostitute, and murder by charm (182-89); just measures (193); rejecting one who consults ventriloquists (196); and crop failure due to God's curse (285).

Nevertheless, although the implied audience is the ancient Israelites, a careful reading shows that the overall treatment of Leviticus makes much more sense if we take the intended audience to be Christians rather than Jews. Note first of all that almost all the passages in the second person cited above address matters that would have been of interest to Christians as well as Jews. The only exception is the mixing of kinds (but see below). Surprisingly few of the ritual precepts of Leviticus are mentioned explicitly. The most striking case is the affirmation of the food laws in lines 28-31, although, as mentioned above, only the laws pertaining to birds are grudgingly listed. Animal sacrifices are briefly considered in a general way in lines 4-9. The laws on postpartum female impurity and the circumcision of male infants are summarized in lines 37-50, as are the offerings for purification from skin afflictions in lines 61-68. The rules for fluxes, defilement of objects by those with a flux, and offerings to purify those who have had a flux are summarized in lines 69-89. The scapegoat ritual is covered in lines 99-107. Some rules pertaining to the high priest are discussed in lines 203-215; as are rules about when a priest's daughter is permitted to consume the sacred food (216-20); inadvertent eating of the sacred food by anyone (lines 221-22); the lighting of sanctuary (223-26); and valuation of vows (298-309). A few other cases are considered below. Some of this material may have been merely of antiquarian interest, but some would have interested Christians for other reasons. Biblical precepts on skin diseases and fluxes might have been viewed as medically significant in a world where they were endemic, and the scapegoat ritual was used frequently in Christian typology.

It is even more instructive, in contrast, to catalogue the portions of Leviticus which were omitted in the *Heptateuchos*. It ignores almost the entirety of Chapters 1-9, which deal with the minutiae of various sacrifices and also with the ordination of the Aaronids as priests; most of the food laws in Chapter 11; the rules for sacrificing animals meant for food at the sanctuary in Chapter 17; the rules for peace offerings in

19:1-8 and the reference to sabbaths and the sanctuary in 19:30; the command to stone anyone who offers a child as a human sacrifice, and rules on adultery, incest, bestiality, menstrual defilement, cleanness, uncleanness, and holiness in Chapter 20 (some of which were already covered in the paraphrase of Chapter 18); most of the priestly and sacrificial laws in Chapter 22; all references to the Jewish festivals in Chapter 23; rules for making the bread of the Presence and rules for execution and implementation of the *lex talionis* in Chapter 24; the rules for the festivals and the sabbatical year in 25:1-24; and the reference to the sabbaths of the land in 26:34-35. And, more generally, none of the frequent references to the laws of Leviticus being 'eternal statutes' (e.g., Lev 3:17; 7:34, 36; 10:9, 15; 16:31; 23:14; 24:3) is reproduced in the poem.

Moreover, a Christian agenda is implied by some of the material chosen for mention and, especially, by some of the misreadings and reinterpretation of passages in Leviticus. The contents of Leviticus 17 are ignored except for vv. 13-14, the precept against eating blood (lines 108-13).[74] It may not be a coincidence that this is one of the very few ceremonial rules from the Old Testament which is ratified in a New Testament document (Acts 15:29). The rules against mixed kinds in Lev 19:19 prohibit the interbreeding of cattle, but in lines 166-67 this precept is replaced with the rule against yoking an ox and an ass together, which is found in Deut 22:10. It may also not be a coincidence that the latter passage, rather than the former, is alluded to metaphorically in the New Testament in 2 Cor 6:14. The limitations on using the fruit of newly planted trees in Lev 19:23-25 are reinterpreted in lines 178-81, which read, 'As often as sprouts are grafted into a woody trunk, do not by any means pick the fruit after three full years, but consecrate it to God Most High, because the fifth year shall give it to you by law for eating with permitted foods.'[75] The issue is now the eating of the fruit of shoots grafted onto another tree. It may be that this change was introduced to make the passage more relevant as background to Paul's metaphorical use of grafted shoots in Romans 11. It has already been noted above that the rules in Lev 21:5-

---

[74] Josephus ignores 17:1-9, whose rules presumably were not followed in his day, but he does include the material on animals who die naturally in vv. 15-16. [75] *Insita siluestri quotiens sunt germina trunco,/carpite post ternos nequequam poma decembres,/sed summo sacrate deo; quia quintus edendi/iura dabit uobis licitis cum uictibus annus.* [76] Josephus also democratizes the rule about not marrying a prostitute, so perhaps not too much should be made of this point.

9 against a priest shaving his head or beard or cutting himself in mourning for the dead and against his marrying a prostitute or an adulteress are democratized in lines 197-203 to apply to everyone.[76] It is perhaps also worth noting that the blaspheming half-breed Israelite of Leviticus 24 is made a full-blooded Hebrew and is called a 'senseless Jew' (*Iudaeus iners*) in line 231 (the only place in the poem to use the word Jew), a change and an epithet easier to imagine emanating from a Christian than a Jew.

In sum, the internal evidence of the *Leviticus* portion of the *Heptateuchos* confirms the external evidence and leaves little doubt that it is a Christian work. It is a careful summary of the contents of Leviticus, written with an astonishing sympathy for the material from a Christian author, but it ignores all references to sacrifice, sabbath, festivals, and the eternal nature of the Levitical laws. A Jew might pass over some of these things, but it is hard to imagine one ignoring all of them. Much of what is covered is of potential interest to Christians, a few passages may be doctored to make them more relevant to Christians, and the single use of the word 'Jew' is quite uncomplimentary.

All this granted, the *Leviticus* poem is an extraordinary and in some ways disquieting example of a Christian composition with an Old Testament theme. It seems to include no (or almost no) Christian signature features; it presents Jewish law and ritual in a very sympathetic light and offers criticism of them only obliquely, by omission or minor modification. If it had been removed from its context and transmitted independently, one could envisage it being misread as a Jewish pseudepigraphon. Indeed, as noted above, Fontaine was tempted to read the *Heptateuchos* as a Jewish work. Only a close and subtle reading of the *Leviticus* poem, combined with other information such as the Christian references elsewhere in the *Heptateuchos* and close readings of other parts of the whole poem, demonstrates its Christian origin and agenda. It is thus a useful worst-case scenario: an extended portion of a Christian work on the Old Testament which does not betray its Christian origin by obvious Christian signature features. Any Old Testament apocryphon or pseudepigraphon that we suspect to be of Jewish origin should have its evidence measured against it.

REFLECTIONS ┄┄ ┄┄ In this section of the Chapter One I have demonstrated that, within larger works, Christians could and did write extended passages covering whole episodes from the Old Testament in which they inserted no Christian signature features whatever. Moreover, some of these texts drew on rabbinic and other Jewish traditions, and all of them dealt sympathetically with themes normally thought of as 'Jewish,' including circumcision, the holy seed of the chosen people, and even the book of Leviticus. They did so because, in the scheme of things as they saw it, the Old Testament had its place in the history of salvation and, when they chose to write on Old Testament matters, they wrote with respect for the integrity of a dispensation they now regarded as past and finished.

This attitude, of course, was the exception, and the vast majority of Christian works on the Old Testament introduced Christian signature features through allegory, hermeneutical reflections, apologetic reworking, or other means. But the exception is important: the texts collected here isolate a strain of Christian thought that supports the thesis that Christians could have written Old Testament pseudepigrapha without introducing any Christian signature features therein.

One could reasonably object that these texts do not *prove* that Christians wrote whole works on the Old Testament without any allusions to Christianity: in all three cases the whole work does include Christian signature features, and one could take the position that the works were meant to be read as a whole and that the writers need not have introduced explicitly Christian elements into each episode as long as they established their Christian credentials somewhere in the work. I grant the force of this argument, but I would raise the following points in return. First, the fact remains that these passages show that Christians sometimes drew on Jewish traditions about the Old Testament and sometimes treated Jewish matters with sympathy from within the narrative world of the Old Testament. Therefore, arguments for the Jewish origins of a document on the basis of these features must be advanced with considerable caution. Second, in the nature of things one can always

---

[77] One Syriac manuscript of the sixth or seventh century contains translations of the Hebrew Bible and related works, including a Syriac version of Book 6 of the *Jewish War*. The text is attributed to Josephus but also referred to as the fifth book of the Maccabees. The Syriac text is available in Antonio Maria Ceriani, *Translatio syra pescitto Veteris Testamenti: ex codice Ambrosiano sec. fere VI, photolithographice edita, curante et adnotante* (Milan: Pogliani, 1876-83), f. 320v-330r, and was published with an introduction and German translation by Heimann Kottek in *Das sechste Buch Bellum Judaicum* (Berlin, 1886). A better transcription by Paul Bedjan is found in an appendix in *Homiliae Selectae Mar-Jacobi Sarugensis* (5 vols.; Paris: Harrassowitz, 1905), 1:770-837. See Heinz Schreckenberg, *Die Flavius-Josephus-Tradition in Antike und Mitteralter* (ALGHJ 5; Leiden: Brill, 1972), 61-62. [78] Peiper, CSEL 23, 'Hilarii,' 240-54; 'Marii Victorini Afri,' 255-69. For the

argue that Christians *must* have included Christian signature features somewhere in anything that they wrote, and any work lacking them must be Jewish. But this seems to me to be an extreme position to take, and the evidence of this section weakens its persuasiveness. Third, it is worth noting that we have positive evidence for an Old Testament pseudepigraphon being created by extracting a section of a larger work and treating it as a work on its own, inasmuch as Book 6 of Josephus' *Jewish War* was circulated in Syriac as the fifth book of the Maccabees.[77] It is possible that other works in our corpus of Old Testament pseudepigrapha either extracted and incorporated parts of earlier works or else were extracted from larger works and then were treated as an independent unit. The *History of the Rechabites* within the *Story of Zosimus* seems to be an example of the former, while the *Biblical Antiquities* of Pseudo-Philo, which ends at an odd point and contains no narrative conclusion, could conceivably be an example of the latter. In addition, some works, such as the *Testament of Moses*, have come down to us in obviously damaged and incomplete form. In all three contingencies we cannot rule out the possibility that the complete work from which the surviving text was extracted was explicitly Christian. Such cases would be a nearly exact analogy to the process to which I have subjected Ephrem's commentaries and the *Heptateuchos* here.

5

A PROBABLE CHRISTIAN WORK THAT LACKS ANY CHRISTIAN SIGNATURE FEATURES

The last document to be considered in this chapter is another Latin epic poem, *De Martyrio Maccabaeorum*, a work of 389-394 lines (about twenty-eight hundred Latin words). In the earliest surviving manuscript, a sixth-century palimpsest in Italian, perhaps northern Italian, script, it is anonymous. An eighth-century manuscript is also anonymous, but the manuscripts of the tenth and eleventh century attribute it to Hilarius, and later tradition also ascribed it to Marius Victorinus Afrus. It seems reasonable to assume with Herzog that it circulated anonymously until it was attributed pseudepigraphically to a known author by Carolingian editors. The date of composition is not certain but is probably roughly the same as the other Latin biblical epic pseudepigrapha, that is, sometime in the fourth to sixth centuries. Peiper published two versions with minor variations and of slightly different length.[78] My comments below focus on the first, the longer of the two, although taking into account relevant textual variants from the second.

The poem is based on the story of the seven martyrs and their mother (2 Maccabees 6-7), but reworks it freely. Although the surviving manuscripts associate the poem with the Christian feast day of the Maccabees (1 August),[79] the work itself has no Christian signature features at all. All other Latin biblical epics of this period contain such features, although sometimes very few of them, and can safely be accepted as Christian compositions. Kartschoke argues that it is a Christian work, although he notes that Ebert seemed to have reservations about whether this was so.[80] I shall explain below why I believe the contents of the story are consistent with Christian authorship and are better explained as such.

At the opening of the poem we are told that the very wealthy king Antiochus of Syria wished to change the faith of the just so as to mix them with a hostile people and that in his kingdom were a mother and her seven children who were born of the holy people. Antiochus first offered the mother vast rewards if she and her family would abandon their former customs and adopt new ones, but she refused. He then threatened her with the torture of her children but she did not fear the king and disdained his threats. Antiochus was enraged and commanded that her seven children be burned alive in order of age, from oldest to youngest. She exhorted the first to be strong and to conquer the king with silence, and he died in the fire. She remained anxious for her other children. Antiochus ordered the executions to continue and, after the mother exhorted him to bear the brief pains of the fire in the knowledge that Antiochus would have to feel eternal fires, the second son died laughing in the flames. The mother promised Antiochus that greater punishments would come to him soon, then the third son came forward

manuscripts, see ibid., xx-xxii. See also Mag. Clemens Weidmann, 'Das Carmen de Martyrio Maccabaeorum' (Ph.D. diss., University of Vienna, 1995). This unpublished dissertation, which contains an introduction to De Martyrio Maccabaeorum, a critical text, a German translation, and a commentary, came to my attention too late to be taken fully into account here. The sixth-century manuscript was not available to Peiper (Weidmann, 'Das Carmen,' 100-105). ⸻ [79] ⸻ '. . . versus in natali (natalem) Machabaeorum' (Peiper, CSEL 23, 240 and 254; Weidmann, 'Das Carmen,' 106). Cf. Kartschoke, Bibeldichtung, 108, and Weidmann, 'Das Carmen,' 45. ⸻ ⸻ [80] ⸻ Kartschoke, Bibeldichtung, 38-39, 105-11, esp. 105. ⸻ ⸻ [81] ⸻ . . . meminisse dei legemque tenere, / non a rege datam, sed quam deus arbiter orbis / tradidit et mundi rector, Mosesque petitam / accepit populoque dedit. ⸻ ⸻ [82] ⸻ Virtute id cum lege data mihi uincere certum est.

and she encouraged him too, after which he died without the flames harming his body. The mother told Antiochus that neither she nor her children would be cowed by his punishments, and he commanded that the fourth son be executed. After his mother addressed him, telling him to be strong and to remember the patriarchs and his race that would endure, he too died without the fire burning him. At this point the ministers of the king were horrified by his cruel actions and cursed him in their own minds. Antiochus taunted the mother to enjoy the funeral rites of her children and then commanded the execution of the fifth son. She told the boy to be strong and promised him the victory, then he too rushed into the flames, dying as his body extinguished them. The mother held back her distress and made herself be joyful, but at the same time she fretted over her two youngest sons and whether they too would have the strength to persevere. She exhorted the sixth to be strong beyond his years and to be a model to future generations, and he too died, extinguishing the flames. Despite her exhaustion, the mother prayed at length over her last and youngest son, summarizing the stories of creation, the Exodus, and the wandering in the wilderness and asking God to strengthen him lest the baby of the family be missing among his brothers. Then she addressed the boy, promising him that if he would persevere he would be safe among his brothers and warning him that, if not, there would be no one left to care for him anyhow. The boy prayed to God that he might conquer the king and then leaped into the flames and died. The mother, having seen all of her sons conquer, collapsed and died, and she and her children were received among the saints.

On the one hand, as I have already noted, this document contains no Christian signature features. The closest one might come to finding one is the repeated mention of 'saints' (*sancti*) throughout (lines 25, 62, 318, 358, and 394), but as I have shown above in discussing Augustine's sermon, this usage is also found in ancient Judaism. On the other hand, there are a number of elements that might be taken at first glance to be Jewish signature features, most of them in the speeches of the mother. She exhorts her sons to be mindful of their race, Israel (lines 92, 168, 286-88, 368, 375), and the holy seed of Abraham (lines 167-68); the people to which they were born (line 341); and their native land (line 375). She also tells one son 'to remember God and to hold on to the Law, not given by the king, but which God, the Judge of the globe and the Master of the world transmitted and accepted the prayers of Moses and gave it to the people'[81] (lines 247b-50a). In line 32 she also says, 'It is certain that by virtue with the Law it is given to me to conquer.'[82]

Nevertheless, a careful application of the criteria set out in Chapter One greatly weakens the case for taking these features as indications of a Jewish origin. First, as I mentioned, most are put in the mouth of the mother and are the sort of things an ancient Christian author would have expected her to say; such an author would regard them to have been valid in the mother's time, before the coming of Christ, but not in the author's own time. The narrator also refers to her people as 'the holy people' (line 3) and 'the people of God,' but according to Christian theology the Jewish people were both during the Old Testament period. Second, the treatment of the Law is very generic and, indeed, superficial. A Christian author would agree that the Law was revealed to Moses and was valid at that time, although it was superseded by Christ. Naturally, the last point would not be put in the mouth of the mother, and the author evidently sees no need to make it either. More tellingly, unlike either 2 Maccabees (6:18, 21, etc.) or 4 *Maccabees* (5:2 etc.), this version of the story never makes clear that the sin the martyrs resisted and died rather than commit was to eat pork that had been used in an idolatrous sacrifice. Rather, we are told merely that the king required the mother to change her customs and adopt other ones (lines 11-12) and she urges her children to keep her customs (60) and precepts (85) and to hold on to the Law (247). The characters and the narrator show a curious lack of interest in the specifics of the situation. None of them ever makes clear exactly what the king is demanding that the children do or the mother is urging them not to do. This omission would be very strange in a Jewish work, but it makes perfect sense in a Christian one. The author wanted to encourage the audience to value martyrdom but did not wish to distract them with the fact that these martyrs died for a Jewish food law no longer required of Christians and in fact looked down on by them.[83]

[83] The author might have made an issue of the fact that the food was sacrificed to idols (cf. Rev 2:14, 20), but the New Testament attitude to this practice is equivocal (cf. 1 Corinthians 8) and thus food sacrificed to idols may not have seemed a good rallying point in support of martyrdom. [84] Kartschoke, *Bibeldichtung*, 106-111. [85] Cf. the comments of Weidmann, 'Das Carmen,' 41-45, who also regards it as a Christian composition. [86] Another potential example is 'A Syriac Verse Homily on Elijah and the Widow of Sarepta' published by S. P. Brock in *Mus* 102 (1989): 93-103. This poem of 158 lines retells the story of Elijah and the widow without including any Christian signature features. The editor views the manuscript's attribution of the work to Ephrem with skepticism, although he thinks it may have been composed in the fifth century CE. One could in theory insist that it might be a Jewish composition, although this does not seem very likely and certainly was not suggested by the editor.

In addition, Kartschoke argues for direct dependence of *De Martyrio Maccabaeorum* not only on *4 Maccabees*, which would not affect my case one way or the other, but also on a sermon by Gregory of Nazianzus, whose presentation of the mother's exhortations to the sons is strikingly similar to lines 52-56 and 370 of the poem. Kartschoke also argues that the 'Freude in Leiden' theme of the poem is both decisively Christian and also characteristic of Gregory's treatment of the story.[84]

In sum, the content of *De Martyrio Maccabaeorum* makes best sense if it is interpreted as a Christian composition.[85] In addition, it was transmitted as part of a corpus of epic texts by or attributed to Christian authors and was taken, at least by the Carolingian editors, to be itself a Christian composition, a kind of metrical commentary on a scriptural story. If this is correct, the work is a remarkable example of a Christian writing that retells an Old Testament story without including any Christian signature features.[86]

6

CONCLUSIONS

This chapter has adopted an empirical approach to the problem of whether Christians wrote Old Testament pseudepigrapha and whether such works written by them must always have contained Christian signature features. It has asked not what Christians might have written or what they were capable in theory of writing, but what we can learn from some literary works actually written by them which retold Old Testament narratives or otherwise made use of Old Testament traditions. My interest has not been to limit the range of possibilities but to establish that certain scenarios were possible by showing that models for them really exist in surviving ancient Christian literature. The examples presented here have been selected as the most interesting out of those I have examined. Most of the works I looked at were available in modern editions and translations into modern languages, and there remains much material that I have not considered. A specialist in patristics or other branches of late antique Christian literature might well find more and better examples.

Nevertheless, the case studies presented here give us a great deal of useful information. I have shown that Christians wrote Old Testament pseudepigrapha in various genres; that the fourth-century church historian Eusebius of Caesarea seems to have found nothing objectionable to attributing a work with no Christian signature features (*De Monarchia*) to a Christian author; and that a Syriac Christian translator updated

Basil's Greek *Hexaemeron* to make it look both more Christian and more doctrinally congenial.

Christians sometimes told Old Testament stories for the sake of the story, including Christian signature features only incidentally in such a way that one could be tempted to remove them by redaction criticism. This is not to deny that redaction criticism is a useful tool when applied with proper methodological controls (as Tigay and other authors in *Empirical Models for Biblical Criticism* have ably demonstrated), but rather it shows that the presence of easily detachable Christian elements in a work on the Old Testament is not *in itself* a sufficient reason to treat them as secondary. In larger works, Christians also sometimes embedded retellings of whole episodes from the Old Testament, including Noah's Flood, the Joseph story, the early life of Moses, and even the book of Leviticus, without using Christian signature features in the episodes, although the larger works as a whole did include at least a few such features.

Christian retellings of Old Testament stories sometimes sound, as least superficially, as though they could be Jewish. There are a number of reasons for their giving this impression. Ephrem drew extensively on rabbinic and other Jewish traditions about the Bible. Christian authors strove, at least sometimes, to maintain the narrative integrity of the stories they retold, making the Old Testament characters speak as the author thought they really would have spoken, or presenting elements of the old dispensation sympathetically because these elements were theologically valid in Old Testament times. So a writer like Ephrem could condemn Moses' wife for not circumcising her son even though he would have been hostile to Christian Judaizers of his own time who required the circumcision of gentile Christians. It is, therefore, very important for us, when we read Old Testament pseudepigrapha, to pay close attention to what the characters of the story say, versus what the narrator says, versus what appears to be the perspective of the actual author. The three need not hold the same views, and a close and sensitive reading is sometimes necessary to tell the views apart. In addition, ideas that sound explicitly Christian on the surface often turn out to have close parallels in ancient Jewish literature. Such features include human 'saints,' the appeal to faith as a chief virtue, and angels as ministering spirits.

It is worthwhile to ask how the methodological principles for isolating boundary-maintaining Jewish works outlined in Chapter One measure up when applied to the Christian texts singled out in this chapter. I think it is fair to say that if these principles are applied with care, they come out well. Augustine's sermon on Micah 7 and Psalm 72 lacks anything that could be considered a Jewish signature feature and contains one Christian signature feature that one might be able to challenge if so inclined. Chrysostom's sermon on Joseph contains no Jewish signature features and a couple of Christian ones. The retelling of the story of Noah in Ephrem's Commentary on Genesis contains neither Jewish nor Christian signature features. Both the sermons and the excerpt from the commentary are parts of corpora whose named authors are universally accepted, so their Christian origin is secure. But if they or Old Testament pseudepigrapha with comparable profiles of signature features had been transmitted independently in Christian manuscripts with no authorial attribution, we still would have no reason to take them as Jewish works if we applied my methodology to them.

Chrysostom's sermon on Abraham accepts that the patriarch should have a multitude of descendants who are to possess the land, and that God ordained the Levitical priesthood. Ephrem makes positive statements about circumcision in both the Joseph story and his retelling of the early life of Moses. In both works these statements could be argued to be Jewish signature features. Chrysostom's sermon also includes two Christian signature features, while the three extended excerpts from Ephrem's commentaries contain none. In both cases, the author is known beyond dispute. The apparent Jewish signature features are matters that Christians, even those as hostile to Judaism as Chrysostom and Ephrem, accepted as legitimate matters during the time of the Old Testament. There is nothing that indicates that the authors approve of them in their present as political statements or as rituals to be practiced. There is no pattern of extensive or pervasive Jewish signature features of more than one type in either. If they or pseudepigrapha with a like profile of signature features had been transmitted anonymously, application of my methodology would lead us to conclude that there was no good reason to posit a Jewish origin for any of them.

The Latin biblical epics present considerably greater difficulties. Were the *Leviticus* portion of the *Heptateuchos* transmitted as a separate work, we would have a poem that covered an Old Testament book that is entirely devoted to Jewish laws and rituals, some of which are presented with apparent approval, and this poem arguably contains no Christian signature features at all. Indeed, if we consider the *Heptateuchos* as a whole, we see that it paraphrases a large part of the Old Testament and exhibits only very few Christian signature features. Mainly for this reason, Fontaine has raised the possibility that it is the product of a Western Jew or a Judaizing Christian. I have argued that careful exegesis of the *Leviticus* section shows that it was written by a Christian who maintained the viewpoint of the narrator of Leviticus but who revealed his or her own agenda and interests by what in Leviticus was emphasized, what was altered, and what was omitted. Of the texts considered in this chapter, the *Leviticus* poem would present the greatest challenge to my methodology and the greatest danger of its generating a false positive. The extended and sympathetic treatment of Jewish ritual would argue in favor of its being a Jewish work, but I believe careful attention to how the ritual is treated and to other factors, such as the hint of suppressed hostility toward Jews in the story of the blaspheming Hebrew, would prevent us from mistaking *Leviticus* for a Jewish work.

Although no one seems ever to have argued that *De Martyrio Maccabaeorum* is of Jewish origin, this may only be because it has not until now come to the attention of collectors of Old Testament pseudepigrapha. But although this text lacks any Christian signature features and the mother of the seven martyrs does express nationalist concerns and order her children to obey the law, the author might be expected to put such words in the mother's mouth, and indeed to refer to the Jewish people as God's holy people *in her time*, and the work never makes explicit what transgression the king expects the martyrs to commit. All in all, my methodology finds no good evidence that this work is anything but a Christian composition.

One could with internal consistency insist that the *Heptateuchos* and *De Martyrio Maccabaeorum* are Jewish compositions on the grounds that the first contains either few and redactionally secondary Christian signature features and the second has no such features at all, and that they both show some sympathy toward Judaism. This has actually been suggested for the *Heptateuchos*. As I have explained, I believe to assert this for either would be incorrect and, indeed, wrong-headed. If I am right, two important points need to be emphasized. First, the *Leviticus* portion of the *Heptateuchos* provides us with a Christian retelling of a biblical book that contains a very high density of explicitly Jewish concerns, perhaps the highest in the Bible. Nevertheless, even setting aside the context of *Leviticus* in the *Heptateuchos*, careful exegesis lays bare its Christian origin. As we evaluate the surviving Old Testament pseudepigrapha in the next two chapters to decide which are Jewish works, we will do well to keep in mind *Leviticus* as the superficially most Jewish-sounding Christian work we have been able to identify and to test other works against it. Second, *De Martyrio Maccabaeorum* is an example of a complete ancient Christian work on an Old Testament subject which is entirely devoid of Christian signature features. If there is one case, there may well be others.

I recognize that some may dispute my understanding of both Latin epics, although I do not think a very persuasive case can be mounted against it. But the sermon by Augustine provides us with evidence that is nearly as interesting. Even though it is a publicly preached sermon by a famous Christian author, it is based entirely on straightforward, if philosophically inclined, exegesis of two Old Testament passages; it makes no reference to any explicitly Christian doctrine; it does not quote the New Testament or any other Christian work; and the single allusion to a New Testament passage is so attenuated that we could plausibly dismiss it as coincidental.

In sum, this chapter has given us a considerably more sophisticated and empirically based understanding of how ancient Christians used the Old Testament when they wrote about it. It gives us good reason to believe that they may have written books about the Old Testament without alluding explicitly to Christianity and has also suggested some strategies for identifying such books as Christian nonetheless. It has eliminated some of the traditional criteria for establishing Jewish authorship – such as extensive use of Jewish exegesis and rare, peripheral mention of Christian matters – by pointing to these features in indubitably Christian texts. Much of the evidence has force not just in itself, but also *a minori ad maius*: if we find Christian sermons and commentaries whose explicit purpose was to edify a Christian congregation or readership, but which nearly entirely ignore explicitly Christian matters when dealing with the Old Testament, how much more might we expect anonymous authors of parabiblical Old Testament narratives and revelations to ignore such matters when they hoped to persuade their audience of the genuineness of the story or the revelation?

This chapter concludes the theoretical portion of this book. The next two chapters will apply what we have learned thus far to the surviving corpus of Old Testament pseudepigrapha. Chapter Three will comment individually on all such works that I regard to be of boundary-maintaining Jewish origin. Chapter Four will comment on some texts whose origin is debatable.

CHAPTER THREE

I

INTRODUCTION

Up to this point, the discussion in this book has been mostly theoretical. I have looked at the problem of the Christian transmission of Jewish pseudepigrapha from the perspective of standard historical criticism (Chapter One) and in light of empirical models (Chapter Two). This chapter and the next will take the knowledge gained from these theoretical approaches and apply it to specific texts. The objective of this chapter is to establish a corpus of pseudepigrapha that can be assigned Jewish authorship[1] beyond reasonable doubt. I will pay some attention to the manuscript context and possible reasons for Christian transmission, both vast subjects for each work which can only be touched upon, but I will focus mainly on elements within the texts that are dissonant with a Christian origin and point toward authorship by ethnic Jews. Chapter Four looks at a number of Old Testament pseudepigrapha that have

---

[1] For my purposes here I include proselytes (i.e., gentiles fully assimilated into the Jewish community) in the category of ethnic Jews. See Chapter One for discussion of the problem.

[2] Gabriele Boccaccini has argued that the Epistle of Enoch actually was produced in two editions. The 'proto-Epistle,' which included the Apocalypse of Weeks, was a pre-sectarian work written in the mid-second century and consisted of 91:1-94:5 and 104:7-105:2. Somewhat later, the mainstream Essene movement added 94:6-104:6 to produce the Epistle of Enoch as known from our Ethiopic and Greek sources. Boccaccini notes that the Aramaic Qumran fragments give evidence only for the first edition, the Proto-Epistle of Enoch. See his *Beyond the Essene Hypothesis: The Parting of the Ways Between Qumran and Enochic Judaism* (Grand Rapids, Mich.: Eerdmans, 1998), 104-13, 131-38. It should be noted, however, that if the reconstructions of the Greek fragments of the Epistle from Qumran Cave 7 are correct, this cave included a Greek text of the final version of the Epistle of Enoch. See G.W. Nebe '7Q4 — Möglichkeit und Grenze einer Identifikation,' *RevQ* 13/49-52 (1988): 629-633; Ernest A. Munro, Jr., 'The Greek Fragments of Enoch from Qumran Cave 7 (7Q4, 7Q8, & 7Q12 = 7QEn gr = Enoch 103:3-4, 7-8),' *RevQ* 18/70 (1998): 307-12; Émile Puech, 'Notes sur les fragments grecs du manuscrit 7Q4 = 1 Hénoch 103 et 105,' *RB* 103 (1996): 592-600; James R. Davila, 'Enochians, Essenes, and Qumran Essenes,' in *Enoch and Qumran Origins: New Light on a Forgotten Connection* (ed. Gabriele Boccaccini; Grand Rapids, Mich.: Eerdmans, forthcoming).

Jewish Pseudepigrapha

been argued to be of Jewish origin, but cannot, in my view, be proved to be such, and explores the reasons for uncertainty about their origins.

In Chapter One, I established a group of Old Testament Apocrypha and pseudepigrapha transmitted by Christians which can also be shown to be Jewish on the basis of external criteria. These survive in complete form only in translations extant in Christian manuscripts. But fragments of the original Aramaic of the Book of the Watchers, the Astronomical Book, the Book of Dreams, the Epistle of Enoch (the last perhaps also in Greek),[2] have been recovered from the Jewish context of the Qumran Library, as have fragments of the original Hebrew of *Jubilees*, the Greek of the Epistle of Jeremiah, and Aramaic and Hebrew fragments of Tobit. Likewise, fragments of the original Hebrew of Ben Sira have been recovered from Qumran, Masada, and the Cairo Geniza. I take the Jewish origin of these works for granted here and will not discuss them further.

It is instructive and not a little disquieting to note that of these certainly Jewish works the Book of the Watchers and the Epistle of Enoch display no Jewish signature features and one could debate whether the Book of Dreams contains any. In addition, the Epistle of Jeremiah is a very short work and, although it does refer to female purity issues regarding menstruation and childbirth in v. 29, it is not long enough to display a consistent pattern of Jewish signature features. Were we lacking the external evidence, we would suspect that the Epistle of Jeremiah was Jewish, but we could be much less certain about the other three. That being the case, I should underline that the results of this chapter are meant to be positive: it surveys the pseudepigrapha that I believe can be shown on internal grounds to be of Jewish origin. If a pseudepigraphon is not covered in this chapter, it does not mean that it is not Jewish, only that I cannot with currently available evidence *show* with confidence that it is Jewish. Again, some pseudepigrapha whose origin is debatable will be discussed in Chapter Four. But the importance of the positive results must be underlined as well: in the first two chapters I laid out a series of methodological principles that started from the premise that it was more important to eliminate false positives (assigning a Jewish origin to non-Jewish works) than false negatives (failing to assign a Jewish origin to a Jewish work if our evidence is inconclusive). This chapter demonstrates that even after the application of these principles to the Old Testament pseudepigrapha that have been transmitted only by Christians, we are left with a substantial corpus of pseudepigrapha that are very likely to be Jewish. These include the *Letter of Aristeas*, *2 Baruch*, the Similitudes of Enoch, *4 Ezra*, *3-4 Maccabees*, the *Testament* or *Assumption of Moses*, Pseudo-Philo's *Biblical Antiquities*, and the *Psalms of Solomon*. I make no claim that this list is complete. Old Testament pseudepigrapha continue to be recovered and studied and it may be that more verifiably Jewish works transmitted only by Christians will be isolated with further research.

---

2   *ARISTEAS TO PHILOCRATES*

The *Letter of Aristeas* or, if we prefer the title of the manuscripts, *Aristeas to Philocrates*,[3] is a Greek treatise set in the reign of Ptolemy II Philadelphus (285-247 BCE) which claims to relate the story of the translation of the Pentateuch into Greek for the Library of Alexandria. It consists

---

[3] The word 'letter' in the title is also inappropriate because *Aristeas* doesn't fit the format of ancient letters. Moses Hadas notes that the author calls the work a διήγησις in line 1, a type of narrative known from classical rhetoric and defined by Theon and Cicero as a narration setting forth things that happened, or things as they might have happened, i.e., presenting idealized history with a moral to it. See *Aristeas to Philocrates (Letter of Aristeas)* (New York: Harper, 1951), 56-58, 92. [4] H. St. J. Thackeray produced a critical Greek text in 'Appendix: The Letter of Aristeas,' in Henry Barclay Swete and Richard Rusden Ottley, *An Introduction to the Old Testament in Greek* (Cambridge: Cambridge University Press, 1914), 531-606. Hadas reproduces Thackeray's Greek text with his own translation in *Aristeas to Philocrates*. André Pelletier recollated most of the manuscripts and consulted additional material in the critical text he compiled for *Lettre d'Aristée à Philocrate* (SC 89; Paris: Cerf, 1962). For a discussion of the editorial history of Aristeas and its importance for the history of the LXX translation, see Sidney Jellicoe, *The Septuagint and Modern Study* (Ann Arbor, Mich.: Eisenbrauns, 1978 [rpt. of 1968 edition]), 29-58. There are other English translations by Herbert T. Andrews in *APOT*, 2:83-122; and by R. J. H. Shutt in *OTP*, 2:7-34. [5] See also Eusebius' use of *Aristeas* in *Praep. ev.* 8-9 and *Hist ecc.* 5.8 (in the latter quoting Irenaeus); the comments of Epiphanius in *On Weights and Measures* 3-11; and those of Augustine in *Civ.* 18.42-43. [6] Hadas, *Aristeas to Philocrates*, 18-21. [7] Josephus abbreviates the text of *Aristeas*, but there is little indication of deliberate distortion in his treatment. He reads the name Aristeas for Aristeas; his numbers frequently vary from our manuscripts (but with no clear *tendenz*); the details of the king's dedicatory offerings (*Ant.* 12.57-84)

of about 13,400 words. The narrator and implied author is Aristeas, who seems to be a gentile member of the Egyptian royal court and who writes to the narratee, Philocrates his brother, claiming to have been directly involved in the events he reports.[4] It is universally agreed on the grounds of implausibilities and historical errors in the narrative that the work is pseudepigraphic and of a later date, although exactly how much later is not entirely certain.

André Pelletier has divided the surviving manuscripts of *Aristeas to Philocrates* manuscripts into three groups whose archetype would perhaps take us back into the Byzantine period. Josephus paraphrased the work in *Ant.* 12.1-118, reproducing about a third of it, calling it 'the Book of Aristaeus' (evidently working from a manuscript with a variant version of the name), and Eusebius extracted about a quarter of it in *Praeparatio Evangelica* 8.2-5, 9; 9.38, giving it the title 'On the Translation of the Law of the Jews.'

Josephus is thus our earliest source for *Aristeas*. He puts no more emphasis on the translation than did the work itself; the real interest of the story for Josephus seems to be the good relations it shows between Jews and the Egyptian king as well as the king's deep respect for Jewish tradition. These elements were important for the case Josephus was making in Rome that Jews were an ancient nation respected by other ancient Near Eastern traditions and that they were able to get along with neighboring nations, despite the debacle of the revolt against Roman rule in 68-70 C E. Other writers, however seemed most interested in the translation, and it is this aspect of *Aristeas* to which we probably owe its survival. Aristobulus (*apud.* Eusebius, *Praep. ev.* 13.12.2), Philo (*Moses* 2:25-44), Justin Martyr (1 *Apol.* 31), and Irenaeus (*Haer.* 3.21.2) knew the story of the translation, although it is not clear that any of them had read the account in *Aristeas*. Christian writers seemed particularly interested in information on the origin and authority of the Greek scriptures for the obvious reason that they were their scriptures and it was in their interest to promote the Greek version and undermine the authority of the original Hebrew and Aramaic texts.[5]

The content and shape of the original edition of *Aristeas* is a complicated problem, as Hadas has shown.[6] Of 322 total verses, Josephus uses or alludes to vv. 9-81, 172-305 (with 187-292 summarized very briefly in *Ant.* 12.100-102), and 308-21. Perhaps it is not surprising that he would leave out the introduction and conclusion, but it is more problematical to say he deliberately omitted the other material. Given that he showed reasonable care in handling the details of the document,[7] it is at least possible that the journey to Jerusalem and Eleazar's comments (vv. 83-171) were not in the manuscript he had. This may also be true of the defense of ritual hand washing in vv. 306-7.

Even without the external evidence of Josephus, the internal evidence of *Aristeas*, including both editions of the work if there were two, is decisive for establishing that the writer was Torah-observant and extremely interested in the fate of the Jewish people. In vv. 12-27 we are told of the release by Ptolemy Philadelphus of the Jewish slaves who had been deported to Egypt in the time of his father. The release is presented as instigated by Aristeas out of humanitarian concern. Whatever the historical basis for this episode, the account in Aristeas shows concern for Jews.[8] The Jewish Law is the object of the translation and is mentioned repeatedly. Aristeas and his colleagues affirm to the king that the laws were established for all the Jews (v. 15) and the high priest Eleazer affirms that the good life consists of observing the laws (v. 127). There is much interest in the details of the temple cult and its furnishings (vv. 40, 42, 45, 51-82) and its priesthood (vv. 83-99). The land of Judea is described in somewhat exaggeratedly laudatory terms (vv. 100-20).[9] Eleazer gives an apology for the dietary laws in which he says that they were given to prevent the Jewish people from mixing with other peoples and being exposed to bad influences (vv. 128-42); he gives symbolic moralizing interpretations of these laws and the purity regulations (vv. 144-70); and he refers to mezzuzot and phylacteries as special markers to remind 'us' (the Jewish people) of God (vv. 158-59). The text assumes that all these laws and customs are to be observed by Jews. Kosher food is provided for the translators (vv. 181-82). Aristeas also mentions two

---

are sometimes different, but this whole passage is very difficult and Josephus may not have understood it much better than we do; he gives the name of the high priest as Elisha (Elissaios) not Eleazar (*Ant.* 12.97). All these could be variants in the *Aristeas* manuscript Josephus had before him rather than deliberate changes by Josephus. Otherwise, he makes a small alteration of the sense of v. 18 in *Ant.* 12.23; he adds a little of own material from another source in *Ant.* 12.43-44; he adds an interpretive comment in *Ant.* 12.91; he waters down the curse on anyone who alters the translation in *Ant.* 12.109; and makes perhaps one or two other small changes. But basically he seems to have summarized the text he had before him. See André Pelletier, 'Josephus, the Letter of Aristeas, and the Septuagint,' in *Josephus, the Bible, and History* (ed. Louis H. Feldman and Gohei Hata; Detroit: Wayne State University Press, 1989), 97-115. __ __[8]__ For the historical background see Hadas, *Aristeas to Philocrates*, 28-32, 98-109. __ __[9]__ Hadas, *Aristeas to Philocrates*, 138-49.

nonscriptural Jewish rites: an annual holiday celebrating the arrival of the translators and coinciding with a victory over Antigonus (v. 180; also mentioned by Philo in *Moses* 2:41-42) and manual ablutions in the sea before prayer (vv. 305-6).

Josephus regarded the putative first edition of the work as genuine and the added material in the putative second edition has a high density of Jewish signature features. The text Josephus had must have been old in his time, since he was fooled into believing *Aristeas* was actually a product of the mid-third century BCE, although it was written long enough after that date for the writer not to have accurate knowledge of some important historical matters regarding the reign of Ptolemy II. A good guess for the date of composition of the putative first edition might be 100 BCE plus or minus 125 years. It would be very difficult to refine the date further with any confidence. If there was only one edition, this would be the range of possible dating for its composition. If there was a second edition (the one that survives in our manuscripts), it is difficult to assign it a date. Josephus did not have it, so it may well (but need not) have been composed after his time. Eusebius knew the second edition, so it must have existed by the early fourth century CE.

The content of the first edition (or the whole work if there was only one edition) and its acceptance by Josephus point strongly in the direction of *Aristeas* being written by a boundary-maintaining Alexandrian Jew. It would almost certainly have been written too early to be a Christian composition. One cannot rule out that it might have been written by a gentile proselyte or an especially devoted God-fearer, and the pseudonymous attribution to a gentile author could offer some support to this possibility, but Josephus shows it was accepted in Jewish circles as an accurate representation of Judaism. If there was a second edition, the interpolater was clearly Torah observant and conscious of the need for Jews to keep away from contact with outsiders. The most natural reading is that the author was ethnically Jewish, either by birth or conversion. If the date is after Josephus, one cannot rule out composition by a Jewish-Christian, although there is no positive evidence for this.

In short, the most plausible reading of the evidence is that *Aristeas to Philocrates* was composed by a Torah observant, boundary-maintaining Jew or Jews, perhaps in two editions.

The book of 2 *Baruch* is an apocalypse whose narrator and implied author is Baruch, the scribe of Jeremiah.[10] It is set at the time of the destruction of Jerusalem by the Babylonian army and it relates a series of revelatory experiences granted to Baruch as well as a letter he sent to the nine and a half tribes to encourage them to keep the Law. The book survives complete only in a single Syriac manuscript, Codex Ambrosianus, dated to the sixth or seventh century C E. The whole work consists of about eighty-eight hundred Syriac words. The Epistle of 2 *Baruch* (Chaps. 78-87) is preserved in 36 manuscripts, and two brief excerpts of 2 *Baruch* survive in medieval Jacobite lectionaries. No certain quotations earlier than these lectionaries are extant.[11] A small fragment of a papyrus codex of a Greek version of 2 *Baruch* also survives, containing 12:1-5; 13:1-2, 11-12; and 14:1-3.[12] Despite the separate transmission history of the Epistle of 2 *Baruch*, it is generally agreed that Chapters 1-77 and the Epistle originally constituted a single work.[13] It is also generally agreed that the Syriac is a translation of the Greek, which I accept, and it is widely conjectured that the Greek is in turn a translation from a lost Hebrew original.[14] The problem of secondary translations into Syriac from Greek that was in turn translated from Hebrew is beyond the scope

---

[10] For a critical commentary see Pierre Bogaert, *Apocalypse de Baruch* (2 vols.; SC 144-45; Paris: Cerf, 1969). For English translations see R.H.Charles, 'II Baruch,' *APOT*, 2:470-526; R.H.Charles revised by L.H.Brockington, 'The Syriac Apocalypse of Baruch,' *AOT*, 835-95; and A.F.J.Klijn, '2 (Syriac Apocalypse of) Baruch,' *OTP*, 1:615-52. [11] A photolithographic edition of Codex Ambrosianus was published by Antonio Maria Ceriani in *Translatio syra pescitto Veteris Testamenti: ex codice Ambrosiano sec. fere V I, photolithographice edita, curante et adnotante* (Milan: Pogliani, 1876-83). A critical edition of the Syriac is found in S.Dedering and R.J.Bidawid, *The Old Testament in Syriac According to the Peshiṭta Version* IV.3 *Apocalypse of Baruch, 4 Esdras* (Leiden: Brill, 1973), 2 *Baruch*. The Leiden Peshiṭta edition of the Epistle of 2 *Baruch* is still unpublished. For the Arabic translation see F.Leemhuis, A.F.J.Klijn, and G.J.H.van Gelder, *The Arabic Text of the Apocalypse of Baruch* (Leiden: Brill, 1986) and Fred Leemhuis, 'The Arabic Version of the Apocalypse of Baruch: A Christian Text?' *JSP* 4 (1989): 19-26. Bogaert argues in *Apocalypse de Baruch*, 1:272-80 that the *Epistle of Barnabas* alludes twice to 2 *Baruch* in *Barn.* 11:9 (cf. 2 *Bar.* 61:7) and *Barn.* 16:6 (cf. 2 *Bar.* 32:4). If he is correct, then 2 *Baruch* existed in its Greek form by the early second century C E and the earliest extant reading of it interpreted its contents spiritually rather than literally (cf. Robert A.Kraft, *The Apostolic Fathers: A New Translation and Commentary*, Vol. 3, *Barnabas and the Didache* [New York: Nelson, 1965], 25-26, 117, 131-32). But the wording of the two passages in the *Epistle of Barnabas* is far from identical to the passages in 2 *Baruch* and we cannot be at all sure that the latter is quoting the former in either case. [12] For the

of this chapter. I am content here to flag the problem of the original language of *2 Baruch* as needing more study. If a Hebrew *Vorlage* is confirmed, it will simply add support to the understanding of the work given below on the grounds of its content.

There are many parallels in structure and content between *2 Baruch* and *4 Ezra*, perhaps indicating a literary relationship between them. It is generally accepted that *2 Baruch*, like *4 Ezra*, was written in response to the fall of Jerusalem in the war with the Romans in 70 C E, probably before the Bar Kokhba revolt in 132-135 C E. Given the idiosyncrasies of the viewpoint of *4 Ezra* (see below), it is generally agreed that any influence moved from it to *2 Baruch* rather than the other way around.[15]

Since *2 Baruch* is written in the name of a scriptural character, it stands to reason that the author, whether a Jew or a Christian, would strive to write from Baruch's perspective in Baruch's own time as the author understood it. So in order to establish the origin of *2 Baruch* we must ask not only whether it presents the viewpoint of a Christian author or a Jewish author (or something else), we must ask whether the persona of Baruch is presented the way a Jew, a Christian, or someone else would have presented it. As we have seen in Chapter Two, Christian writers retelling Old Testament stories sometimes made considerable effort to adopt the viewpoint of Old Testament writers. This fact complicates

Greek fragment see Bernard P. Grenfeld and Arthur S. Hunt, *The Oxyrhynchus Papyri,* Part III (London: Egypt Exploration Fund, 1903), 3-7 and Bogaert, *Apocalypse de Baruch,* 1:40-43. The two main criteria for determining Christian authorship of ancient Greek papyri are (1) the use of contracted divine names known as *nomina sacra*; and (2) use of the codex format from the third century C E onward. No divine names survive on the papyrus of the Greek fragments of *2 Baruch*, but the fact that the manuscript was a codex points in the direction of a Christian provenance, although a Jewish provenance is not entirely ruled out. See Eldon J. Epp, 'The Oxyrhynchus New Testament Papyri: 'Not without Honor Except in Their Hometown?' *JBL* 123 (2004): 5-55, esp. p. 20. The presence of both Christians and Jew in Oxyrhynchus is attested during the period in which the manuscript was copied. See the same article and idem, 'The Jews and the Jewish Community in Oxyrhynchus,' a paper presented at the annual meeting of the Society of Biblical Literature in San Antonio, Texas on 22 November 2004. ___ [13] ___ For a recent treatment of the Epistle see Mark F. Whitters, T*he Epistle of Second Baruch: A Study in Form and Message* (JSPSup 42; London: Sheffield Academic Press, 2003). ___ [14] ___ A Hebrew original is accepted, for example, by Charles in *APOT,* 2:472-74 and Klijn in *OTP,* 1:616. Bogaert is not convinced that we need to assume anything behind a Greek original (*Apocalypse de Baruch,* 352-80). ___ ___ [15] ___ For surveys of such issues see James H. Charlesworth, 'Baruch, Book of 2 (Syriac),' *ABD,* 1:620-21, and the bibliography cited therein; and Whitters, *Epistle of Second Baruch,* 149-55. In broad terms, it is reasonably argued that the destruction of the second temple in 70 C E is mentioned in *2 Bar.* 32:2-4 (although the passage is not entirely clear), whereas there is no reference to the Bar Kokhba revolt of 132-35 C E, so the work was composed after the first date and very likely before the second.

our analysis and demands that we read works like *2 Baruch*, which are written in the name of characters from the Jewish scriptures, closely and sympathetically before drawing conclusions about their origins.

One can see how the eschatological scenarios and, especially, the messianic speculations of *2 Baruch* might have appealed to Christians in the early centuries CE.[16] On balance, however, the internal evidence supports the position that *2 Baruch* was written by a Torah-observant Jew. The Mosaic Law is a central concern for the author and the importance of observing it – and the disastrous consequences of failing to observe it – is emphasized repeatedly.[17] It is true that Christian authors are capable of putting such exhortations into the mouths of Old Testament characters, such as the mother of the seven martyrs in *De Martyrio Maccabaeorum*, treated in Chapter Two. Nevertheless, the attitude toward the Law in *2 Baruch* seems to me to go beyond the superficial approval found in such works. First, there is the sheer number of references to the Law. More important, the understanding of it fits best with a Torah-observant attitude. The author condemns Jews who have rejected the yoke of the Law (41:1-3), conceivably even referring to converts to Christianity. In 59:2 there is a reference to 'the lamp of the *eternal law*' (my emphasis), indicating that it is still in force for the writer. According to 77:2 God gave the Law to Israel 'above all the nations.' Chapter 84 has Baruch exhort the nine and a half tribes to remember the commandments of God, Zion, the Law, the Holy Land, and the covenant; not to forget the festivals and the sabbath; and to teach their children the Law. In 66:4-5 Josiah's reforms explicitly include establishment of the festivals and the sabbath and compulsory circumcision, details not found in the scriptural account (cf. 2 Kgs 23 // 2 Chr 34-35). Thus for the author,

---

[16] The excerpting of 44:9-15 and 72:1-73:1 in the Syriac lectionaries indicates that medieval Syriac-speaking Christians valued the work for similar reasons. [17] 3:6; 15:5-7; 17:4; 19:1-3; 32:1; 38:2-4; 41:1-3; 44:2-3, 7, 14; 46:3-5; 48:22, 24, 27, 38, 40, 47; 51:3-4, 7; 54:5, 14; 59:1-2, 4, 11; 66:5; 67:6; 77:2, 15-16; 84:1-10; 85:3, 14. [18] It should be noted, however, that the Jewish people are seen as a good influence on gentiles in *2 Bar.* 1:4 and there seems to be some sympathy expressed for gentile converts in *2 Bar.* 41:3-5 and 72:5. [19] Recent discussions include Nicolae Roddy, "'Two Parts: Weeks of Seven Weeks': The End of the Age as *Terminus ad Quem* for *2 Baruch*," *JSP* 14 (1996): 3-14 and Antti Laato, 'The Apocalypse of the Syriac Baruch and the Date of the End,' *JSP* 18 (1998): 39-46. Roddy finds the calculated date to be 99 CE and Laato argues that it was 139 CE.

the Law explicitly consists of observance of the sabbath, the festivals, and circumcision. One may contrast the treatment of the Law in *De Martyrio Maccabaeorum*, where the specific halakhic issue at stake, the eating of pork offered to idols, is never specified.

The writer also expresses a robust nationalist identity. One might expect either a Jewish or a Christian author to attribute the punishment of Israel to her sins and to promise the punishment of the nations (13:1-12), since this is a scriptural theme (e.g., Jeremiah 27; Zephaniah 1-2), but Baruch also affirms that the people did not mingle with the nations (48:23) and condemns those who did (42:4).[18] Israel is the people whom God elected, a nation that is unequaled (48:20). As noted above, Chapter 84 invokes Zion, the Holy Land, the Law, and the fathers, and commands the exiles of the lost tribes to teach their children about these matters. These passage make best sense if read as the declarations of a Jew expressing his or her ethnic identity.

Although the details are far from clear, the eschatology of *2 Baruch* seems to be consistent with this reading as well. A number of passages deal with eschatological matters. Chapters 26-30 divide the end time into twelve periods (Chapter 27) and appear to calculate the date of the end (Chapter 28).[19] Then we are told that 'the Messiah shall begin to be revealed' (29:3) at the same time that Behemoth and Leviathan shall appear in order to feed the survivors at the commencement of the eschatological earthly paradise. Then we read in 30:1 that 'there shall come about after these things, when the time of the coming of the Messiah has been fulfilled, that he shall return in glory.' The resurrection and blessing of the righteous and the damnation of the wicked shall follow.

Baruch then addressed the people and predicted in Chapter 32 that Zion would be rebuilt but 'that building,' the second temple, would be uprooted once more and would remain a ruin for some time before it was 'renewed in glory' at the eschaton He then carried out an incubation ritual at the site of the Holy of Holies and received a revelatory vision about the end (Chapters 35-40), which a divine audition interpreted as a version of the myth of the four kingdoms, known from the book of Daniel and elsewhere. The fourth kingdom would be uprooted by the eternal rule of the Messiah and its last leader would be judged on Mount Zion by the Messiah and executed.

The vision of the clouds and the waters in Chapter 53 is interpreted as a proleptic history of events from the creation to the eschaton. Chapter 67 describes the destruction of Jerusalem in Baruch's time and

Chapter 68 describes its rebuilding and the restoration of the temple cult. Chapters 69-73 then tell of the time of the end, predicting the usual eschatological trials of war, tribulation, attack by the nations, earthquake, famine, and the like in Chapter 70. We are told in 70:10 that all who survive these trials shall fall into the hands of the Messiah. The Messiah will judge the nations on the basis of how they treated Israel (Chapter 72) and then he will be enthroned and the earthly paradise shall commence (Chap. 73).

Although the Messiah plays a prominent part in the proceedings, there is nothing in the review of history or anywhere else about his virgin birth, earthly ministry, crucifixion, resurrection, or founding of a church, or any other matters that could be applied to the earthly ministry of Jesus. In all three cycles of prediction the Messiah appears at the end time to defeat the forces of evil. It has been argued that 30:1 does refer to Jesus, but I think it is very difficult to interpret the verse in this way. In context, this passage says that the Messiah only begins to be revealed at the time of the end. It is true that the word I have translated as 'coming' is a technical term in Syriac for the advent of Jesus, but this proves nothing more than that the Syriac translator was trying to mold a theologically difficult passage about the Messiah into a reference to Jesus. The coming of the Messiah is only 'fulfilled' 'after these things,' that is, after the establishment of the earthly paradise, and only then does he 'return in glory.' Perhaps the most reasonable interpretation is that the (preexistent?) Messiah returns to God after his earthly advent, just in advance of the general resurrection.[20] It is perhaps not quite impossible that 30:1 is a very cryptic reference to Jesus' first advent and *parousia*, but it is so cryptic and so out of place in context that, if so, it is likely to be a secondary gloss.

It is in light of this evidence that we must evaluate the recent proposal by Rivka Nir to read *2 Baruch* as a composition by a Christian sometime between the end of the first century and the middle of the second.[21] Briefly, she argues that the concepts of the heavenly Jerusalem, the eschatological hope associated with the hiding of the temple vessels,

---

[20] Charles, *APOT*, 2:498; Klijn, *OTP*, 1:631 n. 30b; Bogaert *Apocalypse de Baruch*, 1:413-19, 2:65. [21] Nir, *The Destruction of Jerusalem and the Idea of Redemption in the* Syriac Apocalypse of Baruch (SBLEJL 20; Atlanta: Society of Biblical Literature, 2003).

the destruction of the second temple with no hope expressed for its rebuilding, and the anticipation of bodily and personal resurrection are characteristic of Christianity and not Judaism; that the picture of the Messiah is consistent with Christianity and lacks parallels in Judaism; and that the vision of the clouds and waters presupposes the Christian sacraments of baptism and the Eucharist. I agree with her that the starting point for our understanding of the text should be the Christian context of the surviving manuscripts and we should move backwards from there only as necessary. But when we apply the methods developed in this book to 2 Baruch, it becomes clear that that Christian context does not suffice to explain the work before us, which was clearly written by a Torah-observant Jew. Much of Nir's exegesis and marshalling of parallels with early Christian literature is useful for telling us what 2 Baruch may have meant to its Christian tradents and why they copied and translated the work, but it does not take into account the evidence adduced above which can only be explained in a Jewish context. This is my first objection to her conclusions.

My second objection is that Nir's concept of ancient Judaism is narrow to the point of being procrustean. She limits our Jewish sources to the Bible, the books of the Old Testament Apocrypha, the works of Josephus and Philo, and the early strata of Palestinian Talmudic and Midrashic literature. This means that she excludes not only works of the Old Testament pseudepigrapha which I argue to be Jewish in this chapter (such as 4 Ezra and Pseudo-Philo's Biblical Antiquities), but also works such as Jubilees and the documents from 1 Enoch of which fragments survive in Hebrew and Aramaic among the Dead Sea Scrolls, and even the Qumran Library itself. In some sense opaque to me she seems to regard all of these as 'Christian' rather than 'Jewish.' My reasons for rejecting her view should be clear from my detailed discussion of Judaism and Christianity in Chapter One and her arguments do not stand if her definition of Judaism is rejected.

In summary, the internal evidence indicates that 2 Baruch was written by a Torah-observant author with a Jewish ethnic identity, most likely a boundary-maintaining Jew, writing between the first and second Jewish revolts against Rome. It is perhaps barely possible that the author was a Jewish-Christian who dropped only a single hint of the identification of the Messiah with Jesus in 30:1, but, although this passage remains difficult, the most natural reading of it has nothing to do with Jesus or Christianity.

The Similitudes (or 'Parables') of Enoch is an apocalypse now found embedded in *1 Enoch* as Chapters 37-71, although its content, and that of the texts on either side of it (the Book of the Watchers and the Astronomical Book), shows it to be a self-contained work.[22] It consists of a series of visions granted to the patriarch Enoch about the eschatological judgment of the righteous and the wicked; the coming of an eschatological redeemer who bears the titles 'that Son of Man,' the 'Messiah,' and the 'Chosen One'; and traditions about Paradise and the angels. Curiously, the book ends with the revelation to Enoch that he himself is the messianic Son of Man figure who is enthroned in heaven. The Similitudes of Enoch is preserved only as part of the Ethiopic book of *1 Enoch* and, unlike the other units in this collection, no fragments of the Similitudes survive in any language but Ethiopic. It consists of about

---

[22] The most recent edition of the Similitudes is Michael A. Knibb in consultation with Edward Ullendorff, *The Ethiopic Book of Enoch: A New Edition in Light of the Aramaic Dead Sea Fragments* (2 vols.; Oxford: Clarendon, 1978). There is a critical commentary on the entire collection of *1 Enoch*: Matthew Black in consultation with James C. VanderKam, *The Book of Enoch or 1 Enoch: A New English Edition* (SVTP 7; Leiden: Brill, 1985). The more recent commentary by George W. E. Nickelsburg, *1 Enoch 1: A Commentary on the Book of 1 Enoch, Chapters 1-36; 81-108* (Hermeneia; Minneapolis: Fortress, 2001), covers the Book of the Watchers, the Book of Dreams, the Epistle of Enoch, and the miscellaneous material at the end of the book (with the other works in *1 Enoch* to be covered in the forthcoming second volume). It is the best source at present for general information on the critical study of *1 Enoch*. Other English translations of *1 Enoch* include R. H. Charles, 'Book of Enoch,' *APOT*, 2:163-281; E. Isaac, '1 (Ethiopic Apocalypse of) Enoch,' *OTP*, 1:5-89; M. A. Knibb, '1 Enoch,' *AOT*, 169-319. [23] Nickelsburg, *1 Enoch 1*, 16-17. [24] Ibid., 15-16. [25] For a beginning along these lines, see John Russiano Miles, *Retroversion and Text Criticism: The Predictability of Syntax in an Ancient Translation from Greek to Ethiopic* (SBLSCS 17; Chico, Calif.: Scholars Press, 1985). [26] David Winston Suter, *Tradition and Composition in the Parables of Enoch* (SBLDS 47; Missoula, Mont.: Scholars Press, 1979), 14-23; James R. Davila, 'Of Methodology, Monotheism, and Metatron: Introductory Reflections on Divine Mediators and the Origins of the Worship of Jesus,' in *The Jewish Roots of Christological Monotheism: Papers from the St. Andrews Conference on the Historical Origins of the Worship of Jesus* (ed. Carey C. Newman, James R. Davila, and Gladys S. Lewis; JSJSup 63; Leiden: Brill, 1999), 3-18, esp. p. 12. [27] Alexander, 'The Historical Setting of the Hebrew Book of Enoch,' *JJS* 28 (1977): 156-80, esp. pp. 158-59. [28] M. A. Knibb, 'The Date of the Parables of Enoch: A Critical Review,' *NTS* 25 (1979): 345-59, esp. pp. 349, 356. [29] Cf. M. Black, 'The Messianism of the Parables of Enoch: Their Date and Contribution to Christological Origins,' in *The Messiah: Developments in Earliest Judaism and Christianity* (ed. James H. Charlesworth; Minneapolis: Fortress, 1992), 145-68, esp. pp. 162-65; Davila, 'Of Methodology,' 14, 18. [30] This was suggested to me by Darrell Hannah in an oral communication.

five thousand Ethiopic words. George W. E. Nickelsburg lists forty-nine Ethiopic manuscripts of *1 Enoch* that date from the fifteenth to the nineteenth century. The Similitudes are included in nearly all of them.[23] It is widely agreed that the Ethiopic version of the Similitudes was translated from Greek, perhaps with reference to a Semitic (Aramaic?) original from which the Greek in turn had been translated.[24] I am not qualified to evaluate any claims about the language of the *Vorlage* of the Ethiopic or the original language of the work, and a detailed study of the Ethiopic translation and transmission of biblical and para-biblical Greek and Semitic literature would be needed to decide the question.[25]

It seems clear enough that the Similitudes exercised considerable influence on the Hebrew book of *3 Enoch*, a visionary work in the Hekhalot tradition which retells the story of Enoch, although one can debate whether this influence was direct (e.g., by the author of the core of *3 Enoch* actually having the Similitudes available in its original Hebrew or Aramaic form) or indirect (e.g., based on oral traditions stemming from the Similitudes).[26] P. S. Alexander has demonstrated that the central core of *3 Enoch* (Chaps. 3-15) was in existence by the ninth century C E at the very latest, since its content is summarized by the Karaite author Jacob al-Kirkisani.[27] There are no certain quotations of the Similitudes in antiquity: there may be some connection between *1 En.* 51:1-3 and both *4 Ezra* 7:32 and *L. A. B.* 3:10, but if there is influence, its direction is debatable. Much the same can be said for the similarities between Rev 6:15-16 and *1 En.* 62:3-5.[28] In my view, it is likely that the parable of the sheep and the goats in Matt 25:31-46 is dependent on the Similitudes (and perhaps of a version of the Similitudes which had not yet identified the Messiah with Enoch – see below): it portrays the Son of Man, who is also the King (i.e., Messiah), who judges the nations to eternal life or eternal damnation on his throne of glory in the presence of the angels, a complex of ideas found elsewhere only in the Similitudes.[29] But the parallels are conceptual and involve no verbal quotations and could be debated.

The Similitudes of Enoch shows no interest in Torah observance, makes no mention of the temple cult or priesthood, and gives no indication of any sense of Jewish national or ethnic identity. It is possible that a debate over calendrical matters, perhaps in relation to the solar or lunisolar calendar, is reflected in *1 En.* 41:3-9,[30] although, if so, the issues involved are not laid out clearly. Despite this lack of obvious Jewish signature features, I believe a good case on both internal and external grounds can be made for the Similitudes being a Jewish composition.

On internal grounds, the eschatology of the work is exceedingly difficult to reconcile with any form of Christianity. The fusion of Davidic messianic traditions with Son of Man traditions and elements from the Deutero-Isaianic Servant of Yahweh results in a Messiah who is in many ways similar to early Christological traditions about Jesus in the Gospels.[31] It is true that nothing in the description of the Messiah in the Similitudes is drawn specifically from traditions about Jesus (e.g., the virgin birth, the working of miracles, any element of suffering associated with the Servant traditions, the crucifixion, or the resurrection). But at best this fact is no more than an argument from silence against Christian authorship and it could be maintained that the Christian author left these details out to produce a *vaticinium ex eventu* with a more genuinely antique flavor. Nevertheless, the similarities between the Messiah of the Similitudes and Jesus in themselves provide a strong argument against Christian authorship, since the eschatological Messiah and Son of Man figure in the Similitudes is unambiguously identified with Enoch, not Jesus, in 71:14.[32] I see no way that a Christian author of any sort could

---

[31] J.C.VanderKam, 'Righteous One, Messiah, Chosen One, and Son of Man in 1 Enoch 37-71,' in Charlesworth (ed.), *The Messiah*, 169-91; Davila, 'Of Methodology,' 14-15.
[32] Efforts by Charles (*APOT*, 1:237) and Isaacs (*OTP*, 1:50) to argue that the Similitudes did not identify Enoch with the Messiah are not convincing and have been rejected by other scholars. See, for example, Black, 'The Messianism of the Parables of Enoch,' 145; VanderKam, 'Righteous One,' 177; John J.Collins, *The Scepter and the Star: The Messiahs of the Dead Sea Scrolls and Other Ancient Literature* (New York: Doubleday, 1995), 178. [33] There has been considerable debate on whether the identification of the Messiah with Enoch is original or a secondary development. I am inclined to think that 1 En. 70-71 is a secondary addition and that the original version of the Similitudes ended without identifying the Messiah with a specific person. Perhaps chapters 70-71 were added to defuse possible use of the work by Christians who wished to apply it to Jesus. In any case, the surviving recension of the Similitudes does make the identification and cannot be by a Christian. One could perhaps speculate that the earlier recension was produced by a Christian, who intended the Messiah to be understood as Jesus but refrained from making any clear reference to Jesus, and then a Jewish author added chapters 70-71 to undercut Christian use of the Similitudes. This, however, is an unnecessary and implausible multiplication of hypotheses and, as far as I know, no one has argued it. For a range of viewpoints on the original form of the Similitudes see VanderKam, 'Righteous One,' 177-85; Collins, *The Scepter and the Star*, 178-81; Davila, 'Of Methodology,' 11-12 and n. 15. [34] Milik with the collaboration of Matthew Black, *The Books of Enoch: Aramaic Fragments of Qumrân Cave 4* (Oxford: Clarendon, 1976), 89-98.

have made this identification. I conclude, therefore, that the author of the surviving form of the Similitudes was not a Christian.[33]

On external grounds, the adoption of traditions from the Similitudes in 3 Enoch is exceedingly difficult to explain unless the Similitudes is a Jewish work. The account of the apotheosis of Enoch in 3 Enoch 3-15 clearly presupposes the same basic story as in the surviving form of the Similitudes (not any putative earlier recension), and includes many of the same details. Certainly the most natural reading of the evidence is that the Similitudes, probably in Hebrew or Aramaic form, was transmitted, or at least remembered, in some Jewish circles until the Hekahlot visionaries adopted the strange story of Enoch's exaltation and revised and retold it for their own purposes. It is perhaps not impossible in principle that Jewish tradents could have adopted a bizarre Christian apocalypse written in Greek or Aramaic and made it their own, washing out all trace of any Greek version in transmission of the story, but it does seem extremely unlikely. One could perhaps also posit that the Similitudes was written by a (Greek- or Aramaic-speaking) God-fearer with highly idiosyncratic ideas, but, again, it is difficult to imagine the book being transmitted in Hebrew-speaking Jewish circles unless those Jews found it to be a plausibly Jewish composition. In short, by far the most likely hypothesis is that the Similitudes of Enoch, despite its disinterest in Torah observance, the temple cult, and Jewish ethnicity, is a Jewish composition.

Its date of composition is more difficult to ascertain with any confidence. Traditionally scholars have argued for a date in the first century BCE or first century CE, although J. T. Milik proposed that it was written in Greek c. 270 CE at the time of the Parthian invasion of the West.[34] He argues this first because the work is missing from the surviving fragments of the Qumran library: he posits an original Pentateuch of Enochic works, one of which, the Book of Giants, was later removed by Christians and replaced with the Similitudes. He also argues for the third-century date on the basis of similarities to the New Testament and the *Sibylline Oracles*; the mention of the Parthians and the Medes (= Parthians and Palmyrenes) as eschatological enemies in 1 En. 56:5-7; and the appearance of winged angels in 61:1. His position has been universally rejected. Speculation about an Enochic Pentateuch is hardly decisive; the Similitudes may have been doctrinally uncongenial to the Qumran sectarians; the parallels with other ancient texts are not compelling; the Persians and the Medes are traditional scriptural enemies of Israel and the Parthians and the Medes in the Similitudes are open to many interpretations; and it is difficult to date the advent of the idea of winged angels with any certainty.[35] The general consensus today is that the Similitudes were written in the first or early second century CE, although this conclusion is based on highly impressionistic arguments and should not be taken as firmly established. It is true that the period around the turn of the era gives the best parallels for the kind of apotheosis of human beings found in the Similitudes. And if I am correct in seeing a literary relationship between the Similitudes and Matthew 25:31-46, the influence surely flows from the Similitudes to Matthew rather than the other way around: it would be natural for Matthew to draw on a first-century-or-earlier Jewish apocalypse, but very unlikely for the writer of a later Jewish apocalypse to structure itself around ideas in a Christian Gospel. Finally, the use of Enoch and his revelations as a central theme in Jewish texts is characteristic of the strain of Judaism called 'Enochic' by Gabriele Boccaccini, and it fits in well with the other works in 1 Enoch, all of which were composed before the first century CE.[36] Nevertheless, given our limited knowledge of ancient Jewish sectarianism, I would not rule out the possibility that an Enochic

[35] Jonas C. Greenfield and Michael E. Stone, 'The Enochic Pentateuch and the Date of the Similitudes,' *HTR* 70 (1977): 51-65; Knibb, 'The Date of the Parables of Enoch'; Christopher L. Mearns, 'Dating the Similitudes of Enoch,' *NTS* 25 (1979): 360-69; James C. VanderKam, 'Some Major Issues in the Contemporary Study of 1 Enoch: Reflections on J. T. Milik's *The Books of Enoch: Aramaic Fragments of Qumrân Cave 4*,' *Maarav* 3 (1982): 85-97. Boccaccini has argued that the Similitudes was deliberately omitted from the Qumran library because the Qumran sectarians were hostile to the moderate form of Essenism it represented. See his *Beyond the Essene Hypothesis*, 144-49. [36] Boccaccini, *Beyond the Essene Hypothesis*. I have discussed Enochic Judaism above in Chapter One. [37] The authoritative critical commentary on 4 Ezra is Michael Edward Stone, *Fourth Ezra* (Hermeneia; Minneapolis: Fortress, 1990). Note also the recent comments on '4-5-6 Ezra' by M. de Jonge' in *Pseudepigrapha of the Old Testament as Part of Christian Literature: The Case of the Testaments of the Twelve Patriarchs and the Greek Life of Adam and Eve* (SVTP 18; Leiden: Brill, 2003), 48-52. [38] The most recent edition of the Latin version is A. Frederik J. Klijn, *Der lateinische Text der Apokalypse des Esra* (TUGA 131; Berlin: Akademie-verlag, 1983). The Latin version of 4 Ezra (= 2 Esdras 3-14) consists of about sixty-seven hundred words. [39] Dedering and Bidawid, the 4 Esdras section of *The Old Testament in Syriac According to the Peshitta Version* IV.3 *Apocalypse of Baruch, 4 Esdras*. [40] G. Mussies collects the internal evidence for the existence of a Greek version in 'When Do Graecisms Prove that a Latin Text Is a Translation?' in *Vruchten van de Uithof: Studies opgedragen aan dr. H. A. Brongers ter gelegenheid van zijn afscheid* (Utrecht: Theologisch Instituut, 1974), 100-119. This evidence shows clearly that a Greek version once existed, although, as Mussies points out, it does not rule out the possibility that it was made from the Latin version and then used by the Syriac, or vice versa.

work such as the Similitudes could have been written any time in the early centuries C E.

In any case, we have in the Similitudes a rare and extraordinarily valuable example of a demonstrably Jewish text that shows no interest in Torah observance, the temple cult, or the author's own Jewish identity. Its Jewish origin is shown only by its eschatological content and external evidence about its transmission. If this group or a similar one had produced a text without eschatological content and in which Jews had not maintained some interest, we should probably be unable to prove that it was Jewish. Indeed, it is entirely possible that we have such texts and simply do not know their origin.

FOURTH EZRA

4 *Ezra* is an apocalypse that presents a series of seven visions revealed to Ezra which use the fall of Jerusalem as backdrop to a consideration of fundamental questions about the eternal fate of human beings and divine theodicy.[37] Our chief sources for the text are the Latin and Syriac versions. The oldest Latin manuscript is Codex Sangermanensis, copied in 822 C E. A leaf containing the section 7:[36]-[105] was excised from this manuscript, presumably because the passage in question denies the validity of prayer for the dead. Nearly all the surviving Latin manuscripts lack this passage, indicating that this manuscript was their archetype. The ninth-century Codex Ambianensis, however, does contain them. The Latin version of 4 *Ezra* includes Chapters 1-2 (5 *Ezra*) and 15-16 (6 *Ezra*), passages found in no other textual tradition. This version also identifies the Messiah of 7:28 with 'Jesus,' again, a reading not found elsewhere, and it lacks Ezra's ascent to heaven at the end of the book, which is found in the other versions.[38] The Syriac survives complete only in the sixth- to seventh-century Codex Ambrosianus, along with a few quotations in medieval Jacobite lectionaries. It also has a Christianizing variant in 7:28-29, where it alters what appears to be the original 'four hundred years' of the Messiah's ministry to 'thirty years.'[39] Both internal and external evidence indicate that a Greek version also existed and it is generally assumed that it was the *Vorlage* behind both the Latin and the Syriac.[40] There are a number of early quotations of 4 *Ezra* in Greek. Clement of Alexandria quotes 4 *Ezra* 5:35 in *Strom.* 3.100.1 (regarding the recalcitrance of Israel), assigning it to 'Esdras the prophet,' and seems to allude to 4 *Ezra* 14:21-22, 37-47 in *Strom.* 1.149.3 with reference to Ezra's restoration of the lost scriptures. *Apostolic Constitutions* 2.14.9 quotes

4 Ezra 7:103 without attribution to affirm individual responsibility and 8.7.6 quotes *4 Ezra* 8:23, a hymnic passage to the Lord which is applied without attribution to Christ.[41] Small fragments in Sahidic Coptic survive which seem to have been translated from the Greek, but otherwise the numerous translations into other languages are mostly dependent on the Latin or the Syriac and provide little new information for reconstructing the Greek text.[42] It is widely agreed that the Greek text behind the Syriac, Latin, and Coptic was itself translated from Hebrew.[43] As with *2 Baruch*, I shall reserve judgment on this question. Certainly the Latin displays Semitisms that are consistent with translation from Hebrew, although they may also be consistent with translation from a Greek text deliberately composed in a Septuagintal style to give it a biblical flavor. If the theory of a Hebrew *Vorlage* is upheld, it would be consistent with my conclusions about *4 Ezra* reached on other grounds.

The earliest quotations indicate that Greek-speaking Christians were interested in the work for its apologetic value against Judaism, its esoteric traditions about the transmission of the Old Testament scriptures, and whatever Christological value they could read into it. One could see that Christians would approve of the quasi-Pauline notion of sin (e.g., 7:59 [129]-60 [130]; 9:29-37) and the internal anti-Judaism of the work. Despite its works theology of salvation, it could be seen as a kind of protevangelium that sets the stage for the coming of Jesus. Christians would also have been attracted to the eschatology of the document, even though it is difficult to reconcile with Christianity. But the eschatological signs in 9:1-9 are compatible with Christian expectations (indeed, I wonder if the reference to salvation by faith in v. 7 is a Christian interpolation) and the coming of the Davidic Messiah would have been taken as the second coming of Jesus.

The current consensus is that *4 Ezra* was written in Palestine around

---

[41] M. Black, *Apocalypsis Henochi Graece*; Albert-Marie Denis, *Fragmenta Pseudepigraphorum quae supersunt Graeca* (PVTG 3; Leiden: Brill, 1970), 130-32; Albert-Marie Denis, *Introduction aux pseudépigraphes grecs d'ancien Testament* (SVTP 1; Leiden: Brill, 1970), 194-200. *Barn.* 12.1 may also allude to *4 Ezra* 4:33 and 5:5, where the blood dripping from wood is interpreted as a reference to the crucifixion of Jesus. [42] For a complete survey of the surviving manuscripts and translations of *4 Ezra* see Stone, *Fourth Ezra*, 1-9. [43] Stone, *Fourth Ezra*, 10-11. [44] Stone, *Fourth Ezra*, 9-10. [45] DiTommaso, 'Dating the Eagle Vision of *4 Ezra*: A New Look at an Old Theory,' *JSP* 20 (1999): 3-38.

the turn of the second century CE and that its setting thirty years after the destruction of the first temple (a chronological impossibility if Ezra is involved) is a thin cover for the author's real concern for the theological implications of the recent destruction of the second temple in the first revolt against Rome.[44] Lorenzo DiTommaso, however, has argued for interpolations from the third century in the surviving version of the work. The Eagle Vision in Chapters 11-12 is usually understood to belong in the context of the late first century CE, but DiTommaso believes that, although it was composed at this time, it was updated and redacted c. 218 CE in the reign of Septimus Severus, such that the original is now irrecoverable.[45] If he is correct, this is an important example of a Christian interpolation and reworking of a Jewish pseudepigraphon in which no Christian signature features have been introduced.

4 *Ezra* is replete with Jewish signature features that provide converging lines of evidence that it is a Jewish composition. The importance of the Law of Moses, which has been revealed to Israel and which they are responsible for keeping, pervades the entire work (3:19; 5:27; 7:19, 20, [79]-[81], [89], [94], 63 [133]; 8:12, 29, 56; 9:11, 29-37; 13:42, 54; 14:21-22, 30). It may be fairly remarked that these references do not in themselves prove Jewish authorship, since there are no references to specific laws and even a Christian author would have acknowledged that Jews ought to have kept the Law in the time of Ezra. But the keeping of the Law is a central theme of the book which dovetails with other Jewish signature features. Prominent among them is the special place of Israel in the divine scheme of things. God made an everlasting covenant with Abraham (3:15); though God has destroyed his people, no other nation or tribe had known him or believed his covenants as Israel has (3:33; cf. 5:29; 7:[83]); God has chosen one city, Zion, and one people whom he has loved and given the Law, although this people has now been given over to the many (5:21-30) and given over to the gentiles as a reproach (4:23); although they are now given into the hands of the nations, which are nothing, the world was created for God's people whom he has called his first-born (6:55-59); God made the world for Israel's sake (7:10-11); and Israel is God's people and his inheritance (8:15-16, 26, 45). Although Israel's humiliation before the nations is freely acknowledged, no Christian triumphalism is evident in these passages. On the contrary, the centrality of Israel to God is reaffirmed repeatedly and the oppressing gentiles are dismissed as nothing.

The temple cult, the priesthood, Zion, and the land are also important in the author's worldview. Ezra mourns the destruction of the earthly sanctuary in Jerusalem, 'our city' (3:1), the plunder and pollution of the holy implements, and the murder and enslavement of the priests and Levites (10:20-22). As noted above, Zion is God's one consecrated city (5:25). Ezra is comforted with a vision of the restored Zion (10:38-54), which also figures in the eschatological battle with the nations (13:35-36). The eschatology of 4 Ezra is also inconsistent with Christianity. Not only do the passages on the Messiah fail to refer to the virgin birth, miracle-performing earthly ministry, crucifixion of Jesus, etc., I cannot see any way to reconcile the messianic scenario set out in 7:28-[44] with Christianity. In this passage God's son the Messiah is revealed and is present for four-hundred years, after which he dies, the world is returned to primeval silence for seven days, and the general resurrection and final judgment follow immediately thereafter. Even if we were to accept the reading 'thirty years' in the Syriac (and I think it is clearly secondary), the rest of the scenario simply wouldn't fit. Instead of a first advent culminating in the death and resurrection of the Messiah (i.e., Jesus) and followed by a long but indefinite period before his second advent as eschatological warrior, we have an earthly advent followed by the Messiah's death, a week of primordial chaos, and the general resurrection and the final judgment. No space is allowed for the long period between the ascent of Jesus and his return. This inconsistency with Christian eschatology is obviously due to the fact that the author of 4 Ezra sees the advent and death of the Messiah as still in the future. The Messiah is not Jesus, not even in a veiled *vaticinium ex eventu*.

Various global readings of 4 Ezra have been proposed by one scholar or another over the last century and more, but space permits me to note only one recent one, which is compatible with the analysis above and which I find particularly persuasive. In a 1991 monograph, Bruce W. Longenecker has read 4 Ezra along the following lines.[46] The first part of the book (3:1-9:22) consists of three dialogues between Ezra

---

[46] Longenecker, *Eschatology and the Covenant: A Comparison of 4 Ezra and Romans 1-11* (JSNTSup 57; Sheffield: Sheffield Academic Press/JSOT, 1991). In *2 Esdras* (Guides to Apocrypha and Pseudepigrapha; Sheffield: Sheffield Academic Press, 1995), Longenecker finds more of a covenantal scaffolding in the view finally accepted in 4 Ezra than in his first book, although his interpretation otherwise remains the same. For surveys of other readings see idem, *Eschatology and the Covenant*, 40-49; Stone, *Fourth Ezra*, 23-36.

and the angel Uriel, in which Uriel's position that only a few will be saved is disputed by Ezra. This section is followed by the vision of the woman, who represents the mourning heavenly Jerusalem (9:26-10:59). This vision precipitates a conversion experience in Ezra: his questions are not answered, but he is comforted. The eagle vision (11:1-12:35) is an earlier tradition incorporated into the book but reinterpreted to teach that a remnant of a few worthy ones will be saved at the eschaton (12:34). Only the wise (the same remnant) are worthy of receiving this teaching (12:36-38). In accordance with this new revelation, Ezra (who is, of course, one of the wise who shall be saved) dissembles when he meets with the people in 12:46-49, comforting them because, although they are among the lost, they are not worthy to know it.

The vision of the Man from the Sea (13:1-58), which, like the previous vision, is an earlier tradition incorporated into 4 *Ezra*, is reinterpreted to teach that the ten lost tribes (who kept the Torah even without the temple), along with a remnant of the rest of Israel, shall achieve eschatological salvation. Thus a multitude shall be saved after all, but this is no comfort for Ezra's people, since only a very few of them shall be. In 14:1-48 God agrees to allow Ezra to restore the lost scriptures but warned him to reveal only public knowledge to the people and to save the secrets for the wise (14:26; cf. vv. 5-6). Accordingly, Ezra gives them a traditional prophetic harangue (14:27-36), which, however, fails to reveal to them the secret that only a few of them shall be saved. This secret doctrine is reinforced by the subsequent restoration of the exoteric scriptures (the twenty-four books of the Hebrew Bible) and also seventy esoteric books.

Longenecker's reading makes good sense of the apparent inconsistencies, uneven places, and redactional seams of the books and I suspect that the intent of the original author was something very much like it. But whether or not this is so, the case is overwhelming for 4 *Ezra* as an especially strictly boundary-maintaining Jewish work composed by a Torah-observant author around the end of the first century CE (although perhaps updated by a Christian author in the early third century). Not only does it exclude gentiles from the covenant community and from eschatological salvation, it also excludes most Jews from both. Its focus on Jerusalem and its temple also show that it is not a Samaritan work.

The book of 3 *Maccabees*, inaptly named since it has nothing to do with the Maccabees, is set shortly after the battle of Raphia (217 BCE) and an anonymous narrator tells an unspecified narratee the story of the persecution of the Egyptian Jews by Ptolemy IV Philopator. Ptolemy attempted to enter the Jerusalem temple but was stricken by God with a seizure. In retaliation he first resolved to enslave the Jews in Alexandria unless they offered worship to Dionysus and, when few took up his offer of clemency, he gathered all the Egyptian Jews into an Alexandrian hippodrome to be trampled to death by elephants, but after God foiled four attempts to carry out the mass execution, Ptolemy repented, set the Jews free, and offered praise to their God.

---

[47] Moses Hadas, *The Third and Fourth Books of Maccabees* (2 vols. in one; New York: Harper, 1953), 1:26-27. There are two critical editions of the text: Henry Barclay Swete, *The Old Testament in Greek According to the Septuagint*, vol. 3, *Hosea-4 Maccabees, Psalms of Solomon, Enoch, the Odes* (Cambridge: Cambridge University Press, 1909-12); Werner Kappler and Robert Hanhart, *Maccabaeorum libri I-IV*, fasc. III, *Maccabaeorum liber III* (Septuaginta: Vetus Testamentum Graecum Auctoritate Societatis Litterarum Gottingensis 9; Göttingen: Vandenhoeck & Ruprecht, 1960). Aside from that of Hadas, English translations include Cyril W. Emmet, 'The Third Book of Maccabees,' *APOT*, 1:155-73; H. Anderson, '3 Maccabees,' *OTP*, 2:509-29.   It has been suggested that 3 *Maccabees* is either the excerpted introduction to what was originally a history of the Maccabees, or at least that material has been lost from the beginning. The first possibility is intriguing, given the transmission of the sixth book of Josephus' *Jewish War* as an independent work in Syriac and my thought experiment in Chapter Two of imagining the independent transmission of excerpted passages from other works. Nevertheless, the title may well have become attached to the work merely because it was transmitted alongside the other books of the Maccabees in the manuscripts. For discussion see Emmett, *APOT*, 1:155, 161 and Hadas, *The Third and Fourth Books of Maccabees*, 1:4-5.   [48] Josephus briefly tells a version of the same legend as 3 *Maccabees* in *Ag. Ap.* 2.53-55, placing it during the reign of Ptolemy IX Physcon in the second century BCE.   [49] Emmet, *APOT*, 1:162.   [50] For a survey of the discussion and a bibliography see Anderson, *OTP*, 2:510-12. I cannot agree with him that 'in view of the glorification of the Jerusalem Temple in the book, the Temple is obviously still standing and the destruction that befell it in A. D. 70 has not yet occurred' (p. 510). The temple is glorified just as much after its destruction by Jewish authors such as Josephus and the writers of the Mishnah.   [51] The apostate Jew Dositheus is described with curious restraint in 1:3. Although he was born a Jew, he renounced the Law and his ancestral traditions, and the story describes without further comment how he saved the life of the king. Hadas suggests that in the eyes of the author 'he was nevertheless a Jew by origin and his patriotic deeds should be recorded' (*Third and Fourth Books of Maccabees*, 1:32). There may also be a darker subtext that the well-meaning acts of an apostate drew the baleful attention of the king to Judaism and led to the persecutions narrated in the book.

The original language of *3 Maccabees* is universally recognized to be Greek and it consists of about five thousand Greek words. It survives in the uncial manuscripts Codex Alexandrinus (fifth century C E) and Codex Venetus (eighth-ninth century C E) as well as a number of minuscules, of which the Lucianic copies are less reliable. There is no Latin translation, but translations into Syriac and Armenian survive. The text is well preserved.[47] The date of composition is extremely difficult to narrow down. The story is legendary and must have been written well after the battle of Raphia.[48] In turn, it must have been written long enough before the time of Theodoret of Cyrrhus (c. 393-458) for him to take it as a historical account and summarize it in his commentary on Daniel.[49] Internal evidence for a date is lacking, although it has been argued that linguistic criteria indicate that the most likely period is from the second century B C E to the first century C E.[50] Given the content, an Alexandrian provenance is plausible, although perhaps not quite certain: after all, Josephus, a Palestinian Jew writing in Rome, told the same story.

Greek-speaking Christians would have appreciated *3 Maccabees* for its description of the miraculous triumph of worshipers of the scriptural God when they resisted the persecution of a hostile polytheistic king. These elements doubtless led to its adoption and transmission by the Eastern Church. Nevertheless, the narrative itself is written from a Jewish perspective. Ptolemy's attempt to enter the temple in Jerusalem was treated as an outrage that set the population of Jerusalem up in arms (1:9-29). The high priest Simon, in his prayer, referred to God's 'holy people Israel' (2:6); asserted that God choose Jerusalem and the temple for his name (2:9); and referred to God's love for the house of Israel (2:10). In revenge for his subsequent humiliation, Ptolemy ordered the Alexandrian Jews to accept a brand on their bodies in honor of Dionysus, thus requiring them both to honor another god and to violate the scriptural law against tattoos (Lev 19:28), but most of them resisted (2:27-33). They also incurred enmity for following the Law of their God, notably keeping special dietary laws (3:2-7). When the Jews were miraculously delivered, the king permitted them to celebrate a seven-day festival that was then made an annual holiday (6:30-32, 35-36, 40), one with no scriptural sanction but whose existence Josephus confirms (*Ag. Ap.* §§2.55). The same or another such festival is mentioned in 7:17-20. Moreover, the king even permitted them to execute those Jews who had violated the divine law and to hold a joyful feast afterward (7:10-16).[51] Finally, the concluding doxology of the work,

'Blessed be the Deliverer of Israel for all eternity, amen!' (7:23) is difficult to read, especially in context, as anything but an expression of religious nationalism in which the author identifies him- or herself with Israel.

The transmission of 3 Maccabees solely in Christian circles must be weighed against these features in it. It is perhaps not impossible to imagine a sympathetic Christian author in the first or second century CE adopting an oral version of this legend, retelling it as an example of the people of God resisting idolatry in the dispensation before the advent of Christ, and not including any Christian signature features. But the interest in dietary laws and the descriptions of a historical but nonscriptural Jewish festival point to an author who approves of the observation of both scriptural and local Jewish customs. Moreover, the positive references to Israel as God's beloved people, combined with the bloodthirsty dispatching of those who betrayed the community and the sentiment of the final doxology, point in the direction of an author with a strong sense of Jewish ethnic identity. The focus on the Jerusalem temple and the Jewish Diaspora in Egypt eliminates a Samaritan origin as a serious possibility. We cannot eliminate the possibility of authorship by a Jewish-Christian, but there is no positive evidence in favor of it. The evidence best supports composition by a Torah-observant Egyptian Jew who is very concerned to maintain the boundary between Judaism and gentile idolatry.

---

[52] A critical edition of the Greek text of 4 Maccabees has been published by Swete in *The Old Testament in Greek According to the Septuagint*, vol. 3, *Hosea-4 Maccabees, Psalms of Solomon, Enoch, the Odes*. English translations include R. B. Townshend, 'The Fourth Book of Maccabees,' *APOT*, 2:653-85; Hadas, *Third and Fourth Books of Maccabees* vol. 2; and H. Anderson, '4 Maccabees,' *OTP*, 2:531-64. For additional discussion of text and versions see Townshend, *APOT*, 2:654 and Hadas, *Third and Fourth Books of Maccabees*, 135-36. [53] For discussions of the evidence for the earliest citations of 4 Maccabees see Hadas, *Third and Fourth Books of Maccabees*, 122-27; and David A. deSilva, *4 Maccabees* (Guides to Apocrypha and Pseudepigrapha; Sheffield: Sheffield Academic Press, 1998), 143-55. [54] See Hadas, *Third and Fourth Books of Maccabees*, 95-99; Jan Willem van Henten, *The Maccabean Martyrs as Saviours of the Jewish People: A Study of 2 and 4 Maccabees* (JSJSup 57: Leiden: Brill, 1997), 70-82; deSilva, *4 Maccabees*, 14-18, for reviews of the evidence for the date of 4 Maccabees.

7

The book of 4 *Maccabees* is a philosophical retelling of the story in 2 Maccabees 6-7 of the martyrs of the Maccabean revolt. 4 *Maccabees* thus has nothing to do with the Maccabees themselves, but presumably acquired its title from its paraphrasing of material from 2 Maccabees and its transmission along with 1-2 Maccabees. 4 *Maccabees* survives in the two early uncials Sinaiticus (fourth century C E) and Alexandrinus with the title 'Fourth (book of) Maccabees' (*Μακκαβαίων δ´*), as well as in part (lacking 5:11-12:1) in Venetus, and in some minuscule manuscripts. It is found in many manuscripts of Josephus, where it is attributed to him under the title 'On the Supremacy of Reason' (*Περὶ αὐτοκράτορος λογισμοῦ*). There is universal agreement that 4 *Maccabees* was composed in Greek (and it consists of about seventy-eight hundred Greek words), but a Syriac translation is also extant, as is a Slavonic version and a Latin paraphrase, although the work has not been transmitted in the Latin Vulgate.[52]

4 *Maccabees* has some parallels with the New Testament and early church fathers, but they contain no direct quotations of it, and we cannot rule out that the similarities are due to independent but converging theological developments, oral traditions about the martyrs, shared sources, and the like. Of the suggested parallels, those with Hebrews 11:35b and Origen's *Exhortation to Martyrdom* seem the most persuasive. The earliest undoubted reference to 4 *Maccabees* is by Eusebius in the early fourth century in *Hist. eccl.* 3.10.6, where he attributes it to Josephus. (In the early fifth century, Jerome also takes Josephus to be the author in *Vir. ill.* 13 and *Pelag.* 2.6.) 4 *Maccabees* is also used in sermons on martyrdom by Gregory of Nazianzus and John Chrysostom in the second half of the fourth century.[53] Thus, in broad terms, 4 *Maccabees* should be dated after the time of either the composition of 2 Maccabees or of Jason of Cyrene's larger work that 2 Maccabees epitomizes, since 4 *Maccabees* is dependent on one of these. The existence of 4 *Maccabees* is well attested by the fourth century C E but most scholars would date it to the first or early second century C E.[54] The earliest surviving uses of 4 *Maccabees* mostly focus on the steadfastness of the Maccabean martyrs to their religion in the face of persecution and torture. The relevance of this theme to the early church hardly needs belaboring and it is likely that the extended treatment of the example of these martyrs led to the transmission of the book by Christians. The question we need to consider, therefore, is whether Christian composition suffices to explain the origin of 4 *Maccabees*. More

precisely, we must ask whether such Jewish features as appear in the book can be explained as a sympathetic retelling of the story by a Christian who acknowledged the validity of the old dispensation with Israel in the time of the Maccabean martyrs, even though this Christian author would reject Jewish praxis after the coming of Jesus. I have argued in Chapter Two that the Christian author of *De Martyrio Maccabaeorum* retold the story from just this perspective, so a comparison of 4 *Maccabees* with *De Martyrio Maccabaeorum* should be instructive.

If we take into account all these considerations, the Jewish origin of 4 *Maccabees* is amply demonstrated by its content. The thesis of the book is that reason is sovereign over the emotions, and this thesis is argued by means of a retelling of the martyrdom of the aged priest Eleazer, the seven sons, and their mother, with the philosophical dialogue and commentary built around a lovingly detailed description of the torture of the victims. The martyrs submit to torture and execution rather than obeying the king's order to disobey the Jewish food taboos and eat pork and food sacrificed to idols (4:26, 5:2, 6, 14, 19; 6:15; 8:2; 9:27; 11:16, 25). The writer refers frequently to the Jewish Law and the importance of keeping it. It is true that some of these passages refer to the Law only in very general terms (e.g., 1:17; 2:5-6; 3:20; 9:1-2; 11:5, 12; 13:9, 13, 24; 15:9-10, 31; 16:16; 18:1, 4, 10) and that such references are found also in *De Martyrio Maccabaeorum*. But other passages in 4 *Maccabees* make the content and nature of this Law clear in a way that we do not find in *De Martyrio Maccabaeorum*. The Law includes circumcision (4 *Macc.* 4:23-25). The importance of the food taboos is attested not only by the many passages cited above, but also by 4 *Macc* 1:33-34, which spells out some of the other limitations besides avoidance of pork. Both circumcision and the food taboos must be observed even in the face of persecution and death. The sabbatical year is also assumed to be binding (4 *Macc* 2:8), as is the temple service (4 *Macc* 4:19-20).

The Jewish ethnic identity of the author is clear. In *De Martyrio Maccabaeorum* we find some positive references to the Jewish nation either in the mouths of the characters or even at times in the words of the narrator. Such comments appear frequently also in 4 *Maccabees* (e.g., 9:6,

---

[55] Goldstein, *II Maccabees* (AB 41A; Garden City, N.Y.: Doubleday, 1983), 26-27, 549.
[56] Williams, *Stylometric Authorship Studies in Flavius Josephus and Related Literature* (Jewish

18, 29; 13:18-19; 15:28-29; 17:6, 9-10; 18:5, 23). But 4 *Maccabees* goes far beyond such general statements. A striking indicator of the Jewish identity of the author is the author's use of the first-person plural. The implied author and the implied audience are Torah observant and of Jewish ethnic origin. The implied author and the audience keep the food taboos (4 *Macc* 1:33-34) and observe the Law (4 *Macc* 13:22, 18:1). They are descended from the patriarchs (4 *Macc* 7:19) and ancient Jews (4 *Macc* 3:20) and regard Aaron and Eleazer as fathers (4 *Macc* 7:9, 11). They are of the same nation (4 *Macc* 17:8), identified as Israel (4 *Macc* 17:20-22; 18:1). Nothing like these references is found in *De Martyrio Maccabaeorum*.

It is true that at times ancient Christian authors referred to scriptural worthies in terms of fictive kinship. Compare, for example, the characterization of Abraham as 'our father' in 1 *Clem.* 31:2, and see the discussion of the Wisdom of Solomon in the Excursus at the end of Chapter Four. Nevertheless, one would be hard put to find a Christian work that combined the firmly Jewish ethnic identity of 4 *Maccabees* with its emphasis on Torah observance. The most reasonable reading of the evidence is that the author is a Torah-observant Jew. It is extremely unlikely that the author is a gentile Christian or a God-fearer, although I would not rule out the possibility of Jewish-Christian authorship, even though I see no positive evidence for it.

If 4 *Maccabees* is a Jewish work and if it was composed, as most specialists think, in the first or early second century CE, is it possible that the manuscript tradition that attributes it to Josephus is correct? David S. Williams has pointed out weaknesses in the traditional arguments against Josephan authorship. First, 4 *Maccabees* makes certain errors we might not expect of Josephus and expresses sentiments unlikely to have come from him, yet the supposed mistake about the topography of the temple complex may not be an error and Josephus' works contain many internal contradictions. Second, it has been argued that 4 *Maccabees* is based on 2 Maccabees, yet Josephus did not know 2 Maccabees. But it is not impossible that 4 *Maccabees* used the source of 2 Maccabees rather than 2 Maccabees itself, although this is a minority viewpoint. In addition, it is not universally agreed that Josephus did not know 2 Maccabees. Jonathan A. Goldstein, for example, argued that he did.[55] Third, if 4 *Maccabees* was written before 70 CE, it is unlikely that Josephus could have been the author. But, as we have seen, some scholars place the writing of 4 *Maccabees* in the late first or early second century CE.[56] Williams rightly rejects these arguments as inconclusive.

Any case for Josephan authorship of 4 *Maccabees* is seriously weakened, however, by the fact that the earliest attribution of the work to Josephus is by Eusebius in the early fourth century C E. Between the end of the second century and the middle of the third, a number of writers refer to Josephus, and in the third century Origen quotes frequently from him, mentioning three of his surviving works by name (the *Antiquities*, the *Jewish War*, and *Against Apion*, probably understanding that the *Life* was part of the *Antiquities* rather than a separate work). None of these pre-Eusebian authors associate 4 *Maccabees* with Josephus.[57] It is possible, of course, that Eusebius had correct information that was unavailable to the earlier authors, but this is a very thin thread on which to hang Josephan authorship unless there is substantial internal evidence in 4 *Maccabees* in support of it.

Such evidence, however, is sorely lacking. No one has argued that the style and viewpoint of 4 *Maccabees* has any obvious correspondence to the undoubted works of Josephus. Williams's refutation of the traditional arguments merely leaves the possibility of Josephan authorship open; it does nothing to advance it. On the contrary, Wilson goes on to apply computer-generated stylometric analysis to 4 *Maccabees* to compare its authorial style to that of Josephus. He concludes:

‹Absolute certainty cannot be forthcoming on an issue involving ›
statistical analysis. However remote, the possibility of chance account- ›
ing for the variations observed must be recognized. Yet, in the case of ›
the hypothesis of Josephan authorship of 4 Maccabees, the magnitude ›
of the results obtained through stylometric analysis are overwhelm- ›

Studies 12; Lewiston, N.Y.: Mellen, 1992), 105-120. Some other discussions of the authorship of 4 *Maccabees* include Townshend, *APOT*, 2:656-57; Hadas, *Third and Fourth Books of Maccabees*, 113-15; and deSilva, 4 *Maccabees*, 12-14. ___ [57] ___ See the discussion of the transmission of the works of Josephus below in the excursus to this chapter. ___ [58] ___ Williams, *Stylometric Authorship Studies*, 149. ___ [59] ___ Ceriani, *Monumenta sacra et profana ex codicibus praesertim Bibliothecae Ambrosianae* (Milan: Bibliotheca Ambrosiana, 1861), I 1:55-64. R.H. Charles published an annotated edition and translation in *The Assumption of Moses* (London: Black, 1897), republished and updated in shorter form without the Latin text in 'The Assumption of Moses,' *APOT*, 2:407-24. More recent editions are E.-M. Laperrousaz, 'Le Testament de Moïse,' *Sem* 19 (1970): 1-140; and Johannes Tromp, *The Assumption of Moses* (SVTP 10; Leiden: Brill, 1993). Other English translations include J. Priest, 'Testament of Moses,' *OTP*, 1:919-34 and R.H. Charles, revised by J.P.M. Sweet, 'The Assumption of Moses,' *AOT*, 601-16. ___ [60] ___ Charles, *APOT*, 1:409-10. Laperrousaz reserves judgment on the original language ('Le Testament de Moïse,' 16-25) and Tromp argues for a Greek original (*Assumption of Moses*, 78-85).

ing. The odds against a common population for the Josephan block
and 4 Maccabees, produced by the study of the ten Josephan test
words, are extraordinarily high.

This finding has been confirmed by studying correlation, distinctiveness ratios, word choice, and the frequency of a grammatical con-
struction. Testing in regard to these studies produced statistically
significant scores. By far, the most economical explanation for all the
results is that Josephus had nothing whatsoever to do with the composition of 4 Maccabees.›[58]

The results of computerized statistical analysis are, of course, only as
good as the assumptions behind the analysis and the implementation of
those assumptions, and it may be that someone could challenge Wilson's
results on either account. One could also suggest that 4 *Maccabees* was
written by Josephus when he was a much younger man who held different views and who wrote in a different style from his later works. But
it is fair to say that the only positive evidence for Josephan authorship
of 4 *Maccabees* is the statement of Eusebius and the later agreement of
Jerome and part of the manuscript tradition, and that this evidence is
very weak. I conclude, therefore, that 4 *Maccabees* was almost certainly written by a Torah-observant, boundary-maintaining Jew, who may
have been a contemporary of Josephus, but who was probably not
Josephus himself.

THE LATIN FRAGMENT KNOWN AS THE *TESTAMENT OF MOSES* OR THE *ASSUMPTION OF MOSES*

8

This Latin fragment relates the final admonition of Moses to Joshua
just before Moses' death. The very beginning and an uncertain amount
of material at the end are lost, but it is a fairly substantial fragment (consisting of about 2,150 legible words), so it is worthwhile to see how much
information we can extract from it. The manuscript, which was published by A. M. Ceriani in 1861, was written in the sixth century CE.[59]
The Latin shows some signs of having been translated from Greek and
external evidence supports the existence of a Greek *Vorlage* (see below).
R. H. Charles argued that the Greek had been translated from Hebrew,
but such Semitic idioms as appear in the Latin may indicate nothing
more than translation from biblicizing Greek.[60]

At least two pseudepigrapha dealing with the end of Moses' life
were circulating in antiquity. Both a *Testament of Moses* (Διαθήκη Μωυ-

σέως) and an *Assumption of Moses* (Ἀνάληψις Μωυσέως) are mentioned in lists of biblical apocrypha. In formal terms, the Latin fragment reads well as a testament in which a scriptural character gives final admonitions to family or a successor, and it seems to assume that Moses died rather than being translated to heaven (e.g., *T. Mos.* 1:15), although it has been argued that *T. Mos.* 10:12 is a gloss that implies a heavenly translation. Richard Bauckham has collected all the quotations and allusions relevant to ancient Moses pseudepigrapha and has concluded that some of them refer to the Greek version of our Latin fragment, which was the *Testament of Moses*, while others refer to the *Assumption of Moses*, a different and later work.[61] It is possible that a third, unnamed work was alluded to as well by Clement of Alexandria. The *Testament of Moses* concluded with a dispute between the devil (Sammael) and the archangel Michael over the body of Moses, in which the devil claimed the body on the grounds that Moses had murdered the Egyptian taskmaster. Michael drove the devil away with a rebuke and took the body to the place assigned for its burial. If this passage was originally in the Latin fragment, it is now lost, but the episode is alluded to in Jude 9. In the *Assumption of Moses* the devil claimed Moses' body on the specious grounds that he (the devil) was 'the Master of matter.' Moses' body was buried and his soul assumed to heaven in this story.

Bauckham's reconstruction of the two pseudepigrapha is plausible overall, although, as he himself notes, not all of the evidence can be interpreted consistently along these lines. The most difficult datum for his reconstruction is that the fifth-century church historian Gelasius Cynzicenus quotes a Greek version of *T. Mos.* 1:6, 14 and assigns it to the *Assumption of Moses* (*Hist. eccl.* 2:17:17 and 2:21:17). Initially, this would seem to imply that our Latin fragment ended with a physical or spiritual translation of Moses to heaven. But Bauckham suggests that either Gelazius mistakenly understood two quotations available to him to be from the *Assumption of Moses*, when only one was and the other was from the *Testament of Moses*, or that the *Assumption of Moses* was a revised version of the *Testament of Moses* and also contained the quoted material.

---

[61] Bauckham, *Jude and the Relatives of Jesus in the Early Church* (Edinburgh: Clark, 1990), 235-80. [62] Charles argues that the Epistle of Jude alludes three times to the Greek *Vorlage* of our Latin fragment (*APOT*, 2:412-13) but Laperrousaz ('Le Testament de Moïse,' 51-58)

Either explanation is possible and if the first is correct, we cannot deduce anything about the ending of our Latin fragment from the title assigned to it by Gelasius.

All that said, I am not entirely convinced by Bauckham's argument that our Latin fragment is the *Testament of Moses* that he reconstructs and which was quoted in Jude 9. Three of his four sources, the *Slavonic Life of Moses* 16; (Pseudo-)Oecumenius, *In Jud.* 9; and Cramer's *Catena*, relate only material that would have come from the lost ending of the Latin fragment. Only his first source, the *Palaea Historica*, a Byzantine compendium of scriptural stories which shows acquaintance with ancient parabiblical works, has any potential overlap with the surviving Latin material. I quote Bauckham's translation of its opening lines:

⟨Of the death of Moses. And Moses said to Jesus the son of Nave, › 'Let us go up into the mountain.' And when they had gone up, Moses › saw the land of promise, and he said to Jesus, 'Go down to the people › and tell them that Moses is dead.' And Jesus went down to the people, › but Moses came to the end of his life.⟩

It is not impossible to read this laconic passage as including a summary of the Latin fragment, but it is not obvious that it is a summary of it rather than of an entirely different pseudepigraphon. In *T. Mos.* 1:6, Moses summons Joshua, but he says nothing about going up the mountain or about seeing the promised land and nothing in the text implies that the conversation took place on the mountain rather than before Moses ascended it. It may be that the epitomizer read the Greek version of our Latin pseudepigraphon and read material from Deuteronomy 34 into it, but there is no reason to assume this was the case. Likewise, nowhere in the Latin fragment does Moses say to Joshua, 'Go down to the people and tell them that Moses is dead.' Moses does speak of his own death in 1:15 and 10:11-15; Joshua speaks of Moses' departing from the people in 11:4, 9-14, 19; and Moses speaks of the fate of the people after he is gone in 12:4-13. Again, it could be that the epitomizer is summarizing this exchange rather inaccurately, but we need not assume this. To my mind, the simplest understanding of the passage in the *Palaea Historica* is that it epitomizes another Moses pseudepigraphon, different from both our Latin fragment and the Assumption of Moses. Presumably the pseudepigraphon known to the author of the *Palaea Historica* should be identified as the *Testament of Moses* as reconstructed by Baukham and it is also the work from which Jude quotes. Our Latin fragment is known from elsewhere only in the Greek quotations of Gelasius, which he assigns, evidently wrongly, to the *Assumption of Moses*.[62]

In short, the external evidence gives us no help in determining whether the Latin fragment is a Jewish composition or not. It tells us no more than that the work existed in Greek in Christian circles in the fifth century. We must turn to the internal evidence for more information. The work is set in the time of Moses and consists mostly of the words of either Moses or Joshua, so the question before us is whether it can be explained as a composition by a Christian aiming to write what Moses and Joshua would have said or whether it must be a composition by a Jewish (or some other kind of) author.

Within those parameters, the contents of the work point beyond reasonable doubt to Jewish authorship. Moses' prophecy refers to God's covenant and his oath 'that their seed would never be absent from the land that you gave to them' (3:9). It would be difficult to imagine a Christian writing this or, indeed, a Jew writing it after 70 C E. The author has Moses predict that at the eschaton those who 'confess circumcision' will be crucified and even those who deny it (renounce it?) will be

and Bauckham (*Jude and the Relatives of Jesus*), 275-78 have shown that these parallels are not convincing. [63] Another reading, which I do not find persuasive, is that the work was written during the Maccabean revolt and was updated not long after the time of Herod the Great. But even if this reconstruction is correct, nothing important in my conclusions would need to be altered. See the following essays in George W. E. Nickelsburg, Jr., *Studies on the Testament of Moses* (SBLSCS 4; Cambridge, Mass.: Society of Biblical Literature, 1973): Nickelsburg, 'Introduction,' pp. 5-14, esp. p. 6; John J. Collins, 'The Date and Provenance of the Testament of Moses,' pp. 15-32; Nickelsburg, 'An Antiochan Date for the Testament of Moses,' pp. 33-37; Collins, 'Some Remaining Traditio-Historical Problems in the Testament of Moses,' pp. 38-43; Jonathan A. Goldstein, 'The Testament of Moses: Its Content, Its Origin, and its Attestation in Josephus,' pp. 44-52. Tromp has summarized and commented on this discussion in *Assumption of Moses*, 120-23.
[64] The case for Samaritan authorship has been argued by Klaus Haaker in 'Assumptio Mosis – eine samartanische Schrift?' *TZ* 6 (1969): 385-405. In favor of his position are the parallels between the Latin fragment and some Samaritan traditions about Moses and Joshua, and the lack of mention of later scriptural prophets in the work. However, parallels in Jewish literature can also be found for the material on Moses and Joshua, and the story's focus on Moses may have led the author to concentrate on Moses' prophecies rather than later ones. (In addition, the description of the prayerful figure in 4:1-6 seems to show awareness of intercessory material from the Judean figures Daniel and Ezra.) Moreover, the interpretation of the 'place' in 1:17 as the site of a sanctuary rather than simply a hiding place is unnecessary, and the interpretation of the 'two tribes' as Ephraim and Manasseh and the 'ten tribes' as the other tribes is ingenious but is by no means the most natural reading. It is true that Samaritans had reason to take note of and dislike the Hasmoneans and Herod, but the author pictures the Hasmoneans as defiling their own altar and sanctuary and acting impiously against the Holy of Holies (5:3-4; 6:1), which implies the basic validity of the Jerusalem cult. The author also resents their abuse of the priestly office (5:4;

tortured, while circumcised children will be forced to submit to epis-pasm surgery (8:1-3) and others will be compelled to blaspheme with regard to their own laws and sacrifices (8:5). The author is interested in the Jewish priesthood, seeing the second temple cult as corrupted (5:1-6). The Hasmonean priest-kings are singled out for condemnation (6:1) and the life of Herod the Great is summarized and condemned as well, even though he was not of a priestly line (6:2-6). Nevertheless, at the eschaton Israel will be exalted to live among the stars (10:8-9).

These features point in the direction of a first-century CE Jewish author. The eschatology of the work clinches this identification. Chapter 6 summarizes the 34-year reign of Herod (6:1-6) and alludes to the rule of his sons for shorter periods than his reign (6:7 – this was true of Archelaus but not Antipas or Philip), followed perhaps by an account of the campaign of the Roman governor of Syria, in 4 BCE (6:8-9). We pass from there to an account of the eschatological trials in Chapters 7-8. This material recapitulates events and sufferings typical of the Maccabean period, but evidently projected into the end time.[63] There is no mention of the Great Revolt against Rome of 68-70 CE or the destruction of Jerusalem or the temple. The advent of a priestly 'messenger' (*nuntius* – angel?) is followed by the coming of God in a final eschatological crisis and judgment (10:1-10). The internal evidence points to a date of composition early in the first century CE, probably before the crucifixion of Jesus (by which time both Antipas and Philip had ruled as long as their father).

In sum, although the Latin fragment cannot be identified with any confidence as the *Testament of Moses* quoted by Jude, it does seem to be a work of the very end of the first century BCE or the early part of the first century CE, probably too early to be a Christian composition and in any case no later than the first generation of Christianity. It displays no positive indicators of Christian composition. Its assurance that the Jewish people will remain on their land in perpetuity; its support of circumcision; its interest in the politics of the temple cult in the first century BCE; its interest in eschatology without allusion to Jesus; and its confidence in the eschatological exaltation of Israel point strongly in the direction of Jewish authorship. Indeed, the hostility toward the Hasmoneans and the cult of the second temple may indicate a sectarian origin, although we are given too little information to assign the work to a specific group such as the Essenes. There is little evidence for Samaritan authorship, and what has been adduced so far has not been found convincing.[64] One can perhaps not rule out entirely the possibility of a gentile God-fearer with just this set of interests, but I see no positive evidence in favor of this and such a God-fearer would have to be very well informed about and committed to Judaism. The most reasonable hypothesis is that this Latin fragment about the end of the life of Moses is a Jewish composition written between about 4 B C E and 30 C E or at least before 70 C E.[65]

6:1), which implies that the Jerusalem priesthood was valid in itself. The perspective of the work is thus sectarian Jewish and this fact, combined with the lack of clear Samaritan signature features, renders a Samaritan origin quite unlikely. For discussion see Collins, 'The Date and Provenance,' 16 n. 6; James D. Purvis, 'Samaritan Traditions on the Death of Moses,' in Nickelsburg (ed.), *Studies on the Testament of Moses*, 93-117, esp. pp. 116-17; Tromp, *Assumption of Moses*, 107-108. ____ [65] ____ This conclusion represents the consensus in the secondary literature. See, for example, Charles, *APOT*, 2:411; Laperrousaz, 'Le Testament de Moïse,' 88-99; Priest, *OTP*, 1:920-22; Sparks, *AOT*, 602-604; Tromp, *Assumption of Moses*, 116-19; De Jonge, *Pseudepigrapha of the Old Testament*, 65-68. ____ [66] ____ Pseudo-Philo's *Biblical Antiquities* was reintroduced to the scholarly world by Leopold Cohn in 'An Apocryphal Work Ascribed to Philo of Alexandria,' *JQR* O.S. 1 (1898): 277-332. M. R. James published a translation based on Joannes Sichardus's sixteenth century edition and four manuscripts in *The Biblical Antiquities of Philo: Now First Translated from the Old Latin Version* (London: Society for Promoting Christian Knowledge, 1917). A critical edition based on twenty manuscripts was published by Guido Kisch in *Pseudo-Philo's Liber Antiquitatum Biblicarum* (Publications in Medieval Studies 10; Notre Dame, Ind.: University of Notre Dame, 1949). Another edition drew on all the manuscript evidence and was published with French translation and commentary in *Pseudo-Philon: Les Antiquités Bibliques*, vol. 1, *Introduction et texte critiques*, by Daniel J. Harrington and Jacques Cazeaux, and vol. 2, *Introduction littéraire, commentaire et index*, by Charles Perrot and Pierre-Maurice Bogaert, with the collaboration of Daniel J. Harrington (SC 229-30; Paris: Cerf, 1976). Christian Dietzfelbinger has published a German introduction and translation in *Pseudo-Philo: Antiquitates Biblicae (Liber Antiquitatum Biblicarum)* (JSHRZ 2.2; Gütersloh: Mohn, 1979) and Howard Jacobson has published *A Commentary on Pseudo-Philo's* Liber Antiquitatum Biblicarum: *With Latin Text and English Translation* (2 vols.; AGJU 31; Leiden: Brill, 1996). There is another English translation by Harrington in 'Pseudo-Philo,' *OTP*, 2:297-377. ____ [67] ____ Howard Jacobson, 'Thoughts on the *Chronicles of Jerahmeel*, Ps-Philo's *Liber Antiquitatum Biblicarum*, and Their Relationship,' *Studia Philonica Annual* 9 (1997): 239-63. ____ [68] ____ Daniel J. Harrington, 'The Text-Critical Situation of Pseudo-Philo's 'Liber Antiquitatum Biblicarum,'' *RBén* 83 (1973): 383-88; Harrington and Cazeaux, *Pseudo-Philon*, 1:15-57. ____ [69] ____ Jacobson, *A Commentary*, 269. ____ [70] ____ Daniel J. Harrington, 'The Original Language of Pseudo-Philo's *Liber Antiquitatum Biblicarum*,' *HTR* 63 (1970): 503-14, esp. pp. 503-504. Cf. Bengt Löfstedt, 'Zu den lateinischen Übersetzung von (Ps.) Philons Schriften,' *Eranos* 89 (1991): 101-106; Jacobsen, *A Commentary*, 278-80. ____ [71] ____ Cohn, 'An Apocryphal Work,' 307-308; Harrington, 'The Original Language,' 505-508; Jacobson, *A Commentary*, 222-24. ____ [72] ____ Harrington, 'The Original Language,' 508-14. Cf. Jacobson, *A Commentary*, 215-222, 262. In addition John Strugnell attempts to reconstruct the putative Hebrew *Vorlagen* of two psalms of David in the *Biblical Antiquities* in 'More Psalms of David,' *CBQ* 27 (1965): 207-16.

9

The *Liber Antiquitatum Biblicarum* or *Biblical Antiquities* is a work of re-written scripture which retells scriptural history from Adam up to the time of David.[66] It survives in twenty-one Latin manuscripts ranging in date from the eleventh century to the fifteenth century. Some of the material in the *Biblical Antiquities* also is found in a Hebrew translation of the Latin in the *Chronicles of Jerahmeel*.[67] It appears that the archetype of all surviving Latin manuscripts was an imperfect copy that may have been missing some leaves. Indeed, some commentators believe that the end of the work, the extent of which is unknown, was missing from this archetype and is now lost. The archetype also attributed the *Biblical Antiquities* to Philo of Alexandria, prefacing it with Jerome's *De Philone* and placing after it the Latin translation of Philo's *Questions and Answers on Genesis*: hence the alternate appellation 'Pseudo-Philo.'[68] The earliest certain quotation of the *Biblical Antiquities* of which I am aware is of *L.A.B.* 5:7 by Rabanus Maurus in the ninth century.[69] As will become clear below, this quotation must come well after the time of the work's composition and so it is not of interest to us.

The Latin version of the *Biblical Antiquities* is the earliest surviving form of the text and is generally regarded to be a translation from a Greek version that, in turn, was translated from a Hebrew original. The Latin is idiosyncratic. Daniel J. Harrington finds it to be similar to that of the Old Latin version of the Bible and typologically earlier than post-Vulgate Latin.[70] Evidence for a Greek stratum is based on several considerations. The work contains a great many Greek loan-words transliterated directly into Latin, including Greek forms of most of the proper names, and some passages clearly translate the LXX rather than the Hebrew. Numerous apparent mistranslations and misreadings of the Greek *Vorlage* have also been advanced, although many of these are speculative.[71] Very few of the alleged Grecianisms are syntactical, which somewhat weakens the overall case.

As for a Hebrew stratum behind the Greek, Harrington has assembled an impressive list of passages that misread the Hebrew texts of scriptural passages or understand them differently from the main tradition of the LXX. He also has advanced some cases that seem to be best explained as misunderstandings of a Hebrew *Vorlage* not obviously connected with a scriptural passage. A number of these mistranslations work for Hebrew and not Aramaic whereas none work for Aramaic and not Hebrew.[72]

Moreover, he has shown that the Hebrew text presupposed corresponds more closely to the *Vorlage* of the L X X, and especially of the proto-Lucianic revision of some L X X books, than to the M T, but that in many cases the Latin does not presuppose the Greek of the L X X or any of its known revisions.[73] Regarding the *Vorlage* of the *Biblical Antiquities* he sums up,

‹ The examples presented up to this point are sufficient to establish › that in the biblical texts contained in L A B we are not dealing with the › insertion of a known O L [Old Latin] or L X X text. To suppose that we › are dealing with an unknown Latin or Greek text cannot be ruled out, › but this does involve explaining one unknown by another. A more › reasonable hypothesis is that we are dealing directly with the Hebrew › *Vorlage* of L A B's biblical text through the medium of Latin and Greek › translations. It seems better to suppose that in L A B's present Latin › version we can glimpse the Hebrew biblical texts employed by the › author in the original version of the work. ›[74]

I concur with this judgment. It is not impossible that the work was composed in Greek by a writer who used a Greek translation of the biblical text that had significant variants from the major L X X manuscripts, perhaps a revision of the L X X against poor copies of the Hebrew text or by a translator with a weak knowledge of Hebrew. It could even have

[73] Harrington, The Biblical Text of Pseudo-Philo's *Liber Antiquitatum Biblicarum*,' *CBQ* 33 (1971): 1-17. [74] Ibid., 5-6. [75] For a minimalist statement of the background of the Lucianic revision of the L X X, see Emanuel Tov, *Textual Criticism of the Hebrew Bible* (Minneapolis: Fortress, 1992), 148. For a detailed presentation of the case for a proto-Lucianic recension see Eugene Charles Ulrich, Jr., *The Qumran Text of Samuel and Josephus* (HSM 19; Missoula, Mont.: Scholars Press, 1978). [76] Harrington, The Biblical Text,' 6-7, 16-17. [77] Hannah M. Cotton, 'Ḥever: Naḥal: Written Material,' *EDSS*, 359-61; Hanan Eshel, 'Murabbaʿat, Wadi: Written Materials,' ibid., 583-86; Emanuel Tov, 'Scriptures: Texts,' ibid., 832-36, esp. p. 836. [78] Eugene Ulrich, 'Two Perspectives on Two Pentateuchal Manuscripts from Masada,' in *Emanuel: Studies in Hebrew Bible, Septuagint, and Dead Sea Scrolls in Honor of Emanuel Tov* (ed. Shalom M. Paul et al.; VTSup 94; Leiden: Brill, 2003), 453-64. [79] W. F. Albright, 'New Light on Early Recensions of the Hebrew Bible,' in *Qumran and the History of the Biblical Text* (ed. Frank Moore Cross and Shermaryahu Talmon; Cambridge: Harvard University Press, 1975), 140-46 (rpt. of *BASOR* 140 [1955]: 27-33); Frank Moore Cross, 'The History of the Biblical Text in the Light of Discoveries in the Judaean Desert,' in Cross and Talmon (eds.), *Qumran and the History of the Biblical Text*, 177-95 (rpt. of *HTR* 57 [1964]: 281-99); Eugene Ulrich, 'The Dead Sea Scrolls and the Biblical Text,' in *The Dead Sea Scrolls After Fifty Years: A Comprehensive Assessment* (ed. Peter W. Flint and James C. VanderKam; 2 vols.; Leiden: Brill, 1998-99), 1:79-100, esp. pp. 95-96.

been composed in Latin by an author who made use of an Old Latin translation of such a Greek text. But to posit these intermediate translations would be to introduce unnecessary complexities. The Latin text of Pseudo-Philo is based on something like the Hebrew text behind the LXX and, where we have it for comparison, the proto-Lucianic revision of the LXX, yet it is not based on either of these Greek translations themselves. The simplest explanation is that the writer worked directly from this Hebrew text of the scriptures and so presumably wrote in Hebrew.[75] The evidence discussed above for a Greek stratum behind the Latin supports the view that the Latin was translated from a Greek translation of the Hebrew original of the *Biblical Antiquities*, although the existence or not of a Greek version does not really matter for my purposes. Harrington also suggests that the relationship of the Hebrew biblical text used by the *Biblical Antiquities* to the proto-Lucianic recension, along with some readings in common with the Samaritan Pentateuch, argues that the place of composition was Palestine and the date of composition before about 100 CE.[76] The second point is better supported than the first, although neither is certain. The texts of the scriptural manuscripts in Hebrew recovered from the caves of Naḥal Ḥever and the Wadi Murabbaʿat and deposited during the Bar Kokhba revolt in 132-135 CE belong to the proto-Masoretic recension and show none of the textual variation characteristic of the scriptural manuscripts from Qumran.[77] The textual evidence of the scriptural fragments in Hebrew deposited at Masada c. 73-74 CE is similar, but too sparse to support any generalization about the nature of the scriptural texts used by the Jews who perished there after the Great Revolt.[78] Thus the evidence currently available does not support the survival of scriptural texts significantly variant from the proto-Masoretic text beyond the early second century CE, and therefore points to the composition of the *Biblical Antiquities* before this time. But the geographical provenance of the work is another matter. The theory of local texts proposed by William F. Albright and Frank Moore Cross has not been widely accepted in recent years and cannot provide decisive evidence for a Palestinian origin for the *Biblical Antiquities*.[79]

There is, then, a solid philological case for the *Biblical Antiquities* to have been composed originally in Hebrew by the early second century CE and therefore virtually certainly by a Jew. The internal evidence offers additional support for the Jewish provenance of the work. It frequently mentions the Mosaic Law and its importance (e.g., 12:2, 4;

16:5; 19:1, 9; 21:9-10; 22:5-6; 23:2, 10; 25:3, 13; 29:4; 30:2, 5; 33:3; 34:1; 38:2; 39:6), and it presents the establishing of the covenant with Israel on Mount Sinai as a glorious event (32:7-8). The specific content of the Law is laid out in some detail. It is hinted that Moses was born circumcised (9:14-15). The text reviews the law of sacrifices on the altar (13:2); the laws for leprosy (13:3); and the festivals of Unleavened Bread (13:4), Weeks (13:5), Trumpets (i.e. the New Year) (13:6a); the Day of Atonement (13:6b); and the Festival of the Booth (i.e., Booths) (13:7). It also refers to the celebration of Passover (48:3; 50:2) and presents sabbath observance as obligatory (25:13; 44:6-7). There is a reference to an annual memorial festival in honor of Seila, the daughter of Jephthah, observed on the fourteenth day of a month that the author seems to assume the reader already knew (unless the text is corrupt and the month is lost) (40:8).

One could argue that even a boundary-maintaining Christian could have written positively and fulsomely about the Law as something valid in the Old Testament dispensation while rejecting it for Christians in the writers own time. And it is true that the admonitions to observe this or that law is set in the narrative world of the story and is never addressed directly to the reader. Nevertheless, this interest in specific ritual customs, particularly the festivals and the sabbath, is not found in either the *Leviticus* section of the *Heptateuchos* or the *De Martyrio Maccabaeorum* (see Chapter Two), a difference that at least points away from Christian authorship.

Other features in the *Biblical Antiquities* offer more compelling support for Jewish authorship. There are statements to the effect that the Law and the covenant with Israel are eternal: the covenant with Abraham shall not be broken (4:11); at Mount Sinai God revealed the 'eternal law' (11:2), 'the law of the eternal covenant with the sons of Israel,' and 'eternal precepts that shall not pass away' (11:5); and that an 'eternal light' (evidently the Law) was kindled in Moses (9:8; 19:4). There are also statements that give Israel a special and eternal

---

[80] Cohn, 'An Apocryphal Work,' 306-307; James, *The Biblical Antiquities of Philo*, 27; Kisch, *Pseudo-Philo's Liber Antiqutatum Biblicarum*, 15-18; Dietzfelbinger, *Pseudo-Philo*, 91; Perrot and Bogaert, *Pseudo-Philon*, 2:10; Jacobson, *A Commentary*, 195-97. [81] Ibid., 207, 252-53. [82] Perrot and Bogaert, *Pseudo-Philon*, 2:53-59; Jacobson, *A Commentary*, 247-50.

status in the sight of God: the giving of the Law at Sinai glorified Israel above all other nations (11:1); they are God's chosen nation that he has loved above all others (19:8); God swore an oath not to desert his people forever (30:7); God chose only Israel out of all the nations (31:5); even when God punishes his people he will not reject or hate them forever (49:3). It is difficult to imagine a gentile Christian writing all these passages.

The cumulative evidence, then, suggests strongly that Pseudo-Philo's *Biblical Antiquities* was composed in Hebrew by a Jew by the early second century CE. It is therefore worthwhile to ask whether the attribution to Philo of Alexandria is at all likely. Briefly, the answer is no. Whether or not Philo knew some Hebrew, all of the works assigned to him with any certainty were composed in Greek and used the LXX as their scriptural text. It is very difficult to imagine that he could have written such a substantial document in Hebrew or that Clement and Origen, both residents of Philo's native Alexandria, could have been completely unaware of it if he had. The interests and content of the work are also quite different from those of Philo. It is universally agreed that the *Biblical Antiquities* are not by him and I concur with this consensus.[80]

The author then, was a Hebrew-speaking, Torah-observant and boundary-maintaining Jew. It is perhaps not entirely impossible that the author was a Jewish-Christian, although there is no positive evidence to indicate this. Indeed, the possibility has been raised that the *Biblical Antiquities* engages in a few places in anti-Christian polemic, notable in 32:3, which treats the near sacrifice of Isaac as a unique event, perhaps opposing a Christian typology.[81] This, however, is speculative. The work has some interest in eschatology but its views on such matters remain opaque.[82]

10

THE PSALMS
OF SOLOMON

The *Psalms of Solomon* is a collection of eighteen poetic, perhaps liturgical, works preserved in Greek and Syriac, although scholars usually posit a Hebrew original behind them. The Greek text consists of about five thousand words. It survives in eleven Greek manuscripts, dating from the tenth to the sixteenth century, and in two Syriac manuscripts that date from the tenth and from the fifteenth or sixteenth century, respectively. There are also quotations in three Syriac manuscripts.[83] In addition, the opening list of contents in the Codex Alexandrinus includes 'Eighteen Psalms of Solomon,' although the pages where the work was are now lost. There are numerous parallels between the Greek texts of *Pss. Sol.* 11 and Baruch 4:36-5:9, although it is debated whether one is dependent on the other or they both depend on a common source.[84] I have argued elsewhere that Baruch must have been composed in Greek; if I am correct, then the relationship between the texts must have originated in Greek.[85] If *Pss. Sol.* 11 was composed in Hebrew and then translated into Greek, the likelihood is that the passage in Baruch was composed after the *Psalms of Solomon* had been translated into Greek and this passage is dependent on *Pss. Sol.* 11.

There is a reasonable case that the *Psalms of Solomon* were composed in Hebrew, but it is not as compelling as the case for a Hebrew *Vorlage*

---

[83] The standard editions of the Greek are Oskar von Gebhardt, *Psalmoi Solomontos zum ersten Male mit Benutzung der Athoshandschriften und des Codex Casanatensis* (Leipzig: Hinrichs, 1895) and Henry Barclay Swete, *The Old Testament in Greek: According to the Septuagint*, vol. 3, *Hosea-4, Maccabees, Psalms of Solomon, Enoch, The Odes* (Cambridge: Cambridge University Press, 1930). The long-promised critical edition of the Greek by Robert B. Wright has not yet been published. For the Syriac text see W. Baars, *Psalms of Solomon* in *The Old Testament in Syriac According to the Peshiṭta Version*, vol. 4.6, *Canticles or Odes – Prayer of Manasseh – Apocryphal Psalms – Psalms of Solomon – Tobit – I (3) Esdras* (Leiden: Brill, 1972). For discussions of text-critical issues see Joachim Begrich, 'Der Text der Psalmen Salomos,' *ZNW* 38 (1939): 131-64; M. Delcor, 'Psaumes de Salomon,' in *Dictionnaire de la Bible: Supplément* (ed. L. Pirot and A. Robert; Paris: Letouzey & Ané, 1979), 9:214-45; Robert R. Hahn, *The Manuscript History of the Psalms of Solomon* (SBLSCS 13; Chico, Calif.: Scholars Press, 1982) and Joseph L. Trafton, *The Syriac Version of the Psalms of Solomon: A Critical Evaluation* (SBLSCS 11; Atlanta: Scholars Press, 1985). Critical commentaries include Herbert Edward Ryle and Montague Rhodes James, ΨΑΛΜΟΙ ΣΟΛΟΜΩΝΤΟΣ: *Psalms of the Pharisees, Commonly Called the Psalms of Solomon* (Cambridge: Cambridge University Press, 1891); Joachim Schüpphaus, *Die Psalmen Salomos: Ein Zeugnis Jerusalemer Theologie und Frömmigkeit in der Mitte des vorchristlichen Jarhunderts* (ALGHJ 7; Leiden: Brill, 1977); Kenneth Atkinson, *An Intertextual Study of the Psalms of Solomon* (Studies in the Bible and Early Christianity 49; Lewiston, N.Y.: Mellen, 2001). Other English translations include G. Buchanan Gray, 'The Psalms of Solomon,' *APOT*, 2:625-52; S. P. Brock, 'The Psalms of Solomon,' *AOT*, 649-82; R. B. Wright, 'Psalms of Solomon,' *OTP*, 2:639-70. A translation by Atkinson is also forthcoming in the New English Translation of the Septuagint series. [84] For a summary of the state of the question, see Atkinson, *An Intertextual Study*, 228-29. [85] '(How) Can We Tell if a Greek Apocryphon or Pseudepigraphon Has Been Translated from Hebrew or Aramaic?' (forthcoming in the *Journal for the Study of the Pseudepigrapha*). [86] A detailed case for a Hebrew *Vorlage* behind the Greek *Psalms of Solomon* was laid out already by Ryle and James in *Psalms of the Pharisees*, lxxvii-xcii. For the Syriac translation, see Trafton, *The Syriac Version*, 187-207. Robert B. Wright offers a critical response to Trafton in a review of this book in *JBL* 107 (1988): 131-34.

for Pseudo-Philo's *Biblical Antiquities* (discussed above), since the *Biblical Antiquities* seems to be based on an imperfectly understood Hebrew *Vorlage* of the scriptural text which differed significantly both from the MT and the *Vorlage* of the LXX. There is some evidence for mistranslations of a Hebrew *Vorlage* in the Greek of the *Psalms of Solomon*, and Joseph L. Trafton has argued at length that the Syriac was translated independently from the Hebrew, or at least with reference to both the Hebrew and the Greek, but not everyone has found his arguments convincing.[86] The whole issue of the original language of the *Psalms of Solomon* is in need of a rigorous linguistic, and perhaps computer-aided, analysis (see n. 85). The original language of the work is not of great importance for my analysis here and if it is proved that it was composed in Hebrew, that fact will only reinforce the conclusions reached on other grounds below.

The *Psalms of Solomon* is clearly a collection of Jewish poetic works. Although the Law is mentioned only infrequently (4:8; 10:4; 14:2), the writers identify themselves and their audiences with Israel (7:8-10; 8:26-34; 9:1-2, 8-11; 10:5-8; 17:4-5, 45); they show great interest in God's relationship with Israel (12:6; 14:5; 18:1-3); and they look forward to the eschatological vindication of Israel (17:26-28; 18:5-9). There is also a great deal of hostility toward gentiles (1:1-2, 4-8; 7:2-3, 6; 8:30), who at some point invaded Jerusalem under an evil leader who was punished by God (2:1-29; 8:4-8, 15-21). God sits in judgment over the nations (17:3); the Messiah will purge Jerusalem of gentiles (17:22) and destroy the lawless nations (17:24-25); and God will bring the exiles back to Zion (11:1-9).

The writer or writers are either residents of, or at least very well informed about Jerusalem, and their Jewish identity does not prevent them from distinguishing between the 'righteous' – themselves – and 'sinners' – other Jews rather than gentiles – (e.g., 13:1-12). The Jewish Jerusalemites are presented in highly negative terms: they were more lawless than the gentiles (1:1, 4-8; 8:13); they defiled the sanctuary (1:8; 2:3-5; 8:11-13, 22); they engaged in incest and adultery (8:8-10) and adopted gentile practices (17:1-15). Many of these charges have the air of stock accusations in inter-religious conflict and we need not assume that they give us much objective information about the opponents of the writers. But the charges do give us some insight into the relationship of the writers of the *Psalms of Solomon* to other Jews, and their viewpoint amounts to a sectarian orientation in which they comprise the true Israel over against the fallen Israel of their opponents. It seems difficult to say a great deal more about the community that produced the *Psalms of Solomon*. One school of thought argued that the Pharisees composed them. After the discovery of the Dead Sea Scrolls, some have argued that the *Psalms of Solomon* were produced by the Essenes. A better approach is to assume that the authors belonged to another otherwise unknown sectarian group that had much in common both with the Pharisees and the Qumran sectarians.[87]

The historical references in *Psalms of Solomon* 2 and 8 are widely agreed to deal with the capture of Jerusalem by the Roman general Pompey in 63 BCE, although these passages have also been taken to refer to other figures such as Antiochus Epiphanes, Herod the Great, and Titus. Recently, Kenneth Atkinson has argued that the poems in the *Psalms of Solomon* were composed between about 63 and 30 BCE and redacted into the form we have them now toward the end of this period.[88]

The earliest external reference to the *Psalms of Solomon* may be the echoes of *Pss. Sol.* 11 in the book of Baruch, if that was the direction of influence. If so, the writer of Baruch, whom I argue in the Excursus to Chapter Four to have probably been Jewish (but possibly a God-fearer), was most interested in the psalm's emphasis on the glorious return of the Jewish exiles to Jerusalem. It may be that the failure of the two revolts against Rome in Palestine cooled the Zionist ardor of the Jewish Diaspora and this was a factor leading Jews to lose interest in the *Psalms of Solomon*. We have no early quotations of the work from Christians, but we may conjecture that the speculations about the eschatological advent of a sinless Messiah (*Pss. Sol.* 17-18, esp. 17:36) in a patently Jewish work led Christians to preserve it as a kind of protevangelium.

---

[87] For a summary of the discussion into the early 1990s, see Joseph L. Trafton, 'The *Psalms of Solomon* in Recent Research,' *JSP* 12 (1994): 3-19, esp. pp. 7-8. Since then, important work along the lines of the third view has been done by Kenneth Atkinson in 'Herod the Great, Sosius, and the Siege of Jerusalem (37 B.C.E.) in Psalm of Solomon 17,' *NovT* 38 (1996): 313-22; idem, 'Toward a Redating of the Psalms of Solomon: Implications for Understanding the *Sitz im Leben* of an Unknown Jewish Sect,' *JSP* 17 (1998): 95-112; idem, 'On the Use of Scripture in the Development of Militant Davidic Messianism at Qumran: New Light from *Psalm of Solomon* 17,' in *The Interpretation of Scripture in Early Judaism and Christianity: Studies in Language and Tradition* (ed. Craig A. Evans; JSPSup 33; Studies in Scripture in Early Judaism and Christianity 7; Sheffield: Sheffield Academic Press, 2000), 106-23; idem, '*I Cried to the Lord': A Study of the Psalms of Solomon's Historical Background and Social Setting* (JSJSup 84; Leiden: Brill, 2004).

[88] See Wright, *OTP*, 2:640-41; Atkinson, 'Herod the Great'; idem, 'Towards a Redating.'

The author or authors of the *Psalms of Solomon* were sectarian Jews whose concern with boundary maintenance led them to consider themselves the true Israel and to reject other Jews as impious and impure. It is likely that the work was written before the advent of Christianity and, in any case, the issues that separated these sectarians from other Jews seem to have revolved around perceived defilement of the temple cult rather than any dispute over the acceptance of Jesus as the Messiah.

11

CONCLUSIONS

In Chapter One, I showed on external grounds that Christians transmitted eight ancient Jewish pseudepigrapha and Apocrypha: the Book of the Watchers, the Astronomical Book, the Book of Dreams, the Epistle of Enoch, the book of *Jubilees*, the Letter of Jeremiah, Ben Sira, and Tobit. These works were mostly abandoned by Jews in the early centuries C E, although the Hebrew of Ben Sira continued to be copied into the early Middle Ages and Tobit was later retranslated and reintroduced into Jewish circles. Material derived from *Aramaic Levi* also survives in the Greek *Testament of Levi*, although in substantially altered form. This chapter has applied the methods and gains of Chapters One and Two to isolate nine more ancient Jewish works transmitted by Christians: *Aristeas to Philocrates*, *2 Baruch*, the Similitudes of Enoch, *4 Ezra*, *3-4 Maccabees*, the Latin fragment on Moses, Pseudo-Philo's *Biblical Antiquities*, and the *Psalms of Solomon*. All of these were entirely abandoned by Jews early on, with the possible exception of the Similitudes, some knowledge of which survived in the Hebrew work *3 Enoch*. Therefore, the application of the methods that I have developed in this book provides us with a substantial corpus of seventeen ancient Jewish works, fourteen of them Jewish pseudepigrapha, thirteen of which have been transmitted in complete form (and one as a large fragment) solely in Christian circles. The indicators are that these works have come down to us essentially in the form produced by their original authors, although there is evidence in *4 Ezra* for tampering by Christian tradents. Especially if we focus on major themes and concerns in these works, we can use them with some confidence for reconstructing ancient Judaism. Most of them seem to have been written by Torah-observant Jews who were concerned with boundary maintenance, although the Similitudes is a work of Enochic Judaism which has other concerns. The eight works isolated in Chapter One were all composed before the abandonment of the Qumran caves in 68 C E. There is good evidence that the *Psalms of Solomon*, the Moses fragment, and at least the putative first edition of Greek *Aristeas to Philocrates* were also in existence by the early first century CE and that the *Vorlagen* of *2 Baruch*, *4 Ezra* and the *Biblical Antiquities* had been written by the beginning of the second century CE. It is these works, therefore, that are likely to give New Testament scholars the best information about Judaism in the time of Jesus and the formative years of early Christianity. The remaining works – the Similitudes of Enoch and *3-4 Maccabees* – may have been in existence this early, but a later date of composition cannot be ruled out for them.

There are, of course, numerous Old Testament pseudepigrapha whose origins are less clear, even though many of them are routinely taken to be Jewish. It would be impossible to examine all of them in this book, but Chapter Four will survey some important issues pertaining to six of them. In addition, the following excursus examines the origins of the works attributed to Flavius Josephus and Philo of Alexandria and an Excursus to Chapter Four looks at the question of the origin of the works contained in the Old Testament Apocrypha.

EXCURSUS Observations on Josephus and Philo

The most massive corpora of allegedly Jewish texts transmitted only by Christians are the collections of works attributed to the first-century CE writers Philo of Alexandria and Flavius Josephus. The transmission of these works is relevant to the question of the transmission of the Old Testament Apocrypha and pseudepigrapha, although the problems are also somewhat different. The Apocrypha and pseudepigrapha are

[89] Louis H. Feldman, 'Flavius Josephus Revisited: The Man, His Writings, and His Significance,' *ANRW* 21.2:763-862; Tessa Rajak, *Josephus: The Historian and His Society* (London: Duckworth, 1983); Harold W. Attridge, 'Josephus and His Works,' in *Jewish Writings of the Second Temple Period: Apocrypha, Pseudepigrapha, Qumran Sectarian Writings, Philo, Josephus* (ed. Michael E. Stone; CRINT 2.2; Philadelphia: Fortress, 1984), 185-232; Louis H. Feldman, 'Josephus,' *ABD*, 3:981-98. Secondary literature on Josephus to 1980 is surveyed by idem, *Josephus and Modern Scholarship (1937-1980)* (Berlin: de Gruyter, 1984). Feldman updates this bibliographic survey in 'A Selective Critical Bibliography of Josephus,' in Feldman and Hata (eds.), *Josephus, the Bible, and History*, 330-48. In recent years the University of Münster has sponsored a continuously updated Josephus Bibliography on the Internet at http://www.uni-muenster.de/Judaicum/Josephus/JosephusOnline-e.html.

shorter, usually anonymous works, some of which achieved a canonical or quasi-canonical status in some Christian communities, whereas the Philonic corpus is a collection of mostly philosophical and exegetical treatises and the Josephan corpus a set of longer historiographic works and autobiographic and apologetic treatises. The works of Philo and Josephus are also attributed to named and dated authors who write at times in the first person and about whose lives we are given some information. Neither corpus ever claimed or held scriptural status. The secondary literature on Philo and Josephus is vast and it is beyond the scope of this book to engage in a full-scale investigation of either. Fortunately, this is not necessary, since the Jewish origin of both sets of writings has long since been established on the basis of multiple, converging lines of argument.

Nevertheless, a very brief survey of the case for Jewish authorship of the Josephan and Philonic corpora, along with a review of the spurious and apocryphal works sometimes attributed to them, is in order. In addition I look at one passage by Josephus in the *Antiquities* which paraphrases the book of Leviticus and thus covers the same ground as the Latin poetic paraphrase of Leviticus in the *Heptateuchos*, discussed in Chapter Two. The passage in the *Antiquities* provides some useful information when read alongside the *Leviticus* section of the *Heptateuchos*.

Since part of the evidence for the authentication of the works of Philo comes from Josephus, I begin my analysis with the latter.

JOSEPHUS‒‒ ‒‒Four documents are universally accepted as genuine works by Josephus. The *Jewish War* (*Bellum Judaicum*) chronicles the revolt of the Judeans against the Romans and its suppression in 66-73 or 74 C E. Josephus tells us that he presented the Greek text of the *Jewish War* to Vespasian and Titus, so it must have been written by 79 C E, although the final book, Book 7, may have been published closer to the end of the century. He also mentions an earlier Aramaic version, now lost, whose exact nature and extent remains elusive. The *Jewish Antiquities* (*Antiquitates Judaicae*) surveys all of Jewish history from creation to the eve of the war with the Romans and was written c. 93-94 C E. The *Life* (*Vita*) is an autobiographical account of the life of Josephus with a heavy emphasis on justifying his actions in Galilee during the war and it was probably published around 95 C E. *Against Apion* (*Contra Apionem*), an apology for Judaism in response to anti-Semitic accusations of the Greeks, was probably written around the turn of the century, near the end of Josephus' life.[89]

Overall, there is tolerably good evidence for the text of the works of Josephus, although the large quantity of manuscripts is not necessarily matched by a comparable quality[90] Indeed, it has been asserted that the text of the *Antiquities* is the most corrupt Greek text from antiquity.[91] The *Testimonium Flavianum* (the famous reference to Jesus in *Ant.* 18.63-64) does little to undermine such a conclusion: it seems to indicate that Christians were not above tampering with Josephus' text, although, to be fair, the temptation to do so with this passage must have been unbearable and the Christian reviser has actually acted with considerable restraint, which may well hint that overall the text of the works of

___ 90 ___ Heinz Schreckenberg, *Die Flavius-Josephus-Tradition in Antike und Mitteralter* (ALGHJ 5; Leiden: Brill, 1972). ___ ___ 91 ___ See Feldman's comments on this assertion by Abraham Schalit (Feldman, *Josephus in Modern Scholarship*, 22). ___ 92 ___ For a recent history of the discussion of the *Testimonium Flavianum* see Alice Whealey, *Josephus on Jesus: The Testimonium Flavianun Controversy from Late Antiquity to Modern Times* (Studies in Biblical Literature 36; New York: Lang, 2003). Also see Feldman, 'Flavius Josephus Revisited,' 821-38; and Steve Mason, *Josephus and the New Testament* (Peabody, Mass.: Hendrickson, 1992), 151-84. ___ 93 ___ Schreckenberg, *Die Flavius-Josephus-Tradition*, 69-88; idem, 'The Works of Josephus and the Early Christian Church,' in *Josephus, Judaism, and Christianity* (ed. Louis H. Feldman and Gohei Hata; Detroit: Wayne State University Press, 1987), 315-24; Wataru Mizugaki, 'Origen and Josephus,' in ibid., 325-37; Michael E. Hardwick, *Josephus as an Historical Source in Patristic Literature through Eusebius* (Atlanta: Scholars Press, 1989); Whealey, *Josephus on Jesus*, 7-29. ___ 94 ___ An old but still useful survey of the Judaism of Josephus is James A. Montgomery, 'The Religion of Flavius Josephus,' *JQR* 40 (1920-21): 277-305. More recently, E. P. Sanders has used Josephus as one of his major sources for reconstructing first-century Judaism in *Judaism: Practice & Belief 63 BCE - 66 CE* (Philadelphia: Trinity, 1992). For specific references see the Index of Passages, pp. 567-72. See also Steve Mason, 'Josephus and Judaism,' in *The Encyclopedia of Judaism* (3 vols.; ed. Jacob Neusner, Alan J. Avery-Peck, and William S. Green; Leiden: Brill, 2000), 2:546-63. ___ 95 ___ Magen Broshi, 'The Credibility of Josephus,' *JJS* 33 (1982): 379-84; Zeev Safrai, 'The Description of the Land of Israel in Josephus' Works,' in Feldman and Hata (eds.), *Josephus, the Bible, and History*, 295-324; Benjamin Mazar, 'Josephus Flavius and the Archaeological Excavations in Jerusalem,' in ibid., 325-29; Mordechai Aviam and Peter Richardson, 'Appendix A: Josephus' Galilee in Archaeological Perspective,' in Steve Mason, *Flavius Josephus: Translation and Commentary*, Vol. 9, *Life of Josephus* (Leiden: Brill, 2001), 177-209; Steve Mason, 'Contradiction or Counterpoint? Josephus and Historical Method,' *Review of Rabbinic Judaism* 6 (2003): 145-88. Yigael Yadin presents an overview of Josephus' account of the fall of Masada in light of the archaeological evidence in *Masada: Herod's Fortress and the Zealots' Last Stand* (Tel Aviv: Steimatzky, 1966). Although the Yadin excavations show that Josephus basic account of the Roman siege of the defenders of Masada is correct, it does not follow that the specifics of his story of the breach of the wall and the mass suicide of the defenders can be trusted. See, for example, Shaye J. D. Cohen, 'Masada: Literary Tradition, Archaeological Remains, and the Credibility of Josephus,' *JJS* 33 (1982): 385-405; Raymond R. Newell, 'The Forms and Historical Value of Josephus' Suicide Accounts,' in Feldman and Hata (eds.), *Josephus, the Bible, and History*, 278-94. ___ 96 ___ Shaye J. D. Cohen, *Josephus in Galilee and Rome: His*

Josephus has been treated with respect for the most part.[92] The safest approach when dealing with the works of Josephus is to consider the text of each passage on its own merits, with attention both to textual variants in the manuscripts and to internal factors that may indicate corruption. It must be admitted that, apart from the *Testimonium Flavianum* and related passages, the text of Josephus has often not been approached with this care. Nevertheless, there is no evidence for widespread deliberate distortion of the documents and we can be confident regarding recurrent themes and overall viewpoints in them, whether or not our text of any given passage may be trusted.

Josephus is mentioned by Suetonius in *Vesp.* 5.6.6 and is cited a number of times as a Jewish historian by Christian and non-Christian gentile writers between the end of the second century and the middle of the third. Origen probably knew the whole Josephan corpus and Eusebius certainly did.[93] All of Josephus' works are replete with Jewish signature features of all sorts. The sabbath, circumcision, the Mosaic Law, the purity laws and rituals, the food taboos, the Jewish festivals, the sabbatical year, the Jerusalem temple and its cult and sacrifices, and the Aaronid priesthood (of which Josephus was a member) are all presented as social realities of Josephus' time. Jewish national interests are central to the narratives and he often discusses conflicting religious and nationalistic views and agendas among first-century Jews, including the Pharisees, the Sadducees, the Essenes, the Zealots, the Sicarii, the factions occupying Jerusalem and the temple during the Roman siege, and countless lesser intra-Jewish conflicts and compromises over religious and political issues.[94] His narratives are intertwined inextricably with the history and major figures of the Roman Empire in the first century, such as Julius Caesar, Mark Antony and Cleopatra, Augustus, Tiberius, Gaius, Claudius, Nero, Vespasian, and Titus. Josephus shows a detailed familiarity with the geography of first-century Palestine and many background elements in his narrative have been confirmed by archaeology.[95]

This is not to romanticize the Josephan corpus or present it as an infallible guide to first-century Judaism. Josephus is reasonably faithful to his sources but he is tendentious, self-serving, and frequently self-contradictory. Each statement he makes needs to be weighed in light of the totality of the historical and archaeological evidence. The veracity of data that come only from him is often all but impossible to evaluate except as evidence for the composition and context of his works themselves.[96] But nevertheless, it is not in doubt that Josephus was the author of these four works and that we have their texts in fairly well-preserved form.

Josephus' Apocrypha and Spuria The authenticity of the four documents by Josephus being granted, it must be noted that a number of other works have been attributed to him or to someone with his name, although it is now recognized that none of them was written by him. Eusebius, Jerome, and part of the manuscript tradition claim that Josephus was the author of *4 Maccabees*. I have discussed the reasons for rejecting this claim earlier in this chapter.

A Greek work generally given the title *De Universo*[97] is known from five or six sources. In the *Elenchus* (or *Philosophumena*) the author refers to one of his earlier treatises under this name; a statue found in Rome in the sixteenth century and now in the Vatican Library includes this work in a list of writings by the unnamed subject of the statue; John Philoponus in his work *De Opificio Mundi* attributes this text to 'Josephus the Hebrew;' a fragment of the *Sacra Parallela*, attributed to John Damascene, also gives Josephus as the author; and Photius in the *Bi-*

Vita and Development as a Historian (Columbia Studies in the Classical Tradition 8; Leiden: Brill, 1979). [97] Περὶ τῆς τοῦ παντός οὐσίας according to the *Elenchus*. The other sources give the same title or a similar one. [98] Feldman, *Josephus and Modern Scholarship*, 390; Malley, 'Four Unedited Fragments of the *De Universo* of the Pseudo-Josephus Found in the *Chronicon* of George Hamartolos (Coislin 305),' *JTS* 16 (1965): 13-25. [99] Pierre Nautin, *Hippolyte et Josipe, Contribution à l'histoire de la littérature chrétienne du troisième siècle* (Études et textes pour l'histoire du dogme de la Trinité 1; Paris, 1947); B. Capelle, 'Hippolyte de Rome,' *Recherches de théologie ancienne et médiévale* 17 (1950): 145-74; B. Botte, 'Note sur l'auteur du *De universo* attribué à saint Hippolyte,' *Recherches de théologie ancienne et médiévale* 18 (1951): 5-18; P. Nautin, 'La controverse su l'auteur de l'"Elenchos,"' *Revue d'histoire ecclésiastique* 47 (1942): 5-43; idem, 'L'homélie d'Hippolyte sur le psautier et les œuvres de Josipe,' *Revue de l'histoire des religions* 179 (1971): 137-79; Williams, *Stylometric Authorship Studies*, 151-200. [100] Jacques Moreau, 'Observations sur l'Ὑπομνηστικὸν βιβλίον Ἰωσήππου,' *Byzantion* 25-27 (1955-57): 241-76; Robert M. Grant and Glen W. Menzies, *Joseph's Bible Notes (Hypomnesticon): Introduction, Translation, and Notes* (SBLTT 41; Early Christian Series 9; Atlanta: Scholars Press, 1996). The latter is reviewed with numerous corrections by P.W. van der Horst in *BO* 54 (1997): 195-97. [101] The Iosippos scholia are published by Joseph Ziegler in *Jeremias; Baruch; Threni; Epistula Jeremiae* (Septuaginta: Vetus Testamentum Graecum Auctoritate Academiae Scientiarum Gottingensis 15; Göttingen: Vandenhoeck & Ruprecht, 1976) (note esp. p. 106). This material is also mentioned by Robert Devreesse in *Introduction à l'étude des manuscrits grecs* (Paris: Klincksieck, 1954), 130. The most detailed anal-ysis of these scolia and their origin is by Kipper in 'Josipo (ou Josefo), Traduto Grego Quase Desconhecido,' *Revista de Cultura Biblica* (São Paulo) 5 (1961): 298-307, 387-95, 446-56.

---

bliotheca describes the work, quotes from it, and lists three titles for it, one of which attributes it to Josephus. In addition, William J. Malley has noted four passages in the oldest manuscript of the *Chronicon* of George Hamartolos which are introduced as being by 'Josephus' 'in *The Things According to the Greeks*' (ἐν τοῖς καθ' Ἑλλήνων), and Malley argues that these are additional fragments of the *De Universo*.[98] The attribution to Josephus is rejected because

a the *Elenchus* and the works listed on the Vatican statue are understood by some, but not all, scholars to be by the church father Hippolytus;

b Photius himself was skeptical about Josephan authorship;

c both Photius and the fragment in the *Sacra Parallela* indicate that the *De Universo* mentioned Christ;

d Williams has shown on stylometric grounds that the *De Universo* is not written in the normal style of Josephus.[99]

A Greek work with the title *Notebook of Josephus* (Ὑπομνηστικὸν βιβλίον Ἰωσήππου) survives in a single manuscript (Cambridge Ff. 1.24) and consists of 167 questions and answers on matters pertaining to the scriptures and the early church. It uses the LXX, Josephus, and various church fathers as sources. The most recent editors have dated it to around 400, although its present form includes material that dates from the ninth century or later, and they have suggested Alexandria as a likely provenance. The author may have been named Joseph or the treatise may have acquired the name Josephus because it made extensive use of the works of Flavius Josephus.[100]

A Greek biblical manuscript, Barberinus Gr. 549, preserves 100 citations in marginal notes of a translation of Jeremiah attributed to one 'Iosippos' (Ἰώσιππος). Iossipos is cited occasionally elsewhere and seems to have translated other biblical books. Theodoret of Cyrus refers to him as Ἰωάννης Ἰωσήπος. The translation seems to be independent of the LXX or other Greek recensions, although it shares some readings with the Latin Vulgate and may be indirectly dependent on it. It shares Jerome's messianic exegesis of Jer 38 (32):22 in light of Isa 7:14, making it likely that the author was a Christian. Since the translation is mentioned by Theodoret (d. c. 458) and Jerome does not refer to it, Balduino Kipper argues that it was probably made in the fifth or sixth century CE. It has no connection with Josephus or his works.[101]

In his work *On the Birth of Christ*, Joannes, the eighth-century archbishop of Nicea, includes a forged exchange of letters between Juvenal of Jerusalem, Cyril of Jerusalem, and Pope Julius, in which the Pope cites a book of the chronographer Josephus, allegedly captured by Titus during the Jewish war with Rome, in support of his calculation of the date of birth of Jesus. The forged correspondence reflects debate in the church about the proper date for the celebration of Christmas and on this basis Wolfgang Speyer dates the composition of the letters to the sixth century.[102]

Finally, Speyer notes that an Arabic infancy Gospel refers to 'the book of Joseph the priest, who lived in the time of Christ; some, however, say he was Caiaphas.' Presumably Speyer understands that those who did not identify this Joseph with Caiaphas took him to be Josephus.[103]

Josephus As an Empirical Model ⸺ ⸺ There is one passage in the *Antiquities* of which I wish to take special note: the section in which Josephus summarizes the content of the book of Leviticus (*Ant.* 3.188-286). It is heuristically useful to compare Josephus' treatment of Leviticus with that of the author of the *Heptateuchos* covered in Chapter Two, so I consider the former here as an empirical model functioning as a foil to the latter.

Josephus begins his paraphrase of this material with the appointment of Aaron as high priest, referring to the assembly of the people in Exod 28:1 and Lev 8:1 and expanding considerably the brief speech of Moses in Lev 8:5 (§188-192). Josephus refers briefly to the making of coverings for the Tabernacle and its paraphernalia (§193; an unscriptural detail), then describes the institution of the half-shekel tax according to Exod 30:11-16; 38:25-26 (§§194-96) and the preparation of the anointing oil and perfumes for the divine services as per Exod 30:22-38 and 2 Chr 13:11 (§§197-99), followed by praise of the craftsmen, the consecration of the tabernacle, and its ratification by God's manifestation of his presence (§§200-203; cf. Exod 35:30-36:1; 40:17-34). He proceeds with a description of the consecration ceremony for Aaron and his sons found in Exodus 29 and Leviticus 8-9 (§§204-7) and the story of the ill-fated attempt of Nadab and Abihu at cultic inde-

⸺[102]⸺ Speyer, *Bücherfunde in der Glaubenswerbung der Antike: Mit einem Ausblick auf Mittelalter und Neuzeit* (Hypomnemata 24; Göttingen: Vandenhoeck & Ruprecht, 1970), 139. See also idem, *Die Literarische Fälschung in heidnischen und christlichen Altertum: ein Versuch ihrer Deutung* (Munich: Beck, 1971), 242. The text is published in PG 96:1424-50, esp. cols. 1441-44. ⸺ ⸺[103]⸺ Speyer, *Die Literarische Fälschung*, 241-42. Cf. J. K. Elliott, *The Apocryphal New Testament* (Oxford: Clarendon, 1993), 100, 102.

pendence found in Lev 10:1-7 (§§208-11). There follow an expanded interpretation of Moses' doings in the tabernacle according to Num 7: 89 (§§212-13) and a digression on the Urim and Thummim (§§214-18; cf. Exod 28:30; Lev 8:8; Num 27:21).

Next Josephus summarizes the sacrifices of the twelve tribes according to Numbers 7 and returns to v. 89 to praise the laws revealed to Moses (§§219-23). He then sets out to describe some of the laws concerning purifications and sacred rites (§224). He begins with the latter, summarizing the rules for holocausts for individuals in Leviticus 1 (§§225-27); peace offerings ('thank offerings') in Leviticus 3 (§§228-29); sin offerings, with alternate instructions for the poor, in Leviticus 5 (§230); sacrifices for unwitting sins of lay people in Lev 4:27-35 (§231); sacrifices for deliberate sins in Leviticus 6:1-7 and the sins of rulers in Lev 4: 22-26; public and private offerings of cereal, oil, and wine in Num 15: 4-10 (§§232-34); offerings of fine flour in Lev 2:1-3, 6:14-23 (§235); and some miscellaneous rules concerning sacrifices in Lev 22:27-30 (§236). He moves on to daily, sabbath, and new moon sacrifices (§§237-38; cf. Exod 29:38-42; Num 28:1-15) and then to the major annual festivals: the Festival of Trumpets and the Day of Atonement as per Leviticus 16 and Num 29:1-11 (§§239-43); the Festival of Booths as per Lev 23: 33-43 and Num 29:12-38 (§§244-47); Passover and the offering of first fruits as per Lev 23:5-14 and Num 28:16-25 (§§248-51); and Pentecost as per Lev 23:15-21 and Num 28:26-31 (§§252-53). He then discusses the bread of the Presence in Lev 24:5-9 (§§255-56) and the priestly offering in Lev 6:12-16 (E V 6:19-23) (§257).

As for purification laws, Josephus summarizes the consecration of the Levites in Num 3:5-10 (§258), then moves on to the rules concerning animals fit and unfit for food in Leviticus 11, which he promises to explain in detail in a future work (§259), and the prohibition of the consumption of blood, that which dies of itself, and animal fat, in Lev 7:22-27, 11:39-40, and 17:10-16 (§260). He refers briefly to the laws concerning leprosy, menstruation, and contact with the dead in Leviticus 13-15 and Num 19:1-13 (§§261-64), and accordingly ridicules those who claim that Moses was a leper (§§265-68). Then he summarizes the rules for purification of women after childbirth in Leviticus 12 (§269) and the rite for testing a suspected adulteress in Num 5:11-31 (§§270-73).

Josephus summarizes the laws for personal relationships in Lev 20: 10-21 (§§274-75), the special limits on contact with the dead and the special marriage limitations for priests and the high priest in Lev 21:1-15

($\S\S$ 276-77), the laws concerning physical blemishes for both priests and sacrificial victims in Lev 21:16-23, 22:17-25, and the prohibition against priests drinking wine while on duty in Lev 10:8-11 ($\S\S$ 278-79). Next he gives an account of the sabbatical year in Lev 25:1-7 and the jubilee year in Lev 25:8-34 ($\S\S$ 280-85). He concludes by reaffirming that this law code was by God to Moses on Mount Sinai and passed on to the Hebrews in written form ($\S$ 286).

Josephus' summary of Leviticus is not an exact analogy to the summary of the same book in the *Heptateuchos*. Although they both set out to retell the scriptural narrative, in this section Josephus explicitly organizes his material in certain categories rather than in the order of the text and he regularly draws on other scriptural passages when he finds them to be relevant. Pseudo-Cyprianus, however, covers the material in Leviticus in the biblical order and without reference to other passages. Josephus is also more inclined to add to the text or alter details, although Pseudo-Cyprianus is not entirely immune to this temptation.[104] Nevertheless, a comparison of the two paraphrases of Leviticus is instructive.

Pseudo-Cyprianus adopts the persona of the narrator of Leviticus, speaking in the first person plural about observation of the food taboos and sometimes addressing the reader in the second person, usually (but not quite always) about matters of interest to boundary-maintaining Christians as well as Jews. Like Pseudo-Cyprianus, Josephus usually presents the material in the third person, although not infrequently he speaks in the first person singular, usually to allude to passages elsewhere in the *Antiquities* or in his promised (but never published) work on Jewish customs (e.g., $\S\S$ 188, 205, 206, 209, 214, 215-18, 223, 224, 257; and

---

[104] Some of Josephus' additions and alterations include the references to dew in $\S$ 203; the mention of myrtle in the celebration of Booths in $\S$ 245; the understanding of the priestly offering in Lev 6:19-23 as required twice-daily, whereas the biblical text seems to regard it as a one-time ordination offering ($\S$ 257); the prohibition of the eating of cauls in $\S$ 261; and the expulsion of those with a flux from the city in $\S$ 262. See Chapter Two for changes introduced by Pseudo-Cyprianus. [105] Some of the missing material from Leviticus is included in the paraphrase of the Deuteronomic laws in *Ant*. 4.199-301: the mixing of kinds in Lev 19:19 ($\S$ 228); rules for gleaning in Lev 19:9-10 ($\S$ 231-32); laws concerning whom a priest may marry in Lev 21:7 (which in $\S$ 245, as in the *Heptateuchos*, are democratized to apply to all men, although they are applied specifically to the priests in *Ant*. 3.276); rules against reviling the disabled in Lev 19:14 ($\S$ 276); and the *lex talionis* in Lev 24:19-20 ($\S$ 280).

[first-person plural] 247, 260). He also speaks in the first person plural as a member of the 'people' who observe these laws and who suffer false accusations from outsiders (§§248-50, Passover; §§260-61, food taboos; §268, accusations).

In this summary Josephus omits the following material from Leviticus: the cereal offerings in 2:4-16 (except the rule about salting all sacrifices, which is implied in §227); details regarding offerings for unwitting sins of individuals and the community in Lev 4:1-21; details regarding burnt offerings and sin offerings in 6:9-18, 24-30; miscellaneous rules about how priests should eat the relevant offerings in 10:12-19; the food taboos of Leviticus 11, which receive but a bare mention, but Josephus promises to discuss them at length in his future work; the requirement of the sacrifice of all food animals before the tabernacle in Lev 17:1-9; the moral precepts and miscellaneous rules in Lev 18-19; 20:1-9, 22-27; the rules for who may eat the holy food in 22:1-17; some miscellaneous rules regarding animal sacrifices in 22:26-33; the story of the blaspheming half-breed Israelite in Lev 24:10-23; the blessings and curses in Chapter 26; and the rules for special vows and tithes in Chapter 27.

Given Josephus' agenda, this pattern of omissions makes good sense. He promises to mention 'some few' of the rules for purification and sacrifice and repeatedly promises to come back to them in another work. Although he omits some material on cereal offerings, unwitting sins, burnt offerings, sin offerings, and various rules about the priests, he does give considerable coverage to all these subjects. The requirement to sacrifice all food animals in front of the tabernacle would have been impracticable in his time and presumably it was not followed. Moral precepts were outside his agenda for this passage, so he summarizes some of those in Chapter 20 and ignores the rest. The story of the blaspheming half-Israelite and the material in Chapters 26 and 27 were not relevant to his immediate purpose.[105]

Josephus and the *Heptateuchos* omit some material in common: small parts of the sacrificial instructions and priestly ordination in Lev 1-9; the details of the food taboos in Leviticus 11 (although Josephus promises to cover them later); the sacrificial rules in Lev 17:1-9 (although Jews presumably did not keep them in Josephus' time either); much of the moral and sometimes cultic instruction in Leviticus 18-20 (although both include representative samples); and the *lex talionis* in Leviticus 24. Nevertheless, the contrast between them is striking. The *Heptateuchos* leaves out almost the entirety of the sacrificial rules in Leviticus 1-9 and completely ignores the bread of the Presence, the sabbath, the Jewish festivals, the sabbatical year, and the jubilee year. Josephus covers them all. His interest in the ritual cult marks him out as an observant Jew, just as Pseudo-Cyprian's selective neglect of these matters shows that he or she is not one.

[106] Major bibliographical resources for Philo include Roberto Radice and David T. Runia, *Philo of Alexandria: An Annotated Bibliography 1937-1986* (VCSup 8; Leiden: Brill, 1988) and David T. Runia, *Philo of Alexandria: An Annotated Bibliography 1987-1996* (VCSup 57; Leiden: Brill, 2000). In addition each volume of the *Studia Philonica Annual* contains a bibliographical update for the previous year. Jenny Morris provides a useful overview of Philonic studies in 'The Jewish Philosopher Philo,' in Emil Schürer, *The History of the Jewish People in the Age of Jesus Christ (175 B.C.–A.D. 135)* (3 vols.; rev. ed.; ed. Geza Vermes, Fergus Millar, and Martin Goodman; Edinburgh: Clark, 1973-86), 3.2:809-89. [107] A key work on the text and transmission of Philo is David T. Runia, *Philo in Early Christian Literature: A Survey* (CRINT 3.3; Minneapolis: Fortress, 1993). A special section of *Studia Philonica Annual* 6 (1994) contains several articles in response to Runia's book: Abraham Terian, 'Notes on the Transmission of the Philonic Corpus,' pp. 91-95; Annewies van den Hoek, 'Philo in the Alexandrian Tradition,' pp. 96-99; Robert L. Wilken, 'Philo in the Fourth Century,' pp. 100-102; David Winston, 'Philo's *Nachleben* in Judaism,' pp. 103-10. Note also J. C. M. van Winden, 'Quotations from Philo in Clement of Alexandria's Protrepticus,' *VC* 32 (1978): 208-13; Annewies van den Hoek, *Clement of Alexandria and His Use of Philo in the Stromateis: An Early Christian Reshaping of a Jewish Model* (VCSup 3; Leiden: Brill, 1988); Folkhart Siegert, 'Der armenische Philon: Textbestand, Editionen, Forschungsgeschichte,' *BHT* 100 (1989): 353-69; James R. Royse, *The Spurious Texts of Philo of Alexandria: A Study of Textual Transmission and Corruption* (ALGHJ 22; Leiden: Brill, 1991); Runia, 'References to Philo from Josephus up to 1000 A.D.,' *Studia Philonica Annual* 6 (1994): 111-21, an expanded and corrected version of the list in Runia, *Philo in Early Christian Literature*, 348-56; idem, 'Philonica in the *Catana in Genesim*,' *Studia Philonica Annual* 11 (1999): 113-20; van den Hoek, 'Philo and Origen: A Descriptive Catalogue of Their Relationship,' *Studia Philonica Annual* 12 (2000): 44-121. Clement of Alexandria knew Philo was a philosopher (a 'Pythagorean') who wrote on Jewish matters and published a life of Moses; he probably knew Philo was a Jew; and he was familiar with most of our Philonic corpus. Origen refers to Philo three times by name, calling him a philosopher and praising his intelligence. When he moved from Alexandria to Caesarea in 233, he brought with him copies of nearly the whole corpus of the works of Philo which survive in Greek and these copies were the archetype of virtually the entirety of our Greek manuscript tradition apart from the Greek papyri. Eusebius, bishop of Caesarea, erroneously assumed that Philo had converted to Christianity. He evidently derived his information about Philo from the Episcopal library in Casearea in the fourth century. The post-Eusebian history of the transmission of Philo's works in Christendom cannot occupy us here. In most of the tradition he was erroneously remembered as a convert to Christianity and even a bishop. See J. Edgar Bruns, 'Philo Christianus: The Debris of a Legend,' *HTR* 66 (1973): 141-45; Runia, *Philo in Early Christian Literature*, passim but esp. pp. 5-33; idem, 'Philo of Alexandria and the Beginnings of Christian Thought,' *Studia Philonica Annual* 7 (1995): 143-60. [108] A few such possibilities are collected by Royce in *Spurious Texts*, 146-47. [109] James R. Royse, 'Philo's Divisions of His Works into Books,' *Studia Philonica Annual* 13 (2001): 59-85. [110] Royse, *Spurious Texts*, 145-46. For *Eternity*, see the Norwegian dissertation by Roald

PHILO _____ _____ There is a large corpus of complete or fragmentary treatises whose attribution to Philo is widely, although in some cases not universally, accepted.[106] We also know of a number of Philonic treatises that are now lost. Overall the textual situation of the major works attributed to Philo is tolerably good.[107] The base for the bulk of our manuscript tradition is regrettably narrow, evidently amounting to single exemplars of each work brought out of Alexandria by Origen in the third century. But these exemplars come from Philo's city and it is not unreasonable to assume that the text had been transmitted with care up to that point. Important portions of the Philonic corpus survive only in Armenian, but they at least were translated extremely literally, rendering retroversion of the *Vorlage* more practicable than is usually the case. There is no text-critical or internal evidence for any extensive deliberate tampering with Philo's text by the Christian tradents, although the possibility of corruptions and minor interpolations must be reckoned with for any given passage.[108] Although we must take any given passage on its own terms and apply textual criticism and emendation as seems appropriate, we may assume that the text is our hands is basically reliable and that, at the very minimum, pervasive themes and frequently mentioned ideas in the corpus really do go back to Philo.

Evaluation of the Philonic corpus is further complicated by the fact that, unlike the works of Josephus, the works of Philo have come down to us as a collection of many individual treatises, so we must be mindful of the danger that one or another of them is spurious even though the bulk of the corpus is genuine. Philo himself occasionally makes cross references in one work to another,[109] which is of some help for delineating the genuine works, but often the judgment must be made on the basis of external attestation and style and content of the individual work. Most of the extant treatises are generally accepted as genuine, but doubts have been raised at one time or another concerning *Contemplative Life, Eternity, Providence, Animals,* and *God.*[110] I should be inclined also to take the Philonic authorship of the Armenian fragment of what may be *Concerning Numbers* to be less secure than other treatises. The evidence of these works should perhaps be used with more caution than the rest of the corpus.

As with Josephus, some of the works in the Philonic corpus give us some personal information about Philo. These place him in Alexandria and Rome in the first half of the first century C E. The treatise *Flaccus* tells of the anti-Jewish sentiment in Alexandria which culminated in the persecution of the Jews in 38 C E, aided and abetted by the prefect of Alexandria and Egypt named in the title. The treatise *Embassy* covers the same ground briefly but also deals with the disastrous attempt by the self-divinizing Emperor Gaius to install an enormous statue of himself in the Jerusalem temple. Philo was part of a delegation sent to the Emperor after the pogrom, which tried to persuade him to abandon his plans for the image in the temple, and Josephus mentions Philo's role in these events in *Ant.* 18.259. *Flaccus* and *Embassy* give us some information about the Alexandrian Jewish community and place it in the historical context of figures such as Tiberius, Gaius, Claudius, and Herod Agrippa.

The Jewish nature of the Philonic corpus is clear and pervasive.[111]

Skarsten, 'Forfatterproblemet ved *De aeternitate mundi* i Corpus Philonicum' (Ph. D. diss., University of Bergen, 1987), which argues on the basis of computer analysis of vocabulary that the attribution of *Eternity* to Philo is spurious. This dissertation, which I have not seen, was expanded, translated into English, and published by the University of Bergen in 1996 with the title *An Authorship Problem: De Aeternitate Mundi in Corpus Philonicum*. It was brought to my attention by Torrey Seland in a private communication and he also mentioned it on his Philo of Alexandria weblog (http://philoblogger.blogspot.com/) on 24 September 2004. [111] Philo's beliefs about what precisely Judaism is are complex and cannot be treated in any detail here. Ellen Birnbaum has studied what being a Jew meant to Philo and has concluded that he distinguished between 'Israel' as a 'race' or 'class' (γένος) which 'sees God,' and the 'Jews' who are a 'nation' (ἔθνος) who worship the one God and follow particular customs and laws. The two categories overlap but are not identical, although monotheism is a *sine qua non* for both. It appears that it was possible for gentiles to be members of either group, although the conditions for membership, apart from belief in monotheism, seem not to have been identical. See *The Place of Judaism in Philo's Thought: Israel, Jews, and Proselytes* (BJS 290; Studia Philonica Monographs 2; Atlanta: Scholars Press, 1996). Maren R. Niehoff explores Philo's view of Jewish identity and culture as social constructs in *Philo on Jewish Identity and Culture* (TSAJ 86; Tübingen: Mohr Siebeck, 2001). [112] Alan Mendelson, *Philo's Jewish Identity* (BJS 161; Atlanta: Scholars Press, 1988), 71-75, 115-38; Georg Græsholt, 'Philo of Alexandria: Some Typical Traits of his Jewish Identity,' *Classica et Mediaevalia* 43 (1992): 97-110, esp. pp. 104-110; Sarah Pearce, 'Belonging and Not Belonging: Local Perspectives in Philo of Alexandria,' in *Jewish Local Patriotism and Self-Identification in the Graeco-Roman Period* (ed. Siân Jones and Sarah Pearce; JSPSup 31; Sheffield: Sheffield Academic Press, 1998), 79-105; Niehoff, *Philo on Jewish Identity and Culture*, 17-74, 111-58. [113] Mendelson, *Philo's Jewish Identity*, 1-15, 22-28. Sanders also uses Philo as an important source for his reconstruction of first-century Judaism in *Judaism: Practice & Belief*. For specific references see his Index of Passages, pp. 577-78. Monotheism was, of course, an integral part of Philo's Jewish identity, although it is not relevant for my purposes since Christians accepted the belief in one God as well (although nuanced to accommodate the doctrine of Christ as God incarnate). For Philo's monotheism see Mendelson, *Philo's Jewish Identity*, 29-49; Græsholt, 'Typical Traits,' 100-101. [114] Royse, *Spurious Texts*, 134; Runia, *Philo in Early Christian Literature*, 318-19. [115] Royse, *Spurious Texts*. [116] Ibid., 134-44.

Philo wrote as a Jew and was immersed in Jewish national and political interests, such as those described in the previous paragraph. Jewish ethnic identity among the polytheistic nations was also a significant issue for him. He emphasized the importance of endogamous marriage and presented a highly negative stereotype of the Egyptians, although his view of the Greeks and Romans was much less hostile.[112] He provides evidence for various types of Judaism ranging from the radical allegorists who considered ritual praxis optional, to the literalists who rejected allegorical interpretation of the laws, to secularized Jews who observed the Day of Atonement but otherwise ignored Jewish rituals and festivals, to esoteric movements such as the Essenes and the Therapeutae. Nevertheless, he himself was clearly a boundary-maintaining Jew who did not use his allegorical exegesis as an excuse for neglecting the ritual law.[113]

Philonic Apocrypha and Spuria........ As with Josephus, a number of works and fragments have been attributed to Philo but are generally agreed to be spurious, whether through misunderstanding or deliberate falsification. One of these, the *Interpretatio Hebraicorum nominum*, is now lost. Eusebius lists it as one of Philo's works in *Hist. eccl.* 2.18.7 and Jerome refers to it in the introduction to his translation of the *Onomasticon*, for which it evidently served as a basis. It was a Greek collection of etymologies of Hebrew words and, as such, is unlikely to have been written by Philo, who probably knew little or no Hebrew, although Philo's etymological comments in his works could naturally have misled some into thinking this work was his.[114] The others are still extant. Royse has isolated numerous passages in the catenae and florilegia which are incorrectly assigned to Philo, usually due to misunderstandings and copyist's errors.[115] His book also contains the most up-to-date available survey of Philo apocrypha and is a major source of information here.[116]

The manuscript tradition of Pseudo-Philo's *Liber Antiquitatum Biblicarum* assigns this work to Philo and transmits it with Jerome's *De Philone* and the Latin translation of QG. Philo was taken to be the author of the Wisdom of Solomon as early as the time of Jerome and perhaps in the Muratorian Canon. Both the *Liber Antiquitatum Biblicarum* and the Wisdom of Solomon are universally regarded to be Jewish (I am more confident of this for the second than the first) and non-Philonic. Their authorship is discussed, respectively, in this chapter and in the Excursus at the end of Chapter Four.

The Armenian manuscript tradition ascribes two sermons, on Jonah and on Samson, to Philo. It is generally agreed that neither is by Philo but both are of Jewish origin and from sometime in antiquity. A translation and commentary has recently been published in French and the editors have noted that these sermons are unlikely to be by Philo since they lack his philosophical interests and contradict some of the ideas in his genuine works.[117] Both sermons do seem to be Jewish: note the references to the Law in *De Jona* §§ 4, 115 and to the Jewish ethnic identity of preacher and audience in *De Sampsone* §§ 25, 42. But a full analysis of them is outside the scope of this book.

In 1816 Angelo Mai edited a Greek work whose title indicated that it was Philo's lost treatise *Every Fool is a Slave*. The title, however, did not fit the content and Mai concluded that it belonged to the lost material in the treatise *On the Virtues*, mentioned by Eusebius. Later it developed that

---

[117] Folker Siegert et al., *Pseudo-Philon: Prédications Synagogales: traduction, notes et commentaire* (SC 435; Paris: Cerf, 1999), esp. 33-34; Royse, *Spurious Texts*, 135. [118] Ibid., 136-38. [119] Ibid., 139-40. [120] Ibid., 141-43. [121] Ibid., 143-44. [122] Ibid., 135-36. [123] Ibid., 144.

the text was assigned to the fourteenth-century author George Gemistus Plethon in other manuscripts and Mai subsequently accepted him as the author.[118] A fragmentary Hermetic tractate entitled *Concerning God* (Περὶ θεοῦ) was taken initially to be by Philo, but this was soon demonstrated to be incorrect.[119] According to the late-seventh-century writer Anastasius Sinaita, the third-century writer Ammonius of Alexandria cited a dialogue between the 'unbelieving Jew Philo the philosopher' and Mnason (Acts 21:16). But the legend is dubious and a surviving 'dialogue between the Jews Papiscus and Philo and a Christian monk,' if it is related to the work known to Ammonius, has nothing to do with the historical Philo.[120] It has been suggested that the Greek treatise *De sublimate* (Περὶ ὕψους), also attributed to Longinus, was composed by Philo, but this proposal has not been found convincing so far.[121]

The treatise *De temporibus* (or *Breuiarium de temporibus*), published as a Philonic work by Giovanni Nanni (Ioannes Annius) in 1498, is actually a forgery, perhaps by the same Nanni.[122] Two other extant treatises attributed to Philo, the *De mundo* and the *De mercede meretricis*, consist of excerpts from some of Philo's genuine works.[123]

CHAPTER FOUR

INTRODUCTION

Many Old Testament pseudepigrapha have been argued at one time or another to be of Jewish origin or, more nebulously, to preserve a substantial amount of earlier Jewish tradition. In theory, all but one of the fifty-two works in Charlesworth's two *Old Testament Pseudepigrapha* volumes fall into one of these categories (the exception is *Aḥiqar*). It will be clear by now that I think that many of these pseudepigrapha are Christian compositions whose relationship to earlier Jewish traditions is very tenuous indeed. It is far beyond the scope of this book to discuss all the remaining pseudepigrapha in the Charlesworth volumes, let alone those not included in them. But in this chapter I consider briefly six pseud-epigrapha included by Charlesworth which are widely agreed to be Jewish works or to be based on a demonstrably Jewish *Urtext*. These texts exemplify many of the problems associated with attempts to establish the origins of ancient Old Testament pseudepigrapha and they must suffice as illustrations of how the methods advanced in this book dis-

---

¹ Editions of the Greek text include Charles Alexandre, *Oracula Sibyllina* (2 vols.; Paris: Didot, 1841-56); Aloisius Rzach, *Oracula Sibyllina* (Leipzig: Tempsky, 1891); Johannes Geffcken, *Die Oracula Sibyllina* (GCS 8; Leipzig: Hinrichs, 1902); Valentin Nikiprowetzky, *La troisième Sibylle* (Paris: La Haye, Mouton, 1970). John J. Collins has published an English translation of *Sibylline Oracles* 1-14 and fragments in 'Sibylline Oracles,' *OTP*, 1:317-472. There is an English translation of *Sibylline Oracles* 3-5 by H. C. O. Lanchester in 'The Sibylline Oracles,' *APOT*, 2:368-406 and a German translation by Helmut Merkel of the same three books in *Sibyllinen* (JSHRZ 5.8; Gütersloh, 1998). ² Collins, *The Sibylline Oracles of Egyptian Judaism* (SBLDS 13; Missoula, Mont.: Society of Biblical Literature and Scholars Press, 1974), 21-71; idem, 'The Provenance and Date of the Third Sibylline Oracle,' *BIJS* 2 (1974): 1-18; idem, *OTP*, 1:354-61; idem, 'The Development of the Sibylline Tradition,' *ANRW* 2.20.1:421-59, esp. pp. 430-36; idem, 'The Sibyl and the Potter: Political Propaganda in Ptolemaic Egypt,' in *Religious Propaganda and Missionary Competition in the New Testament World: Essays Honoring Dieter Georgi* (ed. Lukas Borman, Kelly Del Tredici, and Angela Standhardtinger; NTSup 74; Leiden: Brill, 1994), 57-69; Buitenwerf, *Book III of the Sibylline Oracles and Its Social Setting* (SVTP 17; Leiden: Brill, 2003). Collins has replied to Buitenwerf in 'The Third Sibyl Revisited,' in *Things Revealed: Studies in Early Jewish and Christian Literature in Honor of Michael E. Stone* (ed. Esther G. Chazon et al.; JSJSup 89; Leiden: Brill, 2004), 3-19.

Some Pseudepigrapha
of Debatable Origin

mantle many specious arguments for the Jewish origin of some pseud-epigrapha. I present the six works in roughly descending order in terms of the likelihood that a given work is Jewish. The first two (*Sibylline Oracles* 3 and 5) may well be Jewish, although other origins are possible. The next two (*Joseph and Aseneth* and the *Testament of Job*) may be Jewish, although there is no significant positive evidence in favor of this. As for the last two, I think that the *Testament of Abraham* is probably a Christian composition and the *Story of Zosimus* almost certainly is, as are its sources.

SIBYLLINE ORACLES, BOOK 3

The *Sibylline Oracles* stem from a Roman tradition about the ancient Greek prophetess (or prophetesses) who went by the title 'Sibyl.' These oracles were written in Greek hexameter and, according to legend, the best know collection was kept in Rome until it was destroyed in the fire in the temple of Jupiter in 83 B C E, although after the temple was rebuilt it was stocked again with a new collection of *Sibylline Oracles*. Nearly all the pre-Christian polytheistic *Sibylline Oracles* are lost: the surviving collection seems to have been composed almost entirely by writers who associated themselves with Jewish scriptural traditions, whether Jews, Christians, or God-fearers.[1] I focus my comments on two of these books, *Sibylline Oracles* Books 3 and 5.

   Sibylline Oracles 3 is a collection of oracles consisting of 829 lines (about fifty-seven hundred Greek words). Its exegetical difficulties are well illustrated by the different conclusions reached about it by John J. Collins and Rieuwerd Buitenwerf.[2] They agree that the beginning of Book 3 (Collins, lines 1-96; Buitenwerf, lines 1-92) was originally part of another work and does not belong with Book 3 (see below) and that line 776 is a Christian interpolation, but then their ways part. Collins places the composition of the bulk of the oracles in Book 3 (the 'main corpus') in 163-150 B C E, in Egypt, and probably in the circle of Onias the priest, sometime before the Jewish temple in Leontopolis (Helio-polis?) was built. The rest of the work (lines 350-488) consists of 'oracles against various nations,' which Collins assigns to different dates, as late as the first century B C E, with some oracles undateable, and different provenances, including Egypt and Asia Minor. Buitenwerf takes the book to be a literary unity and argues that *Sibylline Oracles* fragments 1 and 3 (quoted by Theophilus at the end of the second century C E) were also originally part of Book 3. He also argues that this composition was written sometime between about 80 and 40 B C E in Asia Minor in the aftermath of the Mithridatic wars. My aim is not to adjudicate between these views or try to advance beyond them – either of which would require a full-scale treatment far beyond the scope of this book – but rather to establish a minimalist range of possibilities for the origins on the basis of the methods worked out in the earlier chapters.

The two manuscript families that contain *Sibylline Oracles* 3 (known as ϕ and ψ) agree in demarcating lines 1-92 as a separate work (λόγος) from lines 93-829, although ψ includes lines 1-92 as part of the same λόγος as Books 1-2. Various notes in the manuscripts at this point in-dicate that the first part of Book 3 has been lost, and this is confirmed by lines 93ff., which begin *in media res*.[3] *Sibylline Oracles* 3 is quoted frequently by early Christian authors, including Theophilus, Athena-goras, Clement of Alexandria, Hippolytus, Pseudo-Justin, Lactantius, Eusebius of Caesarea (dependent on Josephus and Clement), and the Theosophy (dependent on Lactantius), as a genuine ancient prophecy. Since Lactantius seems to have known several Sibylline books and he quotes Book 3 along with fragments 1 and 3 as coming from the work of the Erythrian Sibyl, Buitenwerf argues reasonably plausibly that these two fragments belonged originally to the otherwise lost beginning of Book 3.[4]

At minimum, we can say that *Sibylline Oracles* fragments 1 and 3 existed by the end of the second century C E, when they were quoted by Theophilus, and that material from *Sib. Or.* 3:93-349, 489-829, Collins's

---

[3] Buitenwerf, *Book III*, 65-72. [4] Ibid., 72-91. [5] It is possible that Tatian (c. 160 CE) alludes to *Sib. Or.* 3:419-32 in *Oratio ad Graecos* 41, when he comments that the Sibyl lived before Homer, but he could have gotten this information elsewhere as well. See Buitenwerf, *Book III*, 87. [6] Ibid., 129-30. [7] Unless otherwise noted, all quotations of *Sibylline Oracles* 3 are from Buitenwerf's translation in *Book III*, sometimes with minor orthographic changes.

'main corpus,' is attested from that point on in quotations by various Christian authors. As far as I can tell, lines 350-488, Collins's 'oracles against various nations,' are not quoted by any early Christian author, and this fact offers some support to the theory that they were added to the book secondarily.[5] In the *Chronica,* Eusebius quotes a paraphrase of *Sib. Or.* 3:97-107 by Alexander Polyhistor. The same paraphrase is quoted as from the Sibyl by Josephus in *Ant.* 1:118-19.[6] It is likely, therefore, that at least the unit *Sib. Or.* 3:93-349, 489-829 existed by the late first century B C E and it could well be as early as the second century B C E. It is possible, of course, that lines 350-488 did as well, but we cannot be sure.

The main corpus shows a high density of Jewish signature features, although their exact significance is open to more than one interpretation.[7] It is extremely sympathetic to Jews and Judaism. Jews are 'the people of the great God' (*Sib. Or.* 3:194); they are 'pious men' who live around Solomon's temple and are the offspring of the righteous (213-15); a most righteous race (219); they are praised for avoiding astrology and divination and for caring for righteousness (219-47); they are a 'royal tribe whose race will never stumble' (288-89); they are a 'holy race of pious men' (573) who honor God's temple with sacrifices, they live blissfully under the Mosaic law, are prophets, eschew idolatry, worship God, and avoid immorality (574-600); and God loves them (711).

The Mosaic Law (*νομός*) is mentioned a number of times, but its content is curiously general. God gave the Law to Moses on Mount Sinai on two tablets and commanded the people to follow it (256-60); yet they will be exiled and the temple will fall because they did not keep it, but served idols instead (275-81); nevertheless, they should rely on God's holy laws (284); at the eschaton the Jewish people will live by God's Law, which seems to consist of worshiping God rather than idols and practicing proper sexual morality (573-600, esp. 580 and 600); their enemies shall be punished 'because they acknowledged neither the Law nor the judgment of the great God' (686-87); the gentiles will be converted to the Law and cease to be idolaters (719-23); God will bring about a common Law for the whole human race (757-58); and God is the one who at one time gave a holy Law to the pious (768-69). (Note also 'the word of the great God, the hymn of the Law' [*ἔννομον ὕμνον*]' in 246.) Jewish ritual praxis is scarcely ever alluded to: we are told that the whole earth is offended by Jewish customs (272) and in 591-94 we read that Jews accompanied their morning prayers with ritual ablutions (cf. *Let. Aris.* 305-306). Otherwise, there are no references to circumcision, ritual purity, food taboos, observance of the sabbath and the Jewish festivals, and the like. In effect, as Buitenwerf notes, the Mosaic Law is identified with natural law.[8]

The author does show considerable interest in the Jerusalem temple and its cult. The pious Jewish people live in the vicinity of Solomon's temple (213-15), but it was destroyed because they failed to keep the Law (265-81, 328-29). In 290-94 the Sibyl predicts (as a *vaticinium ex eventu*) the rebuilding of the (second) temple with the help of the Persians; this is the temple that the Babylonians destroyed (302). The Greeks are admonished to offer sacrifices at the temple of God in the future (564-70). The Jewish people will honor God's temple with sacrifices and offerings (573-79). At the time of the coming of the 'King from the sun' (Collins) or the 'king from the East' (Buitenwerf) (652), the kings of the nations will assault the temple but will be defeated (663-92), and afterwards 'all sons of the great God' will reside peacefully around the temple (702-703). Indeed, the gentiles will be converted and will worship in the temple (718-26), and bring offering to the temple, which will become the only place of worship for all future generations (772-80, 808).[9]

These are the elements of the main corpus of Book 3 which can be regarded as Jewish signature features. One entirely reasonable reading of the evidence is that this document originated among Hellenistic, Greek-speaking Jews. It is pro-Jewish, pro-temple, pro-sacrifice, and sings the praises of the Jewish Law. It refers to the nonscriptural practice of ablution before prayers, also attested in *Aristeas to Philocrates*, so the author seems to have knowledge of Judaism which goes beyond the scriptures. Nevertheless, it does not seem to me that a Jewish origin for the work is the only reasonable interpretation of the evidence. One can see how the strong emphasis on monotheism and sexual morality would have appealed to Christian tradents, but it is highly unlikely that the work (apart from line 776) is a Christian composition. Since Alexander

---

[8] Ibid., 339-42, 355-63. [9] The details of the writer's temple ideology and any possible relationship to the temple cult in Leontopolis are outside the scope of this inquiry. For discussions see Collins, *The Sibylline Oracles*, 44-55; Andrew Chester, 'The Sibyl and the Temple,' in *Templum Amicitiae: Essays on the Second Temple Presented to Ernst Bammel* (ed. William Horbury; JSNTSup 48; Sheffield: Sheffield Academic Press, 1991), 37-69, esp. pp. 38-47; Buitenwerf, *Book III*, 353-55.

Polyhistor seems to have known of the main corpus, we should probably date it sometime in the first century B C E at the latest, and quite likely in the mid-second century B C E on the basis of the references to the seventh king of Egypt. But another authorship possibility remains.

Although the writer repeatedly refers to the Law and advocates obeying it, when the contents of the Law are specified they seem mainly to involve proper worship of God, as opposed to idolatry, and sexual morality. Circumcision, the dietary laws, the sabbath, and the Jewish festivals are ignored. This viewpoint could reflect a liberal Judaism that was highly assimilated to its surrounding Hellenistic environment, whether in Egypt, Asia Minor, or elsewhere, but it could also reflect the perspective of a gentile God-fearer who was quite familiar with Judaism but who picked and chose what was appealing for his or her own religion. Such a writer might well have subsumed the Mosaic Law into natural law, considered the Jerusalem temple to be the central locus for the true worship of God, and yet cheerfully ignored any ritual practices that seemed primitive or unsophisticated. The work's interest in the conversion of gentiles supports this possibility. There are repeated appeals to the gentiles to convert. The are admonished not only to change their lifestyle and live righteously, but also to sacrifice in the temple (624-33); the Greeks are warned not to molest Jerusalem if they wish to share in the divine blessings (732-40); they should worship only God and refrain from sexual sins and infanticide (762-66), inasmuch as God 'will raise a kingdom forever among all people' (767-68) and the nations will come to the temple to worship and war shall come to an end (767-95, 808). It may be that the author was a devout gentile who looked forward to the conversion of the nations to a Hellenized and therefore sanitized form of Judaism.

It is true that Josephus alludes to lines 97-107 of the main corpus of *Sibylline Oracles* 3 in the *Antiquities* and it could be argued that this shows that Jews accepted the legitimacy of the main corpus as a true (although, granted, Sibylline and therefore gentile) prophecy about the Jewish people and therefore offers strong support for a Jewish origin. But it appears that Josephus found the passage in Alexander Polyhistor's work and relied on this gentile author's authority for its genuineness and antiquity. We have no evidence that Josephus or any other ancient Jew read or transmitted the main corpus or found it to be a plausible presentation of Judaism or Jewish views. In this case (and in contrast to the case of *Aristeas to Philocrates*), the use of this material by Josephus is not an argument in favor of Jewish origin.

In short, it is possible that the main corpus, apart from a single Christian interpolation, was written either by a highly Hellenized Jew or by a gentile who was much taken with and influenced by Judaism in the second or first centuries BCE. I would not rule either possibility out. If lines 350-488 and fragments one and three were originally part of the main corpus, their contents are consistent with either possibility. If not, they may have originated in Jewish, Christian, or gentile God-fearing circles and they do not give us sufficient information to narrow down the range of possibilities.

3

SIBYLLINE ORACLES, BOOK 5

Sibylline Oracles 5 survives in the manuscript families ϕ and ψ, clearly demarcated as a separate λόγος. It was quoted extensively by Clement of Alexandria (perhaps mediated by a florilegium) and also by Lactantius.[10] It contains 531 lines (about thirty-seven hundred Greek words) and consists of six oracles.[11] The first is a review of history from Alexander the Great to Hadrian (assuming the reference to Marcus Aurelius in line 51 is a gloss).[12] The next four share a common structure consisting of oracles against a nation or nations, the *Nero rediturus* myth, the coming of an eschatological redeemer, and an eschatological judgment (involving fire in all but the first of the four oracles). The sixth oracle presents what seems to be an eschatological scenario involving the building and destruction of a temple to God in Egypt and concludes with a bleak astral battle that consumes the earth and leaves the sky starless. The apparently conscious structuring of the book supports the view that it was composed as a unified work, although the final lines stop very abruptly and it is possible that the ending is lost. It is also widely accepted that lines 256-59, or at least line 257, are a Christian interpolation (but see below).

This is a very difficult and obscure collection of oracles. It has a posi-

---

[10] Buitenwerf, *Book III*, 65-72, 75-77, 79-82. [11] Collins, *Sibylline Oracles*, 73-76; idem, *OTP*, 1:390-91; idem, 'The Development,' 436-38. All quotations of *Sibylline Oracles* 5 in what follows are from the translation of Collins. [12] The positive view of Hadrian in 46-50 combined with the outrage over the destruction of the Jerusalem temple in 70 CE elsewhere in *Sibylline Oracles* 5 implies that it was written before the Bar Kokhba revolt of 132-35, during which Hadrian's troops laid waste to Palestinian Jewry.

tive view of Jews and Judaism. Egypt is condemned 'because you raged against my children who were anointed by God and incited evil against good men' (68-69), although this may refer to scriptural Israel rather than contemporary Jews. But Nero's persecution of Jews is condemned (150-54) and Italy is to be destroyed for Rome's killing of 'holy faithful Hebrews and a true people' (161). During the eschatological crisis of the returning Nero, 'the great city and righteous people' shall be preserved through it all (226-27). The eschatological triumph of 'the divine and heavenly race of the blessed Jews' (249) who inhabit Jerusalem is extolled in lines 248-85.

Likewise, the Jewish temple figures importantly in the writer's theology. Nero is condemned for seizing the Jerusalem temple (although he did not himself have it destroyed; 150-51) and we are told that at the eschaton Judea's children will offer sacrifices to God, presumably in the temple (268). The destruction of the second temple by Titus is also roundly condemned (397-413). The eschatological redeemer shall rebuild the temple (420-25, 432-33). Moreover, the Sibyl predicts that a priest will build a temple to God in Egypt which will be destroyed by the Ethiopians (492-511). It is not entirely clear whether the last prophecy is a *vaticinium ex eventu* concerning the actual Jewish temple in Leontopolis or a genuine prediction of a future Egyptian temple, perhaps inspired by the one in Leontopolis.

Sibylline Oracles 5 does not show the same sustained interest in conversion of the gentiles which we found in *Sibylline Oracles* 3, but the theme is present. In *Sib. Or.* 5:264-66 we are told that at the eschaton the Greeks will have a change of heart to follow the Jewish laws and in 275-80 that mortals will have to give up idolatry or starve. A prediction couched in the past tense says that the new temple to be built by the eschatological redeemer is to be 'visible to all, so that all faithful and all righteous people could see the glory of eternal God' (425-27) and 'East and West sang out the glory of God' (428). At this time sexual sin, murder, and war shall cease (429-31).

Collins reconstructs an entirely plausible scenario around this evidence: *Sibylline Oracles* 5 is a Jewish composition written in Egypt between the Roman destruction of Jerusalem in 70 C E and the Bar Kokhba revolt of 132-135 C E. The writer is no longer sympathetic to Egypt, or indeed to the gentiles in general, and posits a savior figure who comes from heaven rather than being associated with the Ptolemaic dynasty. The reference to the temple in Egypt may indicate that this collection of Jewish oracles emanated from Leontopolis or at least was inspired by the Jewish cult there. The identification of the savior figure with the crucified Jesus in lines 255-59 is at least in part a Christian interpolation.[13]

This reconstruction fits the data well and it is quite possible that it is correct. Nevertheless, it does not seem to me to be the only reasonable reading of the evidence. One point worth considering is whether it is necessary to remove lines 256-59 as a secondary Christian addition. This passage conflates Jesus 'who stretched out his hands on the fruitful wood' (line 257) with the biblical figure of Joshua son of Nun, who caused the sun to stand still. Early Christians were well aware of the correspondence between Jesus' name in the Greek New Testament and the Greek name of Joshua in the L X X and some church fathers made much of the typological correspondences, sometimes carrying them nearly to the point of identification.[14] This passage seems to posit a similar Joshua-Jesus correspondence and makes sense from that perspective. Indeed, deleting line 255 on its own, as Collins proposes, disposes of any Christian connection at the price of creating an entirely hypothetical type of Jewish messianism.[15] We are left with a Jewish savior figure who

---

[13] Collins, *Sibylline Oracles*, 73-95; idem, *OTP*, 1:390-92; idem, 'The Development,' 436-38. [14] Such speculations are first attested in Justin Martyr's *Dialogue with Trypho* (§§75.1-3; 90-91; 106.2; 113.3; 115-120). Robert Kraft collects additional early Christian examples of Jesus-Joshua typology in 'Was There a 'Messiah-Joshua' Tradition at the Turn of the Era?' Online (no pages; copyright 1992): http://ccat.sas.upenn.edu/gopher/other/journals/kraftpub/Christianity/Joshua. Kraft raises the rather speculative possibility that Joshua had already influenced Jewish messianic traditions in the pre-Christian era, but I am basing my comments here on the undoubted fact that Joshua influenced Christian ideas about Jesus. [15] Collins, *OTP*, 1:390, 399 n. e3. [16] The influence of the cult of the Jewish temple in Leontopolis is one explanation for the appearance of the mysterious Egyptian temple in *Sibylline Oracles* 5, but it is not the only possible explanation. It may be that a Greek-speaking Jewish-Christian or gentile God-fearer was familiar with the L X X of Isa 19:18-22 and built an eschatological scenario around these verses with no knowledge at all of Leontopolis. [17] A full discussion of all the Sibyllina is beyond the scope of this chapter, but I will register here my skepticism that any other of the surviving *Sibylline Oracles* can be regarded as Jewish with any confidence. Books 1 and 2 are a very mixed collection of oracles, some of which may be Jewish. Book 4 also seems to be composite, with later material built around an earlier anti-Macedonian oracle that involved the four world empires. I see nothing in Book 4 that points decisively to Jewish authorship. The destruction of Jerusalem in 70 CE is noted in lines 115-29, although it is not clear that the author takes the part of the Jews. Elsewhere (6-11, 27-30) the oracle is hostile to temples in general and the author advocates immersive, propitiatory ablutions (165-69). It is not impossible that the final form of Book 4 comes from a radically Hellenizing, baptizing Jew, but it could equally well

is also identified with Joshua. It is possible that such a figure existed, but we *know* that the Joshua traditions were applied in similar ways to Jesus by Christians, so we trade a well-attested Christological theme for an entirely speculative Jewish messianic one. It would make more sense to delete all four lines, yet I see no compelling reason to do this either. *Sibylline Oracles* 5 as a whole reads comfortably as a work by a Jewish-Christian who was outraged by the Roman destruction of Jerusalem and who put after-the-fact prophecies in the mouth of the Sibyl both to condemn the Romans and the other polytheistic nations and to predict the coming of Jesus as the eschatological redeemer. We have seen in Chapter Two that Christian documents sometimes include very few and easily excisable references to explicitly Christian matters, and *Sibylline Oracles* 5 could be another example of the same phenomenon.

This is one possible reading different from that of Collins. Another would accept the emendation that removes lines 255-59 and understand the remaining document as the product of a gentile God-fearer. Like *Sibylline Oracles* 3, *Sibylline Oracles* 5 shows no interest in circumcision, Jewish dietary rules, the sabbath, or the Jewish festivals, and, insofar as the Jewish Law figures at all (e.g., *Sib. Or.* 5:266), it involves avoidance of idolatry and sexual sins. And, like *Sibylline Oracles* 3, if to a lesser degree, *Sibylline Oracles* 5 teaches that the gentiles will be converted at the eschaton. A devout gentile who believed in the Jews as God's chosen people; revered their temple cult and deplored its destruction; looked for eschatological salvation from the Jewish God; and yet who picked and chose which elements of Judaism to accept and promote, ignoring the more inconvenient and inscrutable ones, would have been capable of writing *Sibylline Oracles* 5.

In sum, at least three understandings of the origins of *Sibylline Oracles* 5 are possible and all of them involve extrapolating backwards to some degree from the surviving manuscripts and the earliest quotations by boundary-maintaining Christians. All three would date the work between c. 70 CE and 132 CE and all three would be sympathetic to the possibilities of an Egyptian provenance and influence by Leontopolitan theology.[16] The first is Collins's reading of the book as a Jewish work. The second, which is the only one to take the text on its own terms without emendation, regards it as a composition by a Jewish-Christian. The third takes it as the product of a devout gentile God-fearer. There is no external evidence to help us choose between them. Given our current knowledge of the Sibylline tradition, I do not believe that any of these possibilities can either be proven or dismissed.[17]

Joseph and Aseneth tells the story of the conversion of Aseneth, the daughter of the Egyptian priest Potiphera, from idolatry to the worship of the true God of the Jewish scriptures, and of her marriage to the patriarch Joseph, along with some of their subsequent adventures. It is an extended expansion of Gen 41:45, told in something resembling the genre of an ancient novel. It survives in several recensions, two of which are contenders for being the closest to the presumed original

come from a God-fearer or a Jewish or gentile Christian. Books 6 and 7 are universally acknowledged to be Christian compositions. The second half of Book 8 is Christian. The origin of the first half of the book is uncertain but the case for Jewish authorship is very weak. The case for Jewish composition of Book 11 is based on the mere mention of Joseph, Moses, and Solomon along with the lack of Christian signature features. Books 12 to 14 are continuations of Book 11. Some of this material is clearly Christian and some of it may be Jewish as well, although arguments for the latter are far from decisive. For discussion of the whole corpus see Collins, 'The Development'; idem, 'The Sibylline Oracles'; and idem, 'Sibylline Oracles,' *ABD*, 6:2-6 and the bibliography cited therein. It seems likely that some of the material in the corpus of *Sibylline Oracles* stems from Jewish circles, but the arguments advanced thus far for large blocks of it being Jewish are not compelling. [18] Philonenko, *Joseph et Aséneth* (StPB 13; Leiden: Brill, 1968). The short recension was translated into English by D.Cook in 'Joseph and Aseneth,' *AOT*, 465-503. [19] Burchard, with Carsten Burfeind and Uta Barbara Fink, *Joseph and Aseneth* (PVTG 50; Leiden: Brill, 2003). Burchard published a provisional Greek text in 'Ein vorläufiger griechischer Text von Joseph und Aseneth,' *DBAT* 14 (1979), 2-53, which was reprinted with accents in Albert-Marie Denis, *Concordance grecque des pseudépigraphes d'Ancien Testament* (Louvain-la-Neuve: Université Catholique de Louvain, 1987), 851-59. Burchard also published a German translation of the provisional Greek text in *Joseph und Aseneth* (JSHRZ 2.4; Mohn: Gütersloh, 1983) and an English translation in 'Joseph and Aseneth,' *OTP*, 2:177-247. See also idem, *Untersuchungen zu Joseph und Aseneth* (WUNT 8; Tübingen: Mohr Siebeck, 1965) and the comments of M. de Jonge in *Pseudepigrapha of the Old Testament as Part of Christian Literature: The Case of the Testaments of the Twelve Patriarchs and the Greek Life of Adam and Eve* (SVTP 18; Leiden: Brill, 2003), 58-62. [20] For an overview of this evidence, see Ross Shepard Kraemer, *When Aseneth Met Joseph: A Late Antique Tale of the Biblical Patriarch and His Egyptian Wife, Reconsidered* (Oxford: Oxford University Press, 1998), 225-44. [21] For example, Philonenko, *Joseph et Aséneth*, 99-109; Burchard, *OTP*, 2:187-88; Randall D.Chesnutt, *From Death to Life: Conversion in Joseph and Aseneth* (JSPSup 16; Sheffield: Sheffield Academic Press, 1995), 71-85; Angela Standhartinger, *Das Frauenbild im Judentum der hellenistischen Zeit: Ein Beitrag anhand von 'Joseph und Aseneth'* (AGJU 26; Leiden: Brill, 1995), 5-20; Edith M.Humphrey, *Joseph and Aseneth* (Guides to Apocrypha and Pseudepigrapha; Sheffield: Sheffield Academic Press, 2000), 115; John J.Collins, 'Joseph and Aseneth: Jewish or Christian?' *JSP* 14 (2005): 97-112. [22] Bohak, Joseph and Aseneth *and the Jewish Temple in Heliopolis* (SBLEJL 10; Atlanta: Scholars Press, 1996). [23] Batiffol, *Le livre de la Prière d'Aseneth* (Studia Patristica. Études d'ancienne littérature chrétienne 1-2; Paris: Leroux, 1889-90), 1-115.

version. The priority of the 'short recension' (essentially text family d, consisting of about eighty-four hundred words) has been defended by Marc Philonenko, who has published a critical edition of this version of the text.[18] The priority of the 'long recension' (of about fourteen thousand words) has been defended by Christoph Burchard, who has published a critical edition of it.[19] The text survives in fifteen Greek manuscripts dating from the tenth to the nineteenth centuries; in two Syriac manuscripts, the older of which (c. 600) is the earliest surviving text of the work; in translations into Armenian, Latin, and other languages; and in a Modern Greek version. It is agreed today that *Joseph and Aseneth* was composed in Greek and I am aware of no one who still argues that the Greek is a translation of a Semitic original.

Knowledge of *Joseph and Aseneth* may be reflected in Egeria's account of her visit to Heliopolis c. 392 CE, although this passage is preserved only in the work of the twelfth-century writer Peter the Deacon. The martyrdom accounts of saints Barbara, Christine, and Irene, which seem to have been composed in the fourth through sixth centuries, may also be dependent on *Joseph and Aseneth*, although this is not certain. The earliest undoubted reference to *Joseph and Aseneth* are the two Syriac manuscripts, which contain a letter that indicates that a certain Moses (evidently Moses of Inghila) translated the work from Greek into Syriac. If the identification of the translator is correct, the Syriac translation of the long recension was made during the second half of the sixth century and the Greek original must have been written somewhat earlier.[20]

A wide range of possible origins for *Joseph and Aseneth* has been proposed, especially in recent years. The most widely accepted view at present is that it is a Jewish composition written in Egypt between the second century BCE and the second century CE.[21] Gideon Bohak has offered a refinement of this position, arguing that the long version is the more original and that the work was probably written in the Ptolemaic period in the mid-second century BCE (but possibly in 70-74 CE) and that it defends and promotes the migration of Onias IV to Egypt to build a Jewish temple in Heliopolis/Leontopolis and establish a Jewish priestly cult there. According to his reading, the mysterious episode of the honeycomb and bees during the angelic visitation to Aseneth (*Jos. Asen.* 16) is an allegory of Onias' migration.[22]

The earliest edition of *Joseph and Aseneth* was published by Pierre Batiffol, who also argued that it was a fourth- or fifth-century Christian work written in Asia Minor.[23] This view was widely adopted initially by scholars, although increasingly throughout the twentieth century an Egyptian Jewish origin was accepted instead. But a view similar to Batiffol's has been recently been defended anew by Ross Shepard Kraemer. Kraemer, with Philonenko, takes the short recension to be the more original and argues for the possibility that *Joseph and Aseneth* was composed no earlier than the third or fourth century C E by a Christian author, although she does not by any means rule out authorship by a Jew or a God-fearer. She regards Syria, Asia Minor, Palestine, and Egypt as possible places of origin. The author is especially interested in late antique mystical cosmologies and practices involving adjuration of divine beings, although the material in *Joseph and Aseneth* cannot be pinned down to a specific religious tradition.[24]

Kraemer has also explored the possibility that *Joseph and Aseneth* was composed in Samaritan circles. She notes that one very late Samaritan source preserves traditions similar to *Joseph and Aseneth* and that Joseph's marriage would be of interest to Samaritans, since their own purity would be dependent on its validity. The term 'Jew' is never used in *Joseph*

---

[24] Kraemer, *When Aseneth Met Joseph.* [25] Idem, 'Could *Aseneth* be Samaritan?' in *A Multiform Heritage: Studies on Early Judaism and Christianity in Honor of Robert A. Kraft* (ed. Benjamin G. Wright; Scholars Press Homage Series 24; Atlanta: Scholars Press, 1999), 149–65, quotation from p. 165. [26] The miniature preceding the text of *Joseph and Aseneth* in M S G has a reference to 'Christ Jesus our Lord.' The expanded version of 2:10 in G (corresponding to a passage in the Modern Greek version) refers to 'the Father and the Son and the Holy Spirit' toward the end. A paranetic addition between 7:6 and 7:7 in M SS F, W, and the Rumanian refers to 'the gospel' (τοῦ εὐαγγελίου). In the same sources, another such addition after 29:9 concludes with a Trinitarian doxology. Family *a* concludes the work after 29:9 with Gen 50:22b-26 L X X and a similar Trinitarian doxology. There is another Trinitarian doxology in the conclusion of the Modern Greek version. See Burchard et al., *Joseph und Aseneth*, 337–58. De Jonge also notes some other possible Christian terminology in *Pseudepigrapha of the Old Testament*, 62 n. 75. It is noteworthy that most of the textual evidence for both recensions of *Joseph and Aseneth* seems to be free of explicitly Christian additions,. Unless we assume that both recensions are originally Jewish, which seems most unlikely, it appears that, whichever recension is original, the Christian tradents who substantially reworked it refrained from introducing overtly Christian material, as did most of the subsequent translators and copyists. [27] E. g., R. T. Beckwith, 'The Solar Calendar of Joseph and Aseneth: A Suggestion,' *JSJ* 15 (1984): 90–111. [28] Collins points out ('*Joseph and Aseneth*: Jewish or Christian?' 102–107) that the issue of intermarriage was much more important in Judaism than in Christianity, and this point supports a Jewish origin. But his argument (ibid., 106, 112) that the conversion of Aseneth would have included baptisim if the work were by a Christian is unconvincing. Christian authors knew full well that baptism was a part of the Christian dispensation and would not have expected to see it in a conversion set in the Old Testament period.

and Aseneth, although 'Hebrew' and 'Israelite' are. She also points to possible parallels in terminology, calendrical reckoning, and angelology with Samaritan sources and proposes a life situation for the work either in the late third-century reform of Baba Rabba or among the Dosithean sectarians. She concludes 'that Samaritan composition of *Aseneth* ought not to be excluded from the list of possibilities.'[25]

I have no intention of adjudicating between these positions and, indeed, I see no way to choose between them given our current state of knowledge. Neither the long nor the short recension of *Joseph and Aseneth* gives us decisive clues as to its origin. Although the manuscripts occasionally include a Christian signature feature, the best texts that can be reconstructed for either the short or the long recension (i.e., the texts of Philonenko and Burchard) do not.[26] Likewise, I see no indubitable Jewish signature features in either recension. It is true that Joseph refrained from eating Egyptian food because 'this was an abomination to him' (*Jos. Asen.* 7:1, both recensions) which, as Burchard notes, is a reversal of Gen 43:32, where we are told that it is an abomination to the Egyptians to eat bread with the Hebrews. But the issue here is not the laws of kashrut *per se*, but the fact that the Egyptian food was strangled and was sacrificed to idols (*Jos. Asen.* 8:5; 11:9, 16; 12:5, long recension; 8:5; 12:5, short recension). These two issues (along with the consumption of blood) were singled out in the early church as matters for concern (Acts 15:19-20, 28-29; 1 Cor 10:14-30; Rev 2:14, 20). Either a Christian or a Jew or a God-fearer could have written these passages in *Joseph and Aseneth*. Aseneth is considered a 'strange woman' who could act as a corrupting influence on Joseph (*Jos. Asen.* 7:5; 8:1, 5, long recension; 7:6; 8:1, 5, short recension), but this is a scriptural theme (e.g., Exod 34:15-16; Num 25:1-2; Deut 7:3-4; 1 Kgs 11:1-13; Prov 2:16; 5:3-6; 6:24-25; 7:5, 14-27; 22:14) which could have been drawn on by any writer familiar with the scriptures who was concerned that outsider women could threaten the boundary-maintenance of the writer's group. It has been suggested that *Joseph and Aseneth* uses a variant of the Qumran solar calendar and, if correct, this would be a good argument in favor of Jewish authorship.[27] But at present the suggestion is speculative. More generally, *Joseph and Aseneth* could be read as a defense of gentile conversion to Judaism, whether aimed at Jews or gentiles, and it has often been read as such. This is a possible interpretation. But a Christian could also have written the story to teach that Christians should not be 'unequally yoked with unbelievers' (2 Cor 6:14) in marriage but should seek the conversion of the idolatrous prospective partner.[28] Likewise, a God-fearer could have composed it to argue the validity of intermarriage between Jews and devout gentiles. In any case, none of these readings take into account the theurgic transformative aspect of the story, which seems central to it, although just what its function is remains far from clear.[29]

The nature of the Joseph story itself may help explain our difficulty in pinning down a specific origin for *Joseph and Aseneth*. The Joseph story is set before the time of Moses and so contains nothing in it pertaining to the Mosaic Law. A nationalist agenda is clearly perceptible in it, but it is presented entirely from the perspective of the patriarchal period, so much so that any attempts to determine when or why the story was written have to be based on subtle clues that are far from decisive. A Jewish writer retelling the story would have no obvious motivation to introduce anachronistic laws, festivals, etc. from the Mosaic Law and such a writer could assume the nationalist themes of the story while leaving them implicit. In fact, the retelling by Philo of Alexandria in his treatise *On Joseph* proceeds in exactly this way. Philo allegorizes the story to demonstrate that Joseph acted as the ideal statesman. The Mosaic Law is ignored, unless we count the laws against premarital sex and adultery (§§42-44), which, of course, remain valid for Christians. There is also reference to 'ancestral practice' for both the Egyptians and the sons of Jacob (§202), but this is a toned-down echo of Gen 43:32. Philo expresses no explicit Jewish nationalism, although the whole work implicitly elevates the Jewish people for producing Joseph, the ideal statesman. Indeed, if we did not know on other grounds that Philo's *On Joseph* was a Jewish work, its contents alone would not rule out its being composed by a Christian or a gentile God-fearer.

Christians, too, would find much in the Joseph story worth retelling. Joseph's steadfastness in the face of adversity, his rejection of the adulterous liaison with Potiphar's wife, and his forgiveness of his brothers are all themes rich with homiletic potential and none of them need be filled out with references to specifically Christian matters, although we can

---

[29] Collins also argues (ibid. 107-109) that the conflict with the son of Pharaoh 'would have had pointed relevance for Jews in Egypt in the last century of Ptolemaic rule' (p. 108) due to historical parallels from that period. This may well be, but it is not a decisive point. Ultimately *Joseph and Aseneth* is a story and it was preserved because readers found it entertaining. It need not be 'relevant' in this sense to anyone, including its original audience, and successful stories are often excitingly implausible. A much later author might well have, intentionally or unintentionally, echoed events of the long-past Ptolemaic period to give the story an archaic and exotic feel.

assume that frequently they would be. In Chapter Two, I have discussed a Greek sermon by John Chrysostom and a section of a Syriac commentary by Ephrem the Syrian which retell the Joseph story with little or no Christianization. Chrysostom's sermon 64 in his first series on Genesis retells the story of Joseph, concentrating on paraphrasing its contents and explaining exegetical difficulties and the motivations of the characters, but also praising Joseph for his virtues and for his forgiveness of his brothers. Chrysostom associates this forgiveness with the New Testament command to forgive one's enemies in a brief passage that could easily be taken as a gloss. Likewise, the Trinitarian doxology could be taken as a secondary accretion, not unlike the similar concluding doxologies in some of the manuscripts of *Joseph and Aseneth*. Ephrem's account in his *Commentary on Genesis* concentrates on a close paraphrase of the Joseph story and sometimes explains and even justifies the motivations of the characters. Strikingly, not only does his retelling refrain from introducing any Christian signature features, it actually introduces the idea of circumcision as a positive, indeed (from the perspective of the Canaanite woman Tamar) enviable Hebrew custom.

A more detailed and wider-ranging study of the treatment of the Joseph story in early Christianity and ancient Judaism might prove even more enlightening for our understanding of *Joseph and Aseneth*. But the discussion here has pointed to other treatments of the Joseph story by both Christian and Jew which follow the scriptural account in such a way that, if we did not have external evidence of a sort lacking for *Joseph and Aseneth*, the internal evidence of these works would be insufficient to pin down their origins. In the case of *Joseph and Aseneth*, serious arguments have been advanced for judging it to be a Christian work of late antiquity; a Jewish work, perhaps even one emanating from the obscure rival temple cult in Leontopolis; a work by a God-fearer; and a Samaritan work. The first involves the least extrapolation from the earliest physical evidence for the document and perhaps should be our working hypothesis for the present, but none of the other possibilities should be dismissed.

THE *TESTAMENT OF JOB*

The *Testament of Job* presents an account of Job's sufferings in typical testamentary form: he relates the events to his children as he sets his affairs in order at the end of his life. Identifying himself with Jobab (cf. Gen 36:33-34), he narrates how he destroyed an idolatrous shrine and in revenge Satan began a vendetta against him, backed by God's authority. Job lost his possessions, his children, his health, and his wife, and endured the attempts of his three friends to comfort him, as well as the insults of Elihu. Nevertheless, Job was vindicated and restored. He divides his estate among his seven sons, presents his daughters with magical sashes that set their minds heavenward and make them speak in celestial tongues, then he dies and his soul ascends to heaven. We are told that his brother Nereus was the author of the book.

The *Testament of Job* survives in four Greek manuscripts dating from the eleventh to the sixteenth century, three manuscripts of an Old Church Slavonic version, and a fragmentary Coptic papyrus of the first half of the fifth century C E.[30] The Greek text is about thirty-five

⸻[30]⸻ An edition of the Greek text was produced by M. R. James in *Apocrypha Anecdota: Second Series* (Texts and studies. Contributions to Biblical and patristic literature 5.1; Cambridge: Cambridge University Press, 1897), lxxii-cii, 103-37. There are two more recent editions of the Greek: S. P. Brock, *Testamentum Iobi*; J.-C. Picard, *Apocalypsis Baruchi Graece* (PVTG 2; Leiden: Brill, 1967), 1-59; Robert A. Kraft, *The Testament of Job According to the SV Text* (Missoula, Mont.: Scholars Press, 1974) (the latter includes an English translation). There is an English translation of the *Testament of Job* by R. P. Spittler in 'Testament of Job,' *OTP*, 1:829-68; another by R. Thornhill in 'The Testament of Job,' *AOT*, 617-48; a French translation by Marc Philonenko in 'Le Testament de Job,' *Sem* 18 (1968): 1-75; and a German translation by Berndt Schaller in *Das Testament Hiobs* (JSHRZ 3.3; Mohn: Gütersloh, 1979). For a survey of the literature to 1989, see Russell P. Spittler 'The Testament of Job: A History of Research and Interpretation,' in *Studies on the Testament of Job* (ed. Michael A. Knibb and Pieter W. van der Horst (SNTSMS 66; Cambridge: Cambridge University Press, 1989), 7-32. ⸻[31]⸻ Schaller, *Das Testament Hiobs*. For a description of the papyrus and a transcription and translation of four fragments see Cornelia Römer and Heinz J. Thissen, 'P. Köln Inv. Nr. 3221: Das Testament des Hiob in koptischer Sprache. Ein Vorbericht,' in *Studies on the Testament of Job*, 33-41. The Coptic manuscript contains readings that are both longer and shorter than the Greek text. ⸻[32]⸻ It has sometimes been suggested that the Greek *Testament of Job* was translated from a Semitic original but this has never been rigorously argued and the case for it seems very weak. Given the Greek text's dependence on the L X X of Job (see next note), a Greek original is likely. Cf. Spittler, *OTP*, 1:830. ⸻[33]⸻ James, *Apocrypha Anecdota: Second Series*, lxxxiv-xciii; Berndt Schaller, 'Das Testament Hiobs und die Septuaginta-Übersetzung des Buches Hiob,' *Bib* 61 (1980): 377-406; Sparks, *AOT*, 618-19. ⸻[34]⸻ Malcolm L. Peel, 'The Treatise on the Resurrection,' in *The Nag Hammadi Library in English* (ed. James M. Robinson; 3rd ed.; San Francisco: Harper & Row, 1988), 52-57. ⸻[35]⸻ Douglas M. Parrot, James Brashler, et al., 'The Discourse on the Eighth and the Ninth,' in ibid., 321-327. ⸻[36]⸻ William R. Schoedel and Douglas M. Parrott, 'The (First) Apocalypse of James,' in ibid., 260-68. ⸻[37]⸻ John N. Sieber, 'Zostrianos,' in ibid., 402-30. ⸻[38]⸻ Antionnette Clark Wire, John. D. Turner, and Orval S. Wintermute, 'Allogenes,' in ibid., 490-500. ⸻[39]⸻ Alexander Böhlig and Frederik Wisse, 'The Gospel of the Egyptians,' in ibid., 208-19; Birger A. Pearson, 'Marsanes,' in ibid., 460-71. ⸻[40]⸻ Marvin Meyer and Richard Smith (eds.), *Ancient Christian Magic:*

hundred words long. An apocryphal *Testament of Job* is also mentioned in the Latin Gelasian Decree in the fifth or sixth century, although it is not certain that our *Testament of Job* is the document in question. The earliest certain source for the work is thus the Coptic version, which should be our starting point for understanding it. The Coptic manuscript consists of 110 fragments and contains the *Testament of Adam*, the *Testament of Job*, the *Testament of Abraham*, and the *Acta Petri et Andreae* in that order, none of them in a good state of preservation. The language is an early, pre-standardized form of the Sahidic dialect. Readable material from Chapters 25-53 of the *Testament of Job* survives, although there seems to be some hope that future technologies will render some material from Chapters 1-24 legible. Unfortunately, this manuscript remains unpublished apart from a few fragments, although Berndt Schaller includes such variants from it as affect the translation in the apparatus to his German translation.[31] Whoever commissioned the manuscript was clearly a Christian who had an interest in stories about both the pre-Israelite patriarchs and the apostles.

It is generally agreed that the *Testament of Job* was composed in Greek rather than Coptic and, since most Sahidic literature of this period was translated from Greek, this seems a reasonable assumption.[32] Until the Coptic version has been fully published and critically compared with the Greek, the question of the original language must remain open, but if for the sake of argument we follow the consensus and assume that Greek is the original language, our earliest context for the work remains Christian circles in Egypt in the early fifth century C E at the latest. And the *Testament of Job* does fit quite comfortably in this context. The Greek text is heavily influenced by the L X X of Job, which, of course, proves nothing one way or another about Jewish or Christian origin. It contains no indubitably Christian or Jewish signature features, although it has been noted that the Greek has some terms that can be argued to be both Christian and later than the first century C E.[33] The interest in glossolalia and spiritual ascents could have roots in the New Testament (e.g., 1 Cor 13:1; 14:1-33; 2 Cor 12:1-5), but it is entirely at home in late antique Egyptian Christianity. The Coptic library from Nag Hammadi features numerous heavenly and spiritual ascents, for example, in the *Treatise on the Resurrection*;[34] the *Discourse on the Eighth and the Ninth*,[35] *The (First) Apocalypse of James*;[36] *Zostrianos*;[37] and *Allogenes*.[38] *Nomina barbara* with mystical import appear in the *Gospel of the Egyptians* and *Marsanes*.[39] Late antique Coptic texts of ritual power also show an interest in celestial ascents[40] and make use of *nomina*

barbara as words of power.⁴¹ The ascetic, world-denying tendencies of
the book are also entirely consonant with Egyptian Christianity. Thus
I see no compelling reason to move backwards from the context of late
antique Egypt to a putative earlier origin for the *Testament of Job* in Jewish circles.

Nevertheless, many scholars take the *Testament of Job* to be a Jewish

Coptic Texts of Ritual Power (San Francisco: HarperSanFrancisco, 1994), #39, 'Spell for ascending
through the heavens,' pp. 66-68. Some of these spells also show considerable interest in the details
of the heavenly realm, with numerous parallels to the heavenly ascents and cosmographies in
Merkavah mysticism or Hekhalot literature. One example in the same volume is #71, 'Rossi's
"Gnostic" tractate against the powers of evil,' pp. 133-46, which deals with angels, seals of power,
multiple firmaments on high, celestial curtains, God's throne, rivers of fire, the four living crea-
tures, and the archangels. ___ ⁴¹ ___ Ibid., #26 'Amulet to protect a house and its occupant from
evil,' pp. 49-50; #38, 'A Gnostic fire baptism,' pp. 63-66; #43, 'Book of ritual spells for medical
problems,' pp. 83-90; #46, 'Spell to heal a foot,' p. 92; #50, 'Amulet to heal and protect a woman,'
pp. 97-98; #64, 'Exorcistic spell to drive evil forces from a pregnant woman,' pp. 120-24; #80,
'Spells for favor, honor, and passion,' pp. 169-70; #133, 'The Coptic hoard of spells from the University of Michigan,' pp. 293-310. ___ ⁴² ___ For example, Marc Philonenko, 'Le Testament de Job
et les Thérapeutes,' *Sem* 8 (1958): 41-53 (the Therapeutae); Ben-Zion Wacholder, 'Job, Testament
of,' *EncJud* 10:129-30 (the Therapeutae); John J. Collins, 'Structure and Meaning in the Testament of Job,' *SBLSP* 1 (1974): 35-52 (Egyptian Judaism); H. C. Kee, 'Satan, Magic, and Salvation
in the Testament of Job,' ibid., 53-76 (early Merkavah Mysticism); Spittler, *OTP*, 1:833-34 (the
Therapeutae with later Montanist editing); Emil Schürer, Geza Vermes, et al., *The History of the
Jewish People in the Age of Jesus Christ* (175 B. C.–A. D. 135) (3 vols; Edinburgh: Clark, 1986): 3.1:552-
55 (a survey of possible Jewish origins). Note also Schaller, who mentions other possibilities but
baldly asserts, '[a]n der jüdischen Herkunft des Testaments Hiobs kann daher kein Zweifel beste-
hen' (*Das Testament Hiobs*, 309); and Pieter W. van der Horst, who acknowledges the Christian parallels to *T. Job* 46–53 but still asserts its Jewish origin on the grounds that Jewish parallels can be
adduced for most of the same features ('Images of Women in the Testament of Job,' in Knibb and
van der Horst (eds.), *Studies on the Testament of Job*, 93-116, esp. p. 109). Likewise, Irving Jacobs argues for a Jewish origin for the *Testament of Job* on the basis on its interest on conversion, missionary activity, and martyrdom – all prominent themes in Christianity ('Literary Motifs in the Testament of Job,' *JJS* 21 [1970]: 1-10). ___ ⁴³ ___ Recent English translations include E. P. Sanders, 'Testament of Abraham,' *OTP*, 1:871-902 and N. Turner, 'The Testament of Abraham,' *AOT*, 393-421.
For a recent critical commentary see Dale C. Allison, Jr., *Testament of Abraham* (Commentaries
on Early Jewish Literature; Berlin: de Gruyter, 2003). ___ ⁴⁴ ___ Ibid., 41-42. Allison notes the
parodic elements in the work and suggests, '[p]erhaps one should call it an "anti-testament"'
(p. 42). ___ ⁴⁵ ___ The two Greek recensions were first published by Montague Rhodes James in
The Testament of Abraham (Texts and Studies. Contributions to Biblical and Patristic Literature
2.2; Cambridge: Cambridge University Press, 1892). More recent editions with translations include Michael E. Stone, *The Testament of Abraham: The Greek Recensions* (SBLTT 2; SBLPS 2; Missoula, Mont.: Society of Biblical Literature, 1972); Francis Schmidt, *Le Testament grec d'Abraham*
(TSAJ 11; Tübingen: Mohr Siebeck, 1986). The Greek text of both recensions is translated into
French by Mathias Delcor in *Le Testament d'Abraham* (SVTP 2; Leiden: Brill, 1973), 89-185.

work, although often its Jewish origin is more assumed than argued, with the discussion focusing on *which* Jewish group or sect produced it.[42] It is true that one can find connections with ancient Judaism in the *Testament of Job*, including parallels with such groups as the Therapeutae and the Merkavah mystics or Hekhalot practitioners. Nevertheless, the features adduced for comparison with these groups can be perfectly adequately accounted for in the Christian context of the earliest manuscript. One can, of course, explain the lack of Jewish signature features by the fact that Job himself is presented in the scriptural book as a non-Israelite and the general interpretation of his story in antiquity, as in the *Testament of Job*, was that he lived in the pre-Israelite period. The author would therefore have had no reason to mention the Mosaic Law, the people of Israel, etc., and to do so would have been anachronistic. But by the same token, the lack of Christian signature features may mean no more than that the Christian writer tried to recreate the atmosphere of Job's time without any out-of-place references to later events. On balance, although composition by a Jew, or for that matter a God-fearer, cannot be ruled out, if we start from the manuscript evidence and move backwards only as needed, no positive evidence compels us to move beyond a Greek work written in Christian, perhaps Egyptian, circles by the early fifth century C E.

6   THE *TESTAMENT OF ABRAHAM*

The *Testament of Abraham* tells the story of the end of Abraham's life: how God sent the archangel Michael to notify Abraham of his death but Abraham refused to accept this decree. He demanded to be shown the entire world first, and he was also taken to the realm of post-mortem judgment. Eventually his soul was extracted during an encounter with the personified figure of Death. The work survives in two main recensions, a long and a short one.[43] The literary genre of the work is debated; it has affinities with both testaments and apocalypses.[44] The earliest surviving version is generally taken to be the Greek (see below), in which 23 manuscripts of the long recension (recension A – about seventy-one hundred Greek words long) and 9 manuscripts of the short recension (recension B – about thirty-two hundred Greek words long) are extant. The Greek manuscripts range in date from the eleventh to the sixteenth centuries C E.[45] There are also two Coptic version, one in Boharic (962 C E) and the other in an early form of Sahidic (first half of the fifth century C E), and versions in Arabic, Ethiopic,

Slavonic, and Romanian, all of which are preserved in late manuscripts.[46]

Even though the earliest evidence for the work is in Sahidic and Boharic Coptic, the nearly universal consensus is that the *Testament of Abraham* was composed in Greek.[47] Both recensions have some Semitisms, although there is a higher density of these in the short recension. The longer recension has a high density of words that seem to be Christian or medieval, although, again, the short recension contains such terms as well. The fifth century Sahidic manuscript is the same one that contains the *Testament of Job* and has been discussed above. Its text of the *Testament of Abraham* is closest to the short recension, although in places it agrees with the long recension against the short recension. Especially given the apparent Semitisms in both Greek recensions, we should perhaps not discount the possibility that the text was composed in

---

[46] The Boharic version of the *Testament of Abraham* is translated by George MacRae in 'The Coptic Testament of Abraham,' in *Studies on the Testament of Abraham* (ed. George W. E. Nickelsburg; SBLSCS 6; N.p.: Scholars Press for the Society of Biblical Literature, 1976), 327-40. The Slavonic version is translated by Donald S. Cooper and Harry B. Weber, 'The Church Slavonic Testament of Abraham,' in ibid., 301-26. The Romanian version is edited and translated by Nicolae Roddy in *The Romanian Version of the* Testament of Abraham: *Text, Translation, and Cultural Context* (SBLEJL 19; Atlanta: Society of Biblical Literature, 2001). The Boharic, Ethiopic, and Arabic versions are translated into French by Delcor in *Le Testament d'Abraham*, 186-267. For an overview of the textual sources for the *Testament of Abraham* see Allison, *Testament of Abraham*, 4-11.

[47] J. T. Milik writes that in his opinion, 'the oldest, and the original, text is preserved in the Coptic recension,' and he appears to mean by this that the *Testament of Abraham* was composed in Coptic and translated into Greek. But he does not argue the case for this position. See Milik, with the collaboration of Matthew Black, *The Books of Enoch: Aramaic Fragments from Qumrân Cave 4* (Oxford: Clarendon, 1976), 105-106, quotation from p. 105. [48] For an overview of the state of the question on the issues touched on in this paragraph, see Allison, *Testament of Abraham*, 12-27. On the basis of his syntax criticism, R. A. Martin has argued the likelihood that both recensions of the *Testament of Abraham* descend ultimately from a Semitic original, although the history of transmission is unclear. ('Syntax Criticism of the Testament of Abraham,' in Nickelsburg [ed.], *Studies on the Testament of Abraham*, 95-120. Elsewhere, I have offered some criticisms of Martin's methodology and shown that it has produced at least one false positive (the book of Baruch) ('[How] Can We Tell If a Greek Apocryphon or Pseudepigraphon Has Been Translated from Hebrew or Aramaic?', forthcoming in the *Journal for the Study of the Pseudepigrapha*), In the case of the *Testament of Abraham* his arguments are not persuasive. Robert A. Kraft rightly criticizes him for using control data from the Hellenistic period on a text whose date is uncertain and whose language has clearly been influenced by the Greek scriptures ('Reassessing the "Recensional Problem" in Testament of Abraham,' in ibid., 121-37, esp. pp. 134-35). This essay by Kraft also presents an important discussion of the possible relationships between the two recensions and the *Urtext* behind them. [49] Allison, *Testament of Abraham*, 23, 238-42. [50] In their current form both the long recension and one family of the short recension

Coptic and translated into Greek, but most early Sahidic literature was translated from Greek and the Greek text of both recensions of the *Testament of Abraham* shows familiarity with the LXX, so a Greek *Urtext* is a reasonable working hypothesis. The relationship between the long and short recensions is complex and neither seems to preserve the *Urtext*. There is debate about which recension is superior. A reasonable mediating position is that the long recension best preserves the content of the original, although the language has been modernized, while the short recension abbreviates the *Urtext* and discards much of the original flow of thought.[48]

There are no certain references to the *Testament of Abraham* earlier than the Sahidic manuscript, so this copy should be the starting point for the discussion. If the original language is Coptic, it becomes extremely likely that the work was composed by a Christian. If we accept that the original language is Greek and that the short recension is an abbreviation of the *Urtext*, we must posit some time for the alterations to the original and the translation into Coptic, so the *Urtext* could scarcely have been composed after the late fourth or early fifth centuries CE. If the reference to the apocryphal books of the three patriarchs in *Apos. Con.* 6:16.3 has a version of our *Testament of Abraham* in mind, a date in the fourth century or earlier is indicated.

We should proceed, therefore, to attempt to read the *Testament of Abraham* as the product of a Greek-speaking, fourth- or early fifth-century Christian, perhaps located in Egypt, and we should take the long recension as our starting point, while acknowledging that it does not reflect the *Urtext* with anything like perfect fidelity. Much of the document is congenial to the late antique Christian context. The long recension echoes the language of Matt 7:13-14 in *T. Abr.* 11:2-11. The influence of Matthew on the parallel passage in short recension 8:3-6 is much less apparent, which raises the possibility that the short recension preserves a more original text. However, even if we accept the short recension as original, it still refers to two gates (8:4-5, 7, 10) which lead to 'life' ($\zeta\omega\eta$) and to 'destruction' ($\dot{\alpha}\pi\dot{\omega}\lambda\epsilon\iota\alpha$) (8:11) and one of which is a 'narrow gate' ($\sigma\tau\epsilon\nu\eta$ $\pi\dot{\nu}\lambda\eta$) that leads to life (9:1, 3).[49] The parallels with Matt 7:13-14 are still striking and, in my opinion, any attempt to deny them would be less convincing than my heuristic attempt in Chapter Two to explain away the influence of Luke 8:17 on Augustine's sermon on Micah 6:6-8 and Psalm 72. One can, of course, argue that the *Urtext* lacked any allusion to Matthew, but this involves special pleading beyond the evidence of the text.[50]

Other features of the *Testament of Abraham* are consistent with a Christian origin. For the most part it is universalistic in its outlook and it shows no interest in Jewish institutions such as the sabbath, circumcision, the Jewish ritual and purity laws, and the Jewish festivals. We do not even find a condemnation of idolatry. The morality is generic and would have been accepted in Jewish, Christian, or gentile God-fearing circles in antiquity: the virtue of hospitality to strangers is praised and the sins of murder, robbery, adultery, and sexual immorality are condemned.

Nevertheless, there are some features of the work that are less readily explained in a Christian context. Dale Allison has made the most recent and comprehensive case for a Jewish *Urtext* behind the surviving recensions of the *Testament of Abraham*. In his judgment, it 'remains overwhelmingly probable that a non-Christian *Urtext* underlies our two recensions.'[51] He argues, first, that three passages in the long recension of the *Testament of Abraham* are based on exegesis of the original Hebrew of Genesis (although not, as he says, on the M T) and that this dependence on the Hebrew 'is consistent with at least parts of RecLng deriving from a Jewish environment.' Later he asserts that, 'given that the L X X was the Bible of the early church, one may doubt the Christian origin of a book containing legends, wholly unattested in Christian writings, which derive from reflections upon the Hebrew Bible.'[52] Indeed, he makes a persuasive case that these three passages presuppose exegesis of the Hebrew rather than the Greek of the L X X. The talking tree of *T. Abr.* 3:3 is probably inspired by a word play on the 'tamarisk' (אשל) tree that Abraham planted according to Gen 21:33, taking it to be

end with Trinitarian doxologies, but there are good grounds for considering them secondary. The conclusion of the long recension admonishes readers to imitate Abraham's hospitality and, virtue, which is hardly the point of the story and must be by a secondary hand. Family E of the short recension omits the Trinitarian portion of the doxology and may be closest to the original ending. See ibid., 409-12. ___ [51] ___ Ibid., 28-29. ___ [52] ___ Ibid., 24 and 29. ___ [53] ___ Ibid., 111-12, 165-67, 347-48. ___ [54] ___ Ibid, 24-26. ___ [55] ___ One argument for the Jewish origin of *T. Abr.* 13, long recension, is that Abel rather than Christ is the enthroned judge of humanity. But there is no clear New Testament doctrine concerning the postmortem judgment of human beings during the Old Testament dispensation and one reasonable scenario for Christians would be to have the martyr Abel (who, as Allison notes, was regarded as a Christ figure by early Christians; *Testament of Abraham*, 282) act in the role of judge. The passage states quite clearly in 13:4 that Abel would judge the world only until 'his (Christ's?) great and glorious *parousia*,' on which see below.

a tree of 'asking' or 'inquiring' (שאל), and by a reinterpretation of the 'oak of Moreh' (אלון מורה) in Gen 12:6-7 as the 'teaching oak' or the like. The resurrected calf of *T. Abr.* 6:5 probably comes from a reading of the Hebrew of Gen 18:8 in which the calf rather than Abraham is understood as the subject of the verb 'to stand' (עמד). And the multiple faces of death in *T. Abr.* 17:14-16 may well be inspired by the inherently plural form of the word פנים in the phrase ויקם אברהם על פני מתו in Gen 23:3, normally translated, 'And Abraham rose up from before his dead' (RSV) or the like.[53] All that granted, I do not see that these passages provide significant evidence that the *Testament of Abraham* is a Jewish composition. It is well established that this work is dependent on Jewish traditions about the death of Moses.[54] The author evidently had access to Jewish midrashic traditions, as was not at all unusual among Christians in antiquity. Knowledge of such matters no more proves a Jewish origin for the *Testament of Abraham* than it does for Ephrem's commentaries on Genesis and Exodus (see Chapter Two above).

Chapter 13 of the *Testament of Abraham* also has some unusual features. In the long recension, Abraham asks Michael to explain the celestial judge, the recording angels, and the fiery angel in the vision of the preceding three chapters. Michael informs him that the enthroned judge is Abel. There follows a curious passage in vv. 4-8 in which we are told that Abel will judge the world until 'his great and glorious *parousia*' (v. 4), at which time something that sounds like the ultimate and final judgment will take place.[55] Nevertheless, there will follow a 'second *parousia*' in which every breathing creature shall be judged by the twelve tribes of Israel (v. 6). In v. 7 we read, 'The third' (τὸ δέ τρίτον), by the Lord God of all they shall be judged and, as for the rest, the end of that judgment is near and the sentence is fearsome and there is none to mitigate it.' Then v. 8 refers to the judgment of the world by 'three judgment seats,' to which it attaches the notion of verification of court testimony by two or three witnesses as per Deut 19:15. The rest of the chapter describes and names the two angels on the right and the left.

It seems likely that there is more than one redactional layer in this chapter. In particular, vv. 4-8a seem intrusive and can be detached without damaging the flow of thought. The two *parousiai* and three eschatological judgments are difficult to reconcile with a Christian viewpoint: there is nothing about Jesus, and the judgment by the twelve tribes of Israel would certainly not be congenial to boundary-maintaining Christians. But by the same token, assigning the passage a Jewish origin raises as many problems as it solves. The word *parousia* in an eschatological context is a Christian usage, and E. P. Sanders's comment that '[t]he term was probably more common in Jewish literature than can now be directly demonstrated' is wishful thinking.[56] Indeed, the entire chapter is replete with Christian terminology. For example, vv. 11-13 are dependent on 1 Cor 3:14-15.[57] If there is a Jewish *Urtext* behind this eschatological scenario, it has been so thoroughly Christianized that it is now irrecoverable, which raises the question why the Christian redactor did not introduce Jesus if the scenario is incompatible with Christianity. The short recension (Chapter 11) has no parallel with anything in the chapter after 13:3 and instead has a passage describing Enoch as the celestial recording scribe. Allison suggests that the short recension may be original here, in which case the material in the long recension is unlikely to be Jewish.[58]

Allison also doubts that Chapter 14 of the long recension (which has no parallel in the short recension) could be from a Christian hand. In it, Abraham's prayer is enough to incline God toward mercy not only toward a person equally balanced between eternal life and destruction (vv. 1-8), but also toward the egregious sinners whom Abraham himself had sentenced to death earlier in the narrative. It may be true, as Allison intimates, that such a liberal 'soteriological optimism' regarding the unbaptized dead is uncharacteristic of the views of the church fathers (I am not qualified to evaluate this claim), but if so, that would hardly prevent every Christian from holding such a view.[59] No clear rulings on the fate of either sinners or the righteous in Old Testament times are passed down in the New Testament and speculation on such matters must have rife among the Christian laity (as it is today) no matter what official positions were adopted by the leadership. Likewise, the notion in *T. Abr.* 14:15 that temporal suffering atones for sin and prevents

[56] Sanders, *OTP*, 1:890 n. 13 a. See Allison, *Testament of Abraham*, 283-84 for a discussion of the linguistic evidence. [57] Ibid., 277-79, 287, 291. [58] Ibid. 277-79. [59] Ibid., 29. [60] Ibid. 306. [61] Allison also posits an earlier, evidently more Jewish, stratum behind long recension Chapter 11 (short recension Chapter 8) in which something like an equal number of people were saved and damned, rather than most being damned as in the current text of both recensions (ibid., 29, 239). But this is speculative and he acknowledges that any putative Jewish original behind this chapter is irrecoverable (ibid., 240). [62] A related possibility is that the *Testament of Abraham* is essentially a Christian composition but it incorporates one or more Jewish sources in the chapters on Abraham's ascent to heaven (10-14). The material that causes difficulty for Christian authorship is concentrated in this section. In this case also, the Jewish source is irrecoverable.

punishment in the afterlife may not appear in patristic theology,[60] but it is found in *1 En* 22:12-13 and *2 Bar.* 78:6, two Jewish works translated and transmitted by Christians, so presumably it was not compellingly objectionable to all Christians.[61]

Taking all this into account, I can envisage a number of possible origins for the *Testament of Abraham* which explain the available evidence. First, Allison may be right and the surviving recensions of the *Testament of Abraham* may go back to a Jewish *Urtext*, presumably emanating from the Greek-speaking Diaspora, perhaps Egypt. The author may have avoided reference to the Jewish Law, ritual, temple cult, priesthood, and festivals because these institutions were post-Abrahamic. Circumcision is not mentioned, even though it is very relevant to the Abraham story, but not every text need mention everything. The Jewish author would presumably be responsible for the archetype behind the confusing eschatological scenario in *T. Abr.* 13:4-8 as well as the statement that the twelve tribes of Israel will judge every creature in *T. Abr.* 13:6 (in both cases in the long recension). The only positive evidence that points clearly toward Jewish authorship is the latter statement. Otherwise, no interest is shown in Jewish nationalism and the eschatology is remarkably universalist. If a Jewish *Urtext* existed, it has been so thoroughly assimilated by the Christian tradents that it is beyond recovery with the data currently available.[62]

A second, and to my mind no less plausible, understanding is that the *Urtext* of the *Testament of Abraham* was composed by a gentile Christian who was less concerned with boundary maintenance than most of the other surviving Christian literature. The author may have had Judaizing tendencies (again, see 13:6, long recension) or may simply have taken seriously the importance of (a presumably converted) Israel in the eschatology of some New Testament passages (e.g., Romans 11 or Revelation 7). The author evidently held the view that intercession by a gloriously renowned Old Testament saint such as Abraham could lead sinners to salvation during the old dispensation. Doubtless this would have been understood as Abraham mediating the grace of Christ in his prayers on behalf of the dead, but this idea was left implicit so as to maintain a convincingly Old Testament atmosphere. The eschatology of 13:4-8, long recension, is no more clearly explained by positing Jewish authorship than by taking the passage as Christian. Once again, in order to maintain the Old Testament atmosphere, the author may have deliberately presented an eschatological scenario whose culmination was essentially indecipherable, yet a Christian reader was given a crucial hint: that the eschatological future (to Abraham's time) would involve two *parousiai* and therefore would relate to the unmentioned Christ (or is the reference to 'his son' in 13:5 a hint that Jesus and not Abel is in view?). The author and the author's intended audience may even have shared additional assumptions that made the meaning of the rest of the passage clearer. Perhaps we should recall 1 Pet 1:10-12, which asserts that neither the Old Testament worthies who received revelations about Christ, his sufferings, and his future glory, nor the angels who mediated these revelations understood them fully.

One may fairly protest that this scenario is entirely hypothetical, and there is some force to this objection. But I would reply first that this understanding of the text's origin explains the data as convincingly as positing Jewish authorship. The lack of interest in Jewish culture and institutions makes sense if the author was a Christian and the difficulties raised by Christian authorship are no greater (nor any less easily explained away) than those raised by Jewish authorship. Second, proposing Christian authorship eliminates the – to my mind unnecessary – additional layer of inference required by arguing for Jewish authorship. If we start with the Christian manuscripts and move backwards and if it develops that we must posit either an unusual form of Judaism or an unusual form of Christianity to explain the text, the unusual form of Christianity requires multiplication of fewer entities. Third, and perhaps most importantly, although the previous paragraph reconstructs

---

[63] OTP, 2:443-61.   [64] Charlesworth, *The History of the Rechabites*, vol. 1, *The Greek Recension* (SBLTT 17; SBLPS 10; Chico, Calif.: Scholars Press, 1982). The Greek text was originally published independently by Montague Rhodes James, 'On the Story of Zosimus,' in *Apocrypha Anecdota* (Texts and Studies. Contributions to Biblical and Patristic Literature 2.3; Cambridge: Cambridge University Press, 1893), 86-108, and by A. Vassiliev (ed.), 'Vita s. Zosimae narratur,' *Anecdota Graeco-Byzantina* pars prior (Moscow, Universitas Caesareae, 1893), xxxviii-xl, 166-79. I have not seen the latter edition. Charlesworth based his text on four Greek manuscripts: the two used by James (one of which goes only to 9:10); one used by Vassiliev (two that he used are now unavailable); and a fourth that lacks one leaf containing 16:8b-21:5a. Other manuscripts are lost or unavailable. The text reconstructed from this evidence consists of about three thousand words in Chapters 1-18 and about another 640 words in Chapters 19-23. In addition, J. Duncan M. Derrett has published a transcript of the Greek text of 11:2b-13:5 (fols. 202v-204r) from an apparently complete copy of the *Story of Zosimus* in Cod. Mus. Brit. Add. 10073, fols. 192v-209r. See his 'Jewish Brahmins and the Tale of Zosimus: A Theme Common to Three Religions,' *Classica et Mediaevalia* 34 (1983): 75-90, esp. 78, 82-85. The text of this manuscript is explicitly Christian, is shorter than the other manuscripts in some places and longer in others, and it requires further study.

a Christian authorship whose exact theological components, although reasonably plausible in themselves, are otherwise unattested, *the Christian transmission of this work in itself compels us to assume that its Christian tradents read it more or less along these lines*. It is abundantly clear that some Christians read the *Testament of Abraham* and copied it, so presumably they found it edifying and useful in some way. They must have found explanations for the jarring elements in it, such as the references to the salvation of unbaptized sinners through Abraham's intercession, the eschatological judgment by the twelve tribes, and the mysterious threefold final judgment involving two *parousiai*. Their explanations must have been similar to the ones I have proposed above, or at least similarly creative. If perforce we must accept such a reading of the *Testament of Abraham* by Christian tradents, why not accept it for a Christian author?

The third possible origin is that a gentile God-fearer composed the *Urtext*, which was then adopted and revised by Christians. This interpretation would explain why the author is sympathetic toward Israel yet indifferent to most Jewish cultural institutions and why the ideas about personal postmortem judgment are based entirely on general moral criteria rather than either Jewish praxis and national fidelity or Christian theology. It may also explain the inscrutability of the eschatological explanations: the author may have made them up, perhaps even combining Jewish and Christian ideas and reformulating them in a way that would make sense neither to Jews nor to Christians. This explanation is very speculative, but I would not rule it out.

In sum, the *Testament of Abraham* is a very difficult text and no explanation of its origins is entirely satisfactory. To my mind, Christian authorship of the *Urtext* offers fewer difficulties, but authorship by a Jew or a gentile God-fearer remains quite possible. In any case, both recensions have been heavily reworked in different ways and if a pre-Christian original ever existed, it cannot be recovered without a fortuitous discovery of new data.

7

THE *STORY OF ZOSIMUS*

The *Story of Zosimus* is a work of late antiquity or the early Middle Ages which was included by James H. Charlesworth in his second *Old Testament Pseudepigrapha* volume with the title *The History of the Rechabites*.[63] Charlesworth published a translation of the Syriac version there and an edition and translation of the Greek version elsewhere.[64] The work tells the story of the hermit Zosimus, who was guided to the Abode of the Blessed where he met a colony of holy naturist Rechabites who were taken to their paradisiacal realm by an angel in the time of Jeremiah. After hearing about their history and lifestyle, Zosimus was returned home. According to the Greek version, being first warned by angels, he was abused by the devil and a host of demons for forty days in their attempt to suppress the written account of his visit to the Abode of the Blessed. Victorious, he drove the devil away, circulated the account of his adventures, lived another thirty-six years, and was ushered to the afterlife by angels.

It is widely agreed that the *Story of Zosimus* is composite and contains core material composed in Jewish circles. I accept the composite nature of the work, but find a Jewish origin for it or its sources to be very unlikely. Most commentators agree that Chapters 19-23 are secondary accretions added to the Greek version by one or more Christian redactors, so I shall largely ignore them. In 1978 Brian McNeil argued that

---

⁶⁵ McNeil, 'The Narration of Zosimus,' *JSJ* 9 (1978): 68-82; quotation from p. 68. The current reference system for the Story of Zosimus, developed by Martin (see n. 66 below), has added versification and divided what was previously Chapter 5 into two chapters. McNeil uses the older system of James's edition and his references are noted parenthetically; otherwise I will use Martin's chapters and versification. ⁶⁶ McNeil's reason for finding the allusions to be secondary is that they are out of context and inapt. However, scriptural allusions or even quotations in ancient literature frequently take no account of the original context of a passage, so there is no particular reason to think that these allusions are redactional rather than from the hand of the original author. ⁶⁷ Martin, 'The Account of the Blessed Ones: A Study of the Development of an Apocryphon on the Rechabites and Zosimus (The Abode of the Rechabites)' (Ph. D. diss., Duke University, 1979), esp. 169-70. ⁶⁸ James H. Charlesworth, assisted by P. Dykers, *The Pseudepigrapha and Modern Research* (Missoula, Mont: Scholars Press, 1976), 223-28. ⁶⁹ OTP, 2:444-45. ⁷⁰ Ibid., 2:445. ⁷¹ Derrett, 'Jewish Brahmins,' 75-78, 85-87, quotation from p. 78. Ronit Nikolsky concludes that *Story of Zosimus* 11, which she isolates as a separate episode and calls 'The Conduct of the Blessed,' is dependent on some form of the work by (Ps.?) Palladius. See her 'The Provenance of *The Journey of Zosimus* (also known as *The History of the Rechabites*)' (Ph. D. diss., Hebrew University, 2003 [in Hebrew]), 67-85. ⁷² Knights, '"The Story of Zosimus" or "The History of the Rechabites"?' *JSJ* 24 (1993): 235-45; idem, 'Towards a Critical Introduction to "The History of the Rechabites,"' *JSJ* 26 (1995): 324-42; idem, '*The History of the Rechabites* – an Initial Commentary,' *JSJ* 28 (1997): 413-36; idem, 'A Century of Research into the Story/Apocalypse of Zosimus and/or the History of the Rechabites,' *JSP* 15 (1997): 53-66; idem, 'The *Abode of the Blessed*: A Source of the *Story of Zosimus*?' *JSP* 17 (1998): 79-93. Knights's unpublished doctoral dissertation also deals at some points with the *Story of Zosimus*: Christopher Hammond Knights, 'The Rechabites in the Bible and in Jewish Tradition to the Time of Rabbi David Kimḥi' (2 vols.; Ph. D. diss., University of Durham, 1988).

Chapters 1-17 are 'a light Christian reworking of a Jewish text.'[65] He finds only Chapter 13 (Narr. 12) to be a Christian passage. He argues that the allusions to the New Testament in 5:4 and to the *Protevangelium of James* in 7:8 (Narr. 6) are secondary additions and he attributes the allusions to the book of Acts in 10:4-5 (Narr. 9) to assimilation by a 'translator' (what is translated from what to what remains unclear).[66] He also takes the reference to the 'son of God' in 16:2 (Narr. 15) to be to Michael rather than Christ. He takes this Jewish work to originate among Philo's Therapeutae (on whom more below).

In 1979 Charlesworth's student, Elbert Garrett Martin, completed a doctoral dissertation on the *Story of Zosimus* (which he called the *Account of the Blessed Ones*).[67] He takes the original and Jewish core of the work to be Chapters 8-10 (minus a number of secondary verses and phrases). A Jewish redactor added Chapters 11-12 and 14-15 (minus 11:1; 15:3; and part of 15:10). Then Christian redactors added 13:1-5, 16:1-7, followed by Chapters 1-7 and 17-18 and brief additions throughout. The Syriac version also has a number of its own additions and variations. Charlesworth himself published a rather different reconstruction in 1976 in which he found Chapters 7-9 to be the central core,[68] but in his 1986 introduction to his translation of the Syriac version he appears at least sympathetic to Martin's reconstruction, although his analysis differs in details and he does not explicitly endorse Martin's conclusion that Chapters 8-10 are the original core.[69] He cautiously declines to attribute the work to a particular provenance and regarding its origins he writes '[a]t this stage in our work it is best to suggest only that sections of this document are Jewish or heavily influenced by Jewish traditions, and that they may antedate the second century A.D.'[70] In 1983 J. Duncan M. Derrett pointed to parallels between the *Story of Zosimus* 11 and (Ps.?) Palladius, *De Vita Bragmanorum*, a fifth century C E or later account of the ancient Brahmins combined with a conversation between Alexander the Great and an Indian sage. The parallels with the *Story of Zosimus* are in the first section, on the Brahmins. Derrett concludes that the two works 'have a common ancestor in terms of thought, if not of dependence verbatim.'[71]

In the 1990s Chris Knights published several articles on the *Story of Zosimus* in which he advanced a full reconstruction of the redaction history of the work.[72] He noted that the unit consisting of Chapters 8-10, which had already been isolated by Martin, had clear redactional seams immediately before and after it. In 7:14 Zosimus asks to know about the 'administrations' ($\delta\iota o\iota\kappa\acute\eta\sigma\epsilon\iota\varsigma$) of the Blessed Ones, a question answered at length in Chapters 11-16 but ignored in 8-10, which tells the history of the group's transfer to their abode in the time of Jeremiah. The transitions before and after 8-10 flow much better in the Syriac version, which implies that it has smoothed out the difficulties of the Greek. Chaps. 8-10 concern the Rechabites, who are not mentioned elsewhere in the work; these chapters lack the distinctive vocabulary of the rest of the work; Zosimus does not appear in them; and the chapters seem not to be present in the Ethiopic and Armenian versions.[73] References in these chapters to the Rechabites being commanded to go naked (8:3-5; 9:9) are probably secondary insertions, since nudity was frowned upon in ancient Judaism, the nudity of the Blessed Ones is mentioned elsewhere in the work, and some passages in 8-10 which should mention the nudity do not (9:8; 10:2). The mysterious references to avoidance of honey may also be secondary.[74]

The implication is that Chaps. 8-10 is not the original core of the *Story of Zosimus*, but an independent unit that was inserted into an already existing version of it. Knights finds the original core of the work in Chaps. 11-12, 14-16:7, a unit that he entitles the *Abode of the Blessed*. Three main factors lead him to this conclusion. First, this speech by the Blessed Ones addresses its listeners in the plural, which is inappropriate if Zosimus is in mind. Second, Zosimus himself is never mentioned in the unit. Third, Chapter 13 is a secondary Christian addition that mentions Lent, Easter, and the resurrection of Christ.[75] Thus Knights reconstructs the full redaction history of the *Story of Zosimus* along the following lines: a Jewish work, the *Abode of the Blessed* (Chaps. 11-12, 14-16:7), formed the original core and was in existence in a Greek form before about 850 CE, when the Canon of Nicephorus Homolegata mentions the *Apocalypse of Zosimus*. The *Abode of the Blessed* was expanded by a Christian author or authors to include Chapters. 1-7, 13, and 16:8-18:5, additions that transformed the story into a travelogue of the hermit Zosimus. Then the Greek *History of the Rechabites* (Chaps. 8-10), also a Jewish work, was inserted between Chapters 7

---

[73] Knights's arguments are summarized in 'The *Abode of the Blessed*,' 80-81. See also '"The Story of Zosimus,"' 237-40. [74] Knights, '"The Story of Zosimus,"' 240-41; idem, 'The *History of the Rechabites*,' 419-20, 428, 429. [75] Knights, 'The *Abode of the Blessed*,' 83-84, 86. [76] 'The *Abode of the Blessed*,' 85. [77] Ibid., 85-86. [78] Ibid., 86, his emphasis.

and 11, with minor changes introduced into it to harmonize it with the rest of the story. Last of all, Chapters 19-23 were added to the Greek version.

I am largely persuaded by Knights's redactional analysis: he makes a good case for the independent preexistence of both the *Abode of the Blessed* and the *History of the Rechabites* and for their incorporation into the *Story of Zosimus* in the order indicated. I wish, however, to challenge his case for either of these earlier works being Jewish compositions. Although redactional analysis of the work has varied among scholars, the arguments they have advanced for a Jewish origin refer to material found either in the *Abode of the Blessed* or the *History of the Rechabites*, so I will consider each in turn as a potential Jewish document.

THE ABODE OF THE BLESSED ‥‥‥ ‥‥‥ Knights writes that '[i]t may be reasonably claimed … that *Ab. Bles.* is Jewish,'[76] yet his efforts to argue the case are surprisingly perfunctory. He asserts that a number of apparently Christian passages *could* be Jewish. He reasonably points out that 12:3 says that the Blessed Ones are *not* naked, but wear the garment of immortality, and so the statement is compatible with a Jewish origin. It may be that the references in 4:1, 5:2-3, 8:3-5 and 9:9 are inspired by 12:3; and 5:2-4 is also equivocal about the nakedness of the Blessed Ones. The two interpolations in the *History of the Rechabites* seem to misunderstand and take the nakedness of the Blessed Ones as literal and unequivocal. Knights also cites 2 *En.* 22:8, 3 *En.* 12:2-3; *T. Job* 48:3 and the *Martyrdom and Ascension of Isaiah* as Jewish parallels for the concept of the 'garment of immortality,' although only the second can be classed with confidence as Jewish. Still, he is right to assert that 12:3 need not by any means be by a Christian.[77]

He is on much weaker ground in his treatment of Chapter 16, which refers to 'the Son of God himself,' the 'church,' and the 'Eucharist.' It is true that 'none of these terms is *of necessity* Christian.'[78] Son of God is an angelic title and can also be used of human beings, but this is the Son of God *himself*, evidently a unique case, surely referring to Christ. Likewise, the Greek word ἐκκλησία need not mean 'church,' but this is its most natural meaning in a document transmitted by Christians, and the word εὐχαριστία can mean 'thanksgiving' as well as Eucharist, but the natural meaning in the context of believers arriving at church would surely be the latter rather than the former. Knights writes, '[t]hus all the words in *Stor. Zos.* 16 which appear, at first sight, to be Christian, are not assuredly so. The description *could* be a Jewish one, and I would suggest (like McNeil) that there is every reason to argue that it is.'[79] In fact, there is little reason to do so and, in any case, he does *not* argue this, he simply asserts the possibility. The most natural reading of the chapter by far is that it refers to explicitly Christian themes. Yet this material cannot be readily excised as secondary and it leads us to the conclusion that the *Abode of the Blessed* is a Christian work.

As far as I am aware, only one positive argument has been advanced in favor of the Jewish authorship of the *Abode of the Blessed*. McNeil has pointed out that a passage in the Talmud *Yerushalmi* (*y. Yeb.* 6.6) parallels the rules for the sexual asceticism of the Blessed Ones.[80] The Talmudic passage requires that a man produce two children before he may 'withdraw from the duty of propagation' and reports some debate on what exactly is meant by 'two children.' The *Abode of the Blessed* 11:6-8 (Narr. 10) describes much the same custom for the Blessed Ones: after a couple produce two children they separate and become celibate, although it adds that one of the children marries and the other remains a virgin, an idea lacking in the *Yerushalmi* passage and one that undercuts the purpose of the ruling.[81] The concepts are similar but there is no reason to assume that this idea came directly from the Talmud or even Jewish tradition. Asceticism was a matter of widespread interest in the ancient world and such ideas could have arisen and been discussed in many circles. The parallel is interesting but by itself it proves nothing.

---

[79] Ibid., 87, his emphasis. [80] McNeil, 'The Narration of Zosimus,' 72-73. [81] If each couple produces only two children and half of all the children do not reproduce, the community will shrink by fifty percent each generation until no one is left. This verse (11:8) is missing in Cod. Mus. Brit. Add. 10073, either because it is a secondary addition, or because a scribe recognized the problem with it and deleted it. [82] 'Towards a Critical Introduction,' 327-30; 'The History of the Rechabites,' 418-19, 420, 422, 424, 425, 427, 432. [83] Ibid., 429. [84] Ibid., 416-19; 'The Rechabites in the Bible and in Jewish Tradition,' 2:45-55. The rabbinic texts are *Mekhilta de Rabbi Simeon* to Exod 18:27; *Tanhumah Shemini* 5 // *Tanhumah Buber Shemini* 14; *Sifre Numbers* 78; and *Yalkut Shim'oni* to the Prophets 38. [85] 'The History of the Rechabites,' 429-30; 'The Rechabites in the Bible and in Jewish Tradition,' 2:45-55. The rabbinic texts are *Mekhilta de Rabbi Simeon* to Exod 18:27; *Sifre Numbers* 78; and *Yalkut Shim'oni* to the Torah 169. [86] 'The History of the Rechabites,' 434-36; 'The Rechabites in the Bible and in Jewish Tradition,' 2:97-98.

Knights rightly takes the original language of this work to be Greek, inasmuch as it uses the Septuagint, and he also rightly regards such Semitisms as appear in it as Septuagintalisms.[82] The Greek of 9:10 appears to echo Peter's words in the story of the transfiguration of Jesus in Mark 9:5 and parallels, but Knights simply raises the possibility, without argument, that it is 'another Christian insertion into the text.'[83] His main positive arguments involve connections with late rabbinic passages, almost all of which date to after the rise of Islam, in some cases long after. According to *Story of Zosimus* 8:3 the father of the Rechabites, 'Aminadab,' heard Jeremiah's preaching and in response commanded the Rechabites to adopt their peculiar lifestyle. Knights points out that some rabbinic passages report that 'Jonadab' ordered his followers to follow the prescribed lifestyle as a result of hearing Jeremiah's preaching.[84] If we assume that 'Aminadab' is a corruption of 'Jonadab,' it may be that this detail – and it is only a detail – derives from knowledge of late Jewish midrash, but it is equally possibly that it arises from an independent reading of Jeremiah 35 which took the Jonadab son of Rechab mentioned there to be a contemporary of Jeremiah, and by implication understood the Jonadab son of Rechab in 1 Kgs 10:15-23 to be a different person. Likewise, Jeremiah 35 does not make it explicit that the commands of Jonadab had divine authority behind them, but some rabbinic texts and one textual tradition of the *History of the Rechabites* 10:3 take this view.[85] But this is a natural deduction and requires no genetic influence.

The *History of the Rechabites* 10:5-9 describes how an angel delivered the Rechabites from prison and led them through and then across a river to the land they currently inhabited, which was then surrounded by water and a wall of cloud. Three rabbinic passages also refer to the exile of the Rechabites. *Pesikta Rabbati* 31 identifies them with those from 'the land of Sinim' who will return to the Holy Land at the eschaton according to Isa 49:12 (and who, by implication, are currently in exile). According to the *Midrash Aggadah* to Num 24:22 the Rechabites were sent to the 'dark mountains' by God at the time of the destruction of the temple. And 2 *Alphabet of Ben Sira* 28 asserts that 'the descendants of Jonadab live in Paradise where they entered alive.'[86] The separate traditions are not very close to the *History of the Rechabites* but if we combine them in just the right way they are somewhat more impressive: the Rechabites were taken away to a paradisiacal realm by God at the time of the destruction of the temple. It may be that the writer of the *History* of the Rechabites was aware of a Jewish tradition to this effect (if one ever existed at all), although it seems equally possible that the rabbinic texts echo a non-Jewish tradition like the one found in the *History of the Rechabites*. There is no evidence for a literary connection and it is not clear in which direction influence, if any, flowed.

Other arguments are weaker or more tangential still. Knights acknowledges that the portrayal of Jerusalem 'may be an entirely stylized one' and gives good reason for thinking so, yet he also asserts that '[t]he centrality of Jerusalem in *The History of the Rechabites* would point to the *place* of composition as being Palestine rather than Babylonia or Egypt or elsewhere in the Diaspora.'[87] It hardly needs to be replied that an interest in Jerusalem in biblical pseudepigrapha is likely enough on its own terms and tells us nothing about a text's provenance. Likewise, McNeil notes that Jeremiah figures in a number of extracanonical Jewish texts and suggests that the *Story of Zosimus* draws on 'common legends and traditions' rather than having a genetic connection with any of the known works.[88] This is likely enough, but all the Jeremianic works he cites were known to and transmitted by Christians, who doubtless developed their own body of Jeremiah legends.

Finally, McNeil also proposes that the Jewish core of the *Story of Zosimus* was written in the circle of the Therapeutae on the grounds that 'if it be accepted that the Narration is a statement of the ideals of a Jewish community, then the group whose ideals it fits with the minimum of difficulty is the Therapeutae.'[89] This is circular reasoning. Jew-

---

[87] 'Towards a Critical Introduction,' 332, his emphasis. [88] 'The Narration of Zosimus,' 74. [89] Ibid., 81. [90] Alexander Golitzin, 'Recovering the "Glory of Adam": "Divine Light" Traditions in the Dead Sea Scrolls and the Christian Ascetical Literature of Fourth-Century Syro-Mesopotamia' in *The Dead Sea Scrolls as Background to Postbiblical Judaism and Early Christianity* (ed. James R. Davila; STDJ 46; Leiden: Brill, 2003), 275-308. See also Chapter Two above. [91] McNeil, 'The Narration of Zosimus,' 75, 80-81; idem, 'Asexuality and the Apocalyse of Zosimus,' *HeyJ* 22 (1981): 172-73; Knights, 'Towards a Critical Introduction,' 337-38; idem, 'The Abode of the Blessed,' 93. In the penultimate reference Knights notes some passages in which the Rechabites are taken as models for monastic communities. The early Christian writers had a positive view of the Rechabites and referred to them several more times. Hegesippus tells us that when James the brother of Jesus was being stoned, one of the Rechabites, who are identified as a priestly family to which Jeremiah testified, protested (Eusebius, *Hist. eccl.* 2.23); the Rechabites are held up as an example by John Chrysostom for not disobeying their father's command (*Hom. Acts* 5:34) and as people approved by the prophets (*Hom. Matt.* 12:38-39 4); and Jerome extols the asceticism of the Rechabites in *Jov.* II.3.15 and calls them 'holy men' in *Epist.* 52.3.

ish provenance is the point he sets out, but fails, to demonstrate. On the contrary, he notes that the work rejects calendrical observances (Chap. 12; Narr. 11), and with them by implication the sabbath and the Jewish festivals, and that it never refers to the Jewish Law. The Therapeutae explicitly observe festivals, we may assume they kept the Torah, and we are not told that they had any interest in angels, all of which McNeil acknowledges make the identification problematical. As for the worship of the Blessed Ones, we learn that they pray (11:4); they commune with the angels and rejoice over the righteous and intercede for sinners (12:6-9); they observe Lent and Easter (13:1-5, in contradiction to 12:1); and that after joyful funeral services shared with the angels (15:5-16:4) they worship in church and celebrate the Eucharist (16:5-7). It is only with painful contortions that this picture can be reconciled with any form of Judaism.

What then are we to make of the *Story of Zosimus?* It should be clear by now that I am not persuaded that any level in its redactional history is Jewish. I take the original core to be the *Abode of the Blessed* (Chaps. 11:1-16:7) and see no reason to delete any of the surviving text of those chapters as secondary. This work is dependent in some way on the traditions about the Brahmins found also in *De Vita Bragmanorum*. Around the *Abode of the Blessed* was constructed the journey of the hermit Zosimus in Chaps. 1-7 and 16:8-18:5, which make somewhat more of the nudity of the Blessed Ones than the original document. Then the *History of the Rechabites* (Chaps. 8-10), an originally independent unit, was added and adjusted slightly by the addition of the commands for the Rechabites to remove their clothing and probably the addition of the plural address to the 'sons of men.' There are clear indications of Christian authorship in the *Abode of the Blessed* and the chapters on Zosimus the hermit, and perhaps in the *History of the Rechabites* as well. And the fact that there are rabbinic parallels to some material in both the *Abode of the Blessed* and the *History of the Rechabites* proves nothing. The parallels are not close and, even if we take them to reflect Jewish influence, many Christian writers in late antiquity were well acquainted with Jewish traditions.[90]

Both McNeil and Knights have pointed to reasons why the *Abode of the Blessed*, the *History of the Rechabites*, and the redacted forms of the *Story of Zosimus* would have been appealing to monastic circles and might well have been adopted and transmitted in them.[91] I would go further and suggest the likelihood that they were *both* composed *and* transmitted in such circles or in circles sympathetic to monasticism and the ascetic lifestyle. (It is perhaps worth noting that both the *Abode of the*

Blessed and the redacted form of the *Story of Zosimus* address themselves to all 'the sons of men' to defend the strange ascetic lifestyle of the Blessed Ones.) Monastic Christianity is the first context in which we should try to understand these texts and I see no need to seek an earlier, Jewish origin for any of them.[92]

8

CONCLUSIONS

The most persuasive cases for a Jewish origin for any of these works has been that of Collins for the main corpus of *Sibylline Oracles* 3 and for *Sibylline Oracles* 5 as originating among Egyptian Jewry, perhaps in ancient Leontopolis. Nevertheless, the main corpus of *Sibylline Oracles* 3 could plausibly be assigned to a gentile God-fearer in the first century B C E and *Sibylline Oracles* 5 to either a Jewish-Christian or a gentile God-fearer between the first and second Jewish revolts in the late first and early second centuries C E. Serious cases have been made for placing the origin of *Joseph and Aseneth* in Jewish circles (including Heliopolis/Leontopolis) before about 200 C E, or in Christian, Samaritan, or gentile God-fearing circles in late antiquity. The position that requires the least extrapolation from the surviving manuscripts is that of Christian origin, but the nature of the Joseph story seems to facilitate its retelling without the use of Jewish or Christian signature features, and none of the proposed origins can be dismissed. The most plausible origin

---

[92] This section on the *Story of Zosimus* is a slightly abbreviated and revised form of a paper presented in the Pseudepigrapha Section at the annual meeting of the Society of Biblical Literature in Atlanta in November of 2003 and published online. Since then I have seen Nikolsky's unpublished doctoral dissertation 'The Provenance of *The Journey of Zosimus*,' which independent comes to much the same conclusions as mine. She considers the Greek *Story of Zosimus* (which she calls the *Journey of Zosimus*) to be a unitary Christian composition incorporating earlier sources, all of which are also of Christian origin. She argues that the final form of the work was composed in the late seventh or early eighth century C E by a monk associated with the Judean Desert and that the incorporated source the *History of the Rechabites* was composed in monastic circles in the fourth century C E. See also her articles 'The *History of the Rechabites* and the Jeremiah Literature,' *JSP* 13 (2002): 185-207 (despite the date of the volume, the article was published in 2004) and 'The Adam and Eve Traditions in *The Journey of Zosimos*,' in Chazon (ed.), *Things Revealed*, 345-56. Her arguments in support of a monastic Christian origin for the work and its sources are far more thorough than those offered here, and I find most of her conclusions plausible. I am not convinced, however, that Chapters 19-23 are part of the original Greek composition, since they are missing in the other versions. That is not to deny, however, that the author who added them did so with an eye to the overall structure of the work.

for the *Testament of Job* is Christian circles in Egypt in late antiquity, although a somewhat earlier origin and authorship by a Jew or even a gentile God-fearer cannot be ruled out. The origin of the *Testament of Abraham* is difficult to ascertain. There are elements, especially involving the eschatological speculations in Chapter 13, which are difficult to reconcile with Christian authorship. Nevertheless, this passage, as well as the rest of the book, is replete with Christian terminology, and positing Jewish authorship solves few difficulties while creating more. It is not impossible that a Jewish *Urtext* lies behind the surviving recensions of the *Testament of Abraham*, but if so, this *Urtext* is irrecoverable and positing it does not improve our understanding of the recensions we actually have. They are clearly Christian works of late antiquity, albeit less than orthodox by the standards of the church fathers, and I see no gain in attempting to move behind them to a Jewish *Urtext*. The *Story of Zosimus* and its apparent sources display no positive evidence for Jewish authorship and fit the context of Christian monasticism in late antiquity extremely well, so well that the best hypothesis is that they originated in these monastic circles or circles sympathetic to monasticism.

A number of insights from earlier chapters have informed the conclusions of this one and Chapter Three. I will say more about these in the conclusions to this book. Here I simply note the significance of Kraft's basic perception that our understanding of the Old Testament pseudepigrapha is made clearer if we start from the manuscripts and work backwards from them only as necessary rather than beginning with the default assumption that whatever is not explicitly or inevitably Christian must be Jewish. This shift in perspective changes the questions we ask and how the evidence is weighed, highlights the weaknesses in previous evaluations of these texts, and leads us to keep in view a wider range of possibilities for their origins.

EXCURSUS Observations on
the Old Testament Apocrypha

This book focuses on the Christian transmission of Jewish pseudepigrapha, but this issue is obviously part of a larger problem. The Old Testament Apocrypha and pseudepigrapha have in common that all were ultimately rejected from the scriptural canon of Judaism. The books in the Old Testament Apocrypha are not qualitatively different from those in the pseudepigrapha (indeed, the boundary between Apocrypha and pseudepigrapha is not entirely stable, as noted in the introduction), but the Apocrypha obtained canonical status in most of Christendom in antiquity and retain it today, apart from in the Protestant canon. Although some pseudepigrapha were canonized in some Christian churches (e.g., *1 Enoch* and *Jubilees* in the Ethiopic Church), they were not generally accepted as scripture by Christians. The Old Testament Apocrypha are technically outside the scope of this book and it is generally accepted that all of them are of Jewish origin.[93] For the most part I agree with this conclusion. In Chapter One, I have already established such an origin for three of them on external grounds. Much of the original Hebrew of Ben Sira survives in medieval manuscripts and fragments from Madasa and the Qumran library. Fragments of Tobit in Aramaic and Hebrew have also been recovered from the Qumran library, as has a

---

[93] Recent introductions to the Apocrypha include Daniel J. Harrington, *Invitation to the Apocrypha* (Grand Rapids, Mich.: Eerdmans, 1999) and David A. deSilva, *Introducing the Apocrypha: Message, Context, and Significance* (Grand Rapids, Mich.: Baker, 2002). [94] See *Ant.* 11.1-158 and perhaps 10.70-83; *Ant.* 241-13.214; and *Ant.* 11.184-296, respectively. [95] Carey A. Moore, *Daniel, Esther, and Jeremiah: The Additions* (AB 44; Garden City, N.Y.: Doubleday, 1977), 29. [96] Joseph Ziegler, *Sapientia Salomonis* (Septuaginta: Vetus Testamentum Graecum Auctoritate Societatis Litterarum Gottingensis 12.1; Göttingen: Vandenhoeck & Ruprecht, 1962), 7-38; David Winston, *The Wisdom of Solomon* (AB 43; Garden City, N.Y.: Doubleday, 1984), 64-66. [97] Francis Watson has recently argued at length that in Rom 1:18-32 Paul is engaging on a very detailed level with Wisd 13-14 (*Paul and the Hermeneutics of Faith* [London: Clark, 2004], 404-411). His argument is based mainly on thematic parallels: the opportunity to know the true God was wasted; idolatry is the most fundamental error of humanity and is the root of all other evils; and idolatry leads to divine punishment. But these ideas are scriptural truisms and can be derived from Isaiah 44 (especially vv. 9-20, but much of the rest of the chapter is relevant) combined with other scriptural passages on idolatry which share themes or catchwords with this passage. Notably, Deut 4:16-24 connects with Isaiah 44 via the idea of idols in human form in v. 16 and Isa 44:12-13; Hos 4:11-14 connects via the idea of the 'desires' ($\kappa\alpha\tau\alpha\vartheta\acute{\upsilon}\mu\iota\alpha$) of the idolaters in Isa 44:9; and 2 Kings 21 connects via the catchword 'abomination' ($\beta\delta\acute{\epsilon}\lambda\upsilon\gamma\mu\alpha$) in v. 2 and Isa 44:19. The thematic, verbal, and conceptual parallels between Romans and the Wisdom of Solomon which Watson notes arise from these scriptural passages on idolatry. It may indeed be that Paul engages with the Wisdom of Solomon, in which case the latter could still conceivably be a very early Christian although its Jewish origin would become much more likely. But the Pauline passage shows no awareness of the context of the parallel passage in the Wisdom of Solomon (pertaining to the idolatry of the Egyptians) and Paul and the Wisdom of Solomon may be interacting independently with scripture-inspired Jewish notions about idolatry (Paul applying this sin to all humanity and the author of the Wisdom of Solomon congratulating the audience for not succumbing to it). The Epistle of Jeremiah demonstrates both that ancient Jews engaged in extended reflection on Isaiah 44 and that Christians found these reflections interesting enough to transmit themselves.

very fragmentary copy of the Epistle of Jeremiah in Greek. In addition, the use of 1 Esdras, 1 Maccabees, and Additions to Esther B, C, D, and E by Josephus demonstrates that an important Jewish writer accepted them as Jewish works.[94] In all these cases the internal evidence also supports a Jewish origin. Internal evidence also provides a strong case for regarding most of the remaining Apocrypha as Jewish, including Judith, 2 Maccabees, and the Additions to Esther A and F. All these works contain Jewish signature features and most of them are replete with such features. The contents of the Additions to Daniel are consistent with either Christian or Jewish authorship, but if it is correct that they are written in the same style as the rest of the Old Greek translation of Daniel, the best working hypothesis is that their Semitic originals were included in the *Vorlage* translated into Greek in the pre-Christian period and thus that they are almost certainly Jewish.[95] Nevertheless, in two cases the evidence seems to allow for other possibilities and these two documents, the Wisdom of Solomon and to a lesser degree the book of Baruch, are worth discussing briefly.

THE WISDOM OF SOLOMON The Wisdom of Solomon is a sapiential work that claims pseudonymously to have been written by Solomon. It deals with questions of eschatology and the judgment of the righteous and the wicked (Chaps. 1-5); the nature of wisdom (Chaps. 6-9); and the history of God's dealings with the human race, especially with Israel, from Adam to Israel's wandering in the wilderness (Chaps. 10-19). It was composed in Greek sometime in the Hellenistic period. The earliest complete manuscripts are the uncials Codex Sinaiticus (fourth century C E), Codex Alexandrinus (fifth century C E), Codex Ephraemi Syri rescriptus (fifth century C E; preserved only in part as the bottom layer of a palimpsest), and Codex Venetus (eighth century C E). It also survives in a few small papyrus fragments, the earliest of which go back to third-century Antioopolis; in numerous Greek minuscules; the important Old Latin translation; a Sahidic Coptic translation; a very free Syriac translation; and some other translations and citations of lesser importance.[96] It is very difficult to establish a date of composition. It draws on the L X X translation of Isaiah, which seems to have been done no earlier than the end of the third century B C E. Some relation to the letters of Paul is possible but it is unclear if the similarities are the result of deliberate allusion or, if so, in which direction influence ran. If it could be established that Paul knew the work, its Jewish authorship would, of course, be very probable.[97] Two passages in 1 *Clement* seem to be quotations of the

Wisdom of Solomon, although neither is presented as a quotation of another work. *1 Clem.* 3:4 shares the phrase 'death entered the world' with Wis 2:24 and the two works attribute this entry, respectively, to the agency of 'jealousy' (ζῆλος) or 'envy' (φθόνος). The notion that evil brought death into the world was not unknown in this period (cf. the similar sentiments of Paul in Rom 5:12), but the connection specifically with envy is harder to explain away. *1 Clem* 27:5a is nearly identical with Wis 12:12a, although both combine the LXX of Job 9:19 with Jer 27:44 in slightly different formulations, perhaps with some other passages in mind, and it is not impossible that the two works cite a common written or oral source.[98] Nevertheless, and especially given that we have two apparent quotations, a reasonable reading of the evidence is that *1 Clement* is quoting the Wisdom of Solomon and, therefore, that the latter work was circulating around the end of the first century CE. If so, the writer of *1 Clement* found the Wisdom of Solomon useful for its connecting of the origin of death with envious evil and for its affirmation of the sovereignty of God.

According to Eusebius, *Hist. eccl.* 5.26, Irenaeus quoted the Wisdom of Solomon, evidently citing it by title. Irenaeus also alludes to Wis 6:19 in support of the view that created humanity can take on the immortality of the uncreated God (*Haer.* 4.38.3). The earliest surviving explicit quotation of the Wisdom of Solomon is found in Clement of Alexandria's *Stromateis*. In *Strom.* 5.108.2 he cites the 'Book of Wisdom' (Wis 7:24) as authority, contra the Stoics, that Wisdom rather than God pervades all things. And in *Strom* 6.93.2 he quotes Wis 6:10, 7:16, and 14:2-3 (the last explicitly attributed to Solomon) to support his case for regarding secular branches of Hellenic philosophy such as astronomy and geometry as aspects of Divine Wisdom.

---

[98] Lester L. Grabbe also notes Wis 11:21 and 7:17 and possible parallels, respectively, to *1 Clem* 27:5 and 60:1. See his *Wisdom of Solomon* (Guides to Apocrypha and Pseudepigrapha; Sheffield: Sheffield Academic Press, 1997), 29. [99] Some of these themes are attested in the writings of later Christian authors. See J. Edgar Bruns, 'Philo Christianus: The Debris of a Legend,' *HTR* 66 (1973): 141-45, esp. p. 143; William Horbury, 'The Christian Use and the Jewish Origins of the Wisdom of Solomon,' in *Wisdom in Ancient Israel* (ed. John Day et al.; Cambridge: Cambridge University Press, 1995), 182-96, esp. 192-93. [100] Winston, *Wisdom of Solomon*, 67-68. [101] Horbury, 'The Wisdom of Solomon in the Muratorian Fragment,' *JTS* 45 (1994): 149-59. [102] See the Excursus at the end of Chapter Three for information on the roles of Clement and Origen in the transmission of Philo's works. [103] Winston, *Wisdom of Solomon*, 59-63. [104] Bruns, 'Philo Christianus,' 143.

It appears from these citations that Christians valued the book for its philosophical elements that helped give intellectual credibility to Christianity. It is likely that early Christians also would have appreciated the book's theme of the vindication of the persecuted righteous, which could be taken as a protevangelium of both the suffering of Christ and the suffering of persecuted Christians; its exaltation of wisdom; its opposition to idolatry; and its universalism. The reference to the blessed wood by which righteousness comes (14:7), although referring to Noah's ark, cries out for a typological application to the cross. In 16:26 we find sentiments that would have reminded Christians of Jesus' words to the devil in Matt 4:4 and parallels. And the picture of the Word of God as Divine Warrior (18:15-16) would bring to mind the Parousia of Jesus and passages such as Revelation 19.[99]

Although the Solomonic authorship of the Wisdom of Solomon was accepted by Clement of Alexandria, it was challenged to some degree by Origen and more vigorously by Eusebius, Augustine, and Jerome. The Muratorian Canon, which may have been composed as early as the second century CE or as late as the fourth, lists the Wisdom of Solomon in the New Testament after Jude and 1-2 John and before Revelation, saying that, 'Wisdom was written by the friends of Solomon in his honor.' A widely accepted proposal by Tregelles argues that the Latin is a misunderstanding of a Greek *Vorlage* that attributed the Wisdom of Solomon to Philo, that is, Philo of Alexandria.[100] Tregelles' emendation is possible, although William Horbury has recently argued persuasively against it.[101] In any case, Jerome, in his *Preface to the Books of Solomon*, reports that a number of older writers assigned the Wisdom of Solomon to Philo. Philonic authorship is an interesting possibility but both the external and internal evidence speak against it. The attribution to Philo was unknown to Clement and Origen, both of whom knew the Wisdom of Solomon and had access to Philo's works in his home city of Alexandria.[102] Although there are numerous parallels of thought between the Wisdom of Solomon and the works of Philo, there are substantial differences as well, most notably the lack of Philo's Platonism and love of allegory in the Wisdom of Solomon.[103] J. Edgar Bruns has suggested that the attribution to Philo arose as an element of the Philo Christianus legend, since, as noted above, Christian writers could read the Wisdom of Solomon as containing references to the mysteries of Christian redemption, and assigning the book to Philo would reinforce his status as a convert to Christianity.[104] This may be the correct explanation. Perhaps the possibility of Philo's authorship of the Wisdom of

Solomon cannot be ruled out entirely, but there is very little evidence for it.

It seems to be universally accepted today that the Wisdom of Solomon is a Jewish work. Yet if we proceed as usual and begin with the contexts of the earliest manuscripts and citations, this conclusion is by no means required by the evidence. A key problem is the pseudepigraphic adoption of the persona of Solomon. The writer is clearly attempting to sound authentically like Solomon, despite the gross anachronism of composing the book in Greek. Solomon is the implied author and the implied readers are the Israelites during the United Monarchy. So we must ask to what degree the supposed Jewish elements in the book can be attributed to the fact that it is written from the adopted perspective of Solomon and whether a Christian writer (or someone else, such as a gentile God-fearer) could have adopted the same persona.

If we look for Jewish signature features in the Wisdom of Solomon, the most interesting passages have to do with the people of Israel. The writer, in the guise of Solomon, refers to himself as king of God's people (9:7). The writer claims that idolatry had not misled 'us,' that is, Israel (15:4; contrast 1 Cor 12:2), but given the Solomonic persona adopted, this tells us nothing about the actual author and audience. They are a 'sacred people and a blameless seed' (10:15); God chastens his people but punishes their enemies far more (12:19-22); their trials during the wandering in the wilderness are viewed sympathetically (11:1-14; 11:21-12:2, 19-22; 16:2-7; 18:20-25); they are contrasted both with the idolatrous Egyptian oppressors (10:20; 11:9-20; 12:23-27; 16:5-18:19; 19:1-21) and idolatrous peoples of the promised land (12:3-11); they are the 'holy nation' (17:2) and 'sacred ones' (18:1-2, 5, 9); indeed it was through God's 'sons' that 'the light of the incorruptible Law was to be given to the world' (18:4; cf. 16:6; 18:9). But aside from these references, there is little that can be regarded as explicitly Jewish. We find mention of 'the oaths and covenants of the fathers' in 18:22. The writer refers to God's 'Holy Land' in 12:3. There is a reference to clean uses of pottery in 15:7, which seems to imply some awareness of ritual purity issues, but the comment is metaphorical and cannot be pressed very hard. Aaron's propitiation of God with incense is noted in 18:21, but this is a detail taken from the scriptural story (Num 16:46-47). The writer, speaking as Solomon, refers to his mandate to be king of God's people and to build the temple and altar in Jerusalem (9:8), but these too, of course, are scriptural details.

Our earliest citation of the Wisdom of Solomon comes from *1 Clement*, so it seems reasonable to start with this Christian work as a context for it. Given what we have noted above, could the Wisdom of Solomon have been written in the same circle that produced *1 Clement?* The letter of *1 Clement* was sent around the end of the first century CE by the gentile Christian church of Rome to the church in Corinth to protest the summary dismissal of some senior members of the latter church. We do not know how the letter was received in Corinth, but its preservation and presence centuries later in Codex Alexandrinus implies that it was taken seriously by its recipients.

We may note, to begin with, that, although the writer of *1 Clement* was caught up with issues surrounding the deacons and bishops of the church (*1 Clem.* 42-44) and saw the church's membership and mandate extending to all nations (*1 Clem.* 59:2-4; 65:2), nevertheless this writer adopted scriptural Israel and the patriarchs as ancestors of the church. *1 Clement* 10 summarizes the story of Abraham, quoting with apparent approval the scriptural promises of blessing and fecundity for his seed (Gen 12:1-3; 13:14-16, 15:5-6; *1 Clem.* 10:3-6). Indeed, in *1 Clem.* 31:2 he is called 'our father Abraham.' In *1 Clem.* 29:1-3 the author quotes scriptural passages about the special status of Israel to God, only to identify the author and audience with this Israel in 30:1. Indeed, according to *1 Clem.* 64:1 they are chosen to be God's 'special people' (λαὸς περιούσιος; cf. LXX Exod 19:5 and 23:22). The author also quotes, with apparent approval, scriptural references to the Law (*1 Clem.* 53:2) and the covenant (*1 Clem.* 15:4) and refers, also with every indication of approval, to the priests and Levites who serve at the altar, the high priest, and a number of different types of offerings and sacrifices in the Jerusalem temple (*1 Clem.* 32:2; 40:2-5; 41:2-3). Although the author accepts Paul's authority (*1 Clem.* 47:1-4), and so presumably his abrogation of the Law for followers of Jesus, and although the temple has been destroyed, the writer honors these things in their scriptural contexts.

If we imagine that a member of the circle that produced *1 Clement* was well educated in philosophical matters and set out to write a pseudepigraphic work in the name of Solomon, it seems to me that the product would have notable similarities to our Wisdom of Solomon. The writer would speak with Solomon's voice as understood from a Hellenistic context; would treat matters such as the Law, the temple, and the priesthood with respect because they had scriptural authority and were valid in

Solomon's time; and might well have spoken positively of Israel as God's people with an unexpressed subtext that this adoption as God's people would in due course be transferred to the church. One could argue that the attitude toward Israel in the Wisdom of Solomon is too positive for such an author, and indeed the sins of Israel in the wilderness are glossed over in a way that seems quite untypical for a Christian writer (contrast, e.g., 1 Corinthians 10; Hebrews 3-4; *Barn.* 4:6-8, 14:1-5). Nevertheless, the author's larger agenda in Chapters 11-19 was to show that God rewards his worshipers and punishes idolaters, and a positive presentation of the Israelites over against the Egyptians makes rhetorical sense in that context.[105] The contrast between the Wisdom of Solomon and other, clearly Jewish, works in the Apocrypha is sharp: Ben Sira places himself explicitly in a Jewish context, and Tobit, Judith, and 1-2 Maccabees portray Jews in nonscriptural stories and show a pronounced interest in Jewish identity and, not only the Law and the temple, but the details of the ritual and cultic praxes of both, including nonscriptural Jewish customs and festivals.

In short, I see no compelling reason to move backwards from the context of our earliest quotations of the Wisdom of Solomon in order to ex-

---

[105] The writer of *1 Clement* also emphasizes God's judgment of the Egyptians (17:5; 51:5). The punishment of Dathan and Abiram in the wilderness is mentioned twice (4:12; 51:3-4) but their condemnation is not generalized to the Israelites as a whole. The jealous quarreling of the tribes over the priesthood is mentioned in 43:1-6, but it is implicitly compared to the current strife over ecclesiastical offices in the writer's church and the writer holds up Moses' orderly resolution of the conflict as an example (43:6-44:2). There is no condemnation of Israel in the passage. The only other mention of the sins of Israel in the wilderness comes in *1 Clem.* 53:2-5, which summarizes the story of the golden calf not to condemn the Israelites, but to praise Moses' intercession for them and to hold him up as an example for the church of Corinth in its current crisis. This attitude has some resonance with the emphasis of the writer of the Wisdom of Solomon on God's mercy on the sinful Israelites (11:9, 23; 12:19), especially as the result of the intercession of Moses (16:5-7) and Aaron (18:20-25). [106] Note, for example, that the possibility of Christian authorship is not discussed seriously either by Winston or Grabbe in their books entitled *Wisdom of Solomon*. In an article cited above, Horbury dismisses the possibility almost immediately and constructs an elaborate scenario of Jewish authorship which, if not in itself implausible, is based on scarcely any positive evidence ('The Christian Use,' 182, 194, 196). [107] '(How) Can We Tell If a Greek Apocryphon or Pseudepigraphon Was Translated from Hebrew or Aramaic?' (forthcoming in the *Journal for the Study of the Pseudepigrapha*). [108] Joseph Ziegler, *Jeremias, Baruch, Threni, Epistula Jeremiae* (Septuaginta: Vetus Testamentum Graecum Auctoritate Societatis Litterarum Gottingensis 15; Göttingen: Vandenhoeck & Ruprecht, 1976), 7-10; Carey A. Moore, *Daniel, Esther, and Jeremiah: The Additions*, 255-63.

plain its origin. I find nothing in the work that prohibits or even renders unlikely its having been written by a gentile Christian in the second half of the first century CE. No external evidence proves that the work was ever circulated among Jews and none of the internal evidence demands a Jewish origin. Nevertheless, I would by no means rule out the possibility of composition by a Hellenistic Jew, a God-fearer, or a Jewish-Christian any time in the Hellenistic period up to the second half of the first century. But given the work's interest in Solomon and positive attitude toward the Jerusalem temple and its priesthood, I would eliminate Samaritan origin as a possibility. The biblicizing nature of the work leaves open a wide range of possible origins, none of which should be ignored. It is unfortunate, however, that until now scholars who have written on the Wisdom of Solomon have usually dismissed or ignored most of the possibilities in favor of its composition by a Hellenistic Jew.[106]

BARUCH⸺ ⸺The book of Baruch is a pseudepigraphon attributed to the scribe of Jeremiah in the form of a letter (really a pastiche of biblical passages) by the exiled scribe to his fellow exiles in Babylon. After an introduction (1:1-14), it includes a series of confessional prayers (1:15-3:8), a poem praising wisdom (3:9-4:4) and a psalm of comfort to the exiles (4:5-5:9). It may well be a composite collection incorporating originally separate pieces. It is generally accepted to be a Jewish composition. It survives in Greek as well as Syriac, Latin, and other versions dependent on the Greek. I have argued elswhere that speculation concerning a Hebrew *Vorlage* for part or all of the Greek, despite its virtually universal acceptance by scholars, is ill founded and unconvincing.[107] The Greek text is found in the uncial manuscripts Vaticanus, Alexandrinus, Marchalianus (sixth century CE), Venetus, and presumably was lost from a damaged portion of Sinaiticus. It also survives in very fragmentary papyri going back to the third century CE. In the Greek manuscripts it normally comes between Jeremiah and Lamentations. The earliest reference to it is a quotation of 3:34 by Athenagoras in *Supplication for the Christians* IX in 177 CE.[108] The date of composition is extremely uncertain. If it was composed in Greek, as I believe, it must have originated sometime in the Hellenistic period after the translation of Jeremiah into Greek and before Athenagoras. The external evidence for its origin is thus not very helpful.

Since this book is placed in the mouth of Baruch, the author was clearly trying to speak with Baruch's voice, to the extent that much of the wording is lifted directly from the LXX of Jeremiah and other scriptural texts. Given this implied authorship and biblicizing tendency, we must ask whether anything in the book points to the real author being a Christian, a Jew, or something else. This is not an easy question to answer. Many passages that might be Jewish are also generically scriptural and could equally well have been written by a Christian striving to sound like an Old Testament character. These include references to the Law of Moses (2:2, 27-28; 4:12-13; cf. 1:18 and 2:10); to festivals (1:14); to the temple (2:26; 3:24); to the people of God and Jerusalem (4:4-5, 21-35) and to the return of the Jewish people from exile (4:36-37; 5:5). Christians would have appreciated the implicitly anti-Jewish theme of Israel's sins in Chapters 1-2, 3:1-8, but this is a scriptural theme that was also taken up in Jewish literature such as the Dead Sea Scrolls and 4 Ezra. Both Christians and Jews would have approved of the polemic against idolatry.

Nevertheless, a few passages do point in the direction of Jewish authorship and against Christian authorship. In Bar 2:17-18 the author denies the afterlife in a way that is entirely scriptural (Pss 6:5; 30:9; 88:5; Isa 38:18) and is attested in ancient Jewish literature (e.g., Sir 17:27-28) yet is extremely difficult to imagine coming from the pen of any sort of Christian. The prayer in Bar 2:27-35 expresses a very positive view of the repentance, restoration, and increase of Israel, including the assertions in v. 35 that God has made an eternal covenant with Israel and will never remove them again from their ancestral land. Despite its scriptural antecedents it is very difficult to imagine this verse being written after 70 CE or by a boundary-maintaining Christian. We also find the assertion that the Law continues forever in Bar 4:1. It seems that we can rule out a Christian origin for Baruch. The few Jewish signature features in the book point toward Jewish compostion before the first Jewish revolt against Rome, although composition by a God-fearer remains a viable possibility as well.

CHAPTER FIVE

This book has built on Kraft's insight that the proper place to begin the study of Old Testament pseudepigrapha that have been transmitted by Christians is with the earliest physical evidence for the existence of these works: the manuscripts that contain them. (And, I would add, the earliest certain quotations of them in Christian literature.) We should try to understand these texts first in the same historical context as that of the earliest manuscripts and quotations and, proceeding from the known to the unknown, move backwards to earlier contexts only as required by the evidence. In this book I have asked what criteria and methods we should use to isolate positive evidence (as opposed to arguments from silence) which might persuade us to move backwards to an older context, especially a Jewish one, for such works.

In Chapter One, I set out some intuitively obvious external criteria for isolating Jewish texts and identified a preliminary corpus of the Judean Desert Scrolls (some fully preserved only in versions transmitted by Christians), and the Tannaitic rabbinic texts. On the basis of these (and with some attention also to the works of Philo and Josephus, whose Jewish origin is defended later in the book) I explored the situation of ancient Judaism in relation to the gentile world, both Christian and otherwise. Consistently I found a continuum of belief and practice between Judaism and Christianity and between Judaism and non-Christian gentile religions. Some Jews and Christians were concerned with religious boundary maintenance, but many took a more eclectic if not syncretistic approach to their religion, and it is impossible to be sure what the ratio of the latter to the boundary-maintainers was. The implication for the study of the Old Testament pseudepigrapha is that we have a reasonable prospect of isolating boundary-maintaining Jewish works from other literature, but works written by Jews with less rigid views would be correspondingly harder to distinguish. Accordingly, I proposed a group of 'signature features,' or identifying characteris-

Conclusions

tics, a pervasive pattern of which in a work is likely to indicate that the work is a product of boundary-maintaining Judaism.

Chapter Two makes use of empirical models to ask whether Christians wrote Old Testament pseudepigrapha that either lacked Christian signature features entirely or included only a few that could easily be eliminated by redaction criticism. A look at selected Christian sermons, scriptural commentaries, and poetic epics shows that Christians did write Old Testament pseudepigrapha, that at least some did not find it incoherent that a Christian could write a work that dealt with Old Testament themes and yet never mentioned a Christian doctrine or quoted the New Testament or other early Christian literatures, and that Christians did update explicitly Christian works to make them look more Christian or more doctrinally acceptable. Christians did indeed sometimes retell stories from the Jewish scriptures while including few and peripheral Christian signature features or even no Christian signature features at all, either as an episode in a larger work such as a commentary on a scriptural book or even in a complete work that retells a specific story. Christians also sometimes drew on rabbinic or other Jewish exegetical traditions when retelling stories from the Jewish scriptures. However, none of the texts considered in this chapter contain a clear pattern of Jewish signature features as worked out in Chapter One. Some contain a few of these, in contexts where Christians regarded them as valid for the Old Testament dispensation, even though no longer acceptable in the Christian writer's present. Nevertheless, a close and methodologically sophisticated reading of these texts confirms their Christian origin. The implication is that if even retellings of Old Testament events in Christian sermons, commentaries, and poems – works intended to edify a Christian audience – occasionally could be mistaken for Jewish works, how much more might we expect that some Old Testament pseudepigrapha (or better, Christian apocrypha) composed by Christians who might have good reason to hide their authorship could be readily misunderstood to be Jewish.

229 In Chapter Three, I applied the methodological principles and ad-

vances of the first two chapters to the surviving corpus of Old Testament pseudepigrapha and argued, mostly on the basis of internal criteria, that nine of them are largely intact ancient Jewish pseudepigrapha beyond reasonable doubt. These are: *Aristeas to Philocrates*; *2 Baruch*; the *Similitudes of Enoch*; *4 Ezra*; *3-4 Maccabees*; the Latin Moses fragment (the *Assumption/Testament of Moses*; Pseudo-Philo's *Biblical Antiquities*; and the *Psalms of Solomon*). The Excursus to this chapter also looked briefly at the works of Josephus and Philo.

Chapter Four analyzed six Old Testament pseudepigrapha that are widely understood to be entirely or substantially Jewish compositions. It concludes that *Sibylline Oracle* 3 (main corpus) and 5 may be Jewish works, but other possibilities should not be dismissed. (The case for a Jewish origin for *Sibylline Oracles* 4 and some of the other Sibyllina is weaker than for these two.) *Joseph and Aseneth* and the *Testament of Job* may be Jewish compositions, but positive evidence is lacking and too much weight is given to the argument from silence that they lack indubitable Christian signature features. The two surviving recensions of the *Testament of Abraham* are Christian and there is no convincing evidence for a Jewish *Urtext* behind them. Both the *Story of Zosimus* and its sources are almost certainly Christian rather than Jewish. The Excursus on the Old Testament Apocrypha argued that, although it is possible that all the Apocrypha are of Jewish origin, Baruch could also be by a God-fearer and the Wisdom of Solomon could also be by a first-century gentile Christian and could have other origins as well.

The positive results of this book are the formulation of more rigorous methodologies for determining whether an ancient literary work (especially an Old Testament pseudepigraphon) is of Jewish, Christian, or other origin, and the establishment of a corpus of pseudepigrapha transmitted solely by Christians which can be shown beyond reasonable doubt to be Jewish. It has also confirmed as an ancillary contribution that most of the Old Testament Apocrypha and the works of Philo and Josephus are as well. It is true that this much simply reinforces what we already thought we knew. But the methods developed here articulate far more clearly how we know what we know and what we do not know,

---

[1] But we should bear in mind that there was some sort of Aramaic *Vorlage* of the *Jewish War*.

and establish the conclusions more critically and rigorously than previous efforts. It is important to note that despite the skeptical nature of this approach, it is constructive and is by no means nihilistic: it points to a substantial corpus of Jewish works of whose origin we can be quite confident.

This corpus provides us with a fair range and variety of ancient Jewish literature. It includes a number of Greek compositions (the works of Josephus[1] and Philo, *Aristeas to Philocrates*, 2-4 *Maccabees*, the Epistle of Jeremiah, the Additions to Esther B and E); one work composed in Hebrew whose original is entirely lost (Pseudo-Philo's *Biblical Antiquities*); and some smaller pieces (the Additions to Daniel) which seem likely to derive from a Semitic *Vorlage* of uncertain nature. All of the other Jewish pseudepigrapha and Apocrypha considered here have been assigned Semitic *Vorlagen* at one time or another, but none on conclusive grounds.

Many of these works are witnesses to a Torah-observant form of Judaism (Philo, Josephus, *Aristeas to Philocrates*, 2 *Baruch*, 1-4 *Maccabees*, Pseudo-Philo, and Judith) and a few seem to represent a sectarian (i.e., they define themselves as truly Jewish in contrast to other Jewish groups) form of Torah-observant Judaism (4 *Ezra*, the Latin Moses fragment, and the *Psalms of Solomon*). In addition, we have isolated one Enochic (and therefore not Torah-observant) Jewish work (the Similitudes of Enoch). The Additions to Esther and Daniel are too short to give us conclusive evidence for their affiliations within Judaism, although they do not show obvious signs of being sectarian or Enochic. My approach is geared toward isolation of boundary-maintaining Jewish works but, nevertheless, the Similitudes of Enoch and perhaps the additions to Daniel do not belong obviously to this category.

The geographic origins of these works are very hard to determine and much of what has been written on this has reached confident conclusions on the basis of far too little evidence. Josephus was a Palestinian Jew who wrote in Rome. Internal evidence points strongly in the direction of the *Psalms of Solomon* being a Judean work as well. Philo, of course, was an Alexandrian Jew. Beyond that, it is generally accepted that 2 *Baruch*, 4 *Ezra*, the Latin Moses fragment, Pseudo-Philo, Judith, 1-2 Maccabees, the Additions to Daniel, and perhaps some of the Additions to Esther are of Palestinian origin and that 3-4 *Maccabees* and some of the Additions to Esther are Diaspora works. Except in the cases of Josephus, Philo, and the *Psalms of Solomon*, I do not believe that we can be certain about the geographical origins of any of these, but if we assume for the sake of argument that the consensus is correct, the implication is that Diaspora Judaism is not very well represented. There is no particular reason to assume that Diaspora Jews would have produced fewer Apocrypha and pseudepigrapha than Palestinian Jews, so if our skewed sample is not fortuitous, its content may provide indirect evidence that Palestinian Judaism had a stronger leaning toward boundary maintenance than Diaspora Jews and therefore that such Diaspora Jewish Apocrypha and pseudepigrapha as survive are correspondingly more difficult to identify as such. This is very speculative, but it coheres with the fact that it is by nature extremely difficult to confirm that a work transmitted only by Christians is Jewish unless that work represents boundary-maintaining Judaism.[2]

This book has also produced negative results: the methods developed and applied have raised significant doubts about the Jewish origins of a number of texts that are widely accepted to be Jewish, including the relevant sections of the *Sibylline Oracles* and the *Story of Zosimus*, as well as the full texts of *Pseudo-Phocylides*, *Joseph and Aseneth*, the *Testament of Job*, the *Testament of Abraham*, and the *Wisdom of Solomon*. Space and time did not permit analysis of other pseudepigrapha, but I concur with the doubts expressed in recent publications about the alleged Jewish origins of the *Lives of the Prophets*, the *Testaments of the Twelve Patriarchs*, and

---

[2] If we include Jewish Apocrypha and pseudepigrapha that survive intact only in Christian manuscripts but which are also extant in fragments from Qumran and the Cairo Geniza, we may add two works composed in Hebrew (*Jubilees* and Ben Sira); four works composed in Aramaic (the Book of the Watchers, the Astronomical Book, the Book of Dreams, and the Epistle of Enoch); one that was composed either in Hebrew or in Aramaic (Tobit); and one preserved only in Greek, although some would argue it has a Semitic *Vorlage* (the Epistle of Jeremiah). Of these, Jubilees and Tobit represent Torah-observant Judaism; the four works later incorporated into 1 *Enoch* represent Enochic Judaism; Ben Sira is a sapiential work with relatively little interest in the Mosaic Torah; and the Epistle of Jeremiah is too short for its affiliation to be clear. Ben Sira is a Palestinian work. The geographic origins of the others are not clear, but the Enochic texts are widely thought to be Palestinian as well. There is no consensus regarding the place of origin of Tobit or the Epistle of Jeremiah. Thus the inclusion of these works in our corpus provides us with a somewhat wider range of linguistic origin and a greater theological variety, although little, if any, persuasive additional evidence for Diaspora Judaism. [3] David Satran, *Biblical Prophets in Byzantine Palestine: Reassessing the 'Lives of the Prophets'* (SVTP 11; Leiden: Brill, 1995); M. de Jonge, *Pseudepigrapha of the Old Testament as Part of Christian Literature: The Case of the* Testaments of the Twelve Patriarchs *and the Greek* Life of Adam and Eve (SVTP 18; Leiden: Brill, 2003).

the *Life of Adam and Eve*.[3] Much of the work that has been done to date about the origins of various Old Testament pseudepigrapha needs to be rethought and I hope to revisit this question for a number of specific texts in the future.

As for methodological gains, the major contribution of this book is to set out a process for evaluating the origins of pseudepigrapha transmitted by Christians more critically than has been done before, with special attention to what Jews and Christians actually said and wrote. We have learned to look for converging lines of evidence involving clusters of specific traits ('signature features') which signal boundary-maintaining Jewish authorship. We have learned that Christian works can sometimes be indistinguishable from Jewish ones and can even have traits that seem Jewish. And we have learned to resist the tendency, found all too frequently in previous scholarship, to latch onto Jewish authorship of a work whenever such authorship is a possibility at all and to treat it as the one and only option when other interpretations of the evidence and other origins for the work are equally possible or even more likely. In general, the approach in this book allows us to articulate more clearly what we know and do not know, and how we know what we know and why we do not know what we do not know.

Finally, it is worthwhile to offer some general observations for New Testament scholars and others who do not specialize in Jewish texts transmitted only by Christians but whose research leads them to make use of these texts. Other literary sources for ancient Judaism include the Judean Desert Scrolls, the Jewish inscriptions, the Tannaitic rabbinic texts, and some quotation-fragments preserved by Eusebius and other authors. Each corpus has its own contribution to make and its own special problems. I have discussed some of these issues, but by and large the methodology of using these other literary corpora as background material for other fields is beyond the scope of this book.

The focus of this book has been on Jewish pseudepigrapha, but many of its results apply also to the Old Testament Apocrypha and the works of Josephus and Philo, all of which were also transmitted solely by Christians. Most of these texts are useful for Jewish background to the New Testament. Obviously, pseudepigrapha and Apocrypha that can be assigned to the pre-Christian era on external grounds (mainly fragmentary survival among the Dead Sea Scrolls) come under this category. These include the Book of the Watchers, the Astronomical Book, the Book of Dreams, the Epistle of Enoch, Ben Sira, Tobit, and the Epistle of Jeremiah. So do the works of Philo and Josephus, dated to the first century C E. Other Jewish works that can be assigned to the beginning of the second century C E or earlier include (the first edition of?) *Aristeas to Philocrates*; *2 Baruch*; the Latin Moses fragment; the *Psalms of Solomon*; *4 Ezra*; Pseudo-Philo; 1 Esdras; Judith; 1-2 Maccabees; the Additions to Esther B, C, D, and E; and, less certainly, the Additions to Daniel. Other Jewish works may belong to this early period, although they may also have come from somewhat later and so be less immediately relevant for New Testament background. These include the Similitudes of Enoch, *3-4 Maccabees*, and Additions to Esther A and F. But all of these works may be treated as Jewish compositions from the early centuries C E or earlier, beyond reasonable doubt.

Some other books are fairly likely to be of Jewish origin, such as Baruch, some of the Sibyllina, and the Wisdom of Solomon. It is possible that Joseph and Aseneth, the Testament of Job, and *Pseudo-Phocylides* also are Jewish compositions, and a few other pseudepigrapha not discussed in this book may be as well (e.g., the Prayer of Manasseh, *Jannes and Jambres*, the *Apocalypse of Zephaniah*, etc.), although very little in the way of a positive case can be made for any of them. If these books are drawn on for Jewish background to the New Testament or in general for evidence of Judaism in antiquity, they should be used with caution and their data should not form the basis of theories and reconstructions that are otherwise unsupported.

Even if a document has been shown to be Jewish beyond reasonable doubt, we cannot necessarily assume that its text has come down to us undisturbed by its Christian copyists. We have evidence that Josephus' *Testimonium Flavianum* has been altered. The reference to the Messiah in *4 Ezra* 7:28-29 has been Christianized in some manuscript traditions and there is reason to believe that the Eagle Vision in Chapters 11-12 has also been altered by a Christian tradent. Moreover, some of these works survive complete only in translation, sometimes secondary translation, and even with the best of intentions a translator may not understand or render a *Vorlage* perfectly. The safest approach is therefore to focus on major themes and repeated ideas in these documents rather than isolated details or proof-texts of individual verses.

Jewish pseudepigrapha transmitted by Christians are a precious resource for our reconstruction of Judaism through late antiquity. When they are used with proper methodological caution alongside our other sources, they make an important contribution to our understanding of both Judaism and the religious traditions it has influenced, especially early Christianity.

References are repeated when relevant to more than one category. The categories are listed in alphabetical order. Unless otherwise noted, all abbreviations are those found in Patrick H. Alexander et al., *The SBL Handbook of Style* (Peabody, Mass.: Hendrickson, 1999).

APOCRYPHA, NEW TESTAMENT

Böhlig, Alexander, and Frederik Wisse. 'The Gospel of the Egyptians.' In Robinson (ed.), *The Nag Hammadi Library in English*, 208-19.

Elliott, J. K. *The Apocryphal New Testament: A Collection of Apocryphal Christian Literature in an English Translation*. Oxford: Clarendon, 1993.

Junod, Éric. 'Apocryphes du NT ou apocryphes Chrétiens anciens?' *ETR* 58 (1983): 409-21.

——. '"Apocryphes du Nouveau Testament": une appellation erronée et une collection artificielle.' *Apocrypha* 3 (1992): 17-46.

Parrot, Douglas M., James Brashler, et al. 'The Discourse on the Eighth and the Ninth.' In Robinson (ed.), *The Nag Hammadi Library in English*, 321-327.

Pearson, Birger A. 'Marsanes.' In Robinson (ed.), *The Nag Hammadi Library in English*, 460-71.

Peel, Malcolm L. 'The Treatise on the Resurrection.' In Robinson (ed.), *The Nag Hammadi Library in English*, 52-57.

Robinson, James M. (ed.). *The Nag Hammadi Library in English*. 3rd ed. San Francisco: Harper & Row, 1988.

Schoedel, William R., and Douglas M. Parrott. 'The (First) Apocalypse of James.' In Robinson (ed.), *The Nag Hammadi Library in English*, 260-68.

Sieber, John N. 'Zostrianos.' In Robinson (ed.), *The Nag Hammadi Library in English*, 402-30.

Wire, Antoinnette Clark, John. D. Turner, and Orval S. Wintermute. 'Allogenes.' In Robinson (ed.), *The Nag Hammadi Library in English*, 490-500.

APOCRYPHA, OLD TESTAMENT

General

Charles, R. H. (ed.). *The Apocrypha and Pseudepigrapha of the Old Testament in English*. Vol. 1, *Apocrypha*. Oxford: Clarendon, 1913. Abbreviated as *APOT*, 1.

deSilva, David A. *Introducing the Apocrypha: Message, Context, and Significance*. Grand Rapids, Mich.: Baker, 2002.

Harrington, Daniel J. *Invitation to the Apocrypha*. Grand Rapids, Mich.: Eerdmans, 1999.

Baruch

See under 'Daniel, Esther, and Jeremiah, Additions To'

Ben Sira/Ecclesiaticus

Yadin, Yigael. *The Ben Sira Scroll from Masada*. Jerusalem: Israel Exploration Society/The Shrine of the Book, 1965.

Daniel, Esther, and Jeremiah, Additions to

Moore, Carey A. *Daniel, Esther and Jeremiah: The Additions*. AB 44. Garden City, N.Y.: Doubleday, 1977.

WORKS CITED

1-2 Maccabees

Goldstein, Jonathan A. *I Maccabees*. AB 41. Garden City, N.Y.: Doubleday, 1976.
———. *II Maccabees*. AB 41A. Garden City, N.Y.: Doubleday, 1983.

Solomon, Wisdom of

Grabbe, Lester L. *Wisdom of Solomon*. Guides to Apocrypha and Pseudepigrapha. Sheffield: Sheffield Academic Press, 1997.
Horbury, William. 'The Wisdom of Solomon in the Muratorian Fragment.' *JTS* 45 (1994): 149-59.
———. 'The Christian Use and the Jewish Origins of the Wisdom of Solomon.' In *Wisdom in Ancient Israel*, 182-96. Edited by John Day et al. Cambridge: Cambridge University Press, 1995.
Winston, David. *The Wisdom of Solomon*. AB 43. Garden City, N.Y.: Doubleday, 1984.
Ziegler, Joseph. *Sapientia Salomonis*. Septuaginta: Vetus Testamentum Graecum Auctoritate Societatis Litterarum Gottingensis 12.1. Göttingen: Vandenhoeck & Ruprecht, 1962.

BAR KOKHBA ERA MATERIAL

Benoit, P., J. T. Milik, R. de Vaux, et al. *Les grottes de Murabba'at/Excavations by the Jordan Department of Antiquities, École Biblique et Archéologique Française and Palestine Archaeological Museum*. DJD 2. Oxford: Clarendon, 1961.
Cotton, Hannah M. 'Hever: Nahal: Written Material,' *EDSS*, 359-61.
Cotton Hannah M., and Ada Yardeni. *Aramaic, Hebrew and Greek Documentary Texts from Nahal Hever and Other Sites, with an Appendix Containing Alleged Qumran Texts (The Seiyâl Collection II)*. DJD 27. Oxford: Clarendon, 1997.
Eshel, Hanan. 'Murabba'at, Wadi: Written Materials,' *EDSS*, 583-86.
Lewis, Naphtali, Yigael Yadin, and Jonas C. Greenfield. *The Documents from the Bar Kokhba Period in the Cave of Letters*, vol. 1, *Greek Papyri; Aramaic and Nabatean Signatures and Subscriptions*. Jerusalem: Israel Exploration Society/Hebrew University of Jerusalem: Shrine of the Book, 1989.
Tov, Emanuel. *The Seiyâl Collection. I, The Greek Minor Prophets Scroll from Nahal Hever (8 Hev XIIgr)*. DJD 8. Oxford: Clarendon, 1990.
———. 'Scriptures: Texts,' *EDSS*, 832-36.
Yadin, Yigael et al. *The Documents from the Bar Kokhba Period in the Cave of Letters: Hebrew, Aramaic, and Nabatean-Aramaic Papyri*. Jerusalem: Israel Exploration Society/Hebrew University of Jerusalem: Shrine of the Book, 2002.
Yardeni, Ada. *Textbook of Aramaic, Hebrew and Nabataean: Documentary Texts from the Judaean Desert and Related Material*. Jerusalem: Hebrew University, Ben-Zion Dinur Center for Research in Jewish History, 2000.

BIBLICAL AND ANCIENT NEAR EASTERN STUDIES

Tigay, Jeffrey (ed.). *Empirical Models for Biblical Criticism*. Philadelphia: University of Pennsylvania Press, 1985.
———. *The Evolution of the Gilgamesh Epic*. Philadelphia: University of Pennsylvania Press, 1982.

Amand de Mendieta, Emmanuel, and Stig
Y. Rudberg. *Basilius von Caesarea: Homilien
zum Hexaemeron.* GCS 2. Berlin: Academie
Verlag, 1997.

Baur, Chrysostomus. *John Chrysostom and His
Time.* 2d ed. London: Sands, 1959-60.

Brock, Sebastian P. *The Luminous Eye: The Spiritual World Vision of Saint Ephrem.* Rev. ed.
Kalamazoo, Mich.: Cistercian Publications,
1992.

———. *Hymns on Paradise: St. Ephrem.* Crestwood,
N.Y.: St. Vladimir's Seminary Press, 1998.

Castagno, Adele Monaci. 'I giudaizzanti di
Antiochia: bilancio e nuove prospettive di
ricerca.' In Filoramo and Gianotto (eds.),
Verus Israel, 304-38.

Donahue, Paul J. 'Jewish Christianity in the
Letters of Ignatius of Antioch.' *VC* 32 (1978):
81-93.

Edwards, Mark. 'Ignatius, Judaism and Judaizing.' *Eranos* 93 (1995): 69-77.

Esler, Philip F. (ed.). *The Early Christian World.*
2 vols. London: Routledge, 2000.

Evans, J. M. *Paradise Lost and the Genesis Tradition.* Oxford: Clarendon, 1968.

Falls, Thomas B. *Writings of Saint Justin Martyr.*
FC 6. Washington, D.C.: Catholic University
of America Press, 1948.

Fontaine, Jacques. *Naissance de la poésie dans
l'Occident chrétien: Esquisse d'une histoire de la
poésie latine chrétienne du IIIᵉ au VIᵉ siècle.*
Paris: Études Augustiniennes, 1981.

Giet, Stanislas. *Basile de Césarée: Homélies sur
l'Hexaéméron.* SC 26. Paris: Cerf, 1949.

Harkins, Paul W. *Discourses against Judaizing
Christians: Saint John Chrysostom.* FC 68.
Washington, D.C.: Catholic University of
America Press, 1979.

Hayman, A. P. 'The Image of the Jew in the
Syriac Anti-Jewish Polemical Literature.'
In Neusner and Frerichs et al. (eds.), 'To See
Ourselves as Others See Us,' 423-41.

Herzog, Reinhart. *Die Bibelepik der lateinischen
Spätantike: Formgeschichte einer erbaulichen

Gattung.* Theorie und Geschichte der Literatur und der schönen Künste, Texte und
Abhandlungen 37. Munich: Wilhelm Fink,
1975.

Hexter, Ralph. 'The Metamorphosis of Sodom:
The Ps-Cyprian "De Sodoma" as an Ovidian
Episode.' *Traditio* 44 (1988): 1-35.

Hill, Robert C. *Saint John Chrysostom: Homilies
on Genesis.* 3 vols. FC 74, 82, 87. Washington
D.C.: Catholic University of America Press,
1985-92.

Jackson, Blomfeld. *The Treatise de Spiritu Sancto,
the Nine Homilies of the Hexaemeron and the
Letters of Saint Basil the Great, Archbishop of
Caesarea.* NPNF² 8. Edinburgh: Clark /
Grand Rapids, Mich.: 1996. Rpt. of 1894 edi-
tion.

Kartschoke, Dieter. *Bibeldichtung: Studien zur
Geschichte der epischen Bibelparaphrase von
Juvencus bis Otfrid von Weißenburg.* Munich:
Wilhelm Fink, 1975.

Kraft, Robert A. *The Apostolic Fathers: A New
Translation and Commentary,* vol. 3, *Barnabas
and the Didache.* New York: Nelson, 1965.

Kriel, D. M. '*Sodoma* in Fifth Century Biblical
Epic,' *Acta Classica* 34 (1991): 7-20.

Lightfoot, J. B., J. R. Harmer, and Michael
W. Holmes. *The Apostolic Fathers: Greek
Texts and English Translations of their Writings.*
2nd ed. Grand Rapids, Mich.: Baker, 1992.

Marcovich, Miroslav. *Pseudo-Justinus: Cohortatio
ad Graecos; De Monarchia; Oratio ad Graecos.*
Berlin: de Gruyter, 1990.

Mathews, Edward G., Jr., and Joseph P. Amar,
with Kathleen McVey. *St. Ephrem the Syrian:
Selected Prose Works.* FC 91. Washington,
D.C.: Catholic University Press of America,
1994.

McVey, Kathleen E., and John Meyendorff.
Ephrem the Syrian: Hymns. CWS. Mahwah,
N.J.: Paulist, 1989.

Meeks, Wayne A., and Robert L. Wilken. *Jews
and Christians in Antioch in the First Four
Centuries of the Common Era.* SBLSBS 13.
Missoula, Mont.: Scholars Press, 1978.

Meyer, Marvin and Richard Smith (eds.). *Ancient Christian Magic: Coptic Texts of Ritual

Power. San Francisco: HarperSanFrancisco, 1994.

Migne, J.-P. *Patrologia Graeca*, vols. 53-54, *S. P. N. Joannis Chrysostomus IV.* Paris, 1862.

Morisi, Luca. *Versus de Sodoma.* Edizioni e saggi universitari di filologia classica 52. Bologne: Pàtron Editore, 1993.

Murray, Robert. *Symbols of Church and Kingdom.* London: Cambridge University Press, 1975.

Nodes, Daniel J. *Doctrine and Exegesis in Biblical Latin Poetry.* ARCA 31. Leeds: Francis Cairns, 1993.

Norelli, Enrico. 'Ignazio di Antiochia combatte veramente dei cristiani giudaizzanti?' In Filoramo and Gianotto (eds.), *Verus Israel*, 220-64.

Novatian. 'On the Jewish Meats' (*De cibis Judaicis*). *ANF*, 5:645-50.

Otto, Ioan. Carol. Theod. *S. Iustini philosophi et martyris opera quae ferentur omnia.* 2 vols. Jena, 1847-49.

Peiper, Rudolph. *Cypriani Galli Poetae Heptateuchos.* CSEL 23. Prague, 1881.

Reith, G. 'Justin on the Sole Government of God.' *ANF*, 1:290-93.

Roberts, Alexander, and James Donaldson (eds.). *The Ante-Nicene Fathers: Translations of the Writings of the Fathers Down to A.D. 325.* 8 vols. Edinburgh: Clark/Grand Rapids, Mich.: Eerdmans, 1996. Rpt. of 1885-96 edition.

Roberts, Michael. *Biblical Epic and Rhetorical Paraphrase in Late Antiquity.* ARCA 16. Liverpool: Francis Cairns, 1985.

Schoedel, William R. *Ignatius of Antioch: A Commentary on the Letters of Ignatius of Antioch.* Hermeneia. Philadelphia: Fortress, 1985.

Stanton, Graham N. 'Justin Martyr's Dialogue with Trypho: Group Boundaries "Proselytes" and "God-fearers."' In Stanton and Stroumsa (eds.), *Tolerance and Intolerance*, 263-78.

Thelwell, S. 'A Strain of Jonah the Prophet,' 'A Strain of Sodom,' 'Genesis.' *ANF*, 4:127-35.

Weidmann, Mag. Clemens. 'Das Carmen de Martyrio Maccabaeorum.' Ph.D. diss., University of Vienna, 1995.

Wilken, Robert L. *John Chrysostom and the Jews: Rhetoric and Reality in the Late 4th Century.* Berkeley: University of California Press, 1983.

——. 'The Restoration of Israel in Biblical Prophecy: Christian and Jewish Responses in the Early Byzantine Period.' In Neusner and Frerichs et al. (eds.), *'To See Ourselves as Others See Us,'* 443-71.

DEAD SEA SCROLLS

Albright, W. F. 'New Light on Early Recensions of the Hebrew Bible' in Cross and Talmon (eds.), *Qumran and the History of the Biblical Text*, 140-46. Rpt. of *BASOR* 140 (1955): 27-33.

Boccaccini, Gabriele. *Beyond the Essene Hypothesis: The Parting of the Ways Between Qumran and Enochic Judaism.* Grand Rapids, Mich.: Eerdmans 1998.

Crown, Alan D. 'Qumran, Samaritan *Halakha* and Theology and Pre-Tannaitic Judaism.' In *Boundaries of the Ancient Near Eastern World: A Tribute to Cyrus Gordon*, 420-441. Edited by Meir Lubetski, Claire Gottlieb, and Sharon Keller. JSOTSup 273. Sheffield: Sheffield Academic Press, 1998.

Cross, Frank Moore. 'The History of the Biblical Text in the Light of Discoveries in the Judaean Desert,' in Cross and Talmon (eds.), *Qumran and the History of the Biblical Text*, 177-95. Rpt. of *HTR* 57 (1964): 281-99.

Cross, Frank Moore, and Shermaryahu Talmon (eds.). *Qumran and the History of the Biblical Text.* Cambridge: Harvard University Press, 1975.

Davila, James R. *Liturgical Works.* Eerdmans Commentary on the Dead Sea Scrolls 6. Grand Rapids, Mich.: Eerdmans, 2000.

—— (ed.). *The Dead Sea Scrolls as Background to Postbiblical Judaism and Early Christianity.* STDJ 46. Leiden: Brill, 2003.

——. 'Enochians, Essenes, and Qumran Essenes.' in G. Boccaccini (ed.), *Enoch and Qumran Origins: New Light on a Forgotten Connection.*, 356-59. Grand Rapids, Mich.: Eerdmans.

Fletcher-Louis, Crispin. '4Q374: A Discourse on the Sinai Traditions of Moses and Early Christology.' *DSD* 3 (1996): 236-52.

Flint, Peter. 'Scriptures in the Dead Sea Scrolls: The Evidence from Qumran.' In Paul et al. (eds.), *Emanuel*, 269-304.

Flint, Peter W., and James C. VanderKam. *The Dead Sea Scrolls after Fifty Years: A Compre-*

hensive Assessment. 2 vols. Leiden: Brill, 1998-99.

García Martínez, Florentino. *The Dead Sea Scrolls Translated: The Qumran Texts in English.* Leiden: Brill, 1994.

Golitzin, Alexander. 'Recovering the "Glory of Adam": "Divine Light" Traditions in the Dead Sea Scrolls and the Christian Ascetical Literature of Fourth-Century Syro-Mesopotamia.' In Davila (ed.), *The Dead Sea Scrolls as Background,* 275-308.

Kugler, Robert A. 'Some Further Evidence for the Samaritan Provenance of *Aramaic Levi* (*1 QTestLevi; 4 QTestLevi*).' *RevQ* 17/65-68 (1996): 351-58.

Parry, Donald W., and Emanuel Tov (eds.). *The Dead Sea Scrolls Reader.* 6 vols. Leiden: Brill, 2004.

Paul, Shalom M., et al. *Emanuel: Studies in Hebrew Bible, Septuagint, and Dead Sea Scrolls in Honor of Emanuel Tov.* VTSup 94. Leiden: Brill, 2003.

Schiffman, Lawrence H., and James C. VanderKam (eds.). *Encyclopedia of the Dead Sea Scrolls.* Oxford: Oxford University Press, 2000. Abbreviated as *EDSS.*

Ulrich, Eugene. 'The Dead Sea Scrolls and the Biblical Text.' In Flint and VanderKam (eds.), *The Dead Sea Scrolls After Fifty Years,* 1:79-100.

VanderKam, James C. *The Dead Sea Scrolls Today.* Grand Rapids, Mich.: Eerdmans, 1994.

——. 'Greek at Qumran.' In Collins and Sterling (eds.), *Hellenism in the Land of Israel,* 175-81.

GALILEE AND THE GALILEANS

Freyne, Seán. *Galilee from Alexander the Great to Hadrian 323 B C E to 135 C E.* 2nd ed. Edinburgh: Clark, 1998. Originally published in 1980.

——. *Galilee, Jesus and the Gospels: Literary Approaches and Historical Investigations.* Philadelphia: Fortress, 1988.

——. 'Behind the Names: Galileans, Samaritans, *Ioudaioi.*' In Meyers (ed.), *Galilee Through the Centuries,* 39-55.

——. 'Galileans, Phoenicians, and Itureans: A Study of Regional Contrast in the Hellenistic Age.' In Collins and Sterling (eds.), *Hellenism in the Land of Israel,* 182-215.

Gal, Zvi. *Lower Galilee During the Iron Age.* Winona Lake, Ind.: Eisenbrauns, 1992.

Goodman, Martin. 'Galilean Judaism and Judaean Judaism.' *CHJ,* 3:596-617.

Horsley, Richard A. *Galilee: History, Politics, People.* Valley Forge, Penn.: Trinity, 1995.

——. *Archaeology, History, and Society in Galilee.* Valley Forge, Penn.: Trinity, 1996.

——. 'The Expansion of Hasmonean Rule in Idumea and Galilee: Toward a Historical Sociology.' In Davies and Halligan (eds.), *Second Temple Studies III,* 134-65.

Meyers, Eric M. *Galilee Through the Centuries: Confluence of Cultures.* Duke Judaic Studies 1. Winona Lake, Ind.: Eisenbrauns, 1999.

Reed, Jonathan L. 'Galileans, "Israelite Village Communities," and the Sayings Gospel Q.' In Meyers (ed.), *Galilee Through the Centuries,* 87-108.

Schiffman, Lawrence H. 'Was There a Galilean Halakhah?' In *The Galilee in Late Antiquity,* 143-56. Edited by Lee I. Levine. Cambridge: Harvard University Press, 1992.

GOD-FEARERS, PROSELYTES, SYMPATHIZERS, AND SYNCRETISTIC JEWS

Betz, Hans Dieter (ed.). *The Greek Magical Papyri in Translation, Including the Demotic Spells.* 2nd ed. Chicago: University of Chicago Press, 1992.

Cohen, Shaye J. D. 'Respect for Judaism by Gentiles according to Josephus.' *HTR* 80 (1987): 409-30.

——. 'Crossing the Boundary and Becoming a Jew.' In *The Beginning of Jewishness,* 140-74. Rpt. of *HTR* 82 (1989): 13-33.

Copenhaver, Brian P. *Hermetica: The Greek Corpus Hermeticum and the Latin Asclepius in a New English Translation with Notes and Introduction.* Cambridge: Cambridge University Press, 1992.

Donaldson, Terence L. 'Jerusalem Ossuary Inscriptions and the Status of Jewish Proselytes.' In Wilson and Desjardins (eds.), *Text and Artifact in the Religions of Mediterranean Antiquity*, 372-88.

Esler, Philip F. *Community and Gospel in Luke-Acts: The Social and Political Motivations of Lucan Theology*. Cambridge: Cambridge University Press, 1987.

Feldman, Louis H. 'Proselytism by Jews in the Third, Fourth, and Fifth Centuries.' *JSJ* 24 (1993): 1-58.

Festugière, P. *La révélation d'Hermès Trismégiste*. 4 vols. Paris: Lecoffre, 1944-54.

Figueras, Paul. 'Epigraphic Evidence for Proselytism in Ancient Judaism.' *Imm* 24/25 (1990): 194-206.

Finn, Thomas M. 'The God-fearers Reconsidered.' *CBQ* 47 (1985): 75-84.

Fowden, Garth. *The Egyptian Hermes: A Historical Approach to the Late Pagan Mind*. Corrected ed. Princeton, N. J.: Princeton University Press, 1993.

Gager, John G. 'The Dialogue of Paganism with Judaism: Bar Cochba to Julian.' *HUCA* 44 (1973): 89-118.

——. 'Jews, Gentiles, and Synagogues in the Book of Acts.' *HTR* 79 (1986): 91-99.

Gaster, M. 'The Logos Ebraikos in the Magical Papyrus of Paris and the Book of Enoch.' *JRAS* 33 (1901): 109-117.

Halbertal, Moshe. 'Coexisting with the Enemy: Jews and Pagans in the Mishnah.' In Stanton and Stroumsa (eds.), *Tolerance and Intolerance*, 159-72.

Horbury, William. 'A Proselyte's *Heis Theos* Inscription Near Caesarea,' *PEQ* 129 (1997): 133-37.

Kraabel, A. T. 'The Disappearance of the "God-Fearers,"' *Numen* 28 (1981): 113-126.

——. 'Greeks, Jews, and Lutherans in the Middle Half of Acts.' *HTR* 79 (1986): 147-57.

Kraft, Robert. 'Was There a "Messiah-Joshua" Tradition at the Turn of the Era?' No pages. Copyright 1992. Online: http://ccat.sas.upenn.edu/gopher/other/journals/kraftpub/Christianity/Joshua.

Liebeschuetz, Wolf. 'The Influence of Judaism among Non-Jews in the Imperial Period.' *JJS* 52 (2001): 235-52.

Lieu, J. M. 'The Race of the God-Fearers.' *JTS* 46 (1995): 483-501.

——. 'The "Attraction of Women" in/to Early Judaism and Christianity: Gender and the Politics of Conversion.' *JSNT* 72 (1998): 5-22.

McEleney, Neil J. 'Conversion, Circumcision and the Law.' *NTS* 20 (1974): 319-41.

Mitchell, Stephen. 'The Cult of Theos Hypsistos Between Pagans, Jews and Christians.' In *Pagan Monotheism in Late Antiquity*, 81-148. Edited by Polymnia Athanassiadi and Michael Frede. Oxford: Clarendon, 1999.

Niehoff, Maren R. 'Philo's Views on Paganism.' In Stanton and Stroumsa (eds.), *Tolerance and Intolerance*, 135-58.

Nolland, John. 'Uncircumcised Proselytes?' *JSJ* 12 (1981): 173-94.

Norelli, Enrico. 'Ignazio di Antiochia combatte veramente dei cristiani giudaizzanti?' In Filoramo and Gianotto (eds.), *Verus Israel*, 220-64.

Overman, J. Andrew. 'The God-Fearers: Some Neglected Features.' *JSNT*, 32 (1988): 17-26.

Pearson, Birger A. 'Jewish Elements in *Corpus Hermeticum* I (*Poimandres*).' In *Studies in Gnosticism and Hellenistic Religions Presented to Gilles Quispel on the Occasion of His 65th Birthday*, 336-48. Edited by R. van den Broek and M. J. Vermaseren. EPRO 91. Leiden: Brill, 1981.

Preisendanz, Karl. *Papyri Graecae Magicae: Die Griechischen Zauberpapyri*. 2nd ed. 2 vols. Stuttgart: Teubner, 1973-74.

Rajak, Tessa. 'Jews and Christians as Groups in a Pagan World.' In *The Jewish Dialogue with Greece and Rome: Studies in Cultural and Social Interaction*, 355-72. AGJU 48. Leiden: Brill, 2001.

Schäfer, Peter. 'Jews and Gentiles in Yerushalmi Avodah Zarah.' In Schäfer (ed.), *The Talmud Yerushalmi and Graeco-Roman Culture*, 335-52.

Siegert, Folker. 'Gottesfürchtige und Sympathisanten.' *JSJ* 4 (1973): 109-64.

Sperber, Daniel. 'Some Rabbinic Themes in Magical Papyri.' *JSJ* 16 (1985): 93-103.

Stanton, Graham N. 'Justin Martyr's Dialogue with Trypho: Group Boundaries "Proselytes" and "God-fearers."' In Stanton and Stroumsa (eds.), *Tolerance and Intolerance*, 263-78.

Stroumsa, Guy G. 'Tertullian on Idolatry and the Limits of Tolerance.' In Stanton and

Stroumsa (eds.), *Tolerance and Intolerance*, 173-84.

Stuehrenberg, Paul F. 'Proselyte.' *ABD*, 5:503-5.

Tacheva-Hitova, Margarita. *Eastern Cults in Moesia Inferior and Thracia (5th Century BC – 4th Century AD)*. EPRO 425. Leiden: Brill, 1983.

Tyson, Joseph B. 'Jews and Judaism in Luke-Acts: Reading as a Godfearer.' *NTS* 41 (1995): 19-38.

Wilcox, Max. 'The "God-Fearers" in Acts – A Reconsideration.' *JSNT* 13 (1981): 102-22.

Will, Edouard, and Claude Orrieux. *Prosélytisme juif? Histoire d'une erreur*. Paris: Les Belles Lettres, 1992.

Wilson, Stephen G., and Michel Desjardins. *Text and Artifact in the Religions of Mediterranean Antiquity: Essays in Honor of Peter Richardson*. Waterloo, Ontario: Wilfrid Laurier University Press, 2000.

INSCRIPTIONS, JEWISH

Ameling, Walter. *Inscriptiones Judaicae Orientis*, vol. 2, *Asia Minor*. TSAJ 99. Tübingen: Mohr Siebeck, 2004.

Donaldson, Terence L. 'Jerusalem Ossuary Inscriptions and the Status of Jewish Proselytes.' In Wilson and Desjardins (eds.), *Text and Artifact in the Religions of Mediterranean Antiquity*, 372-88.

Figueras, Paul. 'Epigraphic Evidence for Proselytism in Ancient Judaism.' *Imm* 24/25 (1990): 194-206.

Horbury, William. 'A Proselyte's *Heis Theos* Inscription Near Caesarea,' *PEQ* 129 (1997): 133-37.

Kraemer, Ross S. 'On the Meaning of the Term "Jew" in Greco-Roman Inscriptions.' *HTR* 82 (1989): 35-53.

——. 'Jewish Tuna and Christian Fish: Identifying Religious Affiliations in Epigraphic Sources.' *HTR* 84 (1991): 141-62.

Reynolds, Joyce, and Robert Tannenbaum. *Jews and Godfearers at Aphrodisias*. Cambridge Philological Society Supplement 12. Cambridge: Cambridge Philological Society, 1987.

Williams, Margaret. 'The Meaning and Func-

tion of *Ioudaios* in Graeco-Roman Inscriptions.' *ZPE* 116 (1997): 249-62.

Wilson, Steven G. 'ΟΙ ΠΟΤΕ ΙΟΥΔΑΙΟΙ: Epigraphic Evidence for Jewish Defectors.' In Wilson and Desjardins (eds.), *Text and Artifact*, 354-71.

JEWISH-CHRISTIANITY AND
JUDAIZING GENTILE CHRISTIANITY

Alexander, Philip S. '"The Parting of the Ways" from the Perspective of Rabbinic Judaism.' In Dunn (ed.), *Jews and Christians: The Parting of the Ways*, 1-25.

Bauckham, Richard. 'The *Apocalypse of Peter*: A Jewish Christian Apocalypse from the Time of Bar Kokhba.' *Apocrypha* 5 (1994): 7-111.

——. 'Jews and Jewish Christians in the Land of Israel at the Time of the Bar Kokhba War, with Special Reference to the *Apocalypse of Peter*.' In Stanton and Stroumsa (eds.), *Tolerance and Intolerance*, 228-38.

——. 'The Origin of the Ebionites.' In Tomson and Lambers-Petry (eds.), *The Image of the Judaeo-Christians in Ancient Jewish and Christian Literature*, 162-81.

Becker, Adam H., and Annette Yoshiko Reed (eds.). *The Ways that Never Parted: Jews and Christians in Late Antiquity and the Early Middle Ages*. TSAJ 95. Tübingen: Mohr Siebeck, 2003.

Boer, Martinus C. de. 'The Nazoreans: Living at the Boundary of Judaism and Christianity.' in Stanton and Stroumsa (eds.), *Tolerance and Intolerance*, 239-62.

Brown, Raymond E. 'Not Jewish Christianity and Gentile Christianity but Types of Jewish/Gentile Christianity.' *CBQ* 45 (1983): 74-79.

Castagno, Adele Monaci. 'I giudaizzanti di Antiochia: bilancio e nuove prospettive di ricerca.' In Filoramo and Gianotto (eds.), *Verus Israel*, 304-38.

Donahue, Paul J. 'Jewish Christianity in the Letters of Ignatius of Antioch.' *VC* 32 (1978): 81-93.

Dunn, James D. G. *The Partings of the Ways: Between Christianity and Judaism and their Signif-*

icance for the Character of Christianity. London: SCM, 1991.

—— (ed.). Jews and Christians: The Parting of the Ways A.D. 70 to 135. WUNT 66. Tübingen: Mohr Siebeck, 1992.

Edwards, Mark. 'Ignatius, Judaism and Judaizing.' Eranos 93 (1995): 69-77.

Filoramo, Giovanni and Claudio Giantto (eds.). Verus Israel. Nuove prospettive sul giudeocristianesimo. BCR 65. Brescia: Paideia Editrice, 2001.

Harkins, Paul W. Discourses against Judaizing Christians: Saint John Chrysostom. FC 68. Washington, D.C.: Catholic University of America Press, 1979.

Horbury, William. 'The Benediction of the Minim and Early Jewish-Christian Controversy.' In Jews and Christians in Contact and Controversy, 67-101. Rpt. of JTS 33 (1982): 19-61.

Horrell, David G. 'Early Jewish Christianity.' In Esler (ed.), The Early Christian World, 1:136-67.

Horst, Pieter W. van der. 'Jews and Christians in Aphrodisias in the Light of Their Relationship in Other Cities of Asia Minor.' In Essays on the Jewish World of Early Christianity, 166-81. Freiburg, Switzerland: Universitätsverlag/Göttingen: Vandenhoeck & Ruprecht, 1990.

Howard, George. 'The Gospel of the Ebionites.' ANRW 2.25.5:4034-53. Part 2, Principat, 25.2. New York: de Gruyter, 1984.

Jones, F. Stanley. An Ancient Jewish Christian Source on the History of Christianity: Pseudo-Clementine Recognitions 1.27-71. SBLTT 37. SBL Christian Apocrypha Series 2. Atlanta: Scholars Press, 1995.

Kimelman, Reuven. 'Birkat Ha-Minim and the Lack of Evidence for an Anti-Christian Jewish Prayer in Late Antiquity.' In Sanders, Baumgarten, and Mendelson (eds.), Jewish and Christian Self-Definition, 2:226-44, 391-403.

——. 'Identifying Jews and Christians in Roman Syria-Palestine.' In Meyers (ed.), Galilee Through the Centuries, 301-33.

Kinzig, Wolfram. '"Non-Separation": Closeness and Co-operation Between Jews and Christians in the Fourth Century.' VC 45 (1991): 27-53.

Klijn, A. F. J., and G. J. Reinink. Patristic Evidence for Jewish Christian Sects. NovTSup 36. Leiden: Brill, 1973.

Klijn, A. F. J. 'The Study of Jewish Christianity.' NTS 20 (1974): 419-31.

——. 'Das Hebräer- und das Nazoräerevangelium.' ANRW 2.25.5:3997-4033. Part 2, Principat, 25.2. New York: de Gruyter, 1984.

——. Jewish-Christian Gospel Tradition. VCSup 17. Leiden: Brill, 1992.

Lieu, Judith. 'History and Theology in Christian Views of Judaism.' In Lieu et al. (eds.), The Jews among Pagans and Christians, 79-96.

——. '"The Parting of the Ways": Theological Construct or Historical Reality?' JSNT 56 (1994): 101-19.

Malina, Bruce J. 'Jewish Christianity or Christian Judaism: Toward a Hypothetical Definition.' JSJ 7 (1976): 46-57.

Mimouni, Simon C. 'Pour une définition nouvelle du judéo-christianisme ancien.' NTS 38 (1992): 161-86.

——. 'I nazorei a partire dalla notizia 29 del Panarion di Epifanio di Salamina.' In Filoramo and Gianotto (eds.), Verus Israel, 120-46.

Paget, J. Carleton. 'Jewish Christianity.' CAH, 3:731-75.

Pritz, Ray A. Nazarene Jewish Christianity: From the End of the New Testament Period Until its Disappearance in the Fourth Century. StPB 37. Leiden: Brill/Jerusalem: Magnes, 1988.

Reed, Annette Yoshiko. '"Jewish Christianity" after the "Parting of the Ways": Approaches to Historiography and Self-Definition in the Pseudo-Clementines.' In Becker and Reed (eds.), The Ways that Never Parted, 189-231.

——. 'Fire, Blood, and Water: Demonology and Halakha in the Pseudo-Clementine Homilies.' Paper presented at the annual meeting of the American Academy of Religion in Atlanta on 23 November 2003.

Riegel, Stanley K. 'Jewish Christianity: Definitions and Terminology.' NTS 24 (1978): 410-15.

Simon, Marcel. Verus Israel: A Study of the Relations Between Christians and Jews in the Roman Empire (135-425). Oxford: Oxford University Press, 1986. Translation of French original by H. McKeating. Paris: Boccard, 1964.

Taylor, Joan E. 'The Phenomenon of Early Jewish-Christianity: Reality or Scholarly Invention?' *VC* 44 (1990): 313-34.
Tomson, Peter J., and Doris Lambers-Petry
(eds.). *The Image of the Judaeo-Christians.*
WUNT 158. Tübingen: Mohr Siebeck, 2003.
Vana, Liliane. 'La *birkat ha-minim* è una preghiera contro i giudeocristiani?' In Filoramo
and Gianotto (eds.), *Verus Israel*, 147-89.
Van Voorst, Robert E. The Ascents of James: History and Theology of a Jewish-Christian Community. SBLDS 112. Atlanta: Scholars Press,
1989.
Verheyden, Joseph. 'Epiphanius on the Ebionites.' In Tomson and Lambers-Petry (eds.),
*The Image of the Judaeo-Christians in Ancient
Jewish and Christian Literature*, 182-208.
Wilson, Stephen G. 'Gentile Judaizers.' *NTS* 38
(1992): 605-16.

JOSEPHUS, FLAVIUS

Attridge, Harold W. 'Josephus and His Works.'
In Stone (ed.), *Jewish Writings of the Second
Temple Period*, 185-232.
Aviam, Mordechai, and Peter Richardson. 'Ap-
pendix A: Josephus' Galilee in Archaeologi-
cal Perspective.' In Mason, *Life of Josephus*,
177-209.
Broshi, Magen. 'The Credibility of Josephus.'
JJS 33 (1982): 379-84.
Cohen, Shaye J. D. 'Masada: Literary Tradition,
Archaeological Remains, and the Credibility
of Josephus.' *JJS* 33 (1982): 385-405.
——. *Josephus in Galilee and Rome: His Vita and
Development as a Historian.* Columbia Studies
in the Classical Tradition 8. Leiden: Brill,
1979.
——. 'Respect for Judaism by Gentiles according
to Josephus.' *HTR* 80 (1987): 409-30.
Feldman, Louis H. 'Flavius Josephus Revisited:
The Man, His Writings, and His Signifi-
cance.' *ANRW* 21.2:763-862. Part 2, *Princi-
pat*, 21.2. New York: de Gruyter, 1984.
——. *Josephus and Modern Scholarship (1937-1980).*
Berlin: de Gruyter, 1984.
Feldman, Louis H., and Gohei Hata (eds.). *Jo-*

sephus, Judaism, and Christianity. Detroit:
Wayne State University Press, 1987.
——. *Josephus, the Bible, and History.* Detroit:
Wayne State University Press, 1989.
Goldstein, Jonathan A. 'The Testament of
Moses: Its Content, Its Origin, and its At-
testation in Josephus.' In Nickelsburg (ed.),
Studies on the Testament of Moses, 44-52.
Hardwick, Michael E. *Josephus as an Historical
Source in Patristic Literature through Eusebius.*
Atlanta: Scholars Press, 1989.
Mason, Steve. *Josephus and the New Testament.*
Peabody, Mass.: Hendrickson, 1992.
——. 'Josephus and Judaism.' In *The Encyclopedia
of Judaism*, 2:546-63. 3 vols. Edited by Jacob
Neusner, Alan J. Avery-Peck, and William
S. Green. Leiden: Brill, 2000.
——. *Flavius Josephus: Translation and Commen-
tary*, vol. 9, *Life of Josephus*. Leiden: Brill,
2001.
——. 'Contradiction or Counterpoint? Josephus
and Historical Method.' *Review of Rabbinic
Judaism* 6 (2003): 145-88.
Mazar, Benjamin. 'Josephus Flavius and the
Archaeological Excavations in Jerusalem.' In
Feldman and Hata (eds.), *Josephus, the Bible,
and History*, 325-29
Mizugaki, Wataru. 'Origen and Josephus.' In
Feldman and Hata (eds.), *Josephus, Judaism,
and Christianity*, 325-37.
Montgomery, James A. 'The Religion of Flavius
Josephus,' *JQR* 40 (1920-21): 277-305.
Newell, Raymond R. 'The Forms and Historical
Value of Josephus' Suicide Accounts.' In
Feldman and Hata (eds.), *Josephus, the Bible,
and History*, 278-94.
Rajak, Tessa. *Josephus: The Historian and His
Society.* London: Duckworth, 1983.
Safrai, Zeev. 'The Description of the Land of
Israel in Josephus' Works.' In Feldman and
Hata (eds.), *Josephus, the Bible, and History*,
295-324.
Schreckenberg, Heinz. *Die Flavius-Josephus-
Tradition in Antike und Mitteralter.* ALGHJ 5.
Leiden: Brill, 1972.
——. 'The Works of Josephus and the Early
Christian Church.' In Feldman and Hata

(eds.), *Josephus, Judaism, and Christianity*, 315-24.

Ulrich, Eugene Charles, Jr. *The Qumran Text of Samuel and Josephus*. HSM 19. Missoula, Mont.: Scholars Press, 1978.

Whealey, Alice. *Josephus on Jesus: The Testimonium Flavianun Controversy from Late Antiquity to Modern Times*. Studies in Biblical Literature 36. New York: Lang, 2003.

Williams, David S. *Stylometric Authorship Studies in Flavius Josephus and Related Literature*. Jewish Studies 12. Lewiston, N.Y.: Edwin Mellen, 1992).

Yadin, Yigael. *Masada: Herod's Fortress and the Zealots' Last Stand*. Tel Aviv: Steimatzky, 1966.

JOSEPHUS: APOCRYPHA, SPURIA, AND RELATED WORKS

Botte, B. 'Note sur l'auteur du *De universo* attribué à saint Hippolyte.' *Recherches de théologie ancienne et médiévale* 18 (1951): 5-18.

Capelle, B. 'Hippolyte de Rome.' *Recherches de théologie ancienne et médiévale* 17 (1950): 145-74.

Devreesse, Robert. *Introduction à l'étude des manuscrits grecs*. Paris: Klincksieck, 1954.

Grant, Robert M., and Glen W. Menzies. *Joseph's Bible Notes (Hypomnesticon): Introduction, Translation, and Notes*. SBLTT 41. Early Christian Series 9. Atlanta: Scholars Press, 1996.

Horst, P. W. van der. Review of Grant and Menzies, *Joseph's Bible Notes*. BO 54 (1997): 195-97.

Kipper, Balduino. 'Josipo (ou Josefo), Traduto Grego Quase Desconhecido.' *Revista de Cultura Biblica* (São Paulo) 5 (1961): 298-307, 387-95, 446-56.

Malley, William J. 'Four Unedited Fragments of the *De Universo* of the Pseudo-Josephus Found in the *Chronicon* of George Hamartolos (Coislin 305).' *JTS* 16 (1965): 13-25.

Moreau, Jacques. 'Observations sur l' Ὑπομνστικὸν βιβλίον Ἰωσήππου.' *Byzantion* 25-27 (1955-57): 241-76.

Nautin, Pierre. *Hippolyte et Josipe, Contribution à l'histoire de la littérature chrétienne du troisième siècle*. Études et textes pour l'histoire du dogme de la Trinité 1. Paris, 1947.

———. 'La controverse sur l'auteur de l'"Elen-

chos."' *Revue d'histoire ecclésiastique* 47 (1942): 5-43.

———. 'L'homélie d'Hippolyte sur le psautier et les œuvres de Josipe.' *Revue de l'histoire des religions* 179 (1971): 137-79.

Speyer, Wolfgang. *Bücherfunde in der Glaubenswerbung der Antike: Mit einem Ausblick auf Mittelalter und Neuzeit*. Hypomnemata 24. Göttingen: Vandenhoeck & Ruprecht, 1970.

JUDAISM, ANCIENT

Bauckham, Richard. 'Apocalypses.' In Carson et al. (eds.), *Justification and Variegated Nomism*, 1:135-87.

Boccaccini, Gabriele. *Middle Judaism: Jewish Thought, 300 B.C.E.–200 C.E.* Minneapolis: Fortress, 1991

———. *Roots of Rabbinic Judaism: An Intellectual History, from Ezekiel to Daniel*. Grand Rapids, Mich.: Eerdmans, 2002.

Bremmer, Jan M. 'Review Article: The Manifest and Hidden Heritage of Judaism.' *JSJ* 31 (2000): 45-64.

Carson, D. A., Peter T. O'Brien, and Mark A. Seifrid (eds.). *Justification and Variegated Nomism*, vol. 1, *The Complexities of Second Temple Judaism*. WUNT 140. Tübingen: Mohr Siebeck, 2001.

Cohen, Shaye J. D. *The Beginnings of Jewishness: Boundaries, Varieties, Uncertainties*. Berkeley, Calif.: University of California Press, 1999.

———. 'Ioudaios, Iudaeus, Judean, Jew.' In *The Beginnings of Jewishness*, 69-106.

———. 'From Ethnos to Ethno-religion.' In *The Beginnings of Jewishness*, 109-39.

Collins, John J. *The Scepter and the Star: The Messiahs of the Dead Sea Scrolls and Other Ancient Literature*. New York: Doubleday, 1995.

Collins, John J., and Gregory E. Sterling (eds.). *Hellenism in the Land of Israel*. Christianity and Judaism in Antiquity 13. Notre Dame, Ind.: University of Notre Dame Press, 2001.

Davies, Philip R., and John M. Halligan. *Second Temple Studies III: Studies in Politics, Class and Material Culture*. JSOTSup 340. Sheffield: Sheffield Academic Press, 2002.

Elliott, Mark Adam. *The Survivors of Israel: A Reconsideration of the Theology of Pre-Christian Judaism*. Grand Rapids, Mich.: Eerdmans, 2000.

Evans, Craig A. 'Scripture-Based Stories in the Pseudepigrapha,' in Carson et al. (eds.), *Justification and Variegated Nomism*, 1:57-72.

Goodman, Martin. 'Modeling the "Parting of the Ways."' In Becker and Reed (eds.), *The Ways that Never Parted*, 119-29.

Hengel, Martin. *Judaism and Hellenism: Studies in Their Encounter in Palestine During the Early Hellenistic Period*. 2 vols. London: SCM, 1974.

Horbury, William. *Jews and Christians in Contact and Controversy*. Edinburgh: Clark, 1998.

Horst, Pieter van der. *Essays on the Jewish World of Early Christianity*. Freiburg, Switzerland: Universitätsverlag/Göttingen: Vandenhoeck & Ruprecht, 1990.

Lieu, Judith M. 'Circumcision, Women, and Salvation.' *NTS* 40 (1994): 358-70.

Lieu, Judith, et al. (eds.). *The Jews among Pagans and Christians in the Roman Empire*. London: Routledge, 1992.

Neusner, Jacob, and Ernest S. Frerichs et al. *'To See Ourselves as Others See Us': Christians, Jews, 'Others' in Late Antiquity*. Chico, Calif.: Scholars Press, 1985.

Neusner, Jacob. *Ancient Judaism and Modern Category Formation: 'Judaism,' 'Midrash,' 'Messianism,' and Canon in the Past Quarter-Century*. Lahnham, Md.: University Press of America, 1986.

—. *The Way of Torah: An Introduction to Judaism*. 4th ed. Belmont Calif.: Wadsworth, 1988.

—. *Judaic Law from Jesus to the Mishnah: A Systematic Reply to Professor E. P. Sanders*. South Florida Studies in the History of Judaism 84. Atlanta: Scholars Press, 1993.

—. 'What is a Judaism? Seeing the Dead Sea Library as the Statement of a Coherent Judaic Religious System.' In *Judaism in Late Antiquity*, part 5, *The Judaism of Qumran: A Systemic Reading of the Dead Sea Scrolls*, 1:3-21. Edited by Alan J. Avery-Peck, Jacob Neusner, and Bruce D. Chilton. 2 vols. HO Section One: The Near and Middle East 56-57. Leiden: Brill, 2001.

Niehoff, Maren R. 'Circumcision as a Marker of Identity: Philo, Origen, and the Rabbis on Gen 17:1-14.' *JSQ* 10 (2003): 89-123.

North, John. 'The Development of Religious Pluralism.' In Lieu et al. (eds.), *The Jews among Pagans and Christians in the Roman Empire*, 174-93.

Rutgers, L.V. *The Hidden Heritage of Diaspora Judaism*. 2nd ed. Contributions to Biblical Exegesis and Theology, 20. Louvain: Peeters, 1998.

—. 'Jewish Literary Production in the Diaspora in Late Antiquity: The Western Evidence.' In *The Hidden Heritage of Diaspora Judaism*, 235-84.

Sanders, E. P., with A. I. Baumgarten and Alan Mendelson (eds.). *Jewish and Christian Self-Definition*, vol. 2, *Aspects of Judaism in the Graeco-Roman Period*. London: SCM, 1981.

Sanders, E. P. *Judaism: Practice and Belief, 63 BCE–66 CE*. London: SCM, 1992.

—. *Jewish Law from Jesus to the Mishnah: Five Studies*. Philadelphia: Trinity, 1990.

Sanders, Jack T. 'When Sacred Canopies Collide. The Reception of the Torah of Moses in the Wisdom Literature of the Second-Temple Period.' *JSJ* 32 (2001): 121-36.

Schürer, Emil. *The History of the Jewish People in the Age of Jesus Christ (175 B.C.–A.D. 135)*. 3 vols. in 4. Rev. ed. Edited by Geza Vermes, Fergus Millar, and Martin Goodman. Edinburgh: Clark, 1973-87.

Smith, Jonathan Z. 'Fences and Neighbors: Some Contours of Early Judaism.' In *Imagining Religion: from Babylon to Jonestown*, 1-18, 135-41. Chicago: University of Chicago Press, 1982.

Stanton, Graham N., and Guy G. Stroumsa (eds.). *Tolerance and Intolerance in Early Judaism and Christianity*. Cambridge: Cambridge University Press, 1998.

Stern, Menahem. *Greek and Latin Authors on Jews and Judaism*. 3 vols. Jerusalem: Israel Academy of Science and Humanities, 1974-84.

Trebilco, Paul R. *Jewish Communities in Asia Minor*. Cambridge: Cambridge University Press, 1991.

Cohen, Shaye J. D. 'Masada: Literary Tradition, Archaeological Remains, and the Credibility of Josephus.' *JJS* 33 (1982): 385-405.

Newell, Raymond R. 'The Forms and Historical Value of Josephus' Suicide Accounts.' In Feldman and Hata (eds.), *Josephus, the Bible, and History*, 278-94.

Ulrich, Eugene. 'Two Perspectives on Two Pentateuchal Manuscripts from Masada.' In Paul et al. (eds.), *Emanuel*, 453-64.

Yadin, Yigael. *The Ben Sira Scroll from Masada.* Jerusalem: Israel Exploration Society and the Shrine of the Book, 1965.

——. *Masada: Herod's Fortress and the Zealots' Last Stand.* Tel Aviv: Steimatzky, 1966.

Yadin, Yigael, Joseph Naveh and Yaacov Meshorer. *Masada: The Yigael Yadin Excavations 1963-1965: Final Reports*, vol. 1, *The Aramaic and Hebrew Ostraca and Jar Inscriptions; The Coins of Masada.* Jerusalem: Israel Exploration Society/Hebrew University of Jerusalem, 1989.

NEW TESTAMENT:
HISTORY AND LITERATURE

Balch, David L. (ed.). *Social History of the Matthean Community: Cross-Disciplinary Approaches.* Minneapolis: Augsburg Fortress, 1991.

Bauckham, Richard. *Jude and the Relatives of Jesus in the Early Church.* Edinburgh: Clark, 1990.

Boyarin, Daniel. *A Radical Jew: Paul and the Politics of Identity.* Berkeley: University of California Press, 1994.

Davies, William David. *The Setting of the Sermon on the Mount.* Cambridge: Cambridge University Press, 1964.

Dunn, James D. G. (ed.). *Paul and the Mosaic Law: The Third Durham-Tubingen Research Symposium on Earliest Christianity and Judaism.* WUNT 89. Tübingen: Mohr Siebeck, 1996.

—— (ed.). *The Cambridge Companion to St Paul.* Cambridge: Cambridge University Press, 2003.

Esler, Philip F. *Community and Gospel in Luke-Acts: The Social and Political Motivations of Lucan Theology.* Cambridge: Cambridge University Press, 1987.

Gager, John G. *Reinventing Paul.* Oxford: Oxford University Press, 2000.

Houlden, Leslie. 'The Puzzle of Matthew and the Law.' In Porter et al. (eds.), *Crossing the Boundaries*, 115-31.

Hummel, Reinhart. *Die Auseinandersetzung zwischen Kirche und Judentum im Matthäusevangelium.* BEvT 33. Munich: Chr. Kaiser, 1966.

Iersel, Bas M. F. van. *Mark: A Reader-Response Commentary.* JSNTSup 164. Sheffield: Sheffield Academic Press, 1998.

Kvalbein, Hans. 'Has Matthew Abandoned the Jews? A Contribution to a Disputed Issue in Recent Scholarship.' In *The Mission of the Early Church to Jews and Gentiles*, 45-68. Edited by Jostein Ådna and Hans Kvalbein. Tübingen: Mohr Siebeck, 2000.

Mack, Burton L. *The Lost Gospel: The Book of Q and Christian Origins.* Shaftsbury, Dorset: Element, 1993.

Orton, David E. 'Matthew and Other Creative Jewish Writers.' In Porter, Joyce, and Orton (eds.), *Crossing the Boundaries*, 133-40.

Overman, J. A. *Matthew's Gospel and Formative Judaism: The Social World of the Matthean Community.* Minneapolis: Fortress, 1990.

Porter, Stanley E., Paul Joyce, and David E. Orton (eds.). *Crossing the Boundaries: Essays in Biblical Interpretation in Honour of Michael D. Goulder.* Biblical Interpretation Series 8. Leiden: Brill, 1994.

Saldarini, Anthony J. *Matthew's Christian-Jewish Community.* Chicago: University of Chicago Press 1994.

Sanders, E. P. *Paul and Palestinian Judaism: A Comparison of Patterns of Religion.* London: SCM, 1977.

Segal, Alan F. *Paul the Convert: The Apostolate and Apostasy of Saul the Pharisee.* New Haven: Yale University Press, 1990.

Sim, David C. 'The Gospel of Matthew and the Gentiles.' *JSNT* 57 (1995): 19-48.

Stanton, Graham. 'Matthew's Christology and the Parting of the Ways.' In Dunn (ed.), *Jews and Christians: The Parting of the Ways*, 99-116.

——. *A Gospel for a New People: Studies in Matthew.* Edinburgh: Clark, 1992.

Watson, Francis. *Paul and the Hermeneutics of Faith.* London: Clark, 2004.

Birnbaum, Ellen. *The Place of Judaism in Philo's Thought: Israel, Jews, and Proselytes*. BJS 290. Studia Philonica Monographs 2. Atlanta: Scholars Press, 1996.

Bruns, J. Edgar. 'Philo Christianus: The Debris of a Legend.' *HTR* 66 (1973): 141-45.

Græsholt, Georg. 'Philo of Alexandria: Some Typical Traits of his Jewish Identity.' *Classica et Mediaevalia* 43 (1992): 97-110.

Hoek, Annewies van den. *Clement of Alexandria and His Use of Philo in the Stromateis: An Early Christian Reshaping of a Jewish Model*. VCSup 3. Leiden: Brill, 1988.

——. 'Philo in the Alexandrian Tradition.' *Studia Philonica Annual* 6 (1994): 96-99.

——. 'Philo and Origen: A Descriptive Catalogue of Their Relationship.' *Studia Philonica Annual* 12 (2000): 44-121.

Mendelson, Alan. *Philo's Jewish Identity*. BJS 161. Atlanta: Scholars Press, 1988.

Morris, Jenny. 'The Jewish Philosopher Philo.' In Schürer and Vermes et al (eds.), *The History of the Jewish People in the Age of Jesus Christ*, 3.2:809-89.

——. *Philo on Jewish Identity and Culture*. TSAJ 86. Tübingen: Mohr Siebeck, 2001.

Pearce, Sarah. 'Belonging and Not Belonging: Local Perspectives in Philo of Alexandria.' In *Jewish Local Patriotism and Self-Identification in the Graeco-Roman Period*, 79-105. Edited by Siân Jones and Sarah Pearce. JSPSup 31. Sheffield: Sheffield Academic Press, 1998.

Radice, Roberto, and David T. Runia. *Philo of Alexandria: An Annotated Bibliography 1937-1986*. VCSup 8. Leiden: Brill, 1988.

Roberts, Colin. *Buried Books in Antiquity*: Habent Sua Fata Libelli. Arundell Esdaile Memorial Lecture 1962. London: The Library Association, 1963.

——. 'Philo's Divisions of His Works into Books.' *Studia Philonica Annual* 13 (2001): 59-85.

Runia, David T. *Philo of Alexandria: An Annotated Bibliography 1987-1996*. VCSup 57. Leiden: Brill, 2000.

——. 'Philo and Origen: A Preliminary Survey.' In *Origeniana Quinta: Papers of the 5th International Origen Congress* 333-39 Edited by R. J. Daly. BETL 105. Louvain: Peeters, 1992.

——. *Philo in Early Christian Literature: A Survey*. CRINT 3.3. Minneapolis: Fortress, 1993.

——. 'References to Philo from Josephus up to 1000 AD.' *Studia Philonica Annual* 6 (1994): 111-21.

——. 'Philo of Alexandria and the Beginnings of Christian Thought.' *Studia Philonica Annual* 7 (1995): 143-60.

Siegert, Folkhart. 'Der armenische Philon: Textbestand, Editionen, Forschungsgeschichte.' *BHT* 100 (1989): 353-69.

Skarsten, Roald. 'Forfatterproblemet ved *De aeternitate mundi* in Corpus Philonicum.' Ph. D. diss., University of Bergen, 1987. (= *An Authorship Problem: De Aeternitate Mundi in Corpus Philonicum*. University of Bergen, 1996.)

——. 'Notes on the Transmission of the Philonic Corpus.' *Studia Philonica Annual* 6 (1994): 91-95.

Wilken, Robert L. 'Philo in the Fourth Century.' *Studia Philonica Annual* 6 (1994): 100-102.

Winden, J. C. M. van. 'Quotations from Philo in Clement of Alexandria's Protrepticus.' *VC* 32 (1978): 208-13.

Winston, David. 'Philo's *Nachleben* in Judaism.' *Studia Philonica Annual* 6 (1994): 103-10.

PHILO: APOCRYPHA AND SPURIA

Royse, James R. *The Spurious Texts of Philo of Alexandria: A Study of Textual Transmission and Corruption*. ALGHJ 22. Leiden: Brill, 1991.

Runia, David T. 'Philonica in the *Catana in Genesim*.' *Studia Philonica Annual* 11 (1999): 113-20.

Siegert, Folker, et al. *Pseudo-Philon: Prédications Synagogales: traduction, notes et commentaire*. SC 435. Paris: Cerf, 1999.

PSEUDEPIGRAPHA, OLD TESTAMENT

General

Black, M. *Apocalypsis Henochi Graece*; Albert-Marie Denis, *Fragmenta Pseudepigraphorum quae supersunt Graeca*. PVTG 3. Leiden: Brill, 1970.

Charles, R. H. (ed.). *The Apocrypha and Pseudepigrapha of the Old Testament in English*, vol. 2, *Pseudepigrapha*. Oxford: Clarendon, 1913. Abbreviated as *APOT*, 2.

Charlesworth, James H., assisted by P. Dykers. *The Pseudepigrapha and Modern Research*. Missoula, Mont.: Scholars Press, 1976.

——. 'Christian and Jewish Self-Definition in Light of the Christian Additions to the Apocryphal Writings,' in Sanders, Baumgarten, and Mendelson (eds.), *Aspects of Judaism in the Graeco-Roman Period*, 27-55, 310-15.

——. *The Old Testament Pseudepigrapha*, vol. 1, *Apocalyptic Literature and Testaments*, vol. 2, *Expansions of the 'Old Testament' and Legends, Wisdom and Philosophical Literature, Prayers, Psalms, and Odes, Fragments of Lost Judeo-Hellenistic Works*. Garden City, N.Y.: 1983-85. Abbreviated as *OTP*, 1-2.

Coleman, Gillis Byrns. 'The Phenomenon of Christian Interpolations into Jewish Apocalyptic Texts: a Bibliographical Survey and Methodological Analysis.' Ph. D. diss., Vanderbilt University, 1976.

Davila, James R. '(How) Can We Tell if a Greek Apocryphon or Pseudepigraphon Has Been Translated from Hebrew or Aramaic?' *JSP* 15 (2005): 3-61.

Denis, Albert-Marie. *Introduction aux pseudépigraphes grecs d'Ancien Testament*. SVTP 1. Leiden: Brill, 1970.

Evans, Craig A. *Noncanonical Writings and New Testament Interpretation*. Peabody, Mass.: Hendrickson, 1992.

Jonge, M. de. *Pseudepigrapha of the Old Testament as Part of Christian Literature: The Case of the Testaments of the Twelve Patriarchs and the Greek Life of Adam and Eve*. SVTP 18. Leiden: Brill, 2003.

Kraft, Robert A. 'Christian Transmission of Greek Jewish Scriptures: A Methodological Probe.' In *Paganisme, Judaïsme, Christianisme: Influences et affrontements dans le monde antique*, 207-26. Paris: Boccard, 1978.

——. 'Setting the Stage and Framing Some Central Questions.' *JSJ* 32 (2001): 371-95.

Metzger, Bruce M. 'Literary Forgeries and Canonical Pseudepigrapha.' *JBL* 91 (1972): 3-24.

Nickelsburg, G. W. E. 'Stories of Biblical and Early-Post-Biblical Times,' in Stone (ed.), *Jewish Writings of the Second Temple Period*, 33-87.

Sparks, H. D. F. *The Apocryphal Old Testament*. Oxford: Clarendon, 1984. Abbreviated as *AOT*.

Speyer, Wolfgang. *Die Literarische Fälschung in heidnischen und christlichen Altertum: ein Versuch ihrer Deutung*. Munich: Beck, 1971.

Stone, Michael E. (ed.). *Jewish Writings of the Second Temple Period: Apocrypha, Pseudepigrapha, Qumran Sectarian Writings, Philo, Josephus*. CRINT 2. 2. Philadelphia: Fortress, 1984.

Wright, Benjamin G. *A Multiform Heritage: Studies on Early Judaism and Christianity in Honor of Robert A. Kraft*. Scholars Press Homage Series 24. Atlanta: Scholars Press, 1999.

Abraham, Testament of

Allison, Dale C., Jr. *Testament of Abraham*. Commentaries on Early Jewish Literature. Berlin: de Gruyter, 2003.

Cooper, Donald S., and Harry B. Weber. 'The Church Slavonic Testament of Abraham.' In Nickelsburg (ed.), *Studies on the Testament of Abraham*, 301-26.

Delcor, Mathias. *Le Testament d'Abraham*. SVTP 2. Leiden: Brill, 1973.

James, Montague Rhodes. *The Testament of Abraham*. Texts and Studies. Contributions to Biblical and Patristic Literature 2. 2. Cambridge: Cambridge University Press, 1892.

Kraft, Robert A. 'Reassessing the 'Recensional Problem' in Testament of Abraham.' In Nickelsburg (ed.), *Studies on the Testament of Abraham*, 121-37.

MacRae, George. 'The Coptic Testament of Abraham.' In Nickelsburg (ed.), *Studies on the Testament of Abraham*, 327-40.

Martin, R. A. 'Syntax Criticism of the Testament of Abraham.' In Nickelsburg (ed.), *Studies on the Testament of Abraham*, 95-120.

Nickelsburg, George W. E. (ed.). *Studies on the Testament of Abraham*. SBLSCS 6. N.p.: Scholars Press for the Society of Biblical Literature, 1976.

Roddy, Nicolae. *The Romanian Version of the Testament of Abraham: Text, Translation, and Cultural Context*. SBLEJL 19. Atlanta: Society of Biblical Literature, 2001.

Sanders, E. P. 'Testament of Abraham.' *OTP*, 871-902.

Schmidt, Francis. *Le Testament grec d'Abraham*. TSAJ 11. Tübingen: Mohr Siebeck, 1986.

Stone, Michael E. *The Testament of Abraham: The Greek Recensions*. SBLTT 2. SBLPS 2. Missoula, Mont.: Society of Biblical Literature, 1972.

Turner, N. 'The Testament of Abraham.' *AOT*, 393-421.

Adam, Apocalypse of

MacRae, G. 'Apocalypse of Adam.' *OTP*, 1:707-19

Adam and Eve, Life of

Johnson, M. D. 'Life of Adam and Eve.' *OTP*, 2:249-95.

Jonge, M. de. *Pseudepigrapha of the Old Testament as Part of Christian Literature: The Case of the Testaments of the Twelve Patriarchs and the Greek Life of Adam and Eve*. SVTP 18. Leiden: Brill, 2003.

Knittel, Thomas. *Das griechische 'Leben Adams und Evas': Studien zu einer narrativen Anthropologie in frühen Judentum*. TSAJ 88. Tübingen: Mohr Siebeck, 2002.

Sharpe, III, John Lawrence. 'Prolegomena to the Establishment of the Critical Text of the Greek Apocalypse of Moses.' Ph. D. diss., Duke University, 1969.

Stone, Michael E. *A History of the Literature of Adam and Eve*. SBLEJL 3. Atlanta: Scholars Press, 1992.

Wells, L. S. 'The Books of Adam and Eve.' *APOT*, 2:123-54.

Aristeas to Philocrates

Hadas, Moses. *Aristeas to Philocrates (Letter of Aristeas)*. New York: Harper, 1951.

Pelletier, André. *Lettre d'Aristée à Philocrate*. SC 89. Paris: Cerf, 1962.

——. 'Josephus, the Letter of Aristeas, and the Septuagint.' In Feldman and Hata (eds.), *Josephus, the Bible, and History*, 97-115.

Thackeray, H. St. J. 'Appendix: The Letter of Aristeas.' In Swete, Henry Barclay, and Richard Rusden Ottley. *An Introduction to the Old Testament in Greek*, 531-606. Cambridge: Cambridge University Press, 1914.

2 Baruch (Syriac Apocalyse of Baruch)

Bogaert, Pierre. *Apocalypse de Baruch*. SC 144-45. Paris: Cerf, 1969.

Charles, R. H. '2 Baruch or the Syriac Apocalypse of Baruch.' *APOT*, 2:470-526.

Charlesworth, James H. 'Baruch, Book of 2 (Syriac).' *ABD*, 1:620-21.

Dedering, S., and R. J. Bidawid. *The Old Testament in Syriac According to the Peshiṭta Version*, IV.3, *Apocalypse of Baruch, 4 Esdras*. Leiden: Brill, 1973.

Klijn, A. F. J. '2 (Syriac Apocalypse of) Baruch.' *OTP*, 1:615-52.

Laato, Antti. 'The Apocalypse of the Syriac Baruch and the Date of the End.' *JSP* 18 (1998): 39-46.

Leemhuis, F., A. F. J. Klijn, and G. J. H. van Gelder. *The Arabic Text of the Apocalypse of Baruch*. Leiden: Brill, 1986.

Leemhuis, Fred. 'The Arabic Version of the Apocalypse of Baruch: A Christian Text?' *JSP* 4 (1989): 19-26.

Nir, Rivka. *The Destruction of Jerusalem and the Idea of Redemption in the Syriac Apocalypse of Baruch*. SBLEJL 20. Atlanta: Society of Biblical Literature, 2003.

Roddy, Nicolae. '"Two Parts: Weeks of Seven Weeks": The End of the Age as *Terminus ad Quem* for *2 Baruch*.' *JSP* 14 (1996): 3-14.

Whitters, Mark F. *The Epistle of Second Baruch: A Study in Form and Message*. JSPSup 42. London: Sheffield Academic Press, 2003.

3 Baruch (Greek and Slavonic Apocalypse of Baruch)

Brock, S. P. *Testamentum Iobi*. J.-C. Picard, *Apocalypsis Baruchi Graece*. PVTG 2. Leiden: Brill, 1967.
Harlow, Daniel C. *The Greek Apocalypse of Baruch (3 Baruch) in Hellenistic Judaism and Early Christianity*. SVTP 12. Leiden: Brill, 1996.

4 Baruch (Paralepomena of Jeremiah)

Robinson, S. E. '4 Baruch.' *OTP*, 2:413-25.

Daniel, Apocalypses of

DiTommaso, Lorenzo. *The Book of Daniel and the Apocryphal Daniel Literature*. SVTP 20; Leiden: Brill, 2005.
Zervos, G. T. 'Apocalypse of Daniel.' *OTP*, 1:755-70.
Henze, Matthias. *The Syriac Apocalypse of Daniel: Introduction, Text, and Commentary* (Tübingen: Mohr Siebeck, 2001).

Elijah, Coptic Apocalypse of

Wintermute, O. S. 'Apocalypse of Elijah.' *OTP*, 1:721-53.

1-3 Enoch

Alexander, P. S. 'The Historical Setting of the Hebrew Book of Enoch.' *JJS* 28 (1977): 156-80.
Black, Matthew, in consultation with James C. VanderKam. *The Book of Enoch or 1 Enoch: A New English Edition*. SVTP 7. Leiden: Brill, 1985.
——. 'The Messianism of the Parables of Enoch: Their Date and Contribution to Christological Origins.' In Charlesworth (ed.), *The Messiah*, 145-68.
Charlesworth, James H. (ed.). *The Messiah: Developments in Earliest Judaism and Christianity*. Minneapolis: Fortress, 1992.
Davila, James R. 'Of Methodology, Monotheism, and Metatron: Introductory Reflections on Divine Mediators and the Origins of the Worship of Jesus.' In *The Jewish Roots of Christological Monotheism: Papers from the St. Andrews Conference on the Historical Origins of the Worship of Jesus*, 3-18. Edited by Carey C. Newman, James R. Davila, and Gladys S. Lewis. JSJSup 63. Leiden: Brill, 1999.
Greenfield, Jonas C., and Michael E. Stone. 'The Enochic Pentateuch and the Date of the Similitudes.' *HTR* 70 (1977): 51-65.
Knibb Michael A., in consultation with Edward Ullendorff. *The Ethiopic Book of Enoch: A New Edition in Light of the Aramaic Dead Sea Fragments*. 2 vols. Oxford: Clarendon, 1978.
——. 'The Date of the Parables of Enoch: A Critical Review.' *NTS* 25 (1979): 345-59.
Larson, Erik W. 'The Translation of Enoch: From Aramaic into Greek.' Ph. D. diss., New York University, 1995.
Mearns, Christopher L. 'Dating the Similitudes of Enoch.' *NTS* 25 (1979): 360-69.
Milik, J. T., with the collaboration of Matthew Black. *The Books of Enoch: Aramaic Fragments of Qumrân Cave 4*. Oxford: Clarendon, 1976.
Munro, Ernest A. Jr. 'The Greek Fragments of Enoch from Qumran Cave 7 (7Q4, 7Q8, & 7Q12 = 7QEn gr = Enoch 103:3-4, 7-8).' *RevQ* 18/70 (1998): 307-12.
Nebe, G. W. '7Q4 – Möglichkeit und Grenze einer Identifikation.' *RevQ* 13/49-52 (1988): 629-633.
Nickelsburg, George W. E. 'Enoch, Levi, and Peter: Recipients of Revelation in Upper Galilee.' *JBL* 100 (1981): 575-600.
——. 'Enochic Wisdom: An Alternative to the Mosaic Torah?' in *Hesed Ve-Emet. Studies in Honor of Ernest S. Frerichs*, 123-32. Edited by Jodi Magness and Seymour Gittin. Atlanta: Scholars Press, 1998.
——. *1 Enoch 1: A Commentary on the Book of 1 Enoch, Chapters 1-36; 81-108*. Hermeneia. Minneapolis: Fortress, 2001.
Puech, Émile. 'Notes sur les fragments grecs du manuscrit 7Q4 = 1 Hénoch 103 et 105.' *RB* 103 (1996): 592-600.
——. 'Sept fragments grecs de la *Lettre d'Hénoch* (1 Hén 100, 103 et 105) dans la grotte 7 de Qumrân (= 7QHéngr).' *RevQ* 18/70 (1998): 313-23.
Suter, David Winston. *Tradition and Composition in the Parables of Enoch*. SBLDS 47. Missoula, Mont.: Scholars Press, 1979.

Tiller, Patrick A. *A Commentary on the Animal Apocalypse of* I Enoch. Atlanta: Scholars Press, 1993.

VanderKam, James C. 'Some Major Issues in the Contemporary Study of 1 Enoch: Reflections on J. T. Milik's *The Books of Enoch: Aramaic Fragments of Qumrân Cave 4.*' *Maarav* 3 (1982): 85-97.

——. 'Righteous One, Messiah, Chosen One, and Son of Man in 1 Enoch 37-71.' In Charlesworth (ed.), *The Messiah*, 169-91.

4-6 Ezra / 2 Esdras

Dedering, S., and R. J. Bidawid. *The Old Testament in Syriac According to the Peshiṭta Version*, I V.3, *Apocalypse of Baruch, 4 Esdras*. Leiden: Brill, 1973.

DiTommaso, Lorenzo. 'Dating the Eagle Vision of 4 Ezra: A New Look at an Old Theory.' *JSP* 20 (1999): 3-38.

Klijn, A. Frederik J. *Der lateinische Text der Apokalypse des Esra*. TUGA 131. Berlin: Akademie-verlag, 1983.

Longenecker, Bruce W. *Eschatology and the Covenant: A Comparison of 4 Ezra and Romans 1-11.* JSNTSup 57. Sheffield: Sheffield Academic Press/JSOT, 1991.

——. *2 Esdras*. Guides to Apocrypha and Pseudepigrapha. Sheffield: Sheffield Academic Press, 1995.

——. 'Locating 4 Ezra: A Consideration of Its Social Setting and Functions.' *JSJ* 28 (1997): 271-93.

Mussies, G. 'When Do Graecisms Prove that a Latin Text Is a Translation?' In *Vruchten van de Uithof: Studies opgedragen aan dr. H. A. Brongers ter gelegenheid van zijn afscheid*, 100-119. Utrecht: Theologisch Instituut, 1974.

Stone, Michael E. *Fourth Ezra: A Commentary on the Book of Fourth Ezra*. Minneapolis: Fortress, 1990.

Ezra, Greek Apocalypse of

Stone, M. E. 'Greek Apocalypse of Ezra.' *OTP*, 1:561-79.

Ezra, Vision of

Mueller, J. R., and G. A. Robbins. 'Vision of Ezra.' *OTP*, 1:581-90.

Isaiah, Ascension of

Bauckham, Richard. 'The Ascension of Isaiah: Genre, Unity and Date.' In *The Fate of the Dead: Studies on the Jewish and Christian Apocalypses*, 363-90. NTSup 93. Leiden: Brill, 1998.

Knight, Jonathan. *The Ascension of Isaiah*. Guides to Apocrypha and Pseudepigrapha. Sheffield: Sheffield Academic Press, 1995.

Historians, Greek Fragments of

Holladay, Carl R. *Fragments from Hellenistic Jewish Authors*, vol. 1, *Historians*. SBLTT 20. SBLPS 10. Chico, Calif.: Scholars Press, 1983.

——— Artapanus

Collins, J. J. 'Artapanus.' *OTP*, 2:889-903.

——— Cleodemus Malchus

Doran, R. 'Cleodemus Malchus.' *OTP*, 2:883-87.

——— Eupolemus and Pseudo-Eupolemus

Doran, R. 'Pseudo-Eupolemus.' *OTP*, 2:873-82.

Wacholder, Ben Zion. *Eupolemos: A Study of Judaeo-Greek Literature*. Cincinnati, Ohio: Hebrew Union College – Jewish Institute of Religion, 1974.

Job, Testament of

Brock, S. P. *Testamentum Iobi.* J.-C. Picard, *Apocalypsis Baruchi Graece*. PVTG 2. Leiden: Brill, 1967.

Collins, John J. 'Structure and Meaning in the Testament of Job.' *SBLSP* 1 (1974): 35-52.

Horst, Pieter W. van der. 'Images of Women in the Testament of Job.' In Knibb and Van der Horst (eds.), *Studies on the Testament of Job*, 93-116.

Jacobs, Irving. 'Literary Motifs in the *Testament of Job.' JJS* 21 (1970): 1-10.

James, M. R. 'The Testament of Job.' *Apocrypha Anecdota: Second Series*. Texts and Studies. Contributions to Biblical and Patristic Literature 5.1, lxxii-cii, 103-37. Cambridge: Cambridge University Press, 1897.

Kee, H. C. 'Satan, Magic, and Salvation in the Testament of Job.' *SBLSP* 1 (1974): 53-76.

Knibb, Michael A., and Pieter W. van der Horst (eds.). *Studies on the Testament of Job*. SNTSMS 66. Cambridge: Cambridge University Press, 1989.

Kraft, Robert A. *The Testament of Job According to the SV Text*. Missoula, Mont.: Scholars Press, 1974.

Philonenko, Marc. 'Le Testament de Job et les Thérapeutes.' *Sem* 8 (1958): 41-53.

———. 'Le Testament de Job.' *Sem* 18 (1968): 1-75.

Römer, Cornelia, and Heinz J. Thissen. 'P. Köln Inv. Nr. 3221: Das Testament des Hiob in koptischer Sprache. Ein Vorbericht.' In Knibb and Van der Horst (eds.), *Studies on the Testament of Job*, 33-41.

Schaller, Berndt. *Das Testament Hiobs*. JSHRZ 3.3. Mohn: Gütersloh, 1979.

———. 'Das Testament Hiobs und die Septuaginta-Übersetzung des Buches Hiob.' *Bib* 61 (1980): 377-406.

Spittler, R. P. 'Testament of Job.' *OTP*, 1:829-68.

———. 'The Testament of Job: A History of Research and Interpretation.' in Knibb and Van der Horst (eds.), *Studies on the Testament of Job*, 7-32.

Thornhill, R. 'The Testament of Job.' *AOT*, 617-48.

Wacholder, Ben-Zion. 'Job, Testament of.' *EncJud* 10:129-30.

Joseph and Aseneth

Batiffol, Pierre. *Le livre de la Prière d'Aseneth*. Studia Patristica. Études d'ancienne littérature chrétienne 1-2, 1-115. Paris: Leroux, 1889-90.

Beckwith, R. T. 'The Solar Calendar of Joseph and Aseneth: A Suggestion.' *JSJ* 15 (1984): 90-111.

Bohak, Gideon. *Joseph and Aseneth and the Jewish Temple in Heliopolis*. SBLEJL 10. Atlanta: Scholars Press, 1996.

Burchard, Christoph. *Untersuchungen zu Joseph und Aseneth*. WUNT 8. Tübingen: Mohr Siebeck, 1965.

———. 'Ein vorläufiger griechischer Text von Joseph und Aseneth.' *DBAT* 14 (1979), 2-53. Reprinted with accents in Denis, Albert-Marie. *Concordance grecque des pseudépigraphes d'Ancien Testament*, 851-59. Louvain-la-Neuve: Université Catholique de Louvain, 1987.

———. *Joseph und Aseneth*. JSHRZ 2.4. Mohn: Gütersloh, 1983.

———. 'Joseph and Aseneth.' *OTP*, 2:177-247.

Burchard, Christoph, with Carsten Burfeind and Uta Barbara Fink. *Joseph and Aseneth*. PVTG 50. Leiden: Brill, 2003.

Chesnutt, Randall D. *From Death to Life: Conversion in Joseph and Aseneth*. JSPSup 16. Sheffield: Sheffield Academic Press, 1995.

Cook, D. 'Joseph and Aseneth.' *AOT*, 465-503.

Humphrey, Edith M. *Joseph and Aseneth*. Guides to Apocrypha and Pseudepigrapha. Sheffield: Sheffield Academic Press, 2000.

Kraemer, Ross Shepard. *When Aseneth Met Joseph: A Late Antique Tale of the Biblical Patriarch and His Egyptian Wife, Reconsidered*. Oxford: Oxford University Press, 1998.

———. 'Could Aseneth be Samaritan?' In Wright (ed.), *A Multiform Heritage: Studies on Early Judaism and Christianity in Honor of Robert A. Kraft*, 149-65.

Philonenko, Marc. *Joseph et Aséneth*. StPB 13. Leiden: Brill, 1968.

Standhartinger, Angela. *Das Frauenbild im Judentum ser hellenistischen Zeit: Ein Beitrag anhand von 'Joseph und Aseneth.'* AGJU 26. Leiden: Brill, 1995.

Jubilees

VanderKam, James C. *The Book of Jubilees*. Guides to Apocrypha and Pseudepigrapha. Sheffield: Sheffield Academic Press, 2001.

3-4 Maccabees

deSilva, David A. *4 Maccabees.* Guides to Apocrypha and Pseudepigrapha. Sheffield: Sheffield Academic Press, 1998.

Hadas, Moses. *The Third and Fourth Books of Maccabees.* 2 vols. in one. New York: Harper, 1953.

Henten, Jan Willem van. *The Maccabean Martyrs as Saviours of the Jewish People: A Study of 2 and 4 Maccabees.* JSJSup 57. Leiden: Brill, 1997.

Kappler, Werner, and Robert Hanhart. *Maccabaeorum libri I-IV.* Septuaginta: Vetus Testamentum Graecum Auctoritate Societatis Litterarum Gottingensis 9. Göttingen: Vandenhoeck & Ruprecht, 1960.

Swete, Henry Barclay. *The Old Testament in Greek According to the Septuagint,* vol. 3, *Hosea-4 Maccabees, Psalms of Solomon, Enoch, the Odes.* Cambridge: Cambridge University Press, 1909-12.

Williams, David S. *Stylometric Authorship Studies in Flavius Josephus and Related Literature.* (Jewish Studies 12. Lewiston, N.Y.: Mellen, 1992).

Menander, Sentences of the Syriac

Baarda, T. 'The Sentences of the Syriac Menander.' *OTP,* 2:583-606.

Moses, Assumption *or* Testament of

Bauckham, Richard. *Jude and the Relatives of Jesus in the Early Church.* Edinburgh: Clark, 1990.

Ceriani, A. M. *Monumenta sacra et profana ex codicibus praesertim Bibliothecae Ambrosianae,* I 1:55-64. Milan: Bibliotheca Ambrosiana, 1861.

Charles, R. H. *The Assumption of Moses.* London: Black, 1897.

Collins, John J. 'The Date and Provenance of the Testament of Moses.' In Nickelsburg (ed.), *Studies on the Testament of Moses,* 15-32.

——. 'Some Remaining Traditio-Historical Problems in the Testament of Moses.' In Nickelsburg (ed.), *Studies on the Testament of Moses,* 38-43.

Goldstein, Jonathan A. 'The Testament of Moses: Its Content, Its Origin, and its Attestation in Josephus.' In Nickelsburg (ed.), *Studies on the Testament of Moses,* 44-52.

Laperrousaz, E.-M. 'Le Testament de Moïse.' *Sem.* 19 (1970): 1-140.

Nickelsburg, George W. E., Jr. (ed.). *Studies on the Testament of Moses.* SBLSCS 4. Cambridge, Mass.: Society of Biblical Literature, 1973.

——. 'Introduction.' In Nickelsburg (ed.), *Studies on the Testament of Moses,* 5-14.

——. 'An Antiochan Date for the Testament of Moses.' In Nickelsburg (ed.), *Studies on the Testament of Moses,* 33-37.

Purvis, James D. 'Samaritan Traditions on the Death of Moses.' In Nickelsburg (ed.), *Studies on the Testament of Moses,* 93-117.

Tromp, Johannes. *The Assumption of Moses.* SVTP 10. Leiden: Brill, 1993.

Poets, fragments of pseudo-Greek

Attridge, H. 'Fragments of Pseudo-Greek Poets.' *OTP,* 2:821-30.

Holladay, Carl R. *Fragments from Hellenistic Jewish Authors,* vol. 2, *Poets.* SBLTT 30. SBLPS 12. Atlanta: Scholars Press, 1989.

——— Ezekiel the Tragedian, *Exagoge*

Collins, Nina L. 'Ezekiel, the Author of the *Exagoge*: His Calendar and Home.' *JSJ* 22 (1991): 201-11.

Horst, Pieter van der. 'Moses' Throne Vision in Ezekiel the Dramatist.' *JJS* 34 (1983): 21-29.

——. 'Some Notes on the *Exagoge* of Ezekiel.' *Mnemosyne* 37 (1984): 354-75.

Robertson, R. G. 'Ezekiel the Tragedian.' *OTP,* 2:803-19.

——— *Orphica*

Lafargue, M. 'Orphica.' *OTP,* 2:795-801.

——— Theodotus

Daise, Michael. 'Samaritans, Seleucids, and the Epic of Theodotus.' *JSP* 17 (1998): 25-51.

Fallon, F. 'Theodotus.' *OTP*, 2:785-93.

Patriarchs, Testaments of the Twelve
(*including* Aramaic Levi)

Hollander, H.W., and M. de Jonge. *The Testaments of the Twelve Patriarchs: A Commentary.* SVTP 8. Leiden: Brill, 1985.

Jonge, M. de (ed.). *Studies on the Testaments of the Twelve Patriarchs: Text and Interpretation.* SVTP 3. Leiden: Brill, 1975.

Jonge, M. de. *The Testaments of the Twelve Patriarchs: A Study of their Text, Composition and Origin.* 2nd ed. Assen/Amsterdam: Van Gorcum, 1975.

——. *Pseudepigrapha of the Old Testament as Part of Christian Literature: The Case of the Testaments of the Twelve Patriarchs and the Greek Life of Adam and Eve.* SVTP 18. Leiden: Brill, 2003.

Kee, H. C. 'Testaments of the Twelve Patriarchs.' *OTP*, 1:775-828.

Kugler, Robert A. 'Some Further Evidence for the Samaritan Provenance of *Aramaic Levi* (*1QTestLevi; 4QTestLevi*).' *RevQ* 17/65-68 (1996): 351-58.

Pseudo-Philo, Biblical Antiquities

Cohn, Leopold. 'An Apocryphal Work Ascribed to Philo of Alexandria.' *JQR O.S.* 1 (1898): 277-332.

Dietzfelbinger, Christian. *Pseudo-Philo: Antiquitates Biblicae (Liber Antiquitatum Biblicarum).* JSHRZ 2.2. Gütersloh: Mohn, 1979.

Harrington, Daniel J. 'The Original Language of Pseudo-Philo's *Liber Antiquitatum Biblicarum*.' *HTR* 63 (1970): 503-14.

——. The Biblical Text of Pseudo-Philo's *Liber Antiquitatum Biblicarum*.' *CBQ* 33 (1971): 1-17.

——. 'The Text-Critical Situation of Pseudo-Philo's "Liber Antiquitatum Biblicarum."' *RBén* 83 (1973): 383-88.

Harrington, Daniel J., and Jacques Cazeaux. *Pseudo-Philon: Les Antiquités Bibliques,* vol. 1 *Introduction et texte critiques.* Sc 229. Paris: Cerf, 1976.

Jacobson, Howard. *Commentary on Pseudo-Philo's 'Liber Antiquitatum Biblicarum,'* with Latin text and English translation. 2 vols. AGJU 31. Leiden: Brill, 1996.

——. 'Thoughts on the *Chronicles of Jerahmeel,* Ps-Philo's *Liber Antiquitatum Biblicarum,* and Their Relationship.' *Studia Philonica Annual* 9 (1997): 239-63.

James, M. R. *The Biblical Antiquities of Philo: Now First Translated from the Old Latin Version.* London: Society for Promoting Christian Knowledge, 1917.

Kisch, Guido. *Pseudo-Philo's Liber Antiqutatum Biblicarum.* Publications in Medieval Studies 10. Notre Dame, Ind.: University of Notre Dame, 1949.

Löfstedt, Bengt. 'Zu den lateinischen Übersetzung von (Ps.) Philons Schriften.' *Eranos* 89 (1991): 101-106.

Perrot, Charles, and Pierre-Maurice Bogaert, with the collaboration of Daniel J. Harrington. *Pseudo-Philon: Les Antiquités Bibliques,* vol. 2, *Introduction littéraire, commentaire et index.* SC 230. Paris: Cerf, 1976.

Strugnell, John. 'More Psalms of David.' *CBQ* 27 (1965): 207-16.

Pseudo-Phocylides

Horst, P.W. van der. *The Sentences of Pseudo-Phocylides.* SVTP 4. Leiden: Brill, 1978.

——. 'Pseudo-Phocylides.' *OTP*, 2:565-582.

Sibylline Oracles

Alexandre, Charles. *Oracula Sibyllina.* 2 vols. Paris: Didot, 1841-56.

Buitenwerf, Rieuwerd. *Book III of the Sibylline Oracles and Its Social Setting.* SVTP 17. Leiden: Brill, 2003.

Chester, Andrew. 'The Sibyl and the Temple.' In *Templum Amicitiae: Essays on the Second Temple Presented to Ernst Bammel,* 37-69. Edited by William Horbury. JSNTSup 48. Sheffield: Sheffield Academic Press, 1991.

Collins, John J. *The Sibylline Oracles of Egyptian Judaism.* SBLDS 13. Missoula, Mont.: Society of Biblical Literature and Scholars Press, 1974.

——. 'The Provenance and Date of the Third Sibylline Oracle.' *BIJS* 2 (1974): 1-18.

——. 'Sibylline Oracles.' *OTP*, 1:317-472.

——. The Development of the Sibylline Tradition.' *ANRW* 2.20.1:421-59. Part 2, *Principat,* 20.1. New York: de Gruyter, 1984.

——. 'Sibylline Oracles.' *ABD*, 6:2-6.

——. 'The Sibyl and the Potter: Political Propaganda in Ptolemaic Egypt.' In *Religious Propaganda and Missionary Competition in the New Testament World: Essays Honoring Dieter Georgi*, 57-69. Edited by Lukas Borman, Kelly Del Tredici, and Angela Standhardtinger. NTSup 74. Leiden: Brill, 1994.

——. 'The Third Sibyl Revisited.' In *Things Revealed: Studies in Early Jewish and Christian Literature in Honor of Michael E. Stone*, 3-19. Edited by Esther G. Chazon, David Satran, and Ruth A. Clements. JSJSup 89. Leiden: Brill, 2004.

Geffcken, Johannes. *Die Oracula Sibyllina*. GCS 8. Leipzig: Hinrichs, 1902.

Lanchester, H. C. O. 'The Sibylline Oracles.' *APOT*, 2:368-406.

Merkel, Helmut. *Sibyllinen*. JSHRZ 5.8. Gutersloh, 1998.

Nikiprowetzky, Valentin. *La troisième Sibylle*. Paris/La Haye: Mouton, 1970.

Rzach, Aloisius. *Oracula Sibyllina*. Leipzig: Tempsky, 1891.

Solomon, Odes of

Charlesworth, James H. 'Odes of Solomon.' *OTP*, 2:725-71.

Harris, Rendel, and Alphonse Mingana. *The Odes and Psalms of Solomon*, vol. 1, *The Text with Facsimile Reproductions*. Manchester: Manchester University Press, 1916.

Solomon, Psalms of

Atkinson, Kenneth. 'Herod the Great, Sosius, and the Siege of Jerusalem (37 B. C. E.) in Psalm of Solomon 17.' *NovT* 38 (1996): 313-22.

——. 'Toward a Redating of the Psalms of Solomon: Implications for Understanding the *Sitz im Leben* of an Unknown Jewish Sect.' *JSP* 17 (1998): 95-112.

——. 'On the Use of Scripture in the Development of Militant Davidic Messianism at Qumran: New Light from *Psalm of Solomon 17*.' In *The Interpretation of Scripture in Early Judaism and Christianity: Studies in Language and Tradition*, 106-23. Edited by Craig A. Evans. JSPSup 33. Studies in Scripture in Early Judaism and Christianity 7. Sheffield: Sheffield Academic Press, 2000.

——. *An Intertextual Study of the Psalms of Solomon*. Studies in the Bible and Early Christianity 49. Lewiston, N.Y.: Mellen, 2001.

——. *'I Cried to the Lord': A Study of the Psalms of Solomon's Historical Background and Social Setting*. JSJSup 84. Leiden: Brill, 2004.

Baars, W. *Psalms of Solomon* in *The Old Testament in Syriac According to the Peshiṭta Version*, vol. 4.6, *Canticles or Odes — Prayer of Manasseh — Apocryphal Psalms — Psalms of Solomon — Tobit — 1 (3) Esdras*. Leiden: Brill, 1972.

Begrich, Joachim. 'Der Text der Psalmen Salomos.' *ZNW* 38 (1939): 131-64.

Delcor, M. 'Psaumes de Salomon.' In *Dictionnaire de la Bible: Supplément*, 9:214-45. Edited by L. Pirot and A. Robert. Paris: Letouzey & Ané, 1979.

Gebhardt, Oskar von. *Psalmoi Solomontos zum ersten Male mit Benutzung der Athoshandschriften und des Codex Casanatensis*. Leipzig: Hinrichs, 1895.

Gray, G. Buchanan. 'The Psalms of Solomon.' *APOT*, 2:625-52.

Hahn, Robert R. *The Manuscript History of the Psalms of Solomon*. SBLSCS 13. Chico, Calif.: Scholars Press, 1982.

Ryle, Herbert Edward, and Montague Rhodes James. ΨΑΛΜΟΙ ΣΟΛΟΜΩΝΤΟΣ: *Psalms of the Pharisees, Commonly Called the Psalms of Solomon*. Cambridge: Cambridge University Press, 1891.

Schüpphaus, Joachim. *Die Psalmen Salomos: Ein Zeugnis Jerusalemer Theologie und Frömmigkeit in der Mitte des vorchristlichen Jarhunderts*. ALGHJ 7. Leiden: Brill, 1977.

Swete, Henry Barclay. *The Old Testament in Greek According to the Septuagint*, vol. 3, *Hosea-4 Maccabees, Psalms of Solomon, Enoch, the Odes*. Cambridge: Cambridge University Press, 1909-12.

Trafton, Joseph L. *The Syriac Version of the Psalms*

of Solomon: A Critical Evaluation. SBLSCS 11. Atlanta: Scholars Press, 1985.

——. 'The *Psalms of Solomon* in Recent Research.' *JSP* 12 (1994): 3-19.

Wright, Robert B. Review of Trafton, *The Syriac Version of the Psalms of Solomon. JBL* 107 (1988): 131-34.

Solomon, Testament of

Duling, D. C. 'Testament of Solomon.' OTP, 1:935-87.

——. 'Solomon, Testament of.' *ABD*, 6:117-19.

Zephaniah, Apocalypse of

Wintermute, O. S. 'Apocalypse of Zephaniah.' OTP, 1:497-515.

Zosimus, Story of
(History of the Rechabites)

Charlesworth, James H. *The History of the Rechabites*, vol. 1, *The Greek Recension.* SBLTT 17. SBLPS 10. Chico, Calif.: Scholars Press, 1982.

——. 'History of the Rechabites.' OTP, 2:443-61.

Derrett, J. Duncan M. 'Jewish Brahmins and the Tale of Zosimus: A Theme Common to Three Religions.' *Classica et Mediaevalia* 34 (1983): 75-90.

James, Montague Rhodes. 'On the Story of Zosimus.' In *Apocrypha Anecdota*, 86-108. Texts and Studies. Contributions to Biblical and Patristic Literature 2.3. Cambridge: Cambridge University Press, 1893.

Knights, Chris H. 'The Rechabites in the Bible and in Jewish Tradition to the Time of Rabbi David Kimḥi' 2 vols. Ph. D. diss., University of Durham, 1988.

——. '"The Story of Zosimus" or "The History of the Rechabites"?' *JSJ* 24 (1993): 235-45.

——. 'Towards a Critical Introduction to the "History of the Rechabites."' *JSJ* 26 (1995): 324-42.

——. 'A Century of Research into the Story/ Apocalypse of Zosimus and/or the History of the Rechabites.' *JSP* 15 (1997): 53-66.

——. 'The History of the Rechabites – An Initial Commentary.' *JSJ* 28 (1997): 413-36.

——. 'The *Abode of the Blessed*: A Source for the *Story of Zosimus?' JSP* 17 (1998): 79-93.

Martin, Elbert Garrett. 'The Account of the Blessed Ones: A Study of the Development of an Apocryphon on the Rechabites and Zosimus (The Abode of the Rechabites).' Ph. D. diss., Duke University, 1979.

McNeil, Brian. 'The Narration of Zosimus.' *JSJ* 9 (1978): 68-82.

Nikolsky, Ronit. 'The Provenance of *The Journey of Zosimus* (also known as *The History of the Rechabites*).' Ph. D. diss., Hebrew University, 2003. Hebrew.

——. 'The *History of the Rechabites* and the Jeremiah Literature.' *JSP* 13 (2002): 185-207.

'The Adam and Eve Traditions in *The Journey of Zosimos*.' In Chazon (ed.), *Things Revealed*, 345-56.

Vassiliev, A. (ed.). 'Vita s. Zosimae narratur.' *Anecdota Graeco-Byzantina* pars prior, xxxviii-xl, 166-79. Moscow: Universitas Caesareae, 1893.

RABBINIC AND RELATED LITERATURE

Cohen, Shaye J. D. 'The Rabbinic Conversion Ceremony.' In *The Beginnings of Jewishness*, 198-238. Rpt. of *JJS* 41 (1990): 177-203.

Davila, James R. *Descenders to the Chariot: The People Behind the Hekhalot Literature.* JSJSup 70. Leiden: Brill, 2001.

Margalioth, Mordechai. *Sepher Ha-Razim: A Newly Recovered Book of Magic from the Talmudic Period.* Jerusalem: Yediot Achronot, 1966 (Hebrew).

Meeks, Wayne A. 'Moses as God and King.' In *Religions in Antiquity: Essays in Memory of Erwin Ramsdell Goodenough*, 354-71. Edited by Jacob Neusner. SHR 14. Leiden: Brill, 1968.

Morgan, Michael A. *Sepher Ha-Razim: The Book of the Mysteries.* SBLTT 25. SBLPS 11. Chico, Calif.: Scholars Press, 1983.

Schäfer, Peter. *Synopse zur Hekhalot-Literatur.* TSAJ 2. Tübingen: Mohr Siebeck, 1981.

—— (ed.). *The Talmud Yerushalmi and Graeco-Roman Culture III.* TSAJ 93. Tübingen: Mohr Siebeck, 2002.

Schiffman, Lawrence H. *Who Was a Jew? Rabbinic and Halakhic Perspectives on the Jewish-Christian Schism.* Hoboken, N. J.: Ktav, 1985.

Schultz, Joseph P. 'Angelic Opposition to the Ascension of Moses and the Revelation of the Law.' *JQR* 61 (1970-71): 282-307.

Sperber, Daniel. 'Some Rabbinic Themes in Magical Papyri.' *JSJ* 16 (1985): 93-103.

Stemberger, Günter. *Introduction to the Talmud and Midrash*. Edinburgh: Clark, 1996.

SAMARITANS

Ben Hayyim, Ze'ev. 'Samaritan Hebrew – An Evaluation.' In Crown (ed.), *The Samaritans*, 517-30.

Bóid, R. M. 'The Samaritan Halachah.' In Crown (ed.), *The Samaritans*, 624-49.

Crown, Alan D. (ed.). *The Samaritans*. Tübingen: Mohr-Siebeck, 1989.

——. 'The Byzantine and Moslem Periods.' In Crown (ed.), *The Samaritans*, 55-81.

——. 'Redating the Schism between the Judaeans and the Samaritans.' *JQR* 82 (1991): 17-50.

——. 'Qumran, Samaritan *Halakha* and Theology and Pre-Tannaitic Judaism.' In *Boundaries of the Ancient Near Eastern World: A Tribute to Cyrus Gordon*, 420-441. Edited by Meir Lubetski, Claire Gottlieb, and Sharon Keller. JSOTSup 273. Sheffield: Sheffield Academic Press, 1998.

Crown, Alan D., Reinhard Pummer and Abraham Tal. *A Companion to Samaritan Studies*. Tübingen: Mohr Siebeck, 1993.

Crown, Alan D., and Lucy Davey (eds.). *New Samaritan Studies of the Société d'Études Samaritaines III & IV*. Sydney, Australia: Mandelbaum, 1995.

Daise, Michael. 'Samaritans, Seleucids, and the Epic of Theodotus.' *JSP* 17 (1998): 25-51.

Dexinger, Ferdinand. 'Samaritan Eschatology.' In Crown (ed.), *The Samaritans*, 266-92.

——. 'Samaritan and Jewish Festivals: Comparative Considerations.' In Crown and Davey (eds.), *New Samaritan Studies*, 57-78.

Fossum, Jarl. 'Sects and Movements.' In Crown (ed.), *The Samaritans*, 293-389.

——. 'Dustan and Dosithean Halakha.' In Crown, Pummer, and Tal (eds.), *A Companion*, 78-80.

Grabbe, Lester L. 'Betwixt and Between: The Samaritans in the Hasmonean Period.' In Davies and Halligan (eds.), *Second Temple Studies III*, 202-17. Originally published in *SBLSP* 32 (1993), 334-47.

Hjelm, Ingrid. *The Samaritans and Early Judaism: A Literary Analysis*. JSOTSup 303. Copenhagen International Seminar 7. Sheffield: Sheffield Academic Press, 2000.

——. 'What Do Samaritans and Jews Have in Common? Recent Trends in Samaritan Studies.' *Currents in Biblical Research* 3 (2004): 9-62.

——. *Jerusalem's Rise to Sovereignty in Ancient Tradition and History: Zion and Gerizim in Competition*. JSOT Sup 404. CIS 14. London: Clark, 2004.

Jacoby, Ruth. 'The Four Species in Jewish and Samaritan Tradition.' In *From Dura to Sepphoris: Studies in Jewish Art and Society in Late Antiquity*, 225-30. Edited by Lee I. Levine and Zeev Weiss. Journal of Roman Archaeology Supplementary Series 40. Portsmouth, R. I.: Journal of Roman Archaeology, 2001.

Kraemer, Ross S. 'Could *Aseneth* Be Samaritan?' In Wright (ed.), *A Multiform Heritage*, 149-65.

Kugler, Robert A. 'Some Further Evidence for the Samaritan Provenance of *Aramaic Levi* (*1QTestLevi*; *4QTestLevi*).' *RevQ* 17/65-68 (1996): 351-58.

MacDonald, John. *The Theology of the Samaritans*. London: SCM, 1964.

Macuch, Rudolph. 'Samaritan Languages: Samaritan Hebrew, Samaritan Aramaic,' in Crown (ed.), *The Samaritans*, 531-84.

Magen, Yitzhaq. 'A Fortified City from the Hellenistic Period on Mount Gerizim.' *Qadmoniot* 19 (1986): 91-101 (Hebrew).

——. 'Mount Gerizim – A Sanctuary City.' *Qadmoniot* 23 (1990): 70-96 (Hebrew).

——. 'Mount Gerizim and the Samaritans.' In *Early Christianity in Context: Monuments and Documents*, 91-148. Edited by F. Manns and E. Alliata. Studium Biblicum Franciscanum Collectio Maior 38. Jerusalem: Franciscan Printing Press, 1993.

Magen, Y., L. Tsfania, and H. Misgav. 'The Hebrew and Aramaic Inscriptions from Mt. Gerizim.' *Qad* 33 (120): 125-32 (Hebrew).

Powels, Sylvia. 'The Samaritan Calendar and the Roots of Samaritan Chronology.' In Crown (ed.), *The Samaritans*, 691-742.

Pummer, Reinhard. 'ΑΡΓΑΡΙΖΙΝ: A Criterion for Samaritan Provenance?' *JSJ* 18 (1987): 18-25.

——. 'Samaritan Rituals and Customs.' In Crown (ed.), *The Samaritans*, 650-90.

——. 'How to Tell a Samaritan Synagogue from a Jewish Synagogue.' *BAR* 24.3 (1998): 24-35.

——. 'Samaritan Traditions on the Death of Moses.' In Nickelsburg (ed.), *Studies on the Testament of Moses*, 93-117.

Schiffman, L. H. 'The Samaritans in Tannaitic Halakhah.' *JQR* 75 (1985): 323-50.

Thornton, C. G. 'The Samaritan Calendar: A Source of Friction in New Testament Times.' *JTS* 42 (1991): 577-80.

SEPTUAGINT AND HELLENISTIC GREEK

Note: *works on specific Old Testament Apocrypha and pseudepigrapha are listed under the heading for the specific text.*

Brooke, Alan England, and Norman McLean. *The Old Testament in Greek*. 3 vols. Cambridge: Cambridge University Press, 1906-40.

Greenspoon, Leonard J. 'The Dead Sea Scrolls and the Greek Bible,' in Flint and Vander-Kam (eds.), *The Dead Sea Scrolls after Fifty Years*, 1:101-27.

Grenfeld, Bernard P., and Arthur S. Hunt. *The Oxyrhynchus Papyri,* Part III. London: Egypt Exploration Fund, 1903.

Jellicoe, Sidney. *The Septuagint and Modern Study*. Ann Arbor, Mich.: Eisenbrauns, 1978. Rpt. of 1968 Oxford University Press edition.

Jobes, Karen H. and Moisés Silva. *Invitation to the Septuagint*. Grand Rapids, Mich.: Baker, 2000.

Miles, John Russiano. *Retroversion and Text Criticism: The Predictability of Syntax in an Ancient Translation from Greek to Ethiopic*. SBLSCS 17. Chico, Calif.: Scholars Press, 1985.

Swete, Henry Barclay, with a contribution by H. St. J. Thackeray. *An Introduction to the Old Testament in Greek*. 2nd ed. revised by Richard Rusden Ottley. Cambridge: Cambridge University Press, 1914.

Tov, Emanuel. *Textual Criticism of the Hebrew Bible*. Minneapolis: Fortress, 1992.

VanderKam, James C. 'Greek at Qumran,' in Collins and Sterling (eds.), *Hellenism in the Land of Israel*, 175-81.

SYRIAC

Note: *works on specific Old Testament Apocrypha and Pseudepigrapha in Syriac are listed under the heading for the specific text. Other original-language Syriac texts are listed here and sometimes under other headings.*

Hayman, A. P. *The Disputation of Sergius the Stylite Against a Jew*. 2 vols. CSCO 338-39. Scriptores Syri 152-53. Louvain: Corpus Scriptorum Christianorum Orientalium, 1973.

Thomson, Robert W. *The Syriac Version of the Hexaemeron by Basil of Caesarea*. 2 vols. CSCO 550-51. Scriptores Syri 222-23. Louvain: Peeters, 1995.

Tonneau, R.-M. *Sancti Ephraem Syri: In Genesim et In Exodum commentarii*. CSCO 152-53. Scriptores Syri 71-72. Louvain: Durbecq, 1955.

WEBSITES

Josephus Bibliography on the Internet (University of Münster): http://www.uni-muenster.de/Judaicum/Josephus/JosephusOnline-e.html

Kraft, Robert. 'Was There a "Messiah-Joshua" Tradition at the Turn of the Era?' No pages. Copyright 1992. Online: http://ccat.sas.upenn.edu/gopher/other/journals/kraftpub/Christianity/Joshua.

Philo of Alexandria Weblog (Torrey Seland): http://philoblogger.blogspot.com/

GREEK

CONTENTS

Detailed Table